Betting on Horse Racing

FOR DUMMIES®

by Richard Eng

WILEY

Wiley Publishing, Inc.

Betting on Horse Racing For Dummies®

Published by
Wiley Publishing, Inc.
111 River St.
Hoboken, NJ 07030-5774
www.wiley.com

WILEY

About the Author

At one point in his life, **Richard Eng** was on a responsible career path in the banking business. In 1979, he was making $25,000 a year as a shift supervisor for Union Trust Bank in Darien, Connecticut. However, Eng got a higher calling for a job in professional sports. He left Union Trust and accepted an entry-level position in the publicity department of the New York Racing Association. Eng's first yearly salary in horse racing — $9,000.

Eng worked for the NYRA tracks — Aqueduct, Belmont Park, and Saratoga — until January 1985. During his six years in New York, he worked on some of the greatest horse races of that era: two Triple Crown near misses in the Belmont Stakes with Spectacular Bid in 1979 and Pleasant Colony in 1981; a walkover by Spectacular Bid in the 1980 Woodward; three of trainer Woody Stephens's record five straight Belmont Stakes wins; six Saratoga meetings, including the historic 1982 Travers where the three Triple Crown races winners — Gato del Sol, Aloma's Ruler, and Conquistador Cielo — squared off but were upset by Runaway Groom.

Eng moved on to the new Garden State Park as the Assistant Publicity Director. Garden State was a showcase racetrack built for more than $170 million in Cherry Hill, New Jersey. That spring, Spend a Buck broke with racing tradition. After winning the Kentucky Derby, the connections of Spend a Buck skipped the Preakness and ran him for a $2.6 million payday in the Jersey Derby. Spend a Buck won the Jersey Derby and Horse of the Year honors.

In future years, Eng served as the public relations director at Turfway Park in Florence, Kentucky, for six years; Santa Anita Park in Arcadia, California, for three seasons; and Arlington Park in Arlington Heights, Illinois, for one year.

During the 1990s, Eng did freelance work with ABC Sports and the Breeders' Cup. He also worked four years as a handicapper and writer at Monmouth Park and the Meadowlands. He worked with ABC Sports for seven years on its horse racing and Triple Crown television coverage. Imagine getting paid to attend the Kentucky Derby, Preakness, and Belmont Stakes. In five years working on the Breeders' Cup Newsfeed, Eng witnessed the single most amazing score in horse racing history when his co-workers won $3 million in the 1999 Ultra Pick Six.

In October 1998, Eng became the turf editor and handicapper for the Las Vegas Review-Journal. He writes a weekly horse racing column on what's happening in the sport. Every morning in the Review-Journal, his handicap of the Southern California racing card is a popular feature with race book horseplayers and followers over the Internet. In the evening, he hosts the Race Day Las Vegas Wrap Up radio show five nights a week.

In April 2003, Eng elevated the standing of all public horse racing handicappers in winning the $400,000 Championship at The Orleans handicapping tournament at The Orleans casino in Las Vegas. He and his partner, Louis Filoso, won the first prize of $111,680 for the three-day tournament.

Richard Eng has done a lot in the horse industry since 1979. But the one thing he's glad about is he finally won back the $16,000 pay cut he took to get into the horse racing business.

Dedication

In 1979, you had to see the look on my mom and dad when I told them I was making a career change into horse racing. It's a fact that Chinese people love to gamble. But my parents thought their number three son would earn an honest living at the bank. I dedicate this book to my parents, Bik and Chuck Eng, as well as to my siblings, Patty, Elsie, Peter, Kenny, and Nancy. Add to the list my family through marriage: Sandy, my wife; stepdaughters Carrie and Crissy; and the apple of my eye, grandson Christian.

It's taken a lot of hours and late nights of writing to finish, but it's been well worth it. The final dedications are to three great friends who've supported me in doing this book, but more importantly, were along for the fun ride it's been all these years — Don Barberino, Ralph Siraco, and Tom Varela.

Author's Acknowledgments

I learned early on in my career that no one knows all the answers. The key is having good friends who know all the things that I don't. I could not have written this book without the help of these pros in their respective fields, and I cannot thank them enough: Donald Barberino, Sports Haven; Jim Beers, handicapper and horseman; Trey Buck, American Quarterhorse Association; Rick Hammerle, Santa Anita Park; Floyd Hill, trainer; Carol Hodes, The Meadowlands; John Pawlak, United States Trotting Association; Jerry Porcelli, New York Racing Association; Nick Smith, Ascot Race Course; Tom Varela, Southern California Off-Track Wagering, Inc.; and from the Television Games Network, Bob Baedeker, Pat Bove, Matt Carothers, and Gary Seibel.

The horse photos were provided by Equi-Photo, Inc., Lisa Photo, Inc., Ed Keys of the United States Trotting Association, and photographer Skip Dickstein, a long-time friend who I met during my first Saratoga meeting in 1979.

I want to thank the *Daily Racing Form* for providing the past performances, result charts, and other copyrighted material included in the book. I contribute a Sunday Las Vegas gaming column to the *Daily Racing Form*. *DRF* chairman and publisher Steven Crist has always been supportive of projects meant to help horse racing, and especially with a book like this that reaches out to newcomers. I thank his lieutenants Rich Rosenbush and Dean Keppler for their support. I thank Equibase Company LLC, the sole data collection agency for horse racing, for use of any copyrighted material. I appreciate the feedback from Brisnet, Equiform, Ragozin Sheets, and Thoro-Graph, all companies that help horseplayers win more money.

I also thank my literary agent Jessica Faust, Acquistions Editor Tracy Boggier, Project Editor Chrissy Guthrie, Copy Editor Trisha Strietelmeier, and other fine folks at Wiley Publishing, Inc. who made this book happen. The *For Dummies* books are very popular for good reasons. Wiley understands its audience, researches what subjects are of interest to people, and have great folks working there who know how to make the material fun and interesting to read.

Finally, a lot of my own research was done just doing what I've been doing all these years. I want people to know that if I've ever had a meaningful conversation with them, in some small way, they too contributed to this book.

Publisher's Acknowledgments

We're proud of this book; please send us your comments through our Dummies online registration form located at www.dummies.com/register/.

Some of the people who helped bring this book to market include the following:

Acquisitions, Editorial, and Media Development

Project Editor: Christina Guthrie

Acquisitions Editor: Tracy Boggier

Copy Editor: Trisha Strietelmeier

Editorial Program Assistant: Courtney Allen

Technical Editor: Thomas M. Varela

Editorial Manager: Christine Meloy Beck

Editorial Assistants: Hanna Scott, Nadine Bell, Melissa Bennett

Cover Photos: © Gary Holscher/Getty Images/ Stone

Cartoons: Rich Tennant, www.the5thwave.com

Composition Services

Project Coordinator: Maridee Ennis

Layout and Graphics: Andrea Dahl, Kelly Emkow, Lauren Goddard, Stephanie D. Jumper, Heather Ryan, Julie Trippetti

Proofreaders: David Faust, Jessica Kramer, Joe Niesen, Carl William Pierce, Aptara

Indexer: Aptara

Publishing and Editorial for Consumer Dummies

Diane Graves Steele, Vice President and Publisher, Consumer Dummies

Joyce Pepple, Acquisitions Director, Consumer Dummies

Kristin A. Cocks, Product Development Director, Consumer Dummies

Michael Spring, Vice President and Publisher, Travel

Brice Gosnell, Associate Publisher, Travel

Kelly Regan, Editorial Director, Travel

Publishing for Technology Dummies

Andy Cummings, Vice President and Publisher, Dummies Technology/General User

Composition Services

Gerry Fahey, Vice President of Production Services

Debbie Stailey, Director of Composition Services

Contents at a Glance

Table of Contents

Part II: How the Players and Factors Impact the Race 77

Introduction

● ●

Horse racing may be the most American of all professional sports played today. The horse is indigenous to the North American continent and was used in everyday life by Native American Indians and the first European settlers. When English settlers came to the New World, they imported new breeds of horses. Horses were used for transportation and farming, and they played a big role in the movement west of the Mississippi River. People in the New World began racing their own horses against one another as early as the 1600s. This was nothing new as their ancestors in Europe and Asia had raced horses for centuries.

In *Betting on Horse Racing For Dummies,* I cover the great sport of horse racing from every conceivable angle. I consider it the greatest game around, and hopefully by the end of this book, you'll feel that way, too.

About This Book

Since 1979, I've worked in the horse racing industry in public relations, as a handicapper, and now as the turf editor for the *Las Vegas Review-Journal.* I've met hundreds upon hundreds of newcomers to the sport. The reasons many of them cite for not getting more interested in horse racing are that the sport is hard to learn, is too intimidating, and there isn't a way anybody actually wins any money. Because a vast majority of newcomers echo these words, you know their concerns are real.

The phenomenal popularity from the success of horses like Funny Cide and Smarty Jones in the Triple Crown races in 2003 and 2004, respectively, have whet people's appetites for horse racing. But even though the sport of horse racing enjoys tremendous peaks of interest each spring when these races are run, little is done to capture and nurture that intense curiosity. When the opportunity arose to write *Betting on Horse Racing For Dummies,* I was thrilled to tackle this age-old problem that horse racing faces on a daily basis. (This is called putting your money where your mouth is.)

In horse racing, you have a lot to learn, so much so that it becomes a smorgasbord of raw data — a literal information overload. No wonder you feel intimidated if you try to understand horse racing all in one sitting. What I've tried to do in this book is divide up horse racing into easily digestible pieces. When you get full, just put the book down for a while. Return when you're hungry to find out more.

I wrote *Betting on Horse Racing For Dummies* with the idea of teaching horse racing to newcomers in an "A to Z" fashion. However, I'm positive if you're an occasional or veteran horseplayer, you'll find plenty of meat in these pages to either refresh your own strategies or discover some new ones.

Conventions Used in This Book

You should find the conventions in this book to be pretty straightforward:

- New terms are *italicized* and defined, and there's an in-depth glossary for further definitions in the back of the book.
- When I introduce a new product, a racetrack, or something I want you to find out more about, I often include a Web site address, which appears in monofont.
- Whenever I discuss betting odds, such as two-to-one, I write it this way: 2/1.

What You're Not to Read

I'd love for you to read everything in this book, but if you're short on time or are only interested in the absolute need-to-know info, you can skip the following:

- **Any text marked with a "Technical Stuff" icon:** This icon points out bits of trivia or interesting information that enhances but isn't necessary to your understanding of the topic.
- **Sidebars:** These gray-shaded boxes highlight information that relates to the topic, and they often include personal stories from my experiences in the horse racing and betting world. The info is great, and the stories are all true, but you can skip these sections without worrying about missing out on too much.

Foolish Assumptions

Before writing a word in this book, I made a few ironclad assumptions about you:

- First, you have zero base knowledge about horse racing and betting, which is why I start from square one. Now, if your starting point isn't zero, that's okay, because you can skip some parts. Remember that even if you're a professional handicapper, this book is still chock full of useful ideas.

✔ My second assumption is that you have a $100 betting bankroll for the day. You have no ATM cards, no $20 bills hidden in your shoes, no extra cash you "borrowed" from the family's weekly grocery money — just $100 for the day.

✔ My third assumption is you have at least a slight interest in finding out how and why certain things work in horse racing. For example, commenting on blinker changes on a horse and its impact on your handicapping is one thing. But I assume you want to know how and why blinkers work on the horse so you have a better understanding of how that affects your handicapping. (Wondering what in the heck blinkers are? Don't worry. I get to that eventually.)

How This Book Is Organized

When I organized the Table of Contents for this book, I tried to put myself in the reading chair of a newcomer. Some people like to read every word and devour each thought like a morsel of caviar. Others read a book like it's a 99¢ dinner menu. (Hurry up with the hamburger and small fries, and make it snappy!) Of course, plenty of readers lie somewhere in the middle of these two extremes.

Each chapter is meant to be self-contained, meaning you can read a chapter in the middle of the book and understand it without reading everything before it. And because a winning horseplayer is built up layer by layer, each chapter has a progression from start to finish.

But remember: If you're a newcomer and pick up this book and read just, say, Chapter 15, and then you go to the racetrack tomorrow, I doubt if you'd win without some serious beginner's luck. No form of gambling is ever that easy to master.

Part 1: And They're Off! Horse Racing and the Betting Scene

Part I begins with me telling you everything you need to know (in a nutshell, that is) about betting on horse racing. After you have all that down, you get into the many different types of horse racing. Before you're through with this part, you'll understand how parimutuel wagering works, you'll know how to place a bet, and you'll be familiar with the ins and outs of the racetrack.

Part II: How the Players and Factors Impact the Race

Before you figure out how to handicap, you must understand who, why, and what you're handicapping. You need to be familiar with the horse, jockey, trainer, owner, racing surfaces, and equipment changes. Most handicapping books don't delve into these aspects — let alone dedicate five chapters to them — but I do with the hopes that you see that the handicapping equation is more than just a number.

Part III: Gaining and Keeping a Competitive Edge

If handicapping is comparable to cooking a good meal, then you need to know the ingredients and how to use them. Any horse racing recipe begins with the *Daily Racing Form*. In this part, I show you how to read it and point out key information to look for. Then I introduce betting ideas and money management.

Part IV: Risky Business: Tackling More Advanced Bets

In this part, I bring you into the world of exotic wagers, where your chances of winning go down, but the payoffs go sky high if you do win. And when you're ready for advanced handicapping, these chapters fill you in on which premium products provide the best handicapping help, how to be successful in the big money handicapping tournaments, and how to bet horses at huge odds. Not enough? I even show you how to get a jump start on picking next year's Kentucky Derby winner.

Part V: Playing Different Ponies and Different Venues

Playing the ponies from any place but the racetrack is easier than ever. You can go to your local off-track betting parlor, set up a telephone account with whomever it's allowed and wherever it's legal, or watch the races at home on cable television or over the Internet. If you want to go someplace exotic, try a first-class race book in one of Las Vegas's fine casinos.

Here I also introduce two breeds of horse racing, harness and Quarter Horse, that are as exciting to watch and bet on as the Thoroughbreds.

Part VI: The Part of Tens

The Part of Tens is in all *For Dummies* books, and this book is no exception. Here I've listed for you what I consider the ten best bets and betting angles, the ten best racetracks to visit, and the ten most common betting mistakes. Read the lists, decide whether you agree or disagree, and let me know what you think.

Appendix

Horse racing has its own jargon. To fully understand what I'm talking about or what someone at the racetrack is saying, check out the key words in the glossary.

Icons Used in This Book

If you've ever read a *For Dummies* book before, you know all about icons. They point out bits of information that you should pay particular attention to, or that you can skip altogether in the case of the Technical Stuff icon. Following is a brief description of each icon that appears in this book:

This icon marks useful information that can save you time, money, or both.

This icon marks important information you want to remember.

This icon marks dangerous scenarios and pitfalls to avoid in the world of betting.

This icon marks interesting or advanced material that isn't essential to your understanding of betting on horse racing.

Because I've been in the business for a long time, I've got a few stories to share. This icon highlights those stories.

Where to Go from Here

If you're a complete novice, I recommend reading Chapter 1 for sure. Ideally, you should read from cover to cover. The information is sequenced to take you through the horse racing and handicapping process step-by-step.

For the recreational handicappers, this book is an excellent reference tool. And for professionals, reading *Betting on Horse Racing For Dummies* can be a good refresher course, because as we (I consider myself a professional too, after all) get older, there's a tendency to take short cuts and get sloppy. If you want to bone up on a topic or two, read over the Table of Contents and find the chapters that look interesting and helpful.

And by the way, don't be afraid to take this book to the racetrack with you — or at the very least the Cheat Sheet. Good help is often hard to find. If you have any questions, I can answer them for you so you don't have to look for a racetrack employee. Good luck betting on the horses!

Part I

And They're Off!
Horse Racing and
the Betting Scene

The 5th Wave   By Rich Tennant

Part I

And They're Off

Horse Racing and

the Betting Scene

In this part . . .

Horse racing is unlike any other American spectator sport. You don't pay hundreds of dollars to watch grown up millionaires play a kid's game. In horse racing, you're an active participant, a player in the stands. You're invited to go just about anywhere within the racetrack and enjoy yourself. You decide your level of involvement — meaning as a $2 bettor, a $1,000 horseplayer, or somewhere in between.

In this part, I introduce the different types of horse racing and the inner workings of the horse races. I explain the parimutuel wagering system, outline how to bet and some of the easier bets to make, and paint a word picture of a racetrack so you can take advantage of everything that's available for your enjoyment.

Chapter 1

Playing the Ponies for Pleasure and Profit

Nearly 40 states in the United States conduct some sort of live horse racing. It has been a legal form of gambling a lot longer than casino gambling. In fact, back in the 1940s, horse racing was right up there with baseball and football among the leading U.S. spectator sports. As for horse racing's universal appeal, you can travel to almost any country in the world and find horse racing of some kind going on.

Horse racing has slipped in popularity. But since the mid–1990s, the game has been making a steady comeback. Horses like Funny Cide in 2003 and Smarty Jones in 2004 rode a wave of popularity after winning the Kentucky Derby and Preakness. Both lost the Belmont Stakes to narrowly miss a Triple Crown, but record television ratings were set, and crowds of more than 100,000 people came out to see them try to make history.

Horse racing isn't an easy game to figure out, which is why you've picked up a copy of *Betting on Horse Racing For Dummies*. I try to give you answers about horse racing before you even ask the questions. I focus a lot on betting, but I still take the time to explain the nuances that makes horse racing such a uniquely great game.

Differentiating the Types of Horse Races

Horses have always been a part of American culture. In early times, the animal was used in farming and transportation — so much so that when the automobile was invented, carmakers used the term *horsepower* to define how powerful the car engine was. It was a term that people could easily understand.

Three types of horse racing have evolved in the United States, each of which has its own peculiarities that attract a loyal following:

- **Thoroughbred racing:** This form is by far the most popular and most well-known, thanks to the Triple Crown and Breeders' Cup races, and it's what I focus on throughout the book.

- **Standardbred or harness racing:** In this form of racing, a driver sits behind the horse in a small cart called a *sulky* instead of riding atop the horse like a jockey. Chapter 19 is devoted to harness racing information and handicapping tips.

- **Quarter Horse racing:** These horses are bred for break-neck speed, and the races rarely exceed 870 yards. Head to Chapter 20 for the ins and outs of this exciting form of racing.

All races are run at a racetrack that holds licensed race meets. Each state has a racing commission that ensures that all the rules of racing are being followed. Due to the fact that people are betting on the outcome of horse races, the racing commissions place utmost importance on protecting and policing the integrity of the sport.

Before You Bet: Handicapping the Races

Don't let anyone fool you into believing that betting on horse racing is sheer luck. In any gambling game, having lady luck on your side is always better. But when it comes to handicapping, brains and intellect win out much more often than luck.

Handicapping is the art and science of picking winners. You can do it several ways, though I prefer to stay away from using hat pins, coins, darts, and rabbit feet to pick my horses.

Information is power, and the best place to get horse racing information is from the *Daily Racing Form (DRF)*. The *DRF* is the industry's main daily newspaper that provides independent editorial copy along with the best past performances of all horses racing on any given day. If you're at the racetrack, you'll notice all of the serious handicappers have the *DRF*. Most have studied the races the night before, marking their notes in the newspaper.

Handicapping is a little complex and isn't something you can pick up overnight. If you're new to the game, head to Chapters 11 and 12 for the basics. Then, when you're comfortable, you can try some advanced handicapping techniques, which I discuss in Chapter 16.

Eliminating losers and developing the race shape

When I look at the day's races in the *Daily Racing Form,* the first thing I *don't* do when going through the races is try and pick a winner. Instead, I go through and eliminate the losers. The losers are those horses I think are too slow or overmatched to win that day. Getting the losers out of the way creates a smaller pool from which to pick winners, making your job a lot easier.

Next, I mark in the *DRF past performances,* which is a horse's racing resume, the horses into three categories: speedballs, pace horses, and dead late closers. Each label is self-explanatory. *Speedballs* prefer to take the early lead. Their early position in their past races show mostly "1s," meaning they're in the lead. *Pace horses* stalk the early pace. Their past performances show more "3s" and "4s," indicating their running position. The *dead late closers* lag far back early in the race, so depending on the field size, they're in the back half of the group.

I like to look for the *race shape,* which is how I project the race will be run. For example, if multiple speedball horses are racing, the early pace will be fast, and a speed duel will hurt their chances of winning. Conversely, if only one speed horse is racing, I call this the best bet in horse racing — *lone speed.*

I take into account the overall *class* of each horse. The classier horses win races when facing lesser rivals. Class is something measured in the heart and head of the horse, but at least you can make good judgments by the class of the races they've run in previously. For example, cheap claiming horses exhibit less class than allowance or stakes horses. I cover the class and classification of horse races in Chapter 2.

Taking all factors into account

Winning a horse race is never a one man show. Granted, there's no replacing a fast, talented racehorse. But when you're handicapping the races, the contributions of the jockey, trainer, and owner, and even the reputation of the stable's skilled help — such as grooms and exercise riders — must be taken into account. (See Chapters 7 and 8 for more.)

Publications like the *Daily Racing Form* and the racetrack program print statistics that are paramount to your handicapping. Both publish statistics on the jockeys and trainers. Equipment changes are also duly noted, such as whether the horse has blinkers on or off, is using Lasix medication, is wearing front bandages, and so on. When a trainer makes a change, it's usually a positive sign. At minimum, the change is a signal that the trainer is trying something different to win a race. (Chapter 10 is all about equipment changes.)

In addition, the program and *Daily Racing Form* list the track condition (such as fast, good, muddy, and sloppy for the main track and firm, good, soft, and yielding for the turf course) from race to race so you can see whether a horse runs its best effort on a certain type of dirt or turf surface. (See Chapter 9 for more on track surfaces and conditions.)

Playing the System: Parimutuel Wagering

Parimutuel wagering is the accepted betting system in the United States. The French invented it, and the word *parimutuel* means betting amongst ourselves. In parimutuel wagering, the money wagered goes into a common pool. After deductions are taken out to cover racing expenses and taxes to the state, the remaining money gets paid out to the winners.

The *win odds* on each horse, which reflect the probable win payoff, are determined by the betting public. The more money bet on a horse, the lower its odds. Horses called *long shots* have higher odds because very little money has been bet on them to win. A *tote board* on the infield and displayed on television monitors all around the racetrack relays the odds and potential payoffs for parimutuel wagers.

One of the key points to keep in mind about parimutuel wagering is that you're betting against all the other horseplayers. This type of wagering is opposite of casino gaming where, in most cases, you're playing against the casino or the *house,* as it's also known.

I cover all the nuts and bolts of parimutuel racing in Chapter 3.

Betting with Success

Horse race betting is much different than sports betting, where the odds on a ballgame are 11/10, meaning you bet $11 to win $10. The common bet denomination in horse racing is $2 and has been that way forever. Although it's true that if you bet more money, you can win more money, professional horseplayers follow a different credo: "Bet a little to win a lot."

In horse racing, betting *overlays* is the key to success. Overlays are horses going off at odds higher than their real chances of winning the race. For example, professional horseplayers put their own morning line on each race to determine overlays. When a horse they like is going off at much higher odds (say 10/1) than it deserves (say 5/1), they bet. I don't expect newcomers to make their own *morning line,* which is made by a handicapper who is an employee of the racetrack and reflects how that person thinks the public will bet the race. A simple way to find overlays is to trust the oddsmaker at major racetracks. Then bet on horses that are going off at odds much higher than their morning line.

Starting off simply

Although you can make all kinds of wagers, newcomers should focus on *straight bets,* meaning to win, place, and show. You collect on a *win bet* when your horse finishes first, on a *place bet* if it runs first or second, and on a *show bet* when your horse ends up first, second, or third. The concept is a simple one to grasp. Bet one horse to do one good thing for you to win money.

Chapter 4 is all about placing straight bets, and I even provide step-by-step instructions for calling out a wager if you've never done such a thing before.

Even if you've placed a few bets before, until you get more sophisticated with your handicapping, I wouldn't go much further than wagering on *daily doubles* (linking the winners of two consecutive races), *exactas,* and *quinellas*. In an exacta, you're betting on the first two finishers in exact order. In a quinella, you're betting on the first two finishers in either order (see Chapter 15). In betting, you can use multiple horses, giving yourself a chance to cash a sizeable ticket and still keeping your investment small.

Going for the score

Exotic wagers (see Chapter 15) give you a chance to win a sizeable amount of money with a small investment. A $100 bankroll doesn't give you much leeway to *shoot for the moon,* meaning to win thousands upon thousands of dollars. I recommend initially trying to win your first *prime bet,* meaning a good-sized bet on a horse you really like, and/or a couple *action bets,* which are small wagers just to have a rooting interest. After you win a couple of these bets, you've built up your bankroll and can raise the ante some.

With a small bankroll, the main exotic plays are the quinella, exacta, and daily double. You can also use the *trifecta* and *pick 3* because they can be bet with a $1 unit, but I wouldn't get into the *superfecta* and *pick 4* unless your bankroll has greatly increased. The last two plays produce high rewards but are also very high risk wagers.

The key to *going for a score,* meaning to win a lot of money, isn't necessarily betting a lot of money. The key is beating the favorite in the particular bet you're making. For example, in the daily double, you beat two 6/5 odds race favorites. Your winning horses may pay $10 or $12 win prices. In a natural *parlay,* meaning to take your winnings from one horse and bet it all on the next horse, the $2 daily double returns anywhere between $50 and $72. But because you beat both race favorites, the daily double payoff is overlaid. If the overlay is 25 percent more, the daily double payoff could range between $62 and $90 — not bad for a small investment.

The ultimate wager in going for the score is the *pick 6.* Because it covers six races and is a $2 minimum unit, the cost can be prohibitive. For example, using just two horses in each of the six legs of the pick 6 is a $128 ticket.

My recommendation is to bet the *pick 4.* Using two horses in each of the four legs of the pick 4 costs $16 because it's a $1 unit. That price is much more affordable than the pick 6. Beat a couple race favorites in the pick 4, and you could take home a nice windfall for the night.

Managing your money

Planning your wagers and managing your bankroll with discipline are vital contributors to winning at the horse races — so much so that Chapter 13 (no pun intended) is devoted to that topic. An assumption I made when writing this book is that you have a $100 betting bankroll for the entire day. No ATM withdrawals allowed! If you tap out, no chasing good money after bad.

I like to plan my overall day of gambling so I have some idea how many races interest me. For example, if I really like three horses to win, I must discipline myself to use a percentage of my bankroll on those three horses and races first. If I don't, then I'm using up my bankroll on races I have a lesser opinion about.

I also need to consider how many bets I'd like to make — including action bets, which may be spur of the moment bets on big overlay horses. If I decide I want to make eight bets, here's what I do: I divide eight into my $100 bankroll, which is $12.50 per bet. I factor an additional 50 percent for my three prime wagers ($6.25), which adds up to $18.75. Round down the change, and I bet $18 on each of my three prime plays, totaling $54. I'm left with $46 for the other five plays.

I still have enough flexibility to make a small unplanned action bet or two. In a worse case scenario — meaning all my action bets lose — I've budgeted 54 percent of my bankroll on my strongest plays. If I win one of three, I have a chance to break even. If I win two of three, I make money for the day. If I win all three prime bets, consider it a lady luck afternoon. I also have flexibility if any of my action bets win. For example, say I win $40 on an action bet. Rather than reinvest it all on more action bets, I can grow my prime plays by another $6 each. Now I'm betting $24 each and $72 total on my prime bets. I'm maximizing my chances of winning for the day. This is just one example. An action bet that comes in may win you only $10, or it may win you $90. I want you to understand the principle that some of the profits should be reinvested into your prime plays, which are your strongest plays, and not just frittered away on unplanned action bets.

Only increase the size of your wagers when you're winning. Too often, increasing the size of bets when you're losing is human nature. It's called *chasing your losses* and is considered poor money management discipline. Chasing your losses can turn a bad betting day into a horrendous day. It's generally not a good idea.

Deciding Where to Bet

For the longest time, the racetrack was the only place to go for betting on the horses. Life was much simpler when *simulcasting,* meaning betting on the races away from the racetrack, didn't exist. Now you have hundreds of places to bet horse races, including out of your own home.

The racetrack

The racetrack is the most traditional place to bet on horse racing, and in my opinion, it's the most fun option — at least in terms of the overall experience. In Chapter 5, I take you by the hand and guide you everywhere there's something interesting to see at the racetrack. I give you an idea of how much everything costs, where to sit, where to eat, where to see the horses up close, and so on. I'd be honored if you take me (my book, that is) along for your very first visit to the racetrack.

OTBs and Las Vegas

OTBs (off-track betting parlors) are popular places to bet on horse racing. The good ones offer a lot of amenities, such as fine dining, cushy chairs, plenty of work space, betting terminals at your seat, and so on.

Here's how to find the OTBs near you: Go to the National Thoroughbred Racing Association Web site (www.ntra.com). Click on "Track & Simulcast Facility Locator," and type in your complete address. The search is powered by Mapquest, so you can request text directions or print out a map. If you need additional information, telephone the facility before going there.

In Las Vegas, you can bet on the races in *race books*. These are well-appointed rooms with plenty of seating, well-lit counter space, dozens of television sets, lots of ticket writers to handle your wagers, and something Las Vegas is very famous for — free drinks.

If you're visiting Las Vegas, you don't need a simulcast facility locator. Nearly every casino in town has a race book for the horses. The race book is right next door to the sports book 99 percent of the time. (Yes, betting on sporting events is legal in the state of Nevada.)

Many race books offer contests and twin quinella wagers that can maximize your winning potential. A list of the local contests is printed a couple times a week in the *Daily Racing Form*. Or you can listen to my nightly radio show, the Race Day Las Vegas Wrap Up show, or the morning Race Day Las Vegas show, when you're in town or over the Internet. I give you more Las Vegas horse betting information in Chapter 23.

Home sweet home

I can't think of a better place to play the simulcast races than Las Vegas — unless I'm betting at home, which is now possible. Two national networks, TVG and HRTV, beam the races right into your home. Unfortunately, the two networks have racetrack exclusive contracts. So to see all the available race signals, you need to find a provider that carries both channels, whether you have a cable or a satellite system.

As far as betting, there are many providers of telephone wagering throughout the United States. You need to verify what companies you can legally sign up with in the state you reside. You can also set up betting accounts with Internet companies. You can find a detailed list of bet providers in Chapter 22.

Just for Fun: A Challenge Straight from the Horse's Mouth

You're going to find out pretty fast how much you know about horse racing. Here are ten questions about the sport from simple to not so simple. I gave the test to Mr. Ed, and he aced it.

1. What is the quarter-pole, and where is it located on the racetrack?

2. When the starter presses the button to begin a race, the stall doors spring open and the horses and riders come out. Is the starter turning on or turning off the electricity to open the stall doors?

3. Who was the most famous Australian Thoroughbred racehorse of all time? A Hollywood movie has even been made about him.

4. Name the horse that won the Kentucky Derby the most times.

5. If I bet a trifecta part-wheel, keying one horse to win and putting four other horses underneath, how much does the ticket cost?

6. Every horse racing quiz asks this silly question: How many furlongs are in a mile?

7. Who was "The Ice Man" in the movie *Seabiscuit?* Who played him in the movie?

8. A horse is winning a race very easily. Coming to the finish line, he's startled by a hot dog wrapper and jumps straight up in the air. The jockey grabs the horse around the neck and hangs on. The horse lands on its stomach and slides across the finish line. Does he still win the race?

9. Can a pregnant horse win a race?

10. If I ride "acey-deucy," should you be worried about me?

Now for the answers:

1. The quarter-pole is literally a quarter of a mile from the finish line. It's located at the end of the far turn near the top of the stretch.

2. Racetracks use a heavy duty automotive battery connected to the starting gate. When the starter presses the button, he turns off the electricity, which has been keeping the stall doors shut.

3. Phar Lap. He came to the United States to race and unfortunately died under mysterious circumstances.

4. It's a trick question. The Kentucky Derby is for 3-year-old horses, so you can only run in the race once.

5. $12.

6. Eight.

7. Jockey George Woolf. In the movie *Seabiscuit,* Hall of Fame jockey Gary Stevens played the part of Woolf.

8. Yes. The key is that the jockey stayed on the horse, so the animal carried the correct weight across the finish line.

9. Yes. Mares in foal do race from time to time, and they do win races.

10. I'll be okay. Acey-deucy is a jockey riding style where the right stirrup is shorter than the left stirrup.

Chapter 2

All Horse Races Are Not Created Equal

- -

In This Chapter

▶ Measuring the differences between long and short races

▶ Leveling the playing field in horse racing

▶ Looking at the best of the best: The Triple Crown and the Breeders' Cup

- -

*I*n professional sports like football, baseball, and basketball, every attempt is made to keep the sport honest and to create a competitive balance. This competitive balance, also known as parity, gives the competitors an equal chance of winning. Pro sports strive for parity by maintaining a salary cap or some sort of player cost control. In theory, one team is prevented from buying up all the good players and creating a mismatch of playing talent.

In this chapter, I describe how horse racing establishes its competitive balance, even though all horses are not created equal. I concentrate on Thoroughbred horse racing, even though harness racing and Quarter Horse racing have similar underpinnings. (I cover harness racing in detail in Chapter 19 and Quarter Horse racing in Chapter 20.)

Thoroughbred racing has a system in place in which the owner of a racehorse can find a race that her horse can win. Everything is taken into account, including a horse's age and sex, its racing preferences (dirt versus turf racing, for example), and its class. This is the foundation of horse racing in regards to betting purposes. Horse racing would be an unattractive gamble if the big favorite won every race.

American versus international races

Most horse races outside the United States are run on grass courses. The courses are lush, green, very long, very wide, and in many ways pattern the countryside. Short meets, usually compacted over weekend dates, are run on these courses. The measured amount of racing allows the turf courses a chance to recuperate from a few days of racing (the horses' hooves send divots flying everywhere).

The American version of horse racing is much more commercialized than the rest of the world,

so the majority of races are run on manufactured dirt ovals. American racetracks operate five days a week for months at a time. Grass courses couldn't withstand that kind of daily pounding and stay in safe shape. Thus, dirt tracks were constructed with drainage and banking to handle wet weather.

Maintaining dirt tracks is much easier regardless of whether the weather is rainy, dry, hot, or cold. I cover track surfaces in more detail in Chapter 9.

Race Set-ups: The Long and the Short of It

The wide range of distances in Thoroughbred horse racing makes the formula for picking winners that much more complex. I've seen 2-year-olds race 2 furlongs — a quarter of a mile — all the way up to grass horses go 1½ miles or more.

How far horses can run isn't the real uncertainty in handicapping; how far they can run *fast* is. For example, the Kentucky Derby is 1¼ miles, which is a distance horses seldom, if ever, race. Four-time Kentucky Derby winning trainer D. Wayne Lukas has a pet answer whenever the media asks him whether his horse can last the Derby distance: "They can all go a mile-and-a-quarter; it just takes some of them a lot longer."

When handicapping, you want to find out whether a horse can compete and win at a certain distance. Experienced handicappers can usually answer that question by looking at a horse's *pedigree,* meaning who its sire and dam are. Some horses run their best in short races, while other horses run well in distance races. The greater variety of distances a racetrack's racing office can write, the happier the trainers are in running their horses at that racetrack.

Short races

Short races are known as *sprint races* and are classified as races under 1 mile. That strict definition is used for statistical analysis. However, due to racetrack configurations, there are exceptions to the rule. I believe that a race around one turn qualifies as a sprint. Any race around two turns is a route or distance race (see the following section).

A majority of Thoroughbred racetracks have a 1-mile main track, shaped like an oval, with a ⅞-mile turf (grass) course built inside of it. To allow for a variety of starting distances, many racetracks build *chutes,* meaning extensions of the main track, at the top of the stretch and at the beginning of the backstretch run. Chutes allow the racing office to write one-turn main track races at various shorter distances up to 1 mile.

The exception I refer to are some smaller racetracks where, for example, a 7-furlong race is around two turns. I handicap that as a route race, not a sprint.

The chute at the top of the stretch allows for longer route races up to the classic distance of 1¼ miles (see the next section for more). The key is you don't want to start races going directly into a turn. That creates a major advantage for the inside post positions and hampers the chances of horses starting from the outside posts.

In sprint races, speed from the gate is typically very important. Even if a jockey is riding a dead late closer (see the following section for a definition of *closer*), a good start ensures the horse will be well positioned in the field.

Long races

Races that are 1 mile or longer are called *routes races.* Unlike sprints, which are one-turn races, routes usually go around two turns on the track. When you look out at a racetrack, the first turn, or *clubhouse turn,* is to your right. The second turn, or *far turn,* is to your left.

A one-turn race only uses the far turn. A two-turn race uses the clubhouse turn first and then goes around the far turn.

If a racetrack doesn't have a mile chute down the backside, then a mile race starts at the finish line right in front of the grandstand. Otherwise, a mile race begins at the end of a chute and is a one-turn race.

When races start in front of the grandstand, I strongly urge you to go down on the track apron and watch the start from the rail. You'll literally be a few yards away from the starting gate. Hearing the noise from the horses, riders, and starting gate crew is really exciting. When the starter presses the button to begin the race, a loud bell starts ringing, and the stall gate latches spring open, allowing the horses to leave running. Believe me, there's nothing else like it in sports.

Two-turn races involve a different strategy for the jockey than sprint races. A jockey needs to exhibit patience and a sense of timing, called having "a clock in your head" (see Chapter 7 for more on the jockey). Every horse has a finite amount of energy to expend within the race. Some use it early —called *speed horses*. Some are able to spread their energy out —called *pace horses*. Then other horses like to reserve their energy for the final stages and rally from the back of the pack —called *closers*. I cover these running styles in more detail in Chapter 12.

As you follow horse racing and learn more about it, you'll see that many one-turn horses can't win going around two turns. And the reverse is also true.

Different Levels of Competition at the Racetrack

Just as all horse races are not created equal, neither are all horses. However, racetracks overcome this inequality as best they can by pitting horses of similar ability together for various races. This practice is known as *parity*.

To envision how the horse races are planned by the racing secretary's office, think of a pyramid. (The *racing secretary* is the person in charge of writing the races, assigning weights in handicap races, assigning the number of stalls to trainers, and so on). Each level of the pyramid is a class level. At the base of the pyramid are the *maiden horses,* horses that have never won a race. At the top of the pyramid are the very best horses, called the *stakes horses.* These top horses run in *stakes races,* which offer the most prize money, called *purses*.

In between are the layers of horses that run in *claiming races* — where horses can be bought — and non-selling races. *Non-selling races* come in three types — allowance, optional claiming, and starter handicap races. The goal of the racing office is to write competitive races with full fields of horses. And the goal of the horses is to become stakes horses, but they must win their way up the class ladder, which is called *winning through their conditions. Conditions* are the eligibility requirements of a horse running in a race, such as age, sex, number of wins, and amount of money won.

Horse racing would be awfully boring, and practically unbettable if in every race, one horse is so dominant over the rest of the field that he goes off at 1/5 odds, wins, and pays $2.40. (If you don't understand what I just said about odds and payoffs, head to Chapter 4.)

Racing is seldom a battle of the sexes

Horse racing is the one major sport that has championed equality of the sexes. Female jockeys ride against male jockeys. Female trainers compete against male trainers. Every job at the racetrack can be done by either a man or a woman, and no quarter is given. However, the one group in which females and males rarely compete is the racehorses themselves.

Races are written with gender in mind. Female horses — called *fillies* and *mares* — run mainly against their own sex. Male horses — called *colts, horses,* or *geldings* — usually run against their own kind.

Male horses can't run in female races, but female horses can, at any time, enter and run against males. The only break females might receive is a *weight allowance,* meaning they carry less weight. You often see females run against males in a *stakes race,* which is the highest class of racing (see "Stakes and handicap races: The top of the pyramid," later in the chapter). For example, in the 2004 Breeders' Cup Classic, champion mare Azeri took on the best handicap horses in training and ran a creditable fifth place.

Literally 99.9 percent of all starters in the Kentucky Derby — America's most famous horse race — have been males since its first running in 1875. However, that hasn't stopped a handful of talented fillies from running in the race. A few have even won: Regret in 1915, Genuine Risk in 1980, and Winning Colors in 1988. Way to go, ladies!

In day-to-day horse racing, running a female horse against male horses doesn't make economic sense. Even if the female horse wins, it doesn't earn the horse owner any more purse money above and beyond the normal prize money. Mares have plenty of opportunities to run against their own sex, and the races are easier to win than running against male horses.

Where you see females run more often against males is outside the U.S. racing world — in England, France, Hong Kong, and so on. The racing season is much shorter in these countries, so there are fewer races run and fewer opportunities to win. So, it's much more commonplace for trainers to enter their fillies and mares against males.

At every racetrack, the racing secretary's office produces a *condition book* that outlines all the races coming up in the next two to three weeks. In theory, the condition book mirrors the class levels of horses residing in the barn area. The racing secretary writes the condition book so that every horse has a good chance of winning at least one race in the book.

In this section, I go over the classification of races so you can understand how a racing office puts together the horse racing product that you handicap and bet on regularly.

Maiden races: Where it all begins

Each year, more than 35,000 Thoroughbred racehorses are *foaled* (born). Every foal starts out with the hope that he or she may become a future champion. The reality, however, is that some racehorses are destined for a much brighter future than other racehorses, due to pedigree and training. Every young horse does have one thing in common, though: They all begin as *maidens,* meaning they've never won a race.

Logically enough, races for maidens are called *maiden races.* Within the maiden ranks are different class levels:

- ✔ **Maiden claiming races:** In maiden claiming races, the horses are eligible to be *claimed* (purchased) out of the race by other horsemen. Horses beginning their careers in maiden claiming races have failed to show their *connections* (owner and trainer) enough talent during training, so they begin their career with a lower level price tag.

- ✔ **Maiden special weight races:** These races are the highest level of the various maiden races. Horses entered in maiden special weight races are protected in that another horseman can't claim them out of a race. Maiden special weight races come in many conditions based upon age, sex, surface, and distance. A trainer should be able to find the right spot for his maiden to win — whether it's in a sprint or route race, dirt or turf race, and so on.

The owner and trainer prefer that their horse *breaks its maiden* (wins for the first time) in a maiden special weight. Doing so proves the horse has some quality and may develop into a nice runner. If a horse struggles to *graduate* (win its first race) in a maiden special weight race, it's dropped down in class into maiden claiming races.

One thing to remember as a budding handicapper is not to give up on young horses too soon. To catch long shot priced horses, you need to be a *forgiving handicapper* and forgive a bad race or two. Horses throw in clunker races now and then — especially maidens. To catch good mutuel prices, you need to forgive those bad races and project when the horse will run its best.

Horses run in maiden races to create a larger pool of winners for the next condition. After a horse breaks its maiden, it moves one step up the ladder towards the top of the pyramid to face winners that have broken their maiden and a whole new set of race conditions. Depending on the horse's abilities, it either moves on to claiming races or non-selling races.

Claiming races: Where every horse is for sale

The meat and potato races in horse racing are called *claiming races.* Every horse entered in a claiming race is eligible to be *claimed,* meaning bought out of the race. All you need is an owner's license in that state and money on deposit in a horseman's account. Presto — you can claim a racehorse.

Common sense rules in claiming races, so the competition remains fairly equal. For example, if you own a horse worth $30,000, and your trainer enters it into a claiming race for $10,000, chances are you'll win the race and have the horse claimed from you. The winning purse amount won't be enough to make up the difference of the value of the horse you just lost. In essence, you sold a $30,000 horse to another trainer for $10,000. Make enough negative cash flow transactions, and you'll soon be out of the horse owning business.

Some of the best races to handicap are what I call *hard knocking veteran claimers.* These are older claiming horses that keep running every few weeks. Usually, there are full fields to handicap because the class level is populated with a lot of horses. Depending on the price scale at the racetracks near you, it may be a $35,000 claimer in Southern California and New York, a $20,000 claimer in Kentucky and Florida, or a $10,000 claimer at Philadelphia Park and Mountaineer. This class level is around the median for those racetracks. You'll see a lot of geldings that run every few weeks and grind out purses for their owner and trainer.

You see a certain amount of gamesmanship among the owners and trainers in the claiming game. Claiming a bad-legged racehorse is like buying a lemon of a used car. You need to kick the tires a few times and check under the hood before you buy or bet. Most horses usually run to their true worth. Improving horses move up the claiming ladder, and those horses that don't show improvement drop in class.

Condition levels within claiming races

Because claiming races cover a large category of horses, racetrack offices write conditions within claiming races to equalize the competition while trying to draw full fields of competitive horses.

For example, say at a small racetrack a horse breaks its maiden for a maiden-claiming $12,500 tag. If the horse's next start against winners is in an open (unrestricted)-claiming $10,000 race, it may get beat badly, and here's why. In an open-claiming $10,000 race, the maiden graduate may face veteran horses that have won two, four, six, or even more career starts and are much more advanced.

To remedy this, the racing secretary writes a condition claiming race to give the young horse a chance against its own kind. The horse in this example is better suited for a claiming $10,000 non-winners of two races lifetime condition. That means the horse faces other horses that have also won only one race in their life — their maiden win. That's a perfect example how a racing secretary writes races to create parity and attract competitive fields.

The various kinds of conditions you see in claiming races are for non-winners of two, three, and four races in a lifetime. Another kind of condition is non-winners of a race in a year, six months, or some other time frame determined by the racing secretary. Racing secretaries even write races with conditions that specifically favor a horse if they owe its trainer a favor. Just don't go advertising that. It goes to show there's more than one way to skin a cat.

Stymie and John Henry: Claimers who became champions

Nothing in horse racing captures the human spirit of the rags-to-riches saga more than when claiming horses reach their full potential and develop into stakes winners. It's something to see a *claiming horse,* a horse that anyone can buy out of a race, blossom into a stakes winner that wins the best races at the racetrack. The two racehorses who embody that spirit best are Stymie and John Henry.

Stymie was a mean 2-year-old horse that wouldn't train. His breeder and trainer, Max Hirsch, entered Stymie in claiming races in two of his first three starts. Trainer Hirsch Jacobs claimed Stymie for $1,500 in 1943 and gave him to his wife, Ethel. Things didn't get much better, but at least Stymie broke his maiden in his 14th career start — a maiden claiming $3,000 race at Belmont Park.

Stymie ran in claiming races in 12 of his first 18 career starts. After that, Stymie started another 113 times for Jacobs and never ran for a claiming price again. Stymie showed enough ability to merit a start in the Preakness, the second jewel of racing's Triple Crown (see the section, "The Triple Crown," later in the chapter). He really began to flourish as a 4-year-old, winning seven stakes in 1945 and then seven more in 1947 as a 6-year-old.

In 1946, Stymie won a rare walkover in the Saratoga Cup, meaning he ran uncontested. Stymie fractured a sesamoid in 1948 and was sidelined for 15 months. After a brief return to the races, Stymie was retired as the all-time leading

money-earner with $918,485. That record held for 15 months until the great Citation surpassed him.

John Henry began his career as a 2-year-old in 1978. He didn't run in his first claiming race until spring of that year in his 14th career start. Then, the next five of six starts he made were all in claimers. The last one, however, was his turf debut at Belmont Park, which he won by an astonishing 14 lengths. He never ran for a claiming tag again for the final 64 starts of his career.

John Henry had been sold at sales and privately for very small amounts of money — $1,100, $2,200, $10,000 — and then finally sold for $25,000 (sight unseen!) to bicycle salesman Sam Rubin. John Henry was the very first racehorse owned by Rubin and his wife, Dotty.

The gelding became a major stakes winner on grass first for trainer Bob Donato and then for V.J. "Lefty" Nickerson, who suggested to Rubin that he send John Henry to Ron McAnally to run on the firm turf courses in Southern California.

In 1980, John Henry became a West Coast sensation, reeling off grade 1 wins in the grassy San Luis Rey, San Juan Capistrano, and Hollywood Invitational. The next year he won racing's first seven-figure purse, the 1981 Arlington Million, by a nose over The Bart.

He was named Horse of the Year in 1981 and in 1984. John Henry retired after the 1984 season with career purse earnings of $6,597,947. Not bad for a race horse that nobody wanted.

Read the conditions of a race very carefully. Some horses fit the condition perfectly, and some don't, so think about why certain horses are in a race. You may have to read between the lines by putting yourself in the trainers' shoes. Trainer intent is an important part of handicapping. For example, a shrewd trainer may like to run his claiming horse out of condition when it's ready to win to ensure higher odds. For more on trainer angles, which you need to understand to be a successful handicapper, see Chapter 8.

Moving up in class

When claiming horses perform well and win races, their trainers move them up the claiming ladder to higher price levels. A number of things can happen in this scenario:

- ✔ A horse may peak quickly and then begin to lose form. The only way it remains competitive is to drop down again in class.

- ✔ A horse may plateau and find a nice comfort level where it proves it belongs.

- ✔ A horse may improve through the claiming ranks and move into allowance races (see the section, "Allowance races," later in the chapter) and beyond.

One of the strongest moves you see is when a top-class trainer *double jumps* the horse, meaning she moves the horse up two class levels because it's doing so well. The class rise may be within the claiming ranks, from claiming up to allowance, within allowance conditions, or a move up into a stakes race. In this move, you're bound to get good odds on the horse because the public perceives the animal to be outclassed. Quite the contrary. Betting on an animal in peak condition at a square price in a good spot is the right move. You don't cash every time, but the odds are high enough to be very profitable over the long haul.

Dropping down in class

When horses drop down dramatically in class, a red flag should go up indicating that something is physically wrong with the animal. These horses dropping down in class may not be doing well in training, may not be eating well, and may be going off form, meaning not running at peak efficiency.

If a horse owner claims this horse, he may get stuck with it for a while before it recovers. Sometimes horses like this don't bounce back, and owners get stuck with it forever and are out claiming money. As a horseplayer, if you bet on a drop down horse that doesn't run well, you lose your money.

If you see a $40,000 animal entered for a $10,000 claiming price, be suspicious. Horsemen aren't in the business of giving their animals away for pennies on the dollar. You may want to pass on this horse, because the public usually overbets these kinds of horses, meaning the odds are way too low (also called an *underlay*).

Passing on favorites is okay, especially in the case of drop down claimers. A horse's win odds should reflect its real chances of winning. You get no value in this scenario, so you won't get hurt even if the horse wins.

Non-selling races: Another step up the ladder

If a horse that broke its maiden shows real promise, the preference is to skip the claiming races and move forward into *non-selling races* — races where the entrants can't be claimed. After all, the owner and trainer have a lot invested in each horse and want to protect that investment. Successful claiming horses can also move up to this level if their trainers and owners think they have a shot in this new category. The three categories of non-selling races are allowance, optional claiming, and starter allowance — allowance being the highest level within this category and starter allowance being the lowest.

Allowance races

After a horse wins a maiden special weight race (see "Maiden races: Where it all begins," earlier in the chapter), it jumps up into an *allowance race*. The really nice, young horses strive to win through their conditions. In the first level, they try to win the second race of their career. In the second level, they try to win the third race of their career, and in third level allowance races, they go for the fourth win of their career. After they progress that far, they're ready for stakes competition (see "Stakes and handicap races: The top of the pyramid," later in the chapter).

A good way to describe allowance races is to compare them to minor league baseball. A young ballplayer starts in a rookie league for his first taste of professional baseball. A baseball rookie is comparable to a maiden horse who has never won a race. He plays his way up the ladder, level by level to A, AA, and AAA minor leagues. After he proves himself a polished prospect, he's ready to join the big club in the major leagues. The major leagues are comparable to stakes races. Racehorses need the same kind of development before they start running in stakes races. They learn good habits and learn how to compete by winning their way through their conditions.

The racing office writes lots of allowance races because it wants to graduate young horses up the pyramid and replenish stock (horses) at all competitive levels. The horses that don't make it to the top may slide back, but they're important nonetheless in the racetrack's overall racing program.

If a horse struggles to win and move up in allowance races, it may be forced to run in high claiming races where it can find its own level of competition (see preceding section).

As a handicapper, you should read the conditions of races rather closely. Allowance races can be creatively written with certain horses in mind. For example, part of the condition may be for horses that haven't won a race since December 17. Then you look at each horse's past performance resume in the *Daily Racing Form* (see Chapter 11), and you find a horse that won a race on December 16. Eureka! You found a horse that fits the race condition perfectly. You can then surmise that the conditions of this allowance race were written with this horse in mind. Figure 2-1 gives an example of the conditions for an allowance race at Aqueduct.

Figure 2-1: Allowance race conditions, like this one, can be quite specific.

6 **Aqueduct** *6 Furlongs*(1:074) (F) **Alw 43000N1X** Purse $43,000 (UP TO $8,120 NYSBFOA) For Fillies Two Years Old Which Have Never Won A Race Other Than Maiden Or Claiming Or Which Have Never Won Two Races. Weight, 121 lbs. Non-winners Of A Race Since October 29 Allowed 2 lbs. A race Allowed 4 lbs.

Money allowance races are written for older horses that aren't quite stakes caliber or are stakes horses returning from a long layoff. A money allowance gives the older horses a chance to win without being exposed in a claiming race. A money allowance can draw a quality field and be close to the caliber of a stakes race. This is one more example of how a racing secretary uses eligibility requirements to write conditions for races to satisfy all of the horsemen at the racetrack.

Optional claiming races

The *optional claimer* is a hybrid: It's part allowance race, part claiming race. Bottom line, it opens up more horses for the racing secretary to draw from.

The racing secretary controls the horse-racing product that you and I bet on at the racetrack. The inventory of horses he draws from is stabled at the racetrack or is located in nearby training centers. His goal is to write races with full fields of competitive horses that horseplayers want to bet a lot of money on. An optional claiming race is one more tool at his disposal.

At many racetracks, there's a shortage of good allowance horses. So to overcome the shortage, the hybrid optional claimer is run. The key to making a good marriage in this type of race condition is for the racing secretary to know the quality of the two sets of horses — claiming horses versus allowance horses.

For example, in Southern California, the optional claiming prices begin at $32,000, with increments at $40,000, $50,000, $62,500, $80,000, and up to $100,000. The allowance conditions (see Figure 2-2 for an example) are then written to match up the talent level fairly. In theory, the allowance horse should be the better horse. But plenty of hard knocking claimers try hard every time they race and can upset the competition. For example, an eight-horse optional claiming field may contain four horses running under allowance conditions and four horses running for a claiming price.

Figure 2-2:
Race conditions for an optional claiming race at Aqueduct.

7 **Aqueduct** *6 Furlongs*(1:074) <u>OC 65k/N3X</u> Purse $47,000 (UP TO $8,930 NYSBFOA) For Three Years Old And Upward Which Have Never Won Three Races Other Than Maiden, Claiming, Starter, Or Restricted Or Which Have Never Won Four Races Or Optional Claiming Price Of $65,000. Three Year Olds, 122 lbs.; Older, 123 lbs. Non-winners of $30,000 since October 25 Allowed 2 lbs. Non-winners of a race since October 1 Allowed 4 lbs.

Starter allowance races

Starter allowance races are actually glorified claiming races. The big differences are that the purse is a little higher and the horses aren't exposed to being claimed. The eligibility conditions point to horses that have run in claiming races, as shown in Figure 2-3.

Figure 2-3:
Race conditions for a starter allowance race at Turfway Park.

7 **Turfway Park** *5 Furlongs*(:564) Ⓕ <u>Alw 8000s</u> Purse $10,000 For Fillies And Mares Three Years Old And Upward Which Have Started For A Claiming Price Of $8,000 Or Less In 2003-2004. Three Year Olds, 122 lbs.; Older, 123 lbs. Non-winners Of A Race Other Than Claiming Since November 12 Allowed 3 lbs. Such A Race Since October 12 Allowed 6 lbs.

Starter allowance races reward the hard knocking claimers that aren't good enough to compete in straight allowance races or optional claiming. The purse is higher than in a claiming race and serves as a carrot that lures more horses. As a handicapper, look for claiming horses that have improved so much that they hold a big conditioning advantage over the field.

Stakes and handicap races: The top of the pyramid

At the top of the horse pyramid are the best runners on the grounds — the *stakes horses* and *handicap horses*. These horses have gone up the ladder, breaking their maiden and winning through their allowance conditions, and now they're tackling the best horses at the racetrack. They also face invaders who ship in from other racetracks to try and steal a rich purse.

These are the kind of horses and races you see at the racetrack or OTB and on television in the feature races on weekends and holidays. The racing secretary cards overnight stakes, restricted stakes, non-graded stakes, and stakes graded 3, 2, and 1. These stakes horses are the crème de la crème, the kind you're willing to spend good money to see run.

Here are explanations and examples of each category of stakes race:

- **Grade 1 stakes:** These stakes exemplify the very best races in the country. For example, the Triple Crown races — the Kentucky Derby, Preakness, and Belmont Stakes (see Chapter 18) — are grade 1 stakes. In races of this caliber, you expect to see champion racehorses competing against the very best in their respective divisions. The richest purses tend to be grade 1 stakes, because the best horses follow the money.

- **Grade 2 stakes:** These stakes are considered a cut below grade 1, but they attract a very talented group of horses. A stakes race can move up or down in grade depending on the caliber of horse that runs in it. For example, if a grade 2 stakes has horses in it that normally run in a grade 1 stakes, the race may be upgraded the following year to grade 1 status.

- **Grade 3 stakes:** Another level down from grade 1 and grade 2 stakes, these stakes have a noticeably smaller purse because they attract a lesser caliber of stakes horse. Still, the competition is keen, and the field sizes can be large because the race draws starters from a bigger pool of horses. There are more grade 3 caliber stakes horses than grade 1 caliber horses.

- **Non-graded stakes:** The vast majority of stakes races don't have grades 1, 2, or 3. However, that doesn't mean the horses aren't any good. Quite the contrary. At a major racetrack, a non-graded stakes may be a stepping stone race to a graded stakes. At a smaller racetrack, a non-graded stakes can attract the best horses on the grounds. Any stakes race at any track attracts a very good caliber of racehorse.

- **Restricted stakes:** These stakes are written for horses born in a specific state. For example, there are programs for horses born specifically in California, Florida, Maryland, New York, Ohio, Pennsylvania, and West Virginia, to name a few. So, for example, in a California-bred stakes race, only horses born in California can compete.

✔ **Overnight stakes:** These stakes are written with three days advance notice. In a way, these are high-level glorified allowance races. They carry a higher purse than allowance races. For most stakes races, a horse has to be nominated (pay a fee to become eligible) a month or two before the date it's scheduled to run. This nomination process allows horsemen to point for a race and the marketing and publicity departments at the racetrack to promote the race.

The top stakes are awarded a grading of 1, 2, and 3 to let everybody know what the most important races are. Every racing office has a person called a *stakes coordinator* assigned to recruit horses for these stakes. It's a matter of pride for racetracks to card a big stakes race and have the best horses in their region, and for that matter in the country, participate.

In a Class by Themselves: The Race for the Triple Crown and the Breeders' Cup

Even if a horse is good enough to make it into the stakes and handicap races, he still may not be close to the caliber of elite horses that enter the race for the Triple Crown or the Breeders' Cup. These horses are the absolute best of the best — the stars of the sport. What makes these races so special and hard to reach? Read on to find out.

The Triple Crown

The Triple Crown is strictly for 3-year-old horses. The series consists of the Kentucky Derby, Preakness, and Belmont Stakes. To reach the class level of the Triple Crown, 3-year-old horses must prove themselves in stakes races called *prep races* against other 3-year-old horses. In theory, horses need to run well in the prep races to earn their way to the first leg of the Triple Crown — the Kentucky Derby.

In Chapter 18, I list all the major prep races leading up to the Kentucky Derby. Many of the prep races are grade 1 races (see the preceding section) and carry rich purses as high as $500,000 to $750,000. As stand alone races, the prep races are well worth winning on their own merit.

When horsemen first buy a yearling or a 2-year-old colt, they have in mind a potential Kentucky Derby horse, but 99.9 percent of the colts don't get to the Derby. However, that doesn't keep the horsemen from trying and dreaming.

When Sir Barton won the first Triple Crown in 1919, nobody knew it. That's because the three races weren't linked by the name at that time. In 1930, sportswriter Charles Hatton of the *Daily Racing Form* first coined the phrase Triple Crown to describe the three victories by Gallant Fox, who became horse racing's second Triple Crown champion. Eleven Triple Crown champions have been named, and the honor remains an elusive one. No horse has won the Triple Crown since Affirmed in 1978.

The Breeders' Cup World Thoroughbred Championships

John R. Gaines, an influential Kentucky breeder and owner of Gainesway Farm, founded the Breeders' Cup and first announced it in April 1982. As brilliant as the idea seems now, Gaines had to twist many arms and cajole others to buy into his plan, which was still more than two-and-a-half years away from becoming a reality.

Good things are worth fighting for, though, and eventually the project gained racing industry support. In February 1983, Hollywood Park (in Inglewood, California) was named the first host track of the Breeders' Cup. The reason behind a West Coast site was to take advantage of great Southern California weather and to attract many stars from the entertainment, film, and television industries.

In September 1983, NBC Sports contracted to televise the first Breeders' Cup, guaranteeing all seven races would be shown in a four-hour national broadcast. This was no small feat, because the Saturday event was right in the middle of the college football season.

On November 10, 1984, the inaugural Breeders' Cup was run in front of 64,254 fans at Hollywood Park. Chief's Crown won the first Breeders' Cup event in the Juvenile for 2-year-old horses, and in the end, long shot Wild Again pinballed past Slew o' Gold and Gate Dancer to win a thrilling stretch duel in the Classic, the defining race of the season for older horses.

Now, the Breeders' Cup World Thoroughbred Championships is held every fall. The host racetrack changes each year, but certain venues are part of a rotation. Churchill Downs (Louisville, Kentucky), Belmont Park (Elmont, New York), Gulfstream Park (Hallandale, Florida), Hollywood Park (Inglewood, California), and Santa Anita Park (Arcadia, California) never go long without hosting one. The powers to be at the Breeders' Cup haven't been afraid to think outside the box, either. The event has been held at smaller racetracks such as Arlington Park in Arlington Heights, Illinois; Woodbine in Rexdale, Ontario, Canada; and Lone Star Park in Grand Prairie, Texas. And in 2007, the event will return to the East Coast at Monmouth Park in Oceanport, New Jersey.

Table 2-1 lists the nine races that make up the Breeders' Cup:

Table 2-1	The Nine Races of the Breeders' Cup			
Race	**Purse**	**Distance**	**Surface**	**Conditions**
Steeplechase	$250,000	2⅝th miles	Turf	3-year-olds and up
Distaff	$2 million	1⅛th miles	Dirt	Fillies and mares, 3-year-olds and up
Juvenile Fillies	$1 million	1¹⁄₁₆th miles	Dirt	Fillies, 2-year-olds
Mile	$1.5 million	1 mile	Turf	3-year-olds and up
Sprint	$1 million	6 furlongs	Dirt	3-year-olds and up
Filly & Mare Turf	$1 million	1⅜th miles	Turf	Fillies and mares, 3-year-olds and up
Juvenile	$1.5 million	1¹⁄₁₆th miles	Dirt	2-year-olds
Turf	$2 million	1½ miles	Turf	3-year-olds and up
Classic	$4 million	1¼ miles	Dirt	3-year-olds and up

As a budding horseplayer, circle the Breeders' Cup each fall on your calendar, and don't miss it. The races that day make up the best betting program all year for handicapping and playing the horses. With full fields, talented horses, world class riders, and enough betting opportunities to last a lifetime, the Breeders' Cup is the best day of horse racing bar none.

Chapter 3

Getting a Handle on Parimutuel Wagering

In This Chapter
▶ Figuring out parimutuel wagering
▶ Taking a look at the takeout
▶ Breaking down breakage
▶ Avoiding paying taxes on your winnings

The parimutuel betting system is the foundation for the business of American horse racing as we know it. It has served a purpose of cleaning up the image of horse racing by eliminating bookmakers and putting control of betting into the hands of the racetrack operators.

A Parisian by the name of Pierre Oller is credited with inventing the parimutuel system of betting in 1865. I've researched two origins of the word *parimutuel.* The first is a French word formed from *parier,* which means "to wager," and *mutuel,* which means "shared in common." Thus the phrase "betting amongst ourselves" is a tight, refined meaning of the parimutuel system. The second is a shortened form of "Paris mutuel" denoting where the system originated.

In this chapter, I examine how the parimutuel wagering system works. I define the takeout, look at breakage, and show you how to circumvent the IRS — legally of course — when you win a big horse bet.

Betting Against Other Bettors

Before the advent of parimutuel wagering, horse race betting was done with *bookmakers.* Bookmakers, also known as bookies, are essentially businesspeople that handle gambling bets — mainly on horse racing and sports. Bookmaking is now illegal in the United States, but it's a highly respected business in other parts of the world.

Betting on horse racing back then was easy because it was just straight wagering — win, place, and show. (*Straight wagering* refers to a bet on a single horse, and I cover it in detail in Chapter 4.) Because this era was long before the computer age, betting on multiple horses or multiple races wasn't available. Profits to the bookmakers came in the form of a *vigorish* (also called vig) — a charge taken on bets — and the remainder of the money bet was paid out to winning bettors.

When the Federal government banned bookmakers, *parimutuel wagering* (betting against other bettors) took its place at the racetracks. When you bet on a horse and it wins, your profits come from the losing horseplayers who bet on other horses in the same race. That's the beauty of parimutuel wagering. Horseplayers are betting amongst each other, and if you're smarter than the people around you, you win their money.

The parimutuel system puts a tax on wagering called the *takeout,* which provides the revenues for the horse racing business to pay its bills. The racetrack has to pay for such expenses as overhead costs, the costs of maintaining the racetrack and property, employee wages, and most importantly, *purse money* (the money owners of the racehorses try to win).

Because horse owners need to win enough money to pay their bills, they want to run at racetracks that offer the best purses. Applying the system of supply and demand to horse racing, the bigger the purses, the better the quality and quantity of horses that run at that track. It's a spiral that keeps feeding itself.

In addition to the racetracks and horse owners, the government — local, state, and federal — profits from parimutuel wagering. Depending on the jurisdiction, the government receives a share of the takeout.

The parimutuel wagering system takes care of all parties' needs.

Comparing parimutuel wagering to poker

To best explain parimutuel wagering, I like to compare it to the game of poker. In poker, you're betting against every other player at the card table. The theory is the same in horse racing. You're betting against all the other horseplayers in the parimutuel pool.

When you play poker in Las Vegas or in a card room, the house extracts a percentage of the *ante* (the stake each player puts in the pot) for itself. In horse racing, the equivalent is the takeout (see "Beating the Takeout," later in the chapter). After the percentage is taken out in poker, if you like the cards you hold in your hand, you bet and raise. Similarly, in horse racing, when you think the race has value, you bet into it. The poker play continues until the player with the best hand wins. The same goes in racing, where if you bet the best horse or horses and they run the best, you win.

Bookmakers: Gone in the U.S. but still en vogue in England

At one time, *bookmakers* (people that handle gambling bets) were legal in the U.S. And if they weren't legal, local law enforcement officials accepted bribes from bookies to look the other way. In the late 1890s, bookmakers had a strong hold on horse racing in the U.S. On-track, they'd pay a day rate to the racetrack for the right to be there. Off-track, bookmaking operations took place in pool rooms, cigar stores, and any back rooms protected by law enforcement.

The off-track bookmakers were notorious for cheating their clients. The bookmakers received their information from the racetracks via Western Union. Thus, the bookies had a huge advantage over the horseplayers because they knew the odds, post times, and results. Bookies cheated by selling tickets at lower odds than offered at the racetrack. They also took wagers after the race was run — known as past posting — and duped horseplayers into betting on favorites that had already lost. The bookies bribed jockeys into fixing races by pulling their horses.

The bookmakers' scandalous behavior turned public and government sentiment against horse racing. In the early 1900s, anti-gambling movements spread across the U.S., moving state governments to shut down racetracks. A key moment came in 1908 when Colonel Matt Winn found some old parimutuel machines in a storage room at Churchill Downs in Louisville, Kentucky. He booted out the on-track bookmakers and set up the machines to accept parimutuel wagering. The machines were primitive, but with control back in the hands of the racetrack, the betting was trustworthy.

Little by little, states passed laws allowing racetracks to reopen. Hialeah Park in Miami reopened in 1929. In 1933, Pimlico Race Course in Maryland began using parimutuel machines. The same year, three other states revived horse racing and legalized parimutuel wagering — California, Michigan, and Ohio. Arkansas came back in 1934, Massachusetts in 1935. The last year of bookmaking at Belmont Park was in 1939, and parimutuel wagering began in New York the next spring. Slowly but surely a modernized parimutuel wagering system legislated by state government was replacing on-track bookmaking. Each state also instituted stringent regulatory horse racing commissions to oversee the integrity of the sport.

In England, the past is very much alive, as the bookmakers thrive in English racing. I remember attending the horse races at Newbury Racecourse in England in 1992. A long row of bookmaker podiums lined the racetrack apron, which is a paved area for patrons between the main track and the grandstand. Each bookmaker listed odds on a blackboard for the upcoming races, and you could shop for price.

Being a bookmaker is a fairly reputable business overseas. The competition among companies is fierce, so you the bettor should come out the winner. Most of the English bookmakers have graduated to Internet sites and are accepting new clients from near and far away. The wide array of companies is well known, especially if you've traveled to England recently. The roster of bookmakers includes Bet 365, Blue Square, Victor Chandler, William Hill, Sporting Index, Capital Sports, Bet Direct, PremierBet, Stan James, Sporting Odds, SportingBet, Gamebookers, BetDaq, Bet HiLo, Sporting Options, Paddy Power, Ladbrokes, and Stanley Bet.

The essence of playing poker and betting on horse racing is the same: You bet against all the other players. If you're smarter than the other players, you make money regardless of how much the house deducts from the antes or how much the racetrack takeout is.

Attracting a new gambling audience

A successful horseplayer must acquire two types of skills to win money: handicapping and betting. If forced to choose between which skill I'd rather possess, I'd have to say betting. In Parts III and IV, I cover the subjects of handicapping, betting, money management, and sophisticated handicapping.

I know lots of handicappers who can dissect a horse race with great insight. But they can't construct wagers that'll make them money. On the other hand, I know horseplayers who can take good handicapping information from other sources and build wagers that give them an strong chance of winning money.

Parimutuel wagering is attracting a new gambling audience, because you can win even if you're a good but not great handicapper. If you know that the key to succeeding in the parimutuel wagering system is to find *overlays* (meaning horses going off at higher odds than their actual chance of winning), and you know how to wager to make money, you can rely on various sources to find good handicapping information and still win. In Chapter 12, I discuss finding overlays and using the racetrack morning line to your advantage.

Beating the Takeout

The *takeout,* money deducted from the wagering pool by the host racetrack, is an onerous charge to horseplayers. The *blended rate* (average percent takeout of straight and exotic bets combined) for takeout is about 20 percent, meaning that if you're a median horseplayer (winning and losing money equally), you'll lose 20 percent of your bankroll because of takeout.

To win money betting on horse racing, not only do you need to be a better horseplayer than the masses, but you also must beat the takeout.

In Figure 3-1, you see a pie chart showing where the wagering dollar went for betting on the Santa Anita Park (in Arcadia, California) races.

I live in Las Vegas, where professional gamblers play every kind of game for a living — sports, horse racing, blackjack, slot machines, video poker, craps, you name it. The takeout in casino games is called the *hold,* and casinos compute it to minute fractions to favor them. A professional gambler must know the cost of playing the game and where she can gain an edge to win in the long run. The same is true for a winning horseplayer.

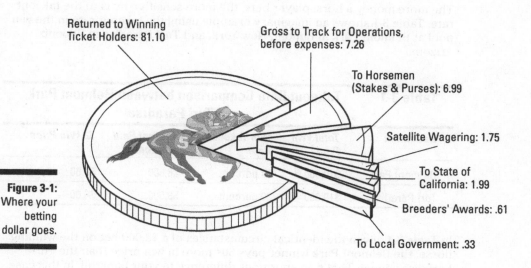

Returned to Winning Ticket Holders: 81.10

Gross to Track for Operations, before expenses: 7.26

To Horsemen (Stakes & Purses): 6.99

Satellite Wagering: 1.75

To State of California: 1.99

Breeders' Awards: .61

To Local Government: .33

Figure 3-1: Where your betting dollar goes.

You'll remember the chart in Figure 3-1 the next time you read in the *Daily Racing Form* that the takeout is being raised to pay for something else — whether it's for insurance, purses, state taxes, or the racetrack itself. When the takeout rate goes up, you're the one footing the bill.

How the takeout rate works

Here I show you how a win price of a horse race is computed, so you understand how the takeout rate works:

✔ In a horse race, the money bet to win goes into the parimutuel win pool. For this example, I use a round number — $10,000 — in the win pool.

✔ If the takeout rate for a win bet is 20 percent, the racetrack deducts $2,000 (20 percent), and the winning bettors receive $8,000 (80 percent).

✔ Say only $400 has been bet on the winning horse. The price for win, place, and show is always posted as a $2 payoff, which means there are just 200 $2 win tickets on the winning horse.

✔ Divide the $8,000 win pool by 200 winning $2 tickets, and you get $40. Thus, a $2 win bet on the above horse returns $40.

Different takeout rates for different types of wagers

The more money a horseplayer bets, the more sensitive he is to the takeout rate. Table 3-1 shows an imaginary example using the takeout rate in the win pool at Belmont Park in Elmont, New York, and Turf Paradise in Phoenix, Arizona.

Table 3-1	Takeout Rate Comparison between Belmont Park and Turf Paradise			
Racetrack	**Total Win Pool**	**Win Takeout Rate**	**Amount Paid to Winners**	**$2 Win Price**
Belmont Park	$10,000	14 percent	$8,600	$8.60
Turf Paradise	$10,000	20 percent	$8,000	$8.00

In Table 3-1, given the identical circumstances of a $2,000 bet on the winning horse, the Belmont Park winner pays 60¢ more in win price than the Turf Paradise winner. That's an enormous difference to your bankroll. In this case, the Belmont Park horseplayer would receive $8,600, and the Turf Paradise horseplayer would just get $8,000. That's a $600 difference in profits to a professional horseplayer.

Table 3-2 shows the takeout percentage rates for various wagers at major U.S. racetracks. Refer to Chapters 4 and 15 for information on these various types of bets.

Table 3-2	Takeout Rates for Selected Racetracks Around the U.S.						
Racetrack	**Win-Place-Show**	**Exacta**	**Trifecta**	**Superfecta**	**Daily Double**	**Pick 3**	**Pick 4**
Arlington Park	17.0	20.5	25.0	25.0	20.5	25.0	25.0
NYRA	14.0	17.5	25.0	25.0	17.5	25.0	25.0
Calder	18.0	20.0	27.0	27.0	20.0	24.0	None
Churchill	16.0	19.0	19.0	19.0	19.0	19.0	19.0

Racetrack	Win-Place-Show	Exacta	Trifecta	Superfecta	Daily Double	Pick 3	Pick 4
California	15.43	20.68	20.68	20.68	20.68	20.68	20.68
Fair Grounds	17.0	20.5	25.0	25.0	20.5	25.0	None
Gulfstream	15.0	20.0	25.0	25.0	20.0	25.0	None
Keeneland	16.0	19.0	19.0	19.0	19.0	19.0	19.0
Laurel Park/ Pimlico	18.0	21.0	25.75	25.75	21.0	25.75	14.0
NJSEA	17.0	19.0	25.0	25.0	19.0	25.0	15.0
Oaklawn Park	17.0	21.0	21.0	None	21.0	21.0	None
Turfway Park	17.5	22.0	22.0	22.0	22.0	22.0	22.0
Turf Paradise	20.0	21.0	25.0	25.0	21.0	25.0	None

NYRA racetracks are Aqueduct, Belmont Park, and Saratoga. California race-tracks include Bay Meadows, Del Mar, Golden Gate Fields, Hollywood Park, Northern California Fairs, and Santa Anita Park. NJSEA racetracks are the Meadowlands and Monmouth Park.

You can find real value in betting into certain wagering pools, depending on where you're betting. At the New York Racing Association (NYRA), straight wagers, exactas, and daily doubles offer the best value in horse racing. Churchill Downs and Keeneland offer value in the trifecta, superfecta, pick 3, and pick 4 (see Chapter 15 for more on these types of exotic wagers). The Maryland Jockey Club that operates Laurel Park and Pimlico, and the New Jersey Sports and Exposition Authority that runs Monmouth Park and the Meadowlands, have low takeouts for their pick 4 bet. A lower takeout means more money is returned to winning horseplayers.

Show plungers

The parimutuel pool can work in your favor when someone bets a large amount of money to show on a horse. (*Betting to show* means your horse must finish first, second, or third in a race for you to collect money.) These bettors are called *show plungers*. (You may also hear *bridge jumper* or *puddle jumper*, which mean the same thing.) I cover this strategy briefly in Chapter 4, but I want to show you the mechanics of why it works and why betting against the show plunger is a smart move to make in parimutuel wagering.

When a horseplayer bets a lot of money to show on a horse, he's banking on the fact that the racetrack must pay a minimum $2.10 show price, even if the large bet creates a *minus show pool,* meaning that there isn't enough money in the pool to pay out all the $2.10 show payoffs and the racetrack must cover the rest. The horseplayer is also banking on the fact the horse on paper is so superior to the rest of the field that at worst he's supposed to finish *in the money*, meaning first, second, or third.

You've probably figured out by now that there are no sure things in life, or in horse racing. Horses going off at short odds like 1/2, 2/5, and even 1/5 do lose. And some even finish out of the money. Betting other horses in the field to show (going against the show plunger) is a low risk bet with a big upside.

Table 3-3 shows an example of a minus show pool. After the 15 percent takeout is subtracted, only $8,500 remains — not enough money to cover all the $2.10 show payoffs. The racetrack must make up the shortage in the pool.

Table 3-3			A Minus Show Pool			
Horse	$2 Show Price	Amount Bet to Show	Show Takeout Rate of 15 %	Show Pool Left	Money Needed for $2.10 Minimum Payoff	Minus Show Pool
A	$2.10	$9,000	$1,350		$9,450	
B	$2.10	$200	$30		$210	
C	$2.10	$200	$30		$210	
Rest of field			$600	$90		
Total		$10,000	$1,500	$8,500	$9,870	$1,370

In Table 3-3, the racetrack must reach into its cash reserves for $1,370 to cover a minus show pool. By law, the racetrack has to pay a minimum $2.10 to show.

Table 3-4 displays the same example, but horse A, the very short price favorite, runs out of the money.

Table 3-4		A Minus Show Pool When the Show Plunger Horse Finishes Out of the Money			
Horse	$2 Show Price	Amount Bet to Show	Show Takeout Rate of 15 %	Show Pool Left	Money Needed for $2.10 Minimum Payoff
B	$28.20	$200	$30		$2,833
C	$28.20	$200	$30		$2,833
D	$56.60	$100	$15		$2,833
Rest of field		$9,500	$1,425		
		$10,000	$1,500	$8,500	$8,500

As you can see in Table 3-4, when the big favorite runs out of the money, the show pool prices are huge. The betting angle is to play other horses to show and root against the big favorite hoping he finishes out of the money.

Simulcast wagering

As the racetracks began to face more competition for the gambling dollar from state run lotteries and Atlantic City casinos (impacting eastern states), experiments were done with simulcast wagering. *Simulcast wagering* means importing the television signal of your horse races to an off-site location for wagering by patrons away from the racetrack.

In 1982, Canadian racing authorities approved the simulcasting of the races from Fort Erie into Woodbine Racecourse in Toronto, Canada. In 1983, Atlantic City was the recipient of the simulcast signal from the Meadowlands in East Rutherford, New Jersey, and the simulcast industry was off and running in the U.S.

Las Vegas jumped into the fray in 1983, and at that embryonic stage, the price of simulcasting

was set at 3 percent of the simulcast wagering, also known as simulcast handle. Although the cost of racing and the takeout have gone up since then, the price of simulcasting from 1983 to the present has remained the same.

How 3 percent came to be the standard rate, I'm not sure. But none of the host racetracks were worried or complained one bit. The prevailing theory of racetrack managers in the 1980s was that simulcast revenue was found money. They believed that horseplayers betting on the races from hundreds, and even thousands of miles away, didn't impact on-track business.

Now, decades later, the reverse is true. Much more money is bet on simulcasting than on the live racing product.

Show plungers have bet as much as $50,000 to $100,000, which raises eye-brows all over the racetrack. You'll look out onto the racetrack and see a disjointed infield tote board where the show pool can be larger than the place pool and even the win pool. If you're going to be a contrarian, this is the time to be one. You have the chance to bet a little to win a lot.

Understanding Breakage

To understand breakage, think about your old pair of blue jeans with a small hole in the pocket, and all your loose change falls down your pants leg and gets lost in the grass. You never know how much money you've really lost.

Similarly, in parimutuel wagering, *breakage* robs you of money that you didn't know you lost. It's like an annoying surcharge that drips into a bank account that states use for different purposes. The money never reaches you, the bettor, and it seldom gets used in a positive way for horse racing. It basically gets sucked out of the system.

Table 3-5 shows how breakage works and steals money from the pockets of horseplayers. I use the same numbers in Table 3-5 as I do earlier in the chapter in Table 3-4.

Table 3-5			**Computing Breakage**			
Horse	*$2 Show Price*	*$2 Show Price before Breakage*	*Reverts to the State Per $2 Bet*	*Amount Bet to Show*	*Money Needed*	*Total Breakage to the State*
B	$28.20	$28.33	$0.13	$200	$2,833	$13
C	$28.20	$28.33	$0.13	$200	$2,833	$13
D	$56.60	$56.66	$0.06	$100	$2,833	$3

As you can see in Table 3-5, the real show price before breakage of horse B is $28.33. States round it down to the lowest 20¢ tier. Thus, the payoff became $28.20, meaning you, the bettor, lost 13¢ of winnings for every $2 wagered. If you bet horse D, you made out a smidgen better. You lost only 6¢ of winnings for every $2 wagered.

Breakage really works against you when the price just misses the higher 20¢ tier. For example, a $2 price before breakage of $2.39 rounds down to $2.20. You lose 19¢ of your winnings. Figure out the breakage over hundreds upon thousands of winning wagers, and it really adds up.

The one state where the horseplayer catches a break on breakage is in New York, which has dime breakage. For example, if you bet on an NYRA racetrack like Aqueduct, Belmont Park, or Saratoga, the payoff prices in Table 3-5 for horse B and horse D would be $28.30 and $56.60 respectively. Horse B's payoff would increase 10¢, but horse D's payoff would be unaffected.

When Uncle Sam Comes to Visit

If you're a horseplayer, sometimes you don't mind paying taxes on your winnings, like after you hit a big score. But what if I told you that you can bet certain ways and avoid paying taxes — and it's completely legal. I know that got your attention.

The U.S. tax threshold on parimutuel wagers is 300/1 odds. So if you win a $2 exotic wager that paid $600, you have to pay tax on it (see Chapter 15 for the details on exotic wagers). When you go to cash the winning ticket, the mutuel clerk asks you for identification to fill out a W-2G form. You get a copy for your files, the racetrack keeps one, and the Internal Revenue Service receives a copy. The IRS then taxes your gambling winnings as earned income.

You can do two things to legally avoid paying taxes on your winnings:

- ✔ Bet $1 unit tickets instead of $2 tickets when possible.
- ✔ Itemize your deductions when you file, and write off your gambling losses against your gambling winnings.

The first strategy comes before you place the bet, and it's very simple. Instead of ordering a $2 ticket, see if you can bet a $1 unit. If you play in $1 units, the tax threshold rises to 600/1 odds. If you still want a $2 ticket, just order it twice by telling the mutuel clerk to repeat the bet.

The second strategy comes into play when you file your Federal tax return. If you've won more than $5,000, the IRS automatically deducts 28 percent of your winnings. You can get that money back — as well as tax on smaller winnings — by itemizing your deductions and writing off your gambling losses against your gambling winnings.

To get your money back, keep good records of your wagering at the racetrack, off-track wagering parlor, and/or casino for the entire year. Keep programs, overnights, your losing tickets, and so on.

Make sure your record keeping is believable. For example, don't record that you bet $10,000 a day when you're really a $2 bettor.

Be accurate. If you itemize your U.S. tax return, the IRS allows you to deduct gambling losses up to the amount of your gambling winnings. It lumps together racetrack and casino gambling winnings on one line item in schedule A, Form 1040. The nature of betting on horse racing is that you're going to lose many more bets than you win, so the IRS easily believes that over the course of a year, a horseplayer will accumulate a lot of losers.

In Las Vegas casinos, if you bet using your *player tracking card* (see Chapter 23), you can request an activity statement. It shows your up-to-date balance of either winning or losing. If your statement is losing, which most are, you can use that in your tax return to offset W-2G earnings.

Everything I've told you in this section is legal, above board, and part of gambling on horse racing and gambling at casinos. It's only fair that if you win some and lose some gambling, you should take advantage of IRS tax laws that benefit you.

Chapter 4

The Skinny on Betting

Making a horse bet can be as simple or as complicated as you want it to be. If you're new to the betting scene, your best bet (no pun intended) is to keep things simple for now.

In this chapter, I introduce you to the simplest bets of all — straight bets — and the different straight betting styles. I clue you in on betting etiquette and show you how to place a bet step-by-step. I also give you some tips on tote board watching.

If you've placed a few bets at the track already, you may want to head to Chapter 15, which discusses exotic wagers.

Starting Off with Straight Bets

Just imagine you're trying to invest money in the stock market. For a safe play, you buy an interest-bearing bond. For higher yields, you purchase some stocks. If you really want to go for it, you invest in futures or options. Horse race betting is structured in a similar manner.

The horseplayer has many kinds of bets available to him. The simplest are *straight bets,* where you bet on a single horse to do one good thing for you. (For those wanting bigger payoffs, try the family of bets called *exotic wagers.* Exotic wagers link up multiple horses in a vertical fashion or multiple races and horses in a horizontal manner. See Chapter 15.)

Straight bets: Win, place, and show

A straight bet refers to three types of wagering: win, place, and show. What do these terms mean? Glad you asked.

- ✔ **A win bet means you bet on a horse to win. (Duh.)**

  One advantage to win betting is that you can see the *win odds* (the value to win) on your horse just by looking at a television screen or the *tote board,* which is the information board located on the infield of the track. For example, if the win odds on the number three horse are 5/2, you know he'll pay out between $7 and $7.80 for every $2 wagered. If you multiply 5/2 win odds by $2 and add your $2 back, you get $7. It can't pay more than $7.80, because if the horse paid $8.00, the win odds would be 3/1. A few racetracks post the probable payoffs in the place and show pools (see the next section).

- ✔ **A place bet means you bet on a horse to come in either first or second place.**

- ✔ **A show bet means you bet on a horse to finish first, second, or third (commonly referred to as finishing *in the money*).**

Place and show pool payoffs

Place and show pools aren't that much different to figure than the win pool. A *pool* is the total amount wagered on a bet, and a *payoff* is the price returned to the winning bettor. The winning payoffs are smaller in the place pool because the top two finishers share the money, and even smaller in the show pool because the top three finishers share it.

The equation for place and show pools is simple but takes some getting used to. You can do the math quickly in your head or jot it down on some scrap paper. Just remember, these figures are estimates. Unlike the win pool, the place and show pools are shared among the top two or three finishers. Here's the equation for figuring an estimated place payoff:

1. **Start with the total amount bet to place and subtract 15 percent for the *takeout* (the percentage withheld from the betting pool by the host track).**

2. **From that total, subtract the place money wagered on your horse and the highest amount of place money bet on another horse to get the profit from the place pool.**

3. **Split the profit amount between the two place horses.**

4. **Divide that amount by the number of $2 place bets on your horse.**

5. **Add $2, and you get your estimate place price.**

The estimate show payoffs are done the same way as the place payoffs. In step 2, subtract the show money wagered on your horse and the two highest amounts of show money bet on other horses. In step 3, divide the profits by three — not two — horses.

What you do with these estimates is make comparisons back to the win payoff. For example, a big favorite may pay $3.60 to win and $3.20 to place. Although I don't advocate betting lots of money on short-priced horses, if you did wager on this animal, I'd recommend a place bet. If the horse loses the race, you'll collect a slightly smaller payoff if the horse finishes second.

Also, at times, the estimated show payoff will be the same or larger than the place payoff. In that case, why not bet to show and take advantage of what I consider an aberration in the betting pools?

These are two ways to bet that are considered safer plays, but you need to do the math yourself if the track doesn't post probable payoffs for the place and show pools.

Dead heats and other sticky situations

Certain things can happen within a race — good or bad — that alter the final outcome or the payoff you receive. For example, once in a while, horses get *disqualified* (moved down in the final order of finish) for interfering with another horse or two. The *stewards* (three judges appointed to officiate the races) decide which horse or horses were bothered and place the offending horse behind them. If this situation occurs, it can change your win, place, and show bet payoffs, or make them losing tickets altogether.

Sometimes the scenario works in your favor. If your horse is the benefactor of a steward's disqualification, moving up in position can improve your straight bets from losers into winners.

Don't discard your mutuel tickets until you're absolutely certain you lost the bet. Many scenarios can occur after a race is run and before it's made official that can change the outcome. For example, a horse can be declared a non-starter, meaning if you bet that horse you're entitled to a refund. A refund means getting the amount of your bet back.

Another situation that can occur is a *dead heat,* where two or more horses literally tie for a finishing position. Table 4-1 illustrates a payout schedule for a dead heat for win.

| Table 4-1 | Payout Schedule for a Dead Heat for Win | | |
Scenario	$2 Win	$2 Place	$2 Show
Dead heat for win	Collect	Collect	Collect
Dead heat for win	Collect	Collect	Collect
Third place finisher	Lose	Lose	Collect

Although a dead heat lowers the payoff you would've received if your horse had won first place, a common saying at the racetrack is that "half a loaf is better than none." Wouldn't you rather win a smaller payoff than throw away a losing ticket?

Styles of wagering straight bets

Most professional handicapping books advise their readers to bet on a horse to win only and to pass on place and show wagering. The reasoning is if you're a good handicapper and can pick a lot of winners, the extra money you bet to win on a horse earns enough profit to compensate for all the lost place and show wagers that you would've cashed.

Although statistical studies bear this strategy out to be true, I believe that beginning horseplayers should bet to place and show.

Newcomers and casual fans most likely play with a modest bankroll. So although studies show that in the long run, win betting is the way to go, newcomers need to experience the enjoyment of cashing tickets and sustaining the bankroll

Different styles of straight betting, such as across the board, parlays, and group parlays, are excellent for newcomers to try. They promote interaction among your group or peers, add to your fun and enjoyment, and hopefully make you some money.

Across the board

A fairly safe way of wagering is to bet a horse *across the board,* meaning you bet an equal amount to win, place, and show. A typical across the board bet costs $6, because it's three different bets: $2 to win, $2 to place, and $2 to show. If your horse wins, you collect all three wagers. The worst case scenario? Your horse ends up in fourth place or worse, called an *out of the money* finish, and all three bets lose.

Simpler bets for a simpler time

If you were betting on horse races in the 1950s, about 95 percent of the money wagered would go into the straight betting pools: win, place, and show. The only exotic wager offered was the *daily double*, linking the winners of the first two races of the day. For example, in 1971, Hollywood Park pioneered the *exacta*, a bet combining the first two finishers in a race. Nowadays, straight pools make up only 30 percent of the parimutuel handle, but they remain a vital source for cashing tickets and keeping the bankroll healthy.

In an across the board bet, the board refers to the infield tote board. After the race, look at the tote board and you see the order of finish and the number of your horse followed by the win, place, and show prices going across. That price, my friend, is how much you collect for a $2 payoff. Table 4-2 shows you how an across the board wager works.

Table 4-2	Cashing an Across the Board Straight Bet		
Result	*$2 Win*	*$2 Place*	*$2 Show*
Your horse wins.	Collect	Collect	Collect
Your horse places.	Lose	Collect	Collect
Your horse shows.	Lose	Lose	Collect
Your horse finishes out of the money.	Lose	Lose	Lose

You come across just as many different betting philosophies as you do horse-players. But one constant I stress is that without a healthy bankroll, you're not going to bet on much of anything. I categorize betting across the board as bankroll building in the sense that unless the horse is a huge long shot, you're not going for a big score. You're trying to win money and grow your bankroll.

For example, if you like a horse that's a juicy 10/1 long shot, you want to maximize your profit. You want your horse to win, of course. But if he runs well and finishes second, which happens a lot in this game, at least you catch decent place and show prices.

Place and show payouts are affected by the odds of the winning horse, which is something you can't control. Your horse shares the place and show pools with the winner, so you're better off if the winner is another long shot and not the favorite. At some point (hopefully soon with the help of this book!), you'll develop skills as a horseplayer and handicapper and will be able to use exotic wagers effectively. But for right now, betting across the board is a lot less stressful. After all, horse racing is supposed to be fun!

Parlays

In horse race wagering, if you take your winnings from one horse and bet it all on a second horse, you are *parlay* betting. Continue this process through two, three, or more races, and the payoff grows to be very large.

Parlay betting is legal and quite common in Las Vegas because it's considered a "house" or "book" bet, meaning that your parlay bet goes up against the *house* (the casino) and not into the parimutuel wagering pool. You find a parlay computer card to fill out in most race books. It saves time and guarantees accuracy, because you're the one filling out the numbers. The *mutuel clerk* (short for parimutuel clerk) just inserts the card into the totalisator machine, and out comes your ticket.

Many racetracks can't offer parlay wagering — not because it's illegal, but because they don't have the software in their totalizator system.

You can do parlay wagering by yourself. Just keep rolling the profits over onto the next horse, which in horse racing is called *let it ride*. Parlaying is a good way of compounding your money when you like a few horses during the day and have a limited bankroll to bet with.

Statistically speaking, the parlay pays less than nearly all multiple race wagers. Now why's that? The answer is simple. In a parlay, the takeout for a straight bet is deducted on every race. So, in banking terms, you lose some of the power of compound interest. In multiple race wagers, the takeout is deducted only once at the time you place the bet, which in the long run is a huge advantage for the horseplayer. (I cover multiple race wagers in more depth in Chapter 15.)

I do, however, recommend parlay play at the New York Racing Association racetracks — Aqueduct, Belmont Park, and Saratoga. Their parimutuel system is legislated to round the *breakage* (the difference between the true mutuel payoff and the rounded down payoff actually paid to the bettor; refer to Chapter 3) down to a nickel, not a dime as with most states.

Group parlay play

I've gone to the races with friends who were newcomers to horse racing. As patient as I try to be, explaining all the nuances of horse race betting and what's going on all around them takes time. Just like you can't become a doctor or a lawyer after studying for a couple of weeks, you can't become a professional horseplayer in one or two afternoons.

Still, I want everyone to participate, have fun, handicap, bet, and especially win. What I like to do is organize a *group parlay,* meaning a parlay wager involving everyone in your group. It's easy to do. Just have everyone in your party kick in a few dollars to form a kitty. How much money is in the kitty doesn't matter; the main thing is everybody participates as an equal partner.

Assign each partner a race to handicap and find a horse to bet on. You don't need all the horses early on. You just go through the progression of the races at the track, one by one. Here's how it works:

1. **The person assigned to the first race gives you her horse. You take the kitty and bet it on that horse to show.**

   Most group parlays are show parlays, meaning you bet to show. Once in a while, you see a place parlay, which is a more aggressive play where your odds of losing go up. You almost never see a win group parlay because staying alive is too hard.

   The partners should agree ahead of time whether they'll play the group parlay all the way through, or if at some point they'll take money from the kitty to ensure a profit. My advice? "No guts, no glory!" Keep all the money in the kitty, and do what Richard Dreyfuss did in the popular horse racing movie of the same name: Just *Let It Ride*.

2. **When the first horse finishes in the money, you've won the first leg, and the group parlay continues. Take your winnings and wager them on a horse in the second race to show.**

   Betting on horse racing is gambling, which means sometimes you lose. If one horse in the parlay loses, the parlay is toast, meaning it's over. Plan B could be to start another group parlay. What happens next is up to you.

3. **If your group parlay runs the gauntlet and cashes in on every race, give each other a pat on the back for a job well done.**

   The groups I've been with have done different things with the winnings. Some divided the profits equally. Others used it to pay for the bar tab or for dinner after the races. Most importantly, group parlays are about having fun at the races as a team, which is a very satisfying feeling.

Placing Your Bet

The way you place your bets is a fairly standard procedure. After you get acquainted with it, you find that betting is like riding a bicycle: You won't forget how to do it.

Options galore: Ways to make your bet

The changes in the way people bet now versus the past parallels what you see in the banking business. Years ago, people only made bank transactions face-to-face with a bank teller. The racetrack was the same way: People only placed bets with a mutuel clerk.

Three cheers for the ABC system

One of the great improvements in modern day horse wagering was the beginning of betting and cashing at the same mutuel window. I'm old enough to remember when the mutuel clerks that cashed your winning tickets were on one side of the mutuel bay and the clerks that sold the tickets were on the other side. To a younger generation, that's like telling your kids that all television sets used to be in black and white or that music used to be played on vinyl records.

Before the new system, waiting in line for a few minutes to cash winning tickets was a huge hassle for bettors. Then they had to go around to the other side of the mutuel bay and wait in line again to bet the next race. On a busy weekend at the racetrack, people could seemingly spend most of the afternoon waiting in lines.

Another problem was the selling windows had specific denominations, so you had to get in betting lines marked "$2 wagers only," "$10 wagers only," and so on. You can bet that more than once a $2 bettor got in the wrong line and had to either bet more money than he wanted to or get out of line and start all over.

With the old system, when a big bettor wanted to make a sizable wager, such as a $1,000 or $2,000 win bet, punching out the tickets took a while because of the dollar denominations at every window. For example, a $1,000 win bet made at a $10 denomination window would literally be punched out by the mutuel clerk as 100 $10 win tickets. If post time was in one minute, the bettor would tell the mutuel clerk to keep punching tickets until the bell rang to start the race. This is where the famous term "punching til the bell"

originated. After the race started and the betting ended, the mutuel clerk counted up the tickets, and the horseplayer paid the money for the tickets. Seeing a horseplayer with a fistful of mutuel tickets in his hand, even if they may have been the $2, $5 or $10 variety, wasn't unusual. You didn't want to be in line behind a "bell ringer," because you'd get shut out from making your own wager.

In 1979, American Totalizator, also known as Amtote, first introduced the All Betting and Cashing (ABC) system to parimutuel wagering. This new system brought a lot of positive changes to making bets.

No longer did horseplayers have to cash winning tickets in one line and make bets in another line. It reduced the time needed to make parimutuel transactions. Now horseplayers can cash their winning mutuel tickets and make new bets against that total at the same time. Also, people can get in any line to make a bet without worrying about the denomination. Whether someone makes a $2 show wager or a $2,000 win bet, the transaction prints out as one mutuel ticket.

The racetracks were delighted when the ABC system was introduced, because it improved their customer service and led to increased wagering by its customers. Racetracks enjoyed cost savings, too, because they needed fewer mutuel clerks on the job.

The modernization of the wagering system eventually led to new types of exotic wagers, which I cover in Chapter 15. The new bet types wouldn't have been possible with the old mutuel machines.

Nowadays, you can bank in person, at an ATM machine, over the telephone, on the Internet, and so on. Horse racing has undergone the same changes. One thing that hasn't changed, though, is you can't bet on credit. If you run out of money at the racetrack or the OTB (off-track betting parlor), you can use your credit card or debit card to get more cash from an ATM machine.

I strongly recommend against using ATM cards at the casino or the racetrack. Getting more cash only promotes poor money management and the bad habit of chasing your losses. I wrote this book with the idea that you have an imaginary $100 betting bankroll for the day. It's enough to have fun with, and if you start out winning, you can always up your bet while you're ahead.

Here are some of the ways you can make a horse bet:

- ✔ **With a mutuel clerk, face-to-face.** Most people like betting with a mutuel clerk. This way of betting is part of the social interaction of the racetrack experience. Being a mutuel clerk is more stressful than you may think, though. Because horse races are *simulcast* (broadcast from racetracks all over the U.S.), *post times* (when the race actually starts) constantly come up, causing horseplayers to try to get a bet down at the last second. Mistakes happen from time to time. Always check your tickets before you leave the mutuel window.

- ✔ **On a self-service computerized betting terminal.** These are ATM-like machines located in convenient locations in the racetrack or OTB. Most have a bill reader to accept cash to start the transaction. Of course, you can also use a winning ticket or a *voucher* (ticket with a cash value) to begin the transaction. The betting menu is displayed right in front of you as you punch your own bets, so you become the customer and the mutuel clerk simultaneously.

The biggest mistake you can make using self-service betting machines is to inadvertently leave your cash voucher in the machine. If someone is lurking nearby and spots it, he can punch out the voucher and have it cashed within 60 seconds. I've made this mistake before, so I'm not immune either. If you realize you left your cash voucher in the machine and it's gone, notify a mutuel supervisor immediately. The mutuel department can trace the voucher and put a hold on it, kind of like a bank can stop payment on a check. If the mutuel department puts a hold on it in time, you can catch the culprit red-handed.

- ✔ **On a portable betting unit.** Some of these units are hand-held, and you can get them from the betting operator for the day. Other types of units are attached to your seat. In either instance, you deposit money at the start of the day to set up a betting account. Then you're free to bet to your heart's desire using what is essentially a small tote machine. When you're done betting for the day, you get a statement of your betting activity and your money back (plus or minus, depending on how your day went).

- ✔ **Over the telephone using a phone betting account.** With phone accounts, either you or an operator punches your bets on a keypad. Operators repeat your bet back to you, and they record your conversation in case of a dispute. When you use your keypad, you're prompted by a computer voice and betting menu. You're mailed a monthly statement. Sometimes you can check your betting history over the Internet. I cover telephone betting accounts in full detail in Chapter 22.

✔ **Online via the Internet.** This type of betting is where the slogan "betting at home in your pajamas" comes from. Online services are available that provide video race feeds showing live horse racing action directly from the racetrack. New U.S. laws prohibit citizens from using their credit cards to fund wagering accounts. Thus, to deposit money in your Internet account, you have to use "snail mail" or an overnight courier service and send in a check or money order. I discuss online betting in Chapter 22.

Rules to bet by

Here are some common sense guidelines that are good for horseplayers to follow, especially when betting person to person:

✔ **Give yourself time by betting early:** Nearly all betting occurs from 10 minutes to post until each race starts. And with simulcasting going on all day, a constant stream of bettors is lined up at the mutuel windows. I suggest you give yourself enough time to get your bet in. Six or seven minutes to post, at minimum, should be enough. If you run out of time and get shut out, meaning you don't get your wager in, don't fret, because another race is right around the corner.

✔ **Write down the bets you're going to make before going to the mutuel window (the place where the mutuel clerk is located).** Writing down bets is especially important if you're making exotic wagers. However, this process is also helpful in preventing you from becoming a horseplayer's worst nightmare: the person handicapping at the mutuel window. Getting stuck behind this person is exasperating. Remember that if you're not sure what you want to bet, you have no business being in line in the first place.

✔ **Speak clearly so the mutuel clerk can hear what you're saying.** The mutuel windows are located side-by-side in a *mutuel bay*. This area is noisy from the crowd, television sets, track announcer, and so on. Betting is an important transaction, and you want to get it right. Mistakes can be very expensive to you if they cost you a winning wager.

✔ **Have your money out and ready to pay for your bets.** This may sound dumb, but many people don't think about it. Because most people make horse bets in the last few minutes before post time, wasting a minute or two fumbling for cash shuts out other horseplayers. Being courteous to the people in line behind you is a good habit, because one day you may be the person in the back of the line.

✔ **Take a few seconds to double-check your tickets for accuracy before leaving the mutuel window.** Usually, you see a sign at the mutuel bay that reads, "A ticket error can't be exchanged after you leave the betting window." This rule is for the protection of both the racetrack and the horseplayers. Mutuel tickets are easy to check, especially if your bets are written down. Make sure the bet is correct — meaning the right racetrack, race number, bet type, and horses. If you think you have a winning bet but find out that the ticket was punched wrong or was called out wrong, you're not going to be happy.

✔ **Count your change at the mutuel window.** If you discover you got short-changed after you leave the mutuel bay, you can go back later to the mutuel clerk. By then, you're at her mercy whether she's honest or not. But remember that this rule works both ways. If you're paid too much money, the mutuel clerk has to make up for the shortage out of his own pocket. Horseplayers have been called many things, but all in all, they're a very honest lot.

✔ **Cash your winning tickets as soon as possible.** Don't give yourself a chance to lose the ticket, or what's happened to me, wash a winning ticket in the laundry.

✔ **After the race, check each ticket to make sure it's a loser.** Any time a scratch happens right before post time, it may affect you. The scratched horse didn't run in the race. If you used the horse on your ticket, you may be entitled to a full or partial refund, depending on the type of wager. Years ago, people called *stoopers* went to the racetrack with large garbage bags, filling them up with discarded mutuel tickets. They went through every discard, looking for winning tickets accidentally thrown away. They often found bets that included a scratched horse where the ticket holder was entitled to a partial or full refund.

Nowadays, racetrack custodians do a good job of sweeping up debris between races, so the stoopers are practically out of business. But the fact remains that thousands of dollars of good tickets are thrown away needlessly. Those tickets are like uncashed winners because they included a scratched horse.

✔ **Tip the mutuel clerk.** You probably don't think about tipping a mutuel clerk, but she may factor into your success at the races. A good clerk punches out your bets accurately and quickly, often times just beating the bell as the races goes off. If you cash a nice bet, it never hurts to give the clerk a small tip to show your appreciation.

Proper procedure: How to call out a wager

When you're ready to bet, whether you're betting in person, over the telephone, or on the Internet, the protocol is the same. Here's how to call out a wager from the top:

1. **State the name of the racetrack.**

   Belmont Park

2. **State which number race it is.**

   race three

3. **State the dollar unit of your bet.**

   $2

4. **State the type of wager.**

   win

5. **Tell the mutuel clerk which horse(s) you want.**

   number 7

Calling out a wager is like calling out a play in an NFL huddle. This fake bet reads like this in real time: "Belmont Park, race 3, $2 to win on number 7."

Watching the Tote Board

The *tote board* is located on the infield facing the racetrack. It shows the race odds; the win, place, and show betting pools for each horse; race payoffs; and fractional running times of the race. Newer tote boards have video monitors built in that actually show the race like a gigantic television screen.

You don't have to be a professional handicapper to learn something by studying the tote board. As the betting money flows into the parimutuel pool, important trends occur and appear on the tote board that tip you off if a horse is live or not. A *live horse* means the public, or maybe the *wiseguys* (a broad term horseplayers use for people who bet smart money), are betting on it.

More money bet to win than to place and show

Here's an easy observation you can make in less than a minute that can tell you an awful lot. A horse that's favored in the win pool should be favored in the place and show pools, too. That doesn't always happen.

Many times, the wiseguys like a horse and bet heavily on it to win. Big bettors play to win and then use the horse they like in exotic wagers. What I look for is a horse that's favored in the win pool but is the third, fourth, or fifth horse in the place and show pools. What that tells me is the horse is bet top heavy in the win pool but light in the place and show pools. That is the way professional horseplayers gamble.

The value comes in betting to place and show, which for newcomers are safer bets to make anyway.

Show plungers: A safe chance to make a score

I cover show plungers in Chapter 3, but I mention them here because the first sign on a show plunger comes from looking at the tote board. A show plunger can bet as much as 99 percent of the show pool on a horse. Usually it's on a horse that's heavily favored to win. The way you try to make a score betting a small amount of money is to bet against the show plunger. Bet one, two, or three other horses in the race to show.

If the favored horse finishes in the money, all the show payoffs will be the minimum $2.10. But if the favored horse runs out of the money (like Patriot Act did, shown in Figure 4-1), your tiny show bets could turn into quite a score.

If you had bet $2 to show on Dynamic Storm, you would have won $254.00, not bad for a $2 show bet. Even a $10 show bet on the second choice in the wagering, Silent Bid, would have won you back $196.

Figure 4-1: Betting against this show plunger would've produced a large return on a small bet.

```
FOURTH RACE        1 1/16 MILES. (1.41 3) MAIDEN SPECIAL WEIGHT . Purse $48,200  (includes $8,700 KTDF – KY TB Devt
Churchill          Fund ) FOR MAIDENS, TWO YEAR OLDS. Weight, 120 lbs. (Preference To Horses That Have Not
                   Started For $30,000 Or Less In Last 5 Starts).
OCTOBER 31, 2004
Value  of Race: $48,200 Winner $30,145; second $9,640; third $4,820; fourth $2,410; fifth $1,185.   Mutuel Pool $594,913.00 Exacta Pool
$210,368.00 Trifecta Pool $202,781.00 Superfecta Pool $75,696.00
Last Raced      Horse             M/Eqt. A. Wt  PP  St   1/4   1/2   3/4   Str  Fin   Jockey              Odds $1
13Oct04 2Kee2   Rush Bay          L    2 120   3   3   3 2    3 1/2   3 1/2   1 1   1 6 1/2   Razo E Jr           10.80
15Oct04 10Kee2  Silent Bid        L b  2 120   6   1   1 2 1/2  1 2   1 1   2 3   2 1/2   Bejarano R           5.60
9Oct04 4Kee6    Dynamic Storm     L    2 120   9   2   4 1    4 1/2  5 hd  4 hd  3 nk   McKee J             86.00
15Oct04 6Kee3   Bavarian Baron         2 120   7   9   10    9 1/2   8 3   7 8   4 1    Borel C H           33.20
9Oct04 7Kee2    Patriot Act       L    2 120   4   5   6 1   6 hd   4 1/2   3 1   5 1/2   Albarado R J          0.20
13Oct04 2Kee3   Thunder Mission   L    2 120  10   8   7 1 1/2  5 1 1/2  5 2   6 1/2   6 hd   Day P               12.80
9Oct04 4Kee3    Fan of the Cat    L b  2 120   5   6   8 2 1/2  8 1   7 2   5 hd  7 12 1/2  Shepherd J           43.30
                Liveinthepresent  L b  2 120   2  10   9 hd  10   9 4   9 10  8 6 1/2   Guidry M            54.00
30Sep04 4TP2    Glenrothes        L b  2 115   8   4   2 3   2 1 1/2  2 hd  8 1/2   9 16 1/2  Hernandez B J Jr5    90.30
2Oct04 6TP7     Wave Land Slew    L    2 120   1   7   5 1 1/2  7 3   10    10    10    Mojica R Jr         124.90
                     OFF AT 2:06 Start Good . Won driving. Track fast.
          TIME :23 3, :48 2, 1:14 1, 1:39 3, 1:46 (:23.76, :48.53, 1:14.31, 1:39.78, 1:46.19)
                         3 – RUSH BAY ................................   23.60   14.60   60.80
$2 Mutuel Prices:        6 – SILENT BID. ..............................            8.20   39.20
                         9 – DYNAMIC STORM. .........................                   254.00
            $2 EXACTA 3–6 PAID $110.80 $2 TRIFECTA 3–6–9 PAID $3,532.20
                      $1 SUPERFECTA 3–6–9–7 PAID $20,437.90

B. c. (Mar), by Cozzene – Seoul , by Deputy Minister . Trainer Amoss Thomas. Bred by Phoebe Ann Mueller Trust (Ky).
   RUSH BAY tracked the pace four wide from early on, reached the front a  quarter-mile out, then won going away under
pressure. SILENT BID gained a clear  lead early, raced near the inside, made the pace until the final quarter and wasn't a mach
for RUSH BAY in the drive. DYNAMIC STORM, within easy striking  distance, raced three or four wide and lacked a closing bid.
BAVARIAN BARON, outrun early, moved inside, rallied from the rail entering the lane and offered a minor gain. PATRIOT ACT
raced within easy striking distance five wide, was  asked for more leaving the five-sixteenths pole and flattened out in the drive.
THUNDER MISSION settled in behind horses, raced three or four wide to  the stretch and was empty in the drive. FAN OF THE
CAT failed to menace. LIVEINTHEPRESENT drifted in at the start bumping WAVE LAND SLEW, then never was  prominent.
GLENROTHES forced the pace four wide for six furlongs and tired. WAVE   LAND SLEW, bumped at the start by
LIVEINTHEPRESENT and forced in, tired upon going a half.
   Owners– 1, Mueller Phoebe A; 2, Baker Robert C and Mack William L; 3, Grum D Janelle; 4, Bavarian Stables LLC; 5, Farish William
S; 6, Stonerside Stable LLC; 7, Champion Racing Stable Inc; 8, Ramsey Kenneth L and Sarah K; 9, Ralls and Foster LLC; 10, Greenwell
Jerry J
   Trainers– 1, Amoss Thomas; 2, Lukas D Wayne; 3, Wiggins Hal R; 4, Million William N; 5, Howard Neil J; 6, Byrne Patrick B; 7,
Tomlinson Michael A; 8, Maker Michael J; 9, McGee Paul J; 10, Greenwell Jerry J

            $2 Pick Three (1–1–3) Paid $1,113.60 ; Pick Three Pool $45,352 .
            $2 Pick Four (7–1–1–3) Paid $10,953.60 ; Pick Four Pool $47,331 .
```

©2005 by Daily Racing Form, Inc. and Equibase Company

Chapter 5

Visiting the Racetrack

I expect a lot of you to be newcomers to horse racing. If so, you're in the majority of Americans who've never seen, much less visited, a racetrack. Racetracks are big places, so they can be intimidating at first.

I also suspect that many of you are sports fans. I know I am. The atmosphere at a racetrack is much different than at a "ball" sporting event. If you go to an NFL, NBA, NHL, or major league baseball game, you purchase a ticket and sit and watch the game. Even the concessionaires bring food and beverage by your seat so you don't have to get up. In horse racing, you're one of the players. You're on your feet a lot, and you're a big part of the action. I love racetracks and have been to every nook and cranny in them.

In this chapter, I give you an in depth look at many of the things that make up a day at the racetrack. From where to sit to where to find out racing statistics, I give you information that you can use to help you handicap, gamble, and just have more fun on your next visit to the races.

Preparing for the Cost of Attending the Races

In addition to spending money on betting, you have to shell out some dough to thoroughly enjoy a day of horse racing. But you get a lot of bang for your buck. Say you went to an NBA or NHL game last night. What did you pay for your tickets? $75 apiece? And you didn't go by yourself, so two seats cost you

$150. You ate dinner at the game? Add another $60. You paid $20 to park the car? Bought a program and yearbook? That's another $20. The costs add up fast and can be very expensive.

For the $250 you spent on an NBA or NHL game for you and a companion, you can take your whole family to the racetrack. You can take good care of them — indulging in everything from valet parking to dessert. And maybe you can even go home with more money than you came with. Talk about a square deal for your entertainment dollar!

Horse racing is one of the best values available for your entertainment dollar. And unlike spectator sports, you're an active participant in horse racing. At the racetrack, $150 easily pays for all your amenities, leaving $100 for gambling on the horses. Would you rather try to win money with that $100 or stuff it into the pocket of some rich basketball or hockey player?

Parking

Here's one general rule for racetrack parking: The closer you want to park to the building, the more it costs. I always thought paying for parking was a waste of money until I started working in Manhattan and had to park my car. Now I consider racetrack parking extremely cheap. At many racetracks, general parking is free. The fee is seldom more than a few dollars — cheaper than going back and forth across the George Washington Bridge.

If you have family and friends with you, I recommend valet parking. Having a winning day at the racetrack and then having someone bring your car to you is a nice feeling! You should budget between $5 and $15 for valet parking, depending on what the racetrack charges, plus a couple bucks to tip the valet.

Admission

Depending on the racetrack, there can be three tiers of admissions — grandstand, clubhouse, and turf club (see "Seating: You Get What You Pay For," later in the chapter). Grandstand admission is free at some racetracks and no more than a few dollars per person at most. You can figure the clubhouse to cost about twice the grandstand price. Some clubhouses have a dress code, so check with the racetrack ahead of time so your party can dress accordingly.

As for the turf club, some racetracks don't have one. Others have a private turf club for members only. And some have a turf club in which you can pay admission for a one-day pass, which can cost anywhere from $10 to $25 per person. Nearly all have a dress code, so please check with the racetrack ahead of time.

Food and beverage

When it comes to food and beverage, a racetrack has it all — from fast food stands to dining room restaurants. If all you need is a hot dog and a beer, you're in luck. If you want filet mignon, you can have that, too.

When it comes to prices, you won't find a 99¢ value menu, but it won't cost you an arm and a leg either. A hot dog and a beer cost between $7 and $10, depending on the track. A thick-carved deli sandwich goes for $6 to $8.

The dining rooms I've been in are reasonably priced, like a mid-level restaurant. Entrees range from $10 up to $30, depending on the type of meal and the racetrack. For example, I had delicious crab cakes for lunch at little Timonium Racetrack in Timonium, Maryland, plus soup, salad, dessert, and iced tea, including the tip, for under $30.

In the summer, you may like to picnic with the family. Most racetracks allow you to bring your own food and beverage. No glass bottles or cans, though. Some summertime racetracks even have barbecue areas set up — first come, first serve.

The cost of food and beverage is affordable, and how much you spend is up to you.

Regardless of where you eat or whether you sit down or stand up, betting windows are always nearby.

Seating: You Get What You Pay For

The best part about going to a racetrack is that most of the seats are free. This practice is an anomaly compared to all other sporting events. In very few instances do seats get pricey in horse racing.

Special events like the Kentucky Derby and the Breeders' Cup World Thoroughbred Championship demand much higher prices. Tickets are difficult to come by for the Derby in particular. Imagine 70,000 or so seats for sale and a half-million people wanting to buy them. Ticket brokers can ask whatever they want for them, and someone will pay the price.

On a day-to-day basis, though, if you want to sit in the best seat at a racetrack, you can. And you get your money's worth.

Turf club

Most major racetracks have a private *turf club* that people can join. A turf club is usually located on an upper floor of the racetrack and is situated at the finish line. In other words, turf club members have a perfect view of the race course.

The turf club concept came from European racing, where turf club members were the elite of society. When they attended the races, the amenities and view of the racing were second to none. Turf clubs are different in present day American racing. At most racetracks, even if you're not a member of the turf club, you can buy a daily pass. Admission may cost up to $25 and require a dress code, but you enjoy the same services as the members. I know one racetrack where the turf club remains private to members only — Keeneland in Lexington, Kentucky. Your best chance of getting in is to know a member and come to the races as an invited guest.

Luxury boxes

Some racetracks, though not all, have *luxury boxes* that you can buy for the season or rent for the day. The first luxury boxes in American sports and horse racing were at Monmouth Park in Oceanport, New Jersey. Monmouth, which was built in 1946, calls them parterre boxes. *Parterre* is a French word for an ornamental flower garden.

Some racetracks call luxury boxes VIP suites, but the idea is the same. They're a fun way for a group of people to enjoy the races in a private setting while drinking, dining, and betting together.

Clubhouse

The *clubhouse* is where most horseplayers go if they take a step up from the grandstand (see the next section). The admission is usually $5 to $10, and you can buy reserved seats. Most clubhouses also have a sit-down restaurant, some facing the race course and some not.

The clubhouse is typically in two areas depending on the architecture of the building. For older racetracks that are built horizontally rather than vertically in multiple stories, the clubhouse section starts just before the finish line and extends toward the first turn, which is also known as the *clubhouse turn*.

In newer racetracks that are built vertically with multiple stories, the clubhouse floors are the higher floors and are above the grandstand floors.

Horseplayers in the grandstand can't enter the clubhouse unless they pay another admission to get in. In most clubhouses, the services and facilities are nicer than in the grandstand — think first class service in an airplane versus coach cabin service.

Grandstand

The majority of racing fans spend their time in the *grandstand.* Admission is just a couple of bucks. At some racetracks, the grandstand admission is free.

Plenty of seating at no cost to the patron is available in the grandstand. Keep in mind that you need space to spread out if you have a couple *Daily Racing Forms* or other handicapping tools. If you're not familiar with the *Daily Racing Form,* I cover it in Chapter 11.

If you're lucky, your racetrack has Las Vegas-style seating counter space, and you're guaranteed to have some room to spread out. In Las Vegas race books, which I cover in Chapter 23, the seats come with counter top space to spread out your handicapping materials.

Some racetracks have state approval to offer casino slot machines. A special area may be designated for this type of gambling in the grandstand. Check and see if your racetrack offers slot machines, and find out where they're located. Hopefully, you don't have to pay to go in.

Track apron

If summer is here, and you want to work on your suntan and handicap the races simultaneously, sitting out on the *track apron* is for you. The track apron is a paved area on the ground floor between the main building and the railing of the main track. Most track aprons have permanent bench seating in place, and it's free.

Many racing fans like to go out on the track apron during the *post parade* when the horses and jockeys parade by on the main track for inspection by the crowd. You get a close look at the horses and jockeys as they walk past. Being outdoors on the apron is also exciting when a race is starting right in front of the grandstand. You're literally a few yards away from the starting gate as the horses are loaded, the jockeys get ready for the start, and they're off! Watching the start of a race up close gives you the feeling of the power, speed, and danger involved in riding a racehorse.

Railbirds on the apron

Horseplayers are called *railbirds,* which is a well deserved nickname. Years ago, when the racetracks were really crowded, a lot of horseplayers were on the track apron. For the post parade and during the race itself, the horseplayers went up to the rail, leaned on it, and watched — thus the term railbirds.

Some of the colorful by-play between the jockeys and racing fans comes from the railbirds. I vividly recall hearing New York horseplayers calling jockey Angel Cordero, Jr. every name in the book after a loss. Thirty minutes later, after Cordero won a race for them, the same guys called him the greatest. You need really thick skin in this business to be a jockey!

Infield

A handful of racetracks have patron areas in the *infield*. The infield is the open area inside the turf course, which in turn is located inside the main dirt track. Just think back to the last Kentucky Derby or Preakness telecast. Remember the camera panning the infield at Churchill Downs showing 50,000 partygoers doing their thing and barely knowing a horse race was going on? Now that's an infield.

For the Kentucky Derby and the Preakness, admission to the infield costs plenty, but for normal racing, it's typically free. For example, the infield at Santa Anita Park is free and absolutely gorgeous, too.

The infield is a very casual place to watch the races from. Looking from the inside toward the grandstand and clubhouse is an interesting perspective. Patrons are used to watching the races from the stands, but when you look back toward the building, you see all the fans silhouetted as the backdrop for the horses.

Many racetracks put family features in the infield, like picnic areas, musical entertainment, children's playgrounds, radio station remotes, and so on.

Typically, an underground tunnel leads to the infield. The reason for the tunnel is for the protection of the main dirt track and turf course and for moving all the people involved.

Accessing Information: The Program and Other Resources

A program at the racetrack is different from the one you pick up at a baseball game. A baseball program has the names and numbers of all the ballplayers, and it's good for the entire series of games between the two teams. At the racetrack, a different group of horses runs each day, so a new program has to be printed everyday.

Program seller booths are located near the entrances to the racetrack. A racetrack program cost between $2 and $5 depending on how fancy it is.

A racetrack program is a necessity to have, not a luxury. It includes information about all the races, horses, jockeys, trainers, and so on for that day's racing. Most importantly, it has the morning line odds of all the horses as determined by the racetrack oddsmaker. The *morning line* is the oddsmaker's prediction of how the public will bet the horses in each race.

Most programs have useful statistics, especially if you're not familiar with the jockeys and trainers. Jockey and trainer statistics include the number of starts; the number of first, second, and third place finishes; the win percentage at the meeting; the amount of purse money won; and so on.

Programs include a map of the building and the grounds, so you know where everything is located. They also list all the executives, so if something happens, you know who to blame.

If you want to have some fun without betting, just watch what other people do with their programs during a race. Some pound them against their legs like they're jockeys whipping a horse. Others smack them into the palms of their other hands. And if their horse loses, some throw them at a television monitor for good measure.

The program serves as a road map for your day at the races. All day long, you mark *scratches* (horses taken out of the race by their trainers) and changes that occur to the races on your program. So you need to be alert and aware at all times. You can access the following sources for important information while at the track:

✔ **Track announcer:** The track announcer gives all the scratches and changes before the first race of the day. You mark them down in your program and continue on. As the day progresses, you mark the results of each race in your program. From time to time, the announcer gives additional updates of late scratches and changes to the card. That voice from above is one of your main sources for information.

- ✔ **Television:** Another key source for racing information is the television. The simulcast feed (the same television signal that's being sent to simulcast locations around the country) has a crawl that runs along the bottom of the screen. The crawl repeats the scratches and changes over and over again. So if you miss the scratch or change the first time, it repeats itself in a couple minutes.

- ✔ **Tote board:** The infield tote board, an information board located inside the turf course, shows the betting pool information for win, place, and show bets (all types of straight bets that are discussed more thoroughly in Chapter 4). In the center is a message board that gives updates throughout the afternoon. The parimutuel prices for the previous race stay up until the next race is ready to run. Then those prices are cleared, so spectators aren't confused about which are the previous race payouts and which are the payouts of the race going off right in front of them.

Watching the Races From Start to Finish

No matter where you sit at the racetrack, you can watch horse racing in two ways: Look out onto the racetrack and watch the live running of the race, or watch the camera coverage on television monitors throughout the building. In this section, I explain the advantages and disadvantages of both.

Looking at the track

You should first get familiar with watching out on the track as the races occur (instead of watching the televisions, as discussed in the next section). The full view gives you a better appreciation of what the horses and jockeys do out there.

Trying to watch races on the main track or the turf course takes the eyes of an eagle, however. When you sit in the grandstand or clubhouse, you're a long way from the action. At a monstrous place like Belmont Park, you can squint at horses a half-mile away. If you have eyes like mine, you squint at an eye chart in the doctor's office that's only 10 feet away!

Many horseplayers bring low-level binoculars to the races to see better. Opera glasses are perfect. Racetracks used to have a binocular stand where you could rent the optics, but most have done away with them to save money.

A big advantage of watching the live race is you can see the entire field from front to back. When horses start to rally from behind, you pick that up immediately. On television, the camera sometimes doesn't pan back far enough to view the end horses. And if it does, the horses may appear so small you can't make out which one is which.

As you watch the race unfold before your eyes, remember that racehorses reach a top speed of 40 miles per hour. You don't sense the incredible speed and danger on television like you do when you look at the live horse race. It's truly an exciting spectacle.

Viewing closed circuit television

Ever since the television age reached American racetracks in the mid-1960s, bringing a pair of binoculars to the races hasn't been quite as crucial. Nowadays, most racetracks' TVs use what's called a *split-screen effect*. You can follow the lead horses on the lower half of the TV screen and see the full field on the upper half of the screen. As a bettor, you want to know where your horse is at all times during the race, so the split-screen effect is quite helpful.

 In Chapter 16 on sophisticated handicapping, I tell how important watching the races closely is, and I don't mean just focusing on the single horse you bet on. Lots of things happen during a race that can help you cash winning tickets in the future.

Understanding the Layout of a Racetrack

The new Arlington Park was reopened in 1989 after a fire destroyed the clubhouse and grandstand in 1985. The old Arlington was a traditional racetrack, meaning the clubhouse started before the finish line and continued right toward the first turn. The grandstand was to the left of the clubhouse and continued toward the top of the stretch — a horizontal design.

Racetracks built since the late 1970s have gone to a vertical design (shown in Figure 5-1), meaning the grandstand is on the lower floors, and the clubhouse and turf club are on the upper floors. There are two reasons for this change:

✔ A vertical racetrack gives all fans a good view of the finish line.

✔ A vertical design leads to an economy of scale, meaning the racetrack uses less land, is cheaper to build, and can be made more comfortable for smaller crowds that come to the races.

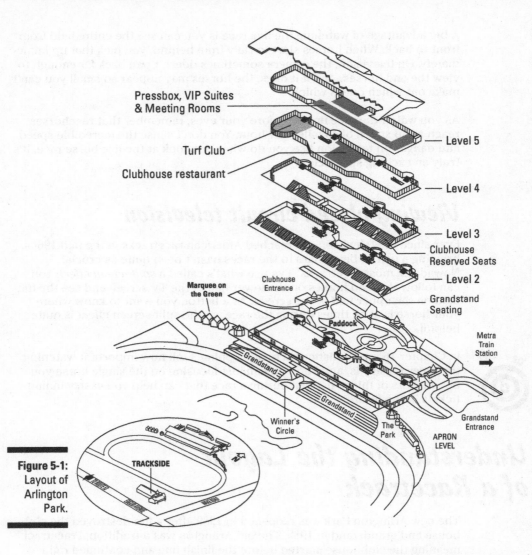

Pressbox, VIP Suites
& Meeting Rooms

Level 5

Turf Club

Clubhouse restaurant

Level 4

Level 3

Clubhouse
Reserved Seats

Level 2

Clubhouse
Entrance

Grandstand
Seating

Marquee on
the Green

Paddock

Metra
Train
Station

Grandstand

Grandstand

Winner's
Circle

The
Park

Grandstand
Entrance

APRON
LEVEL

TRACKSIDE

Figure 5-1:
Layout of
Arlington
Park.

The Arlington paddock and walking ring, like at most racetracks, are behind
the main building. The winner's circle is in front where everyone can see it.
Arlington was designed to handle crowds up to 35,000, but was expanded
with temporary seating to handle 46,118 for the 2002 Breeders' Cup.

Placement of the poles

The prototype of an American racetrack is a one-mile main dirt track with a
⅞-mile turf course built inside of it. Some racetracks — like Belmont Park —

are bigger, and others racetracks, known as *bull-rings* are smaller than a mile circumference.

When jockeys travel to different racetracks for riding engagements, they look for visual clues on the main track and turf course so they know where they are in a race at all times. Those visual clues are called poles.

Tall poles are placed inside the inner rail (the rail denotes the inner most part of the race course), marking the distances around the oval track. The poles are as helpful to the horseplayers watching the race as they are to the jockeys riding in the race.

Furlong poles are placed every ⅛ mile around the racetrack. (A *furlong* equals ⅛ of a mile.) When you hear an announcer call a race, he constantly refers to the *half-mile pole* and the *quarter-pole.* When a horse reaches the half-mile pole, he has four furlongs left to run. The quarter-pole signifies two furlongs to the finish line. The half-mile pole and quarter-pole are two key points in a race for jockey maneuvering, and they let the horseplayers know the exact distances the horses have left to race. Halfway between the furlong poles are smaller *16th-poles.*

The furlong poles are much taller and larger than the 16th-poles, so you can't mistake them. The poles guide the starting gate crew where to position the starting gate for each race. A tractor pulls the starting gate into position, usually about 50 to 100 feet behind the correct pole. For example, a common distance of six furlongs is actually six furlongs and about 50 feet. When the horses leave the starting gate, the timing of the race begins when they reach the six-furlong pole. The 50 feet or so is what's called a *running start* in horse racing. Figure 5-2 shows the layout of the furlong polls.

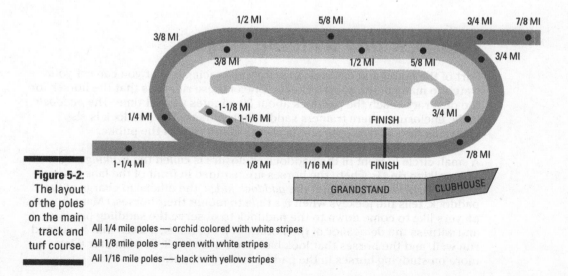

Figure 5-2:
The layout of the poles on the main track and turf course.

All 1/4 mile poles — orchid colored with white stripes
All 1/8 mile poles — green with white stripes
All 1/16 mile poles — black with yellow stripes

The poles are very important for the morning workouts. Horses have timed morning workouts at regular intervals to stay in peak racing condition. Trainers instruct the *exercise riders,* people who ride the horses in the morning, to work their horses a certain distance. For example, in a four-furlong workout, which is a half-mile, the trainer tells the exercise rider to *break off* (meaning start the timed morning workout) at the half-mile pole and finish strong. He may tell the rider to make the distance in an exact time, like 48 seconds for the half-mile workout.

The *finish line pole* is the most distinctive looking pole of all. Some tracks even put a target or bulls-eye on this pole. Every once in a while, you see a jockey misjudge the finish line and stand up too soon, causing him to slow down. With his adrenaline pumping in a furious stretch duel, a jockey sometimes loses his focus. The poles remind him where he is in a race.

Clubhouse and far turn

Looking at the descriptions I give you of a racetrack at the beginning of "Understanding the Layout of a Racetrack," earlier in the chapter, do you know which end is the far turn and which end of the racetrack is the clubhouse turn? Figuring out which is which is like learning to become a sailor, and you're asked which side is starboard and which is port side.

When you face the racetrack from the stands, the *clubhouse turn* is to your right. It's also called the *first turn.* The *far turn* is to your left. The track announcer says during his race call, "The horses are rounding the far turn." In a two-turn route race going a distance of ground, nobody calls it the second turn, even though it is.

Paddock and walking ring

Part of the pomp and circumstance to horse racing is that you can set your watch to many of the sport's rituals. One of these rituals is that the horses for the next race reach the paddock about 20 minutes to post time. The *paddock* is the enclosure where trainers saddle their horses. The paddock is also known as the *saddling area* and is always in full view of the public.

A small circle in front of the paddock enclosure is called the *walking ring.* The walking ring is where the horses are paraded in front of the fans before rider's up. (*Rider's up* is what the *paddock judge,* the official in charge of the paddock, tells the jockeys when it's time to mount their horses.) Many horseplayers like to come down to the paddock to observe the saddling process and witness the demeanor of the horses. A lot of times, horses that look good run well, and the horses that look bad don't do so well. See Chapter 6 for more on studying horses in the paddock and post parade.

Back in the saddle again

In olden days, trainers saddled their horses around trees in the paddock rather than in stalls. It mirrored the European classic style of racing.

Saratoga, in Saratoga Springs, New York, used to do saddling out in the open around trees until the insurance premiums grew too large. The public could get close to the animals being saddled, which was too close for the safety of everyone involved. Now the Saratoga saddling area consists of stalls like most tracks and is fenced in to protect the public.

Two racetracks — Keeneland in Lexington, Kentucky, and Hollywood Park in Inglewood, California — still do saddling in a beautiful tree-lined paddock. Keeneland uses deep hedges and a metal rail to serve as a buffer between the horses and the general public. The classic style remains right down to a large number posted on a tree to signify the number of the racehorse being saddled.

Hollywood Park built a beautiful paddock with a large viewing area for the patrons. The track races on Friday nights, and big crowds make their way downstairs to view the horses up close. They use a white wooden fence to border the paddock, just like at a Kentucky breeding farm.

So kudos to Keeneland and Hollywood for taking an old idea and making it new again for racing fans.

Many a horseplayer has saved money by not betting on a horse he sees acting up in the paddock and walking ring. Acting up means a horse is nervous, fractious, and behaving poorly for his handlers. That loss of energy saps the strength of a horse and shows that he's not mentally prepared to run his best.

The horseplayer who's at the racetrack observing the horse's behavior in the paddock and walking ring in person has a huge advantage. Simulcast horseplayers can easily miss all the commotion, even if the racetrack cameras dutifully show it. In a simulcast facility, horseplayers play many different racetracks. A dozen racetracks may run at the same time. Nobody can watch a dozen television monitors and know what's going on in all the races.

Something you notice in the paddock is that all the owners of the horses come down to watch the saddling. After the trainers finish saddling, they meet with the owners and the jockey riding the horse. Their ultimate goal is to meet again after the race to have their picture taken in the winner's circle.

Winner's circle

The idea of a *winner's circle* originated in horse racing. Like so many other racing terms, the winner's circle has worked its way into daily vocabulary. The winner's circle is located right next to the finish line for all horse racing fans to see.

After winning the race, the horse and jockey are led into the winner's circle to meet up with the winning *connections* — the trainer, owners, and friends. The track photographer lines everyone up to snap a picture. Track photographers make their living selling winner's circle photos to the winning connections.

Most of the public doesn't realize they can order the same winner's circle photos that are sold to the jockeys, trainers, and owners. To order horse-racing photos taken at the racetrack, just call the track photographer. He'll be happy to talk with you, because their business is selling photos.

At some racetracks, like Aqueduct and the Meadowlands, the paddock, walking ring, and winner's circle are in the same location right in front of the grandstand and clubhouse.

The backside

The most interesting part of the racetrack isn't the front side, where the grandstand and clubhouse are, but the backside where the horses are stabled. I suspect 98 percent of horseplayers haven't had a chance to see what goes on behind the scenes on the backside of a racetrack.

What lies behind the stable gate is like a small city. Many of the *grooms* (the workers who take care of the horses) and *hotwalkers* (the people that literally walk horses to cool them down after physical activity) live in dormitories.

The work day starts hours before sunrise at the backside. At the crack of dawn, trainers send their first set of horses to the main track for morning gallops. The backstretch cafeteria is busy all morning (coffee and breakfast sandwiches are big sellers), but by 10 a.m. the track is closed for training. The work isn't finished, though. The horses have to be bathed and brushed, and then it's feeding time for them. The barn help cleans out all the stalls, straightens up the shed row, and puts all the riding equipment away for the day. When the workday is finished, the help relaxes and eats a hearty lunch.

This process goes on seven days a week, 52 weeks a year. Just remember that although people can go on vacation, the horses can't. Someone has to take care of them every day.

The only backside I know that's open to the public is at Keeneland. Many of the bigger tracks like Belmont Park and Santa Anita offer free tram tours of the backside. The tours are fascinating for the novice racing fans. But even the hardcore gamblers should have an appreciation for the behind-the-scenes work that prepares the racehorses.

Rewarding Yourself and Your Family

Racetrack marketing departments work proactively to generate repeat customers and reward those who come out to the races a lot. Even though the gambling dollar primes the parimutuel pump, attracting families is important, because the next generation of horse racing fans will come from them.

Player reward programs

Player reward programs are a knock-off of the player tracking systems used for decades in Las Vegas casinos. Simply put, the gambler fills out a detailed application form to join the rewards program. The information is then entered into a computer. The person receives a card with a magnetic strip. Every time he makes a bet, the card is swiped to credit his account with the amount wagered. From his gross wagering totals, he receives marketing mailers and perks for free racing gifts.

For years, racetracks didn't reward their best horseplayers with anything. Las Vegas showed the world that offering their best customers *comps* — free perks from the hotel like meals, rooms, show tickets, and so on — builds up enormous good will and brand loyalty. Racetracks needed to be dragged into the 20th century kicking and screaming, but now many programs are in place for horseplayers.

The first, and maybe the best, player rewards program in horse racing was the Thoroughbreds Club at Santa Anita. Marketing director Alan Balch started the program in the 1980s, long before other racetracks considered the idea. Club members are called Thoroughbreds, and they're entitled to free programs and track admissions and special promotional giveaway items. They're also sent marketing mailers printed with valuable coupons to use at Santa Anita Park.

Breakfast programs

Many racetracks use the morning training hours as a marketing tool. Some open their doors to the public for free only on the weekends. Others offer a morning program on a daily basis.

Some racetracks put out a big spread for breakfast during morning training hours, and people can eat for a nominal cost. During the workouts, a commentator describes which stakes horses and famous jockeys and trainers are on the main track, and they host interviews with these horsemen.

Some very nice breakfast programs are available at Arlington Park, Belmont Park, Del Mar, Hollywood Park, Santa Anita Park, and Saratoga, to name a few. I recommend you check with your local racetrack to see whether it offers such a program in the morning.

At Santa Anita, you can make early bird advance wagers well before the start of the afternoon races. This is a big convenience for horseplayers with a 9-to-5 job that can't attend the races.

Playgrounds for the kids

Once upon a time, children under 18 weren't allowed into racetracks because of gambling. Those laws were repealed a while back, and now families are more than welcome to attend.

Many racetracks have supervised playgrounds available for kids (another marketing technique). On weekends, some racetracks import carnival activities like pony rides, face painters, and so on, so that dad can catch a break while mom and the kids go play something else, or vice versa.

Part II

How the Players and Factors Impact the Race

The 5th Wave   By Rich Tennant

"Tough race today?"

In this part . . .

*H*orse racing entails 112-pound jockeys atop 1,000-pound animals with minds of their own. In betting on horse racing, the best laid plans can go out the window fast. Therefore, it's important that you get a detailed look at how all the different factors impact the race to help lay the groundwork before you get into handicapping.

In this part, I explain how each racing participant plays a key role in winning horse races. You find out that studying the horses before the race can indicate which horses are ready to win and which ones aren't. You discover that jockeys, trainers, and owners make up the front members of a team of people needed to win horse races, that track conditions on the dirt and turf favor certain kinds of runners, and that equipment changes are important clues to a horse's improvement and even to a horse's sudden form reversal.

Chapter 6

Studying Horses in the Paddock and during Post Parade

*I*n the late 1960s, people wagered on Thoroughbred horse racing at the racetrack. Off-track betting parlors didn't exist, and simulcasting of horse racing didn't occur yet. Now, nearly 90 percent of the parimutuel pools are wagered off-track. Because of the shift towards off-track betting, studying horses in the paddock and during post parade has become a lost art and a hidden advantage to handicappers.

In this chapter, I discuss positive and negative qualities to look for in horses in the paddock and walking ring and on the racetrack during the post parade and warm-ups. Positive signs lend credence to your wagers. Negative signs may cause you to do some rethinking. Studying horses in this manner is a key part of handicapping that's often talked about but seldom practiced.

Dissecting the Anatomy of a Horse

A racehorse is big, weighing in the range of 800 to 1,100 pounds. Remember that fact the next time you hear a bettor complaining about a jockey's ride. The jockey only weighs around 110 pounds, so if a horse has its mind set on doing something, such a small man has a lot of horse to try and control.

The height of a horse is measured in *hands.* A hand is 4 inches in length. Racehorses usually range from 14 to 17 hands tall. The measurement is taken from the ground up to the peak of the *withers.* You can see in Figure 6-1, which shows the anatomy of a racehorse and where all the body parts are located, that the withers can be found at the top of the shoulder.

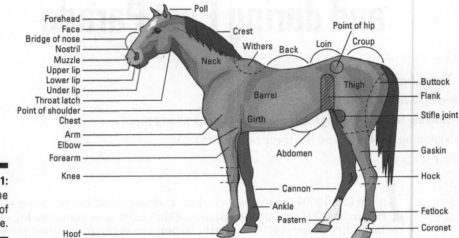

Figure 6-1: The anatomy of a racehorse.

The first time you see a racehorse fully "dressed," keep in mind that all the equipment put on the horse is to

✔ Help the jockey control the horse

✔ Focus the racehorse's attention on running

✔ Help the racehorse overcome bad habits

✔ Aid the racehorse if it has some physical problems

Chapter 10 describes the pieces of equipment worn by a racehorse and their uses.

Examining Horses in the Paddock and Walking Ring

At most racetracks, the *paddock,* where the horses are saddled, and *walking ring,* a circular walk path in front of the paddock, are behind the grandstand

and clubhouse and away from the main track. The horses for each race are walked over from the barn area. Following is the ritual performed for each race, which seldom varies:

✔ **The horse identifier looks at the lip tattoo on each horse to make sure it matches with the horse's foal papers.** *Foal papers* are in essence a horse's birth certificate. The tattoo is like a car license plate made up of a unique sequence of numbers and letters. It's located inside the upper lip of a horse. For the identifier to read the tattoo, he literally flips the horse's lip up. A lip tattoo is permanent, so don't worry about anybody erasing or changing it for purposes of chicanery.

✔ **Each horse is assigned a numbered stall that matches its program number.** The program number is the number assigned to a racehorse for betting purposes. Here the horse is saddled in full view of the public and racing officials.

✔ **Track veterinarians keep an eye on the horses.** They watch the horses from the moment they enter the paddock until they go out onto the race-track for the post parade and warm-up (see "Watching the Horses during the Post Parade and Warm-Up," later in the chapter). The veterinarians continue to watch them until the start to protect the horses and, in turn, to protect the jockeys riding the horses. If the vets sense any problems at all, they can examine the horse up close and recommend to the track stewards that the horse be scratched from the race.

✔ **During the 25 minutes before post time (the time the race starts), the horses in the race are in full view of the betting public at the race-track.** After the horses are in the public's view, you want to examine each horse, looking for positive and negative factors that may affect the horse's performance.

Positive traits to pick from

A trained eye looks for certain qualities in a horse. Having been around horses is helpful, but it's not a prerequisite. You'll get the hang of it with some practice.

Here are the positive traits you want to look for:

✔ **The horse should look healthy.** Some tell tale signs include

• A coat of hair that lies down nicely

• A bright, shiny coloring not caused by moisture but by a natural healthy glow

✔ **A dappled bottom is a sure sign the horse is in excellent health.** A *dapple* is a shiny round spot in a horse's coat.

✔ **Eyes should be clear and bright.** A sharp, edgy look is much better than a dull stare.

✔ **Ears should be alert and pointed, but not in a nervous way.** Ears that are *pricked,* meaning straight up and down or slightly forward, are a good sign.

✔ **You want to see a rounded belly with no ribs sticking out.** Beware of "love handles" like some people have around their waists, because they're caused by fat and aren't good on any athlete — especially a racehorse. The babies — 2-year-old horses — often times have baby fat just like children may have before they grow up.

What isn't worth your wager

In a lot of ways, you can more easily spot horses' negative attributes than you can their positive ones. Horses that look sick or are misbehaving stick out like a sore thumb. Horses can't talk, but their body language indicates whether they're happy being there in the paddock and walking ring.

Here are some things to watch out for:

✔ **The hair on their coats is turned sideways and shows a dull coat.**

✔ **They're hyperactive.** Horses spend so much time in their stalls — up to 23 hours a day — that they can get really excited from being taken out of their stalls. That nervous energy is wasted long before the race starts.

✔ **They react by being unruly or by sulking.** Experienced horses know the routine, but if they're hurting, they're smart enough to know they don't want to be there.

✔ **They exhibit low energy or complete disinterest.** As the horses are led around the walking ring, be wary of horses that are dragging their feet and shuffling up dirt.

✔ **Their ears are pinned back, making them look like a donkey or a mule.** Pinned ears are a sign of indifference or anger and are a sure sign that the horse doesn't want to be there.

If you're interested in finding out more about racehorse body language, I recommend reading *The Body Language of Horses* by Bonnie Ledbetter or watching her video, made with Hall of Fame jockey Chris McCarron, *The Body Language of the Racehorse.* Both are excellent learning tools.

Watching the Horses during the Post Parade and Warm-Up

After the horses are saddled and their jockeys are legged up on top of them, they leave the paddock in post position order for the main track. Most trainers opt to use a *lead pony* (a pony ridden by an outrider) to assist the racehorse and jockey. The lead pony stays with the racehorse right up until post time.

What you like to see are the lead pony and outrider acting in concert with the racehorse and jockey. If the racehorse is acting unruly, it's distracted from focusing its energy and attention on winning the race.

Racehorse viewing increases greatly in the *post parade,* when the horses parade on the racetrack 10 minutes before post time, because it's on the main track in front of the grandstand and clubhouse. Any fans facing that way have a bird's-eye view of the proceedings. All the track's TV monitors show the post parade. It doesn't take much for you to look up at the TV for two or three minutes and look at the horses parading by.

The time after the post parade is an important period for your final inspection. After the post parade is complete, the horses break off and start jogging and warming up. The best way to follow the warm-ups is by using a pair of binoculars. The in-house television cameras can't keep track of up to 14 horses warming up all over the racetrack.

The economics of conditioning

In Chapter 8, I cover the importance of the owner and the trainer. In the pecking order, the owner is more important because he pays all the bills. But to the handicapper, the trainer is the person who has her hands on the pulse of the stable every day.

The ability of the trainer to win is controlled by two things:

✔ Skill

✔ Financial backing

If the trainer has an owner who buys talented horses and pays a fair day rate, then the trainer's skill level should bring out the race horse's full potential. Where this discussion fits into the physicality of horses is when a trainer works *on the cheap,* or cuts corners to save money. Pinching pennies can mean using lower quality feed, skipping on vitamins, passing on certain veterinary care, hiring less qualified help, and so on. These things do add up. A horse from a penny-pinching barn may not look as good or run as well as a horse from a top barn where money is no object and the horse gets premium daily care.

Qualities to bet on

In poker, when you're holding a pair of aces as your hole cards, keeping a "poker face," meaning you're not letting on that you have a good hand, is difficult. I think horse racing is the same way when the groom, trainer, and jockey feel confident about their chances, and the horse is feeling great. Here are a few pointers of positive qualities to look for:

✔ **A nicely made up horse.** If a groom makes the effort to fix up a horse's tail and/or mane, that's a good sign for a couple reasons:

- The groom is conscientious and goes the extra yard taking care of the animals.

- The groom may believe that the horse will run well and hopefully get its picture taken after the race in the winner's circle.

✔ **A bull neck:** This is a sign of pent-up energy waiting to be released. You want to see the horse eager to warm up and playful with the lead pony.

✔ **A smooth, strong, and confident stride.** If a horse is bouncing on its toes and looks playful, that's good. If it's too hopped up, it's wasting valuable energy. And if the race horse is lethargic, forget about it.

✔ **An older horse warming up vigorously.** An older horse may have more physical problems to warm up out of, so his jockey needs to warm him up vigorously to get him loose. I'd be leery if the jockey isn't doing much with an older horse. He may be protecting the horse, which isn't a good sign.

Attributes to avoid in a horse

Horses can't talk, but when they're uncomfortable, you know about it. Here are a few telltale signs that a horse is bothered by something and may not run its best race today.

✔ **Bad behavior.** If a horse won't behave and is giving his jockey a hard time (see Figure 6-2), he may be wasting valuable race energy.

✔ **Excessive sweating.** If the weather is hot and humid, sweating is natural for the horses. But if most of the horses are cool except yours, your horse is probably nervous, which is a bad sign. Keep an eye out for the different types of sweating, which are all caused by nervousness:

- *Kidney sweat* appears as a lather between the horse's hind legs that's created when the horse perspires and rubs up against itself.

- *Lathering* on the horse's neck or underneath the saddle towel appears where there's sweating and rubbing. On the neck, rubbing comes from contact with the leather reins. On the body, the saddle towel is situated between the saddle and the horse's body.

- *Washing out* is different from lathering because it's literally water, or sweat, dripping off the horse's body. Washing out is never good, although once in a long while, a washed out horse wins. In a worst case scenario, a horse sweats so much that it looks like it just took a bath.

✔ **Protruding ribs.** The horse is underweight and probably not eating well. You've heard the phrase "hungry as a horse." If a horse feels great, it eats all its feed and wants more.

Figure 6-2:
A horse acting unruly in the post parade lessens its chances of winning the race.

Photo by Skip Dickstein

Chapter 7

Riders Up: The Importance of a Jockey

In This Chapter

▶ Knowing what makes a good jockey

▶ Weighing the worth of money riders versus rookie riders

▶ Looking at statistics you can bet on

Think of a jockey on a horse like a racecar driver. The horsepower and speed among each car may differ by only 1 or 2 miles per hour, but a good driver continually finishes in the top ten each race because he's more skillful and uses better judgment.

Even though you need a team to win a horse race, the public focuses on the jockey, because that's all people see on race day.

In this chapter, I look at the qualities that make for a good jockey — from certain traits to experience — and what you should look for when viewing a horse race.

Winning Jockeys Share Certain Traits

Jockeys have distinctive riding styles, and it's important to observe and learn them. Some jockeys prefer to take their horses back and come from behind. Others like to send their horses to the early lead.

The behavior and the running style of the horse dictate the jockey's tactics. The better riders cajole their mounts into doing what they want. Fighting with the animal does no good. The horse weighs around 1,000 pounds, and a jockey is about $\frac{1}{10}$ that size. Guess who wins that battle of wills?

The better riders have a knack for putting their horses in position to win by anticipating the action, moving at the right time, and making fewer mistakes. I cover some of these traits, which you should look for when watching the racing action. After a while, you develop a fondness for certain riders and bet on them because you like how they ride a horse.

Fewer mistakes on the track

The racetrack is full of sayings passed down through the ages. Here's one for you: "There are a million ways to lose a race and only one way to win." In preparing to win a horse race, the only part the public really sees is the work of the jockey. Too much emphasis can be placed on the jockey, win or lose.

If a horse isn't in condition for a peak race or just isn't talented enough, the jockey can only do so much. A good rider can always give her horse a chance to do well, but have you ever seen a jockey carry a horse across the finish line? I didn't think so. On the other hand, if a thoroughbred is primed for a top effort and has the most talent in the field, he should win regardless of who's riding him. When a well-meant racehorse gets beat, many times the jockey makes a key error or two that cost the victory.

A good sports comparison is between a racehorse and a baseball pitcher. Baseball analysts like to say that pitching is 90 percent of the game. If a top pitcher throws his "A" game, the other team either gets shut out or barely scratches out a run or two. The pitcher has that much control over the outcome. However, the other 10 percent is still important. A pitcher can throw a great game and still lose 1-0 if his own team doesn't score any runs.

In essence, the racehorse is like a pitcher. If the trainer has his horse in peak condition and he's the fastest horse in the race, he should be about 90 percent on his way to a win. The other 10 percent in horse racing is the jockey and racing luck. If the jockey doesn't make mistakes and gives the horse a chance to run his race, he should win.

Why jockeys are the best-conditioned athletes

Of all the professional sports, which athlete do you think is the best-conditioned? Very few people know the answer, so you can win a bar bet with this one: It's the jockey who rides thoroughbred race horses for a living.

Years ago, the late Dr. Robert Kerlan, who is renowned for his expertise in the treatment of sports injuries, conducted a study to find out, once and for all, which sport has the best-conditioned athletes. To the surprise of many, thoroughbred jockeys graded out the best in his study — better than players from all the "ball" sports and better than any Olympic athletes. In order for a 110-pound rider to control a 1,000-pound horse running at speeds up to 40 miles per hour, he must display an incredible combination of strength, agility, and coordination.

No ride, no money

Jockeys aren't like other pro athletes who sign a contract and earn a salary. Jockeys epitomize workers who get paid for performing well. When a jockey rides a horse in a race, he's paid a fee of about $40 to $50, depending on the jurisdiction. If he wins a race, he'll receive 10 percent of the winner's *purse money* — cash prizes put up by the racetrack that the horses are trying to win. In *stakes races* (big money races for better horses), he may earn a smaller percentage for finishing second or third. When jockeys get injured and can't ride, they earn nothing.

During the course of every race, each rider has decisions to make. If she's riding a slow horse, her decisions may not matter. But if she has a *live horse*, meaning a horse with a solid chance to win, her decisions are critical. The jockeys who make the fewest mistakes win most of the races. In a way, good decision making is a jockey making her own racing luck.

Timing

Horses have different running styles that jockeys must adjust to. *Speed horses*, horses that like to race on the lead, break from the starting gate quickly and are hustled to the front. Unless the rider can cajole the horse to slow down, he's just along for the ride. Other horses are more manageable, so the jockey can *rate* the horse, or ration his speed, so the horse has energy in reserve for the stretch run. And finally, *late running horses*, horses that plod along behind the field, respond to the jockey's request (hopefully!) to accelerate down the stretch.

When a jockey should move with his mount is a key component to winning. The jockey must recognize how fast the pace of the race is — the proverbial "clock in his head." Then he makes adjustments, knowing the style of his own horse, as to whether he needs to move sooner or wait longer.

The best jockeys have an instinct for timing their moves just right. The more horse races you watch, the more you learn from watching the top riders perform day in and day out. How do you know which jockeys are best at judging timing? Just watch the better riders and, more often than not, they're asking their horses to run at the right time and winning more often.

Know this: The top ten riders in the jockey standings typically win 90 percent of the races run at the meet.

The greatest jockey of them all

Hall of Fame rider Laffit Pincay, Jr. retired in 2003 as the world's winningest jockey with 9,530 victories and $237 million in career purse earnings. The number of wins, however, represents only a part of his remarkable story. Stripped from the waist up, Pincay looks like a miniature Incredible Hulk — all muscle, very little body fat. His body is so tight that he broke his collarbone falling off a horse more than a dozen times during his 40-year career.

The main reason Pincay was able to ride as long as he did and win as many races was personal discipline. He avoided many kinds of food and drink that we take for granted, and he exercised religiously — running in hot clothing every morning — all to stay in top shape and keep the weight off.

If Pincay ate a normal amount of food, he'd easily tip the scales at 140 pounds or more. However, he researched and tried so many diets that in the latter stages of his career, he perfected his calorie intake to between 800 and 850 calories a day. That amount is probably less than half of what you and I eat in a day. Four-ounce servings of steak, chicken, or fish were the most Pincay would allow himself. And for a man who loves sweets, at most, he'd eat a few pieces of fruit for dessert.

Pincay got away with riding at 117 pounds because he was such a great rider. Trainers were willing to accept the extra weight on their horses to benefit from Pincay's riding skills. When a Hall of Fame athlete, in any sport, talks about discipline to make it to the top, they better look up the word in the dictionary. Opposite discipline, you'll see a picture of Laffit Pincay, Jr.

Low weight

You probably already know that Americans are bigger now than they were 25 and 50 years ago. Whatever the reason — genetics or diet — each generation weighs more than the last.

In horse racing, jockeys weigh the same now as they did 25 and 50 years ago. The heaviest jockeys weigh about 115 pounds, which is enough to eliminate them from riding many horses assigned a lower weight. In many races you handicap, a horse will carry *overweight* (extra pounds above their assigned weight), because the jockey can't make the assigned weight.

With so many jockeys fighting weight problems, natural lightweights have the edge. The most famous of these lightweights is the late, great Bill Shoemaker, who weighed a feathery 95 pounds soaking wet. Pat Day and Julie Krone are two more Hall of Fame riders who weigh in at 100 pounds.

So when you're judging the daily performance of your favorite jockeys, keep in mind that they're not only stressing about winning races, but they're also stressing because they can't eat very much and have to constantly reduce to make riding weight. Jockeys reduce by spending time in a sweat box or running with added clothes on.

Anticipation

Great athletes in sports have all the tools necessary to succeed. Those tools can vary from sport to sport, but a few are standard. *Anticipation,* the ability to visualize what's going to happen before it happens, is one standard tool.

In horse racing, as you're handicapping, visualize how the race will play out. I call it the *race shape*. Jockeys visualize the race just as handicappers do. They read the past performances of the horses in the *Daily Racing Form,* the horse racing industry's daily newspaper. From the past performances, the jockeys can figure out where each horse is going to be during the running of the race. They also take into consideration the habits of other jockeys and try to guess where they want to place their horses in the race.

The better jockeys anticipate and react faster than their counterparts. If you want to try something fun, watch the race replays and pay attention to the maneuvering going on, especially from the view of the head-on camera. You'll notice that some jockeys are piloting their horse into position to win a race, while others are just hanging on like they're sitting in the rear seat of a taxi-cab. These different racing styles are why riders are often described as either *pilots* or *passengers.* Pilots are in control, anticipating what's going to happen and reacting immediately. Passengers are sitting on their horses hoping things open up for them. You want the pilot on your horse every time.

Considering a Jockey's Experience Level

A lot of positions offer on-the-job training. Just imagine a job where you're a newcomer competing against the very best in the business, and the only allowance given to you is ten fewer pounds.

That's what rookie riders, called *apprentices,* are up against. It's almost like getting your driver's license and then racing in the Indianapolis 500. In this section, I cover the transition from apprentice jockey to one of the elite, a money rider.

Apprentice riders: Are rookie jockeys worth it?

Rookie riders in horse racing are called *apprentices* or *bugboys.* The rules of racing give apprentices a big weight concession — 10 pounds — until they prove themselves by winning a certain number of races. When an apprentice eventually loses her weight concession or *allowance,* as it's also called, she becomes a *journeyman rider,* or full-fledged jockey.

The weight allowance is 10 pounds to start. So, for example, if a horse is assigned a weight of 121 pounds, with a 10-pound bugboy, the weight drops to 111 pounds. Apprentice riders don't get a weight allowance in stakes races.

In the racing program, a small number next to the weight of the horse denotes an apprentice weight allowance. The apprentice starts with a 10-pound allowance. After he wins five races, the allowance is dropped to 7 pounds. After a bugboy wins 35 career races, the weight allowance is 5 pounds for one year starting on the date of his 35th victory. Only an injury can change that one-year time frame, in which case the bugboy can file an appeal with the racetrack stewards for an extension. The stewards are the racing officials who adjudicate each horse race and enforce the rules of racing at the racetrack.

Most bugboys start their career at mid-level to lower-class racetracks. The jockeys at higher-class racetracks like Belmont Park and Santa Anita are the very best in the business. When a rookie rider competes against them, the rookie can look pretty bad in comparison. The 10 pounds don't make up for the lack of experience.

Going to a smaller track reduces the talent deficit between the journeymen riders and the bugboys. Also, trainers at small, lower-class tracks are more apt to give a young rider a chance. In lower-class racing, often times the horse that gets to the lead wins. So if the trainer finds a bugboy who can break sharp from the starting gate and let the horse roll, he'll give him a chance.

Are you asking yourself whether bugboys are worth betting on? The answer can be yes or no. If your horse is a speed horse, the bugboy doesn't have to be very experienced to lead the horse to victory. If the horse either *stalks the pace,* meaning sits a few lengths behind the lead horse, or sits far back and rallies late, then you must ask yourself, is the bugboy a pilot or a passenger (see "Anticipation" earlier in this chapter)? If you need a pilot, and the bugboy isn't ready to be one yet, then I don't advise making the bet.

Money riders: Why trainers seek them out

In big stakes races like the Kentucky Derby or the Breeders' Cup, trainers try to enlist the elite jockeys — or *money riders* — to ride their horses. These jockeys are called money riders because they come through time and time again in pressure situations. When the most money is on the line, they compete like they have ice water in their veins.

In rich stakes, the caliber of the horses is very high. Most any horse entered has a good chance to win given racing luck and a good trip. In normal races, the rider may account for a small percentage toward the outcome. In *rich stakes races* among equally talented horses, the rider makes a big difference.

You know you're great when they change the rules

You can measure greatness in athletics in many ways. No matter how you determine excellence, you can't deny an athlete's greatness when the sport changes the rules because of him. When superstar Lew Alcindor, also known as Kareem Abdul-Jabbar, played center for UCLA, he was so dominant that the NCAA started a new no dunking rule in college basketball. Now that's respect.

In 1976, Steve Cauthen was an apprentice at River Downs in Cincinnati, Ohio. He was so good that he blitzed through his 10-pound and 7-pound weight allowances in no time flat. As a 5-pound bugboy, Cauthen was by far the best jockey at River Downs, and he was only 16 years old.

His jockey agent, Eddie Campbell, knew Cauthen was something special. Campbell convinced New York jockey agent Lenny Goodman in New York to take Cauthen to Aqueduct. Campbell said Cauthen was better than most journeymen in the Aqueduct jockey's room. (Aqueduct, located in Ozone Park, is the winter-time racetrack at the New York Racing Association.)

Goodman put Cauthen on some fast horses, and he won with them immediately. In fact, Cauthen won horses races in bunches — sometimes as many as four, five, and six races in one day. His services were in such demand from trainers that he was listed on multiple horses on the Aqueduct overnight in nearly every race. An *overnight* is a schedule of the races to be run the next day. Goodman had the flexibility to name Cauthen on the best horse in nearly every race.

Goodman was playing within the rules, but eventually enough jockeys, trainers, and agents complained about Cauthen being named on multiple horses. The rules were changed so that a jockey is limited to being named on only two horses in a race. Cauthen was such a polished rider that Goodman called it "stealing" to get the kid to ride someone's horse. It was stealing in that Cauthen was the best rider in the race, he was on the fastest horse, and he was still pulling a 5-pound weight allowance. The other trainers, jockeys, and their agents just didn't think it was fair.

How do you know who the big money riders are? Typically they're the jockeys earning the most purse money. The more money the rider makes winning stakes races, the more in demand he is, and the better horses he'll ride in the future. Just remember that the value of the rider increases as the size of the purse money increases.

Betting by the Book: Statistics

TIP

If you're betting a racetrack where you don't know the jockeys, I recommend you look at the jockey standings and other statistics if available. The jockey standings for racetracks around the country are printed in the pertinent edition of the *Daily Racing Form*. (As many as three daily editions of the *Daily Racing Form* may be printed because of all the national simulcasts.)

Lining up a jockey's mounts: The jock's agent

Behind every successful jockey is . . . a jockey's agent. (I'll bet you were thinking spouse.) The jock's agent does all the hard work for the rider: lining up his mounts with the trainers, getting him to and from out-of-town riding assignments, getting him up in the morning to work horses, making sure he's eating right and not staying out late.

The pay for a jock's agent is good, usually 25 percent of a rider's share of earnings. The hours are long. But when the jockey's not winning enough races, the first person to be fired is the jock's agent. From time to time at any racetrack, the agents for riders move around like musical chairs.

The same information is printed in the racetrack program, too. You see the top ten standings listing each jockey's starts, wins, seconds, thirds, and percentage of winning mounts.

The racetrack program includes interesting jockey statistics on different categories. For example, you may find jockey records for sprint races, distance races, dirt races, grass races, percentage of winning favorites, and ROI (return on investment). These stats give you an idea of a jockey's current form and may clue you in on who's hot and who's not in various categories.

Another source you can access on the Internet is Equibase.com (www.equibase.com) — the statistical hub for the sport of Thoroughbred racing. You can also visit each individual racetrack's Web site, which includes its own jockey standings.

One category of statistics to keep in mind is the top ten standings for the meet at each racetrack. Year after year, meet after meet, the top ten riders at a meet win approximately 90 percent of the races run there.

Comparing Viewpoints

I believe the jockey is important when handicapping races. But some handicappers take a different viewpoint, and I wouldn't be forthright if I didn't mention it.

Some bettors could care less who's riding the horse. In fact, if the jockey is unknown, all the better. They feel that when an unpopular rider is up, the public will shy away from betting on that horse. Thus, the odds are high and juicy.

So the question is, if the horse is 90 percent of the winning equation, do you want a top ten rider or a less fashionable journeyman jockey? The contrarian handicapper will choose the latter. The reason is the odds on the horse will be much higher, even though the less skilled jockey tends to lose some races he's not supposed to because of jockey error.

Chapter 8

Calling the Shots: Trainers and Owners

In This Chapter

▶ Understanding the roles of the trainer and her team

▶ Using a trainer's trends to your betting advantage

▶ Getting acquainted with the owners

*I*n the sport of horse racing, if you stop asking questions, you're begging for trouble. With so much information to learn and so many changes occurring, the educational process never stops.

One question you may be asking right now is, "In a book about betting, why is an entire chapter dedicated to trainers and owners?" Well, when I bet, I'm convinced that trainers and owners are trying to win nearly every time they run a horse. In the occasional start where a horse needs a race for conditioning, you can figure out *tells*. Tells is a poker term for visual cues that a player subconsciously makes showing he's either bluffing or has the *nuts*, meaning a top poker hand. Trainers have tells, but their tells are revealed in the *Daily Racing Form* past performances.

In this chapter, I show you what goes into being a successful trainer, and I clue you in on some of the tells for one of the nation's leading trainers. I also let you know how you can spot trainers' tells and use them to your betting advantage. Finally, I discuss the role of the owner in this winning equation.

Taking the Trainer into Account

During my early days in racing, I asked professional horseplayers this question: If you had a choice to bet on either a hot jockey or a hot trainer, which would you prefer? The majority answered: the *trainer*. A trainer is in charge of the health and well-being of racehorses placed under his care. He trains the racehorses as best he can to develop their talent and win races.

A trainer manages racehorses owned by different people or for groups of people, or she may be a *private trainer,* meaning she works for just one individual or group. In theory, the goal of a trainer is to make a racehorse into a champion. The reality is only a small percentage of racehorses become stakes winners, must less champions.

In this section, I try to paint a word picture that depicts how several people come together to run a barn. A *barn* in this usage refers to a trainer's domain on the backside of the racetrack that includes the horses and the employees who work for him. I get into handicapping angles that are worth following.

A winning team

I started in horse racing in the publicity department at the New York Racing Association (NYRA). One of my early jobs was to get *backstretch notes* — quickie interviews with horsemen that are typed up and distributed to the media. I discovered early on that when I showed up at 8 a.m. to talk with a trainer, he and his barn staff were already in the middle of their workday. Life on the backstretch of a racetrack starts around 4:30 a.m. — well before the sun rises. The horses all have to be fed, galloped or worked out, bathed, and fed again. And those are just the morning chores!

The boss of all this action is the trainer. Consider him the chief executive officer of his barn, because he must deal with the horse owners — the stockholders who pay the bills (see "Owners: There's No Horse Racing without Them," later in the chapter). In addition, he has to deal with people like me in the media. In order to complete the daily operations, the trainer must rely on a team of stable employees that includes the following people:

- ✔ **Assistants:** Just as the name implies, the assistant helps the trainer in managing the day-to-day operations of the stable. If the trainer is busy with owners or the media, the assistant tends to the horses and supervises the barn employees. Depending on how many horses the trainer has under her care, she has at least one assistant and often times more. As the stable gets bigger and bigger, the role of the trainer changes because she spends so much time dealing with the current owners, recruiting new owners, and tending to big picture issues. A top trainer leans on her assistants to make sure everything at the barn runs smoothly.

- ✔ **Grooms:** Grooms are the people who get closest to the horses on a daily basis. They get into the stall with the horses and work on their legs. They brush 'em, clean 'em, and feed 'em. If a horse looks terrific from head to toe, you thank the groom for a job well done. Grooms have to trust the horses, which are often downright ornery. A good groom spends so much time with the horses that he usually starts talking to them like they're Mr. Ed. But the more familiar the groom becomes with a horse, the easier he can spot something wrong. More often than not, the groom is the first person to notice and let his boss know when something is different with a horse.

✔ **Exercise riders:** These workers' role is pretty self-explanatory. Although jockeys work horses in the morning from time to time, the exercise rider's job is to take the horses from the barn to the racetrack for an open gallop. Horses need to be galloped every day, because it allows the horses to open their lungs, get some exercise, and stay fit.

In Chapter 7, I explain that a jockey has a clock in her head, so she knows how fast she's going and how quick the *fractions* — intermediate times taken every furlong or quarter-mile — are in the race she's riding. An exercise rider must also have a clock in his head. When a trainer asks him to do a half-mile in 48 seconds, the rider better hit the number or be pretty darn close. A good exercise rider keeps the trainer informed about the horse's performance during the gallop.

✔ **Hotwalkers:** This position is considered entry level at the barn. After horses race, workout, or gallop, they must cool down by walking. If you can walk straight, hold a shank on a horse, and keep turning left, you have the makings of a good hotwalker.

You can see how every employee contributes to the success of the barn. The hotwalkers, exercise riders, and especially the grooms spend more time with the horses than the trainer does. They must communicate and work as a team, reporting information to the trainer. The trainer has ultimate responsibility for keeping the horses happy and healthy, but he knows he needs good help to win a lot of races.

If the barn isn't winning races, an owner doesn't hesitate to move his horses to another trainer at the drop of a hat. But when the barn is red-hot, a trainer doesn't have to recruit new owners, because they come to him.

A trainer's trends and tells

You can compare a good horse trainer to a good football coach. In football, winning teams do certain things well, mainly because of the coaching philosophy, and they develop tendencies based upon that success. Opposing coaches watch film and chart plays to find those tendencies, so they can establish a game plan that will help them defeat the other team.

Horse racing trainers also develop tendencies that create winning horses. If you want to become a successful horseplayer, you need to find those tendencies in trainers and use them to your betting advantage. In this section, I've included the *Daily Racing Form* past performances for three of trainer Bob Baffert's horses. Baffert, who is stabled in Southern California and races at Santa Anita Park, Hollywood Park, and Del Mar, is one of the leading Thoroughbred horse trainers in the world. His most prestigious wins came in the Kentucky Derby three times, the Breeders' Cup World Thoroughbred Championships three times, and the Dubai World Cup two times.

The three horses cover three different categories for Baffert. Cashmula is a *maiden* colt, meaning he's yet to win his first race. Señor Swinger is a grass runner and a good one at that. Congaree is a dirt horse and a distance runner, meaning he prefers to run in long races around 2 turns. He, like Señor Swinger, is very accomplished in rich stakes races.

You can see at the bottom of the *Daily Racing Form* past performances for Cashmula, Señor Swinger, and Congaree, the word **TRAINER** in all capital letters and in boldface type. These are trainer statistics for Baffert in various categories as compiled by the *Daily Racing Form*. They're the trends or tells for Baffert that used to be hard to come by. Now anyone who buys the *Daily Racing Form* and pays attention to the percentages gains a huge handicapping edge over others who don't use this statistical analysis. The *Daily Racing Form* tracks 34 trends, which cover the last two years. Here I examine the trainer statistics for each of Baffert's horses and explain what they mean. (For more on how to read *DRF* past performances, see Chapter 11.)

Double duty: Trainer and entrepreneur

Every trainer operates his stable a little differently. But one thing is always true: Without talented horses in the barn, the trainer isn't going to win many races.

Trainers can acquire fast racehorses a number of ways, but they need money to buy horses with fashionable *pedigrees* (bloodlines or a horse's family tree) or to aggressively claim horses from other stables. Without cash, a trainer is the same as a small boy pressing his nose against the window of a candy store.

Most of the time, training horses is the easy part of a trainer's job. For a trainer to grow her business, she must also be a salesperson and entrepreneur. Recruiting new owners and dealing with them can be a time-consuming and difficult task. Meeting potential new owners is no different than in other types of sales jobs. It's about building relationships and meeting people. And the only color that counts is green (as in money).

I chose Bob Baffert for this example because he's one of the best trainers in horse racing. The trainer trends show that betting Baffert horses blindly will lead to losing money. Not that he doesn't win a lot of races — around 20 percent — but the odds on his horses are low. So, when Baffert wins a race, there isn't much value for a $2 bet. Remember that to make money betting on horse racing, you need to beat the favorites. In many cases, you'll be trying to beat a Bob Baffert-trained horse to get better value on some long shots.

Checking out Cashmula

Figure 8-1 gives the past performances for Cashmula.

Figure 8-1: Cashmula's past performances.

©2005 by Daily Racing Form, Inc. and Equibase Company

Cashmula is a 2-year-old colt and the type of young, well-bred, expensive horse that Baffert gets to train because of his proven track record in the Triple Crown. The Triple Crown is for 3-year-old horses, so Cashmula is beginning his career with the hope that he'll develop into a quality horse that'll compete in the Triple Crown series the following spring. Cashmula has since been moved to another barn, but the Baffert trainer trends are still accurate:

- **2ndStart(116 .27 $2.30):** *2ndStart* means maiden horses making the second start of their career. The number of horses in this sampling is 116, which is very large for Baffert. The *.27* means he wins with 27 percent of his second time out maiden starters. Thus, Baffert has won with 31 of 116 starters in this category. The return on investment is $2.30 for each $2 bet. A *blind bet,* a bet made with no handicapping at all, of $2 on each starter in this category returns $2.30, which is a very good profit for a minimal amount of work. If you apply some handicapping to this trend, you can improve the return on investment.

- **2YO(202 .17 $.99):** The *2YO* stands for 2-year-old horses. Baffert gets a lot of nice 2-year-olds to train, so the 202 starts by 2-year-old horses is a very large sampling. The *.17* means he wins with 17 percent of his 2-year-old starters. Thus, Baffert has won with 34 of 202 starters in this category.

The return on investment is .99 for each $2 bet, which is lousy. Baffert trains many expensive, highly regarded 2-year-olds. When they do start, the public tends to *overbet* them — meaning the odds on the horses are lower than their real chances of winning the race — because of the good reputation of Bob Baffert. When these horses win, often times they're favored and pay low $2 win prices, contributing to Baffert's terrible return on investment in this category.

✔ **Sprint(603 .21 $1.80):** A *sprint* is considered a distance of less than 1 mile. The 603 starters is a huge sampling that shows that Baffert has a large stable and starts a lot of horses. The *.21* is a healthy win percentage. He has won with 127 of 603 starters in this category. The $1.80 return on investment for a $2 wager is very good for a blind bet, and here's why: With any sort of good handicapping, you should be able to eliminate many starters from this category. Getting the number to break even — meaning $2 — wouldn't take much, and a little more work could get it into the profitable side.

✔ **MdnSpWt(336 .19 $1.54):** *MdnSpWt* means maiden special weight, which is a race for maiden horses carrying a specified amount of weight. The horses are safe from being claimed, meaning purchased out of the race by other horsemen. The *336* is a large sampling of starters in this category. The *.19* is a good win percentage. Baffert has won with 64 of 336 starters in maiden special weight class. The $1.54 return on investment for a $2 bet is a little on the low side.

Surveying Señor Swinger

Check out Figure 8-2 for Señor Swinger's past performances.

Figure 8-2: Past performances of Señor Swinger, a grass runner.

©2005 by Daily Racing Form, Inc. and Equibase Company

Señor Swinger is a talented 4-year-old grass runner privately purchased by Bob Baffert for new owners Robert and Beverly Lewis. The biggest win of the colt's career came on July 24, 2004, in the grade 3 Arlington Handicap at Arlington Park in Arlington Heights, Illinois. Stakes races with a grade 1, 2, or 3 rating are the best races offered in the U.S. He appears to be a cut below grade 1 turf horses. Señor Swinger is competitive though in classy grade 2 and 3 competition. Here are four trainer trends for Señor Swinger:

✔ **31-60Days(261 .21 $1.61):** The *31-60* means horses that are starting with between 31 and 60 days rest since their last race. Baffert has 261 horses that qualify in the past two years. The *.21* is a good win percentage, meaning 55 of 261 starters have won in this category. The $1.61 return on investment for a $2 bet is average considering the large sample.

✔ **Turf(218 .14 $1.54):** *Turf* is self-explanatory and stands for turf racing, also known as grass racing. The number of starters in this category is 218. The win percentage is .14, meaning 31 of 218 Baffert grass starters have won. The $1.54 return on investment for a $2 bet is average.

✔ **Routes(482 .16 $1.10):** *Routes* are races 1 mile and longer. Baffert has 482 starters in this category. The win percentage of .16 means 77 of 482 route starters have won. The $1.10 return on investment is well below average. Baffert horses tend to get overbet by the public, thus his 16 percent winners usually don't pay very much.

✔ **GrdStk(159 .19 $1.48):** *GrdStk* stands for *Graded Stakes*. These are the best stakes races that earn a grade of either 1, 2, or 3. Baffert has 159 starters, of which .19 are winners, meaning 30 of 159 wins in this category. His $1.48 return on investment for a $2 bet is below average.

Considering Congaree

You find Congaree's past performances in Figure 8-3.

Figure 8-3: The impressive past performances of Congaree show what a great racer this horse is.

©2005 by Daily Racing Form, Inc. and Equibase Company

Congaree ranks among the best racehorses that Baffert has ever trained. A multiple grade 1 stakes winner, he has beaten top-class competition. His career earnings of more than $3 million rank him among the elite Thoroughbreds of all-time. His owner, Stonerside Stable, is the racing entity of Robert McNair, who owns the Houston Texans of the National Football League (NFL). Check out the trainer trends for Congaree:

- **61-180(63 .19 $1.02):** The *61-180* stands for horses that are starting with between 61 days and 180 days rest since their last race. Baffert has 63 starters that qualify, of which .19 or 19 percent have won. Of the 12 of 63 winners, $1.02 is the return on investment for a $2 bet. That return on investment is very low for Baffert but is caused by the fact that he starts many favorites in this category, so his winners don't pay much.

- **Route/Sprint(70 .23 $1.28):** *Route/Sprint* means switching from a route race last start to a sprint race today. Baffert has had 70 horses fit this category, of which 23 percent have won. The 16 of 70 winners have paid $1.28 return on investment for a $2 bet. That return is below average.

- **Dirt(689 .20 $1.46):** *Dirt* is self-explanatory, meaning dirt races. Baffert has a gigantic sampling of 689 starters, of which 20 percent have won. His 138 of 689 winners have paid a $1.46 return on investment for a $2 bet. That's not bad considering how large the sample is.

- **Sprint(496 .21 $1.76):** A *sprint* is a race shorter than 1 mile. Baffert has 496 in this category with 21 percent wins. His 104 of 496 wins yielded a $1.76 return on investment for a $2 bet.

- **GrdStk(109 .21 $1.62):** This trend is the same as the final trend for Señor Swinger. This trend is measured earlier in the year, so there are 109 starters in the sampling versus the 159 at the time of Señor Swinger's start.

Owners: There's No Racing without Them

I always thought the most daring people at the racetrack were the jockeys, because horse racing is the only sport where an ambulance follows the participants. (It's true. Next time you're at the racetrack, look out onto the main track. After the horses leave the starting gate, you'll see an ambulance following along the outside rail, going about 35 miles per hour. And you wonder why jockeys have trouble getting health insurance!)

However, one old-time horseplayer told me that the bravest people at the racetrack are the horse owners. He said that most horse owners lose money in the sport. Yet these people walk in with their eyes and wallets wide open, ready to buy racehorses. In this section, I look at why owning horses has such appeal despite the financial risks.

The expenses of horse ownership

The biggest expense an owner must pay is the *day rate* to his trainer for each horse under his care. For example, in Kentucky racing, the day rate ranges from $45 to $80 per day, per horse. From this day rate, the trainer must pay the barn employees and pay for the essentials to care for the horse. Those essentials include feed, vitamins, and supplements for the horse. The owner must also pay out-of-pocket fees outside of the day rate. These fees include veterinarian bills, mortality insurance, blacksmith work, dental work (yes, horses have problems with their teeth), and traveling expenses.

Racing partnerships: The newest trend

The expenses involved in horse ownership are large. One way to own a horse and keep the investment within your means is to join racing partnerships, which are organizations that pool the resources of many people to invest in racehorses. Some of the most reputable racing partnerships include Centennial Farms, Dogwood Stable, Team Valor, and West Point Thoroughbreds. Following is a partnership deal offered by Dogwood that's representative of how these firms work:

✔ Each horse is sold as part of a general partnership. With this set up, favorable tax implications allow for a substantial tax write-off.

✔ Dogwood retains 5 percent interest in each general partnership. Cot Campbell, president of Dogwood, acts as the racing manager.

✔ Four other general partners each own 23.75 percent interest.

✔ The partners must pay a maintenance fee, which is payable quarterly and in advance. A horse costs nearly $45,000 a year to keep in training, so divide that amount among four partners, and divide it again by four quarters of the year.

✔ Profits and tax benefits are allocated equally. Should the horse not measure up, the general partners can vote during a quarterly review to dissolve the partnership.

The average investment in a Dogwood partnership ranges from $25,000 to $75,000. Because most investors dream about winning the Kentucky Derby or the Kentucky Oaks, an emphasis is placed on buying yearlings and 2-year-olds (the types of horses running in these races).

If you'd rather gamble on owning a horse instead of betting on horses, you can contact the racing office at your local racetrack or get more information from the following Web sites:

✔ Centennial Farms: www.centennialfarms.com

✔ Dogwood Stable: www.dogwoodstable.com

✔ Team Valor: www.teamvalor.com

✔ West Point Thoroughbreds: www.westpointtb.com

✔ National Thoroughbred Racing Association: www.ntra.com

✔ Thoroughbred Owners and Breeders Association: www.toba.org

When a horse wins a race, the owner keeps 80 percent, and the jockey and trainer each earn 10 percent of the *purse money* won. The purse money is the cash prize the racetrack puts up for every race. Usually the first five finishers receive a paycheck, though a lion's share — 60 percent of the purse — is paid to the winner.

The joys of owning

Some people get into horse ownership with the idea that it's a hobby, albeit an expensive one, but one with a big upside. The upside is when their 2-year-old outruns his pedigree and wins some nice races. A horse they've claimed improves, wins a few races, and then gets claimed for a much higher price. Or when a horse owner experiences the thrill of winning a horse race and getting his picture taken in the winner's circle with family and friends.

A common perception of horse owners is that they're filthy rich and want to stand out from the crowd. Claims like that couldn't be farther from the truth, although having disposable income does help. Owning horses is one of the most fun things you can do in your life. People who've been very competitive and successful in life point to winning a horse race as an owner as an incredible thrill of unmatched excitement. Racehorse ownership has been compared to owning a pro sports franchise, but at an affordable price.

The owners I know say the friendships they develop with other people make horse owning worth it, even if they've never won a race. A camaraderie is present at the barn, in the owner's box, and in the turf club. Owners have told me that owning a horse bonds a family in a way few things in life can. On days the horse races, family and friends go to the racetrack together to enjoy the day and root their horse on to victory.

Chapter 9

Knowing the Track Surface and Conditions

● ●

In This Chapter

▶ Rating the surface of the main dirt track

▶ Mastering main track maintenance

▶ Understanding turf course ratings

▶ Judging track biases

● ●

1 was channel surfing on my television one night when I saw a race car driver being interviewed. He was talking about the racetrack surface at the speedway, describing it as "kind" and that his car really "grabbed a hold of it." My first reaction was "huh?" I drive my car around Las Vegas and don't think much about the concrete under my tires. But then I realized that the people on the outside of horse racing probably have the same reaction when the jockeys and trainers talk about the racing surfaces in horse racing.

In simplest terms, horses race either on dirt or grass, so what's the big deal? Well, knowing the track surface is a big deal because no two dirt tracks or two grass courses are alike. They may be similar, but not alike. In this chapter, I take a closer look at the two types of racing surfaces and how they factor into handicapping.

Scratching the Surface: Rating the Main Dirt Track

Throughout most of the world, horse racing is conducted *on turf courses.* Most racetracks around the world race short, compact meets that aren't nearly as long or arduous as American campaigns. I must admit, seeing a big field of chestnut and dark bay (brown) horses racing over lush green grass is a wonderful sight.

Unfortunately, though, grass can take only so much pounding and gouging from the horses' hooves. So the solution in the United States for the commercialization of horse racing is *dirt tracks.* Dirt is easier to maintain and can withstand the five-day week schedule in week after week of Thoroughbred racing. Figure 9-1 shows a composite of what a typical main dirt track is made of.

The only ingredient that changes the rating of the main track surface is water. When it rains hard, you see the main track downgraded to a certain level, depending on the amount of moisture. The terminology used in the *Daily Racing Form* past performances or at the racetrack on the infield tote board is the same. In this section, I define the terms for you.

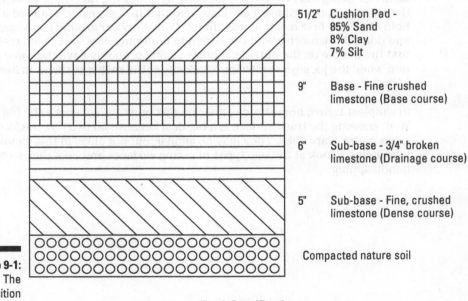

51/2"   Cushion Pad -
85% Sand
8% Clay
7% Silt

9"   Base - Fine crushed limestone (Base course)

6"   Sub-base - 3/4" broken limestone (Drainage course)

5"   Sub-base - Fine, crushed limestone (Dense course)

Compacted nature soil

Figure 9-1: The composition of a main dirt track.

Track Specification
One mile and one eighth oval with chutes for $6^1/_2$, $7/_8$, $7^1/_2$, 1 mile. Track is 90 feet wide through the stretch. Distance from last turn to finish line: 1,049 feet.

Fast

In a perfect horse racing world, all races would be run over a fast track. *Fast* is defined as a dirt track in optimum condition, level with just the right amount of moisture. If you arrive at the racetrack really early — well before the first race — you may get to see the track superintendent and his staff working on the main track. Every racetrack owns or leases a few tractors that are essential for conditioning the dirt surface.

Normal track maintenance includes harrowing the dirt. An oversized harrow is attached to the back of each tractor. The drivers, as a team, sweep around the main track, harrowing a good 50 or 60 feet from the rail out. A finished harrow job leaves a level racing surface with perfect grooves carved into the dirt.

A *harrow* — if you're not familiar with its use in farming — is built of a heavy metal frame with sharp teeth pointing downward into the ground. In this case, the teeth are about four to five inches long. As the harrow is dragged across the racetrack by the tractors, it digs in and breaks up the ground, including any dirt clods that may have formed.

Although too much water degrades the track surface, problems also occur for the track superintendent when too little moisture is in the dirt. On bright sunny days, the main track is commonly watered between every race.

Why the regular watering? Most dirt tracks have a very high percentage of sand in their composition — as much as 80 to 90 percent. The sun and wind evaporate the moisture from the track very quickly. A track that's too dry gets very dusty, and the particles blow away in the wind. However, the main reason for watering is that a dry, sandy track is extremely tiring for the horses to run on. When horses get overextended, they become more injury prone. You hear jockeys complain that the track is "loose and cuppy," where the sand balls up under horse's hooves.

Spraying water over the track keeps the materials moist and binds the surface. A track surface with just the right amount of water is a glib, bouncy surface for horses to run over. Just imagine yourself running along a sandy beach and how difficult getting good footing is. If you run close to the water line where the waves wash up over the sand, the moisture compacts the material, and running becomes much easier.

Good

Good is the next rating down from fast. A *good* surface has a lot of moisture in it, which isn't necessarily a bad thing. In fact, sometimes a good racetrack yields much faster running times than a fast one. The *Daily Racing Form* and some track superintendents use the term *wet fast* when this type of scenario crops up.

A track's rating is subjective. Usually when a wet racetrack can hold up to a harrow, it should be rated fast. But some track superintendents don't see it that way.

A sure sign of a good track is when a *float* is used behind the tractors to smooth out the racing surface. (A float is made of long boards of wood. The amount of pressure it exerts can be controlled by placing weights on top of the wood.) A harrow used on a racetrack with too much moisture in it can leave waves in the dirt, which you don't want. Also, you can't harrow sometimes because the wheel marks from the tractor may sink deep into the mushy cushion, causing an unsafe racing condition. The tractor tire marks are effectively smoothed over by the float as it presses down the wet dirt.

Muddy

Muddy is the next level down from good, and in this case, the racetrack has taken so much rain that it can't be harrowed. Instead, a float is attached to the back of the tractors to flatten out the dirt. A muddy floated track looks like the pancake batter you pour on the griddle. Even the texture is the same, because it can get a little sticky.

Although both good and muddy main tracks are floated, the muddy track absorbs much more water. A horse's hooves sink deeper into a muddy racetrack.

You see a lot of trainers switch to *mud calks* on their horse's shoes when they race on a muddy track. The mud calk is like a cleat on a sports shoe that helps the horse dig into the mushy mud and get much better traction. As a handicapper, you need to pay attention to changes like this. Mud calks improve a horse's footing and thus improve its performance too.

Another handicapping angle you hear about is horses that lose shoes running over a muddy track. The track can get so sticky it literally sucks the shoes right off the horse's hoof — nails and all. That's a legitimate excuse for a horse losing a race over a muddy track. So when you find out about this happening in a horse racing article in the *Daily Racing Form* or another horse racing medium, that horse is worth noting the next time it runs.

You've probably heard about some racehorses being *mudders,* meaning they excel when racing over muddy or sloppy racetracks. Do you know why that is? The number one answer given by horsemen and handicappers is small feet. A horse with small feet can more easily pick its way through the gooey racetrack. Now, you can't walk up to a racehorse, pick up its foot, and look at it. But at least you know the reason why mudders run well on muddy racetracks. Conversely, horses with big feet tend to run poorly on a muddy or sloppy racetrack, but they improve greatly in turf racing. A big foot aids the horse in digging into the grass and ground and pushing off with good traction.

Sloppy

A *sloppy* main track is easy to spot because it'll be raining cats and dogs, and the top of the track surface will be covered in standing water. Sloppy tracks remind you that horse racing goes on like the mailman — rain or shine. Don't be surprised to see horses splashing through water and the returning jockeys covered with dirt from head to toe (see Figure 9-2).

Figure 9-2: Horses splashing through the slop at Saratoga.

Photo by Skip Dickstein

When a track is in sloppy condition, floating is the only way to keep the cushion at an even, level depth so the horses can get over it safely. Floating also helps by squeezing some of the water out of the cushion. More weight is applied atop the float to force the water out of the dirt and down toward the rail where the drains are.

Track superintendents have access to detailed weather forecasts, and when the local weather calls for rain, they have a chance to *seal* the racetrack before the storm hits. They roll the track, creating a tight seal on the top. Rolling takes the air out of the cushion, so if it does rain, the water runs off the top toward the inside where the drainage is. The idea is to press the dirt down, taking the ridges out of it so the water runs off easier.

Speed horses are the kind I like to bet when the racetrack is sloppy. Lots of horses hate when slop is kicked back in their faces and often don't put forth their best effort because of it. The speedball horse is in front and in the clear, and the jockey can place the horse in the best path for firmer footing.

Frozen

You see *frozen* track surfaces from time to time at wintertime racetracks. A main track has between 4 and 6 inches of cushion atop the base. In the winter, moisture can seep into the cushion and freeze up if the track superintendent isn't careful.

To prevent the racing surface from freezing solid, the track crew may have to harrow the racetrack overnight — literally for 15 or 16 hours continuously.

Frozen tracks usually promote the speed horses. The jockeys I've talked to tell me it's like racing on a concrete highway with a couple inches of dirt cushion over it.

When I worked at Turfway Park in Florence, Kentucky, we raced at night in the dead of winter. Our track crew harrowed the main track overnight to prevent freezing. The drivers would rest during the daylight hours, and then we'd race in the evening. After the races were over, the tractors would work overnight once again.

Giving a Little TLC: Main Track Maintenance

In handicapping the races, every piece of knowledge helps. Many handicappers don't really know what goes on with the main track and turf course. The fact that you're reading this chapter will help you understand why tracks play a certain way. Here, I explain some main track maintenance procedures that I think you'll find interesting and useful.

Crowning

I suspect most of you have never set foot on a dirt racing surface before. But you've probably walked onto a football field. The first thing you probably noticed is that the field isn't perfectly level. Most football fields are crowned with the high point in the center sloping toward the low points by the two sidelines. *Crowning* a field helps drainage. Otherwise, when it rains, the water would collect in the center of the field where most of the game is played.

The same philosophy occurs in horse racing. The main track is crowned with the high point by the outside sloping down towards the rail where the drainage ditches are located. Most tracks build the crown out to around 60 feet and then slope the rest towards the outside rail so all the water doesn't run down to the inner rail. This set-up distributes some of the rainwater to the outer rail, too.

Some tracks — like Lone Star Park, Philadelphia Park, and Suffolk Downs — however, don't build any break in their crown. All the rain that falls on the 80-, 90-, or 100-foot wide racetrack flows to the inside — that's an awful lot of water. During heavy rain at those places, I'd rather bet horses I think will run on the outer portion of the racetrack.

The normal crown on the straight part of the main track — front and back sides — has about a 2 percent slope. On the turns, the crown is called *banking*, and its slope is around 4 to 6 percent. Banking on the turns is much steeper to aid the horses in getting around the turns.

Materials in the track

Knowing the materials in the racetrack can help define biases and how well a racetrack will drain. Jerry Porcelli, the former track superintendent with the New York Racing Association (NYRA), shared with me what's done at the New York tracks and what the composition is at some other well-known racetracks.

Because NYRA racing is held at three different tracks — Aqueduct, Belmont Park, and Saratoga — every attempt is made to keep the main tracks as similar and consistent as possible. The composition of the tracks is 90 percent sand, 4 percent clay, and 6 percent silt.

The NYRA track that gets the most rain has the shortest meet — Saratoga. A finer sand that promotes faster drainage is used at Saratoga. (If you've ever lived in or visited the upstate New York town, summer thunderstorms are a very common occurrence.) The finer the sand, the better it packs down when the track superintendent wants to *seal* (roll the track, creating a tight seal on the top) or *float* (to level or smooth by dragging wooden boards over a muddy track) the surface.

Porcelli told me that a soft, soaking rain is a bigger problem than a hard, pouring rain. If the main track is sealed before the rain starts, the hard rain "packs the track down like a million little hammers," and most of the water just runs off. A soft rain seeps in and soaks the ground even further.

Tracks around the country must tailor their main tracks to the weather conditions and the materials that are readily available to them. Suffolk Downs in Boston, Massachusetts, uses a very coarse sand that drains well but doesn't pack well. Lone Star Park races in very hot weather in the Dallas, Texas area. The track make-up is 75 percent sand and much more silt and clay to try and keep the moisture in the track.

Churchill Downs in Louisville, Kentucky, is famous for a main track that dries out in lightning quick fashion. The track uses a very fine sand that packs down really tight — which I know for a fact from working numerous Kentucky Derbies for the network. When the Churchill main track takes a lot of rain, walking on it is like being at the beach near the shoreline. The sand is wet and packed down, and the racing surface is very firm.

Because of the slope of the course, the material on the racetrack has a tendency to slide towards the inside, creating a major bias unless the track crew corrects the situation. You'll notice in rainy weather at almost any racetrack that the speed horses on the lead will race in the four-path (fourth lane), on out.

Blading

An integral part of track maintenance is *blading* the racetrack. When material slides off the crown toward the inner rail, it's important for the track crew to return the material to where it came from. The workers take a *grader* that has a big blade on it and literally push the material back up the slope.

The key for the track superintendent is to have the same depth of cushion from the inside all the way to the outside of the racetrack. Whether the normal depth is 4, 4½, or 5 inches, it should be uniform.

The material on the track naturally comes down the slope due to the force of gravity. The gravity is even more prevalent on the turns with a steeper 4 percent to 6 percent slope. In the summer, after a heavy rain, lots of loose material gets pulled down the slope. You can see that happen in your own yard, out on the street, or at the park. The water runs downhill and pulls material with it.

Blading is done at major racetracks almost every day. Tracks are worked on all day long. They're harrowed in the morning after workouts and in the day-time or nighttime, depending on when the races are.

Making the Grade: Turf Course Ratings

When you see the huge expanse of grass that makes up a track's turf course (see Figure 9-3), you can't help but think about a football field, a baseball park, or even your own backyard if you have a big one. Well, taking care of a grass course is nothing like any of the above. The track superintendent uses a variety of grasses mixed together to give the course added toughness and the ability to stay lush through different growing seasons. During the racing season, the track crew has to cut the grass, roll the ground if it gets uneven, aerate it, and add nutrients, nitrogen, fungicides, insecticides, and of course, water.

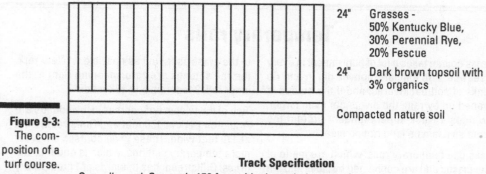

24"   Grasses -
      50% Kentucky Blue,
      30% Perennial Rye,
      20% Fescue

24"   Dark brown topsoil with
      3% organics

Compacted nature soil

Figure 9-3:
The com-
position of a
turf course.

Track Specification
One mile oval. Course is 150 feet wide through the stretch.

The cut of the grass and the amount of moisture in the ground affect the running times. The grass can range in height from 4 inches up to 6 inches high. To come up with a track designation, the track crew walks the turf course. The workers bring a probe and stick it into the ground at intervals all around the course. The reading is very subjective, because what's firm for one crew may be good for another. Yielding for one track superintendent is soft for the next.

Following are the ratings for the quality of a turf course racing surface:

✔ **Firm:** A grass course is firm when it's in optimum condition. If no rain has fallen lately, it's necessary to water the course to maintain growth. The ground underneath the grass is firm to the point of being hard.

✔ **Good:** A good course has taken some rain, but not to the point of being saturated. As horses run over it, the ground has a lot more give. You notice more divots fly up than on a firm course.

✔ **Yielding:** The ground is so moist that it gives way underneath the horses' hooves. You see huge chunks of divots flying back as the horses run. This course is very tiring, and seldom do you see horses win going wire to wire. *Dead late closers* (come-from-behind horses) stay covered up and make one mad dash in the stretch run.

✔ **Soft:** You see this designation more in foreign racing than in the United States. The grass course has been saturated, and the ground is soft to the point of being mushy. The running times are extremely slow because the horses are literally running over a bog.

Temporary rails

A grass course takes a lot of punishment in every horse race. The animals' hooves dig in and rip chunks of sod backwards, and if the course is softened up by rain, the divots get even larger. How does a track superintendent protect the course so it lasts a long racing meet?

Tracks use temporary rails, which are made of white plastic and are connected by pipes into the ground. These rails distribute the wear and tear out over different sections of the turf course and allow the grass to regenerate and stay healthy.

A turf course is built with as many temporary settings as possible to spread the punishment

to the grass as far out as possible. In New York, the rail settings are zero, meaning right at the inner rail, 9 feet out, and 18 feet out.

Two of the widest turf courses in the country are Arlington Park at 150 feet and Gulfstream Park at 170 feet wide. These wide courses allow for more temporary settings, which is good for the grass. Gulfstream has upwards of 11 temporary rail settings.

The use of temporary rails plays a big factor in your handicapping. Historically, when the rails are up, speed horses benefit. And the farther out the rails go, the more they help the speed horses.

 In European racing, you see track designations like "good to yielding." The turf courses are so big that seldom is the track condition uniform all the way around.

Tuning In to Track Biases

A track superintendent's main job is to provide a safe racetrack for the horses, but he also wants a fair racetrack without bias. A member of the track crew measures the depth of the main track every day by driving around in a truck and stopping at every 16th pole to measure. The worker sticks a probe into the dirt cushion at 3-foot, 10-foot, 20-foot, 30-foot and 40-foot marks and writes down the measurement. If the depth isn't uniform, the crew grades (see "Main Track Maintenance," earlier in the chapter) the racetrack until it is. Grading prevents a build up of materials down along the rail.

Despite all this effort, however, over the course of a race meet, certain trends can develop on the main track, turf course, or both that give certain horses an advantage over others.

Main track biases

Following are some of the most common main track biases:

- **Golden rail:** If the rail is *golden,* meaning the speed horses last longer, then as a handicapper, you better pick up on it and use it to your advantage. You'll see the speed horses break from the starting gate and be taken straight to the rail by their jockeys.

    If a golden rail exists, even when a come-from-behind horse wins, this horse needs to spend a good part of the race saving ground on the rail before commencing a rally.

- **Dead rail:** The converse is true when the rail is *dead,* meaning the inside speed horses keep stopping like they're running in quicksand. Any speed horses that win over this track bias will race far off the rail, maybe as far as four or five paths (lanes) from the inside rail. In this case, look for come-from-behind horses to rally wide in the stretch.

- **Pure speed bias:** When you see a pure speed bias racetrack, which path or lane the speed horse runs in doesn't matter. Sometimes you see ridiculous fast fractions like a quarter-mile in less than 22 seconds or a half-mile less than 45 seconds. With a speed bias, the leaders just keep going and don't get caught by the closing horses.

You'll notice with experience that certain tracks have enormous biases due to rain and weather. Two racetracks in particular come to mind: Suffolk Downs in Boston, Massachusetts, and Turf Paradise in Phoenix, Arizona. It's not unusual to see such a significant track bias that the winning horses run out in the middle of the racetrack. In fact, sometimes you don't see a horse run any closer than the five- or six-path, well off the inner rail.

As a horseplayer, be careful about a track bias, because you can easily get fooled. For example, say the speed horse on the rail wins the first three races of the day. Many handicappers will immediately label the main track as favoring inside speed. However, the three winners may have been the best horses in the races regardless. Also, when a jockey rides a speed horse, he tries to break the horse sharp and, regardless of the post, move left towards the rail. Remember that riding the rail is the shortest way to the finish line. Conversely, if the first three winners were rally wide horses, many handicappers will list a dead rail and an outside lane speed bias. Again, the three winners may just be the best horses in the races. And remember that horses that rally from behind, most of the time, rally wide because the jockey doesn't want to get trapped inside behind tiring horses. A general rule of thumb I use is to look at the odds of the winning horses. If they're the favorite or second choice in the wagering, you shouldn't be surprised to see them win.

Staying on the straight and narrow path

When I was the public relations director at Turfway Park, former jockey Brent Bartram taught me something that I still see on wet weather days. Bartram was a strong come-from-behind rider. During one particular hot streak, every one of his winners seemed to rally down the four-path in the stretch. I asked him why that was, and his answer was remarkably simple.

When a tractor is pulling a float over the dirt track, the driver stays the same distance off the rail. Bartram said that after a few races, a lane the width of the tractor's tire starts to firm up. The tractor tire is rolling over this lane again and again, making the ground underneath it tighter and tighter. Bartram tried to get his horse to run over this lane for better footing. He figured if he could gain a neck advantage, it would be worth a few more wins in photo finishes.

Turf biases

Turf biases can exist just like main track biases. Here are a few of the most common to watch for:

- ✔ **Temporary rails:** The most obvious bias is when a track puts up its temporary rails. The farther out the temporary rails are placed, the greater advantage speed horses have.

- ✔ **Cut grass:** Another little known advantage is when the grass course gets mowed. Shorter grass helps the speed horses.

- ✔ **Soft and yielding turf:** Soft and yielding turf really lends itself to closing runners. Horses that set the pace over wet ground can crawl incredibly slow early fractions and still collapse at the top of the stretch.

The type of pedigree to look for on soft and yielding turf is foreign-bred horses from France, England, Germany, and other countries outside the United States. The foreign horses regularly run over yielding and soft ground, so they're used to it. I've heard they have turf feet, meaning big hooves that can get a hold of the ground. I guess it's true.

Chapter 10

Zoning In on Equipment Changes

*I*n order to draw out the potential talent in their horses, trainers use various kinds of equipment. Sometimes, a horse gets injured physically or psychologically, and a piece of equipment becomes necessary to help the horse. Another reason for an equipment change is to control poor behavior or bad habits. Horse trainers are willing to try most anything that's legal to improve a horse's performance and win a race.

Unless you've been lucky enough to spend some time with horses and learn about equipment first hand, many of the equipment changes I cover in this chapter won't be noticeable to the newcomers of horse racing at first. But for a horse trainer trying to win races, and for the horseplayers cashing winning wagers, keeping an eye on all equipment changes is very important.

Blinkers — On or Off

The most common piece of equipment known to horse-racing fans are *blinkers*. Blinkers (see Figure 10-1) are eye shields attached to the horse's bridle or head to block his vision and keep him looking forward on the racetrack. Blinkers are a very simple but effective piece of equipment to improve a horse's performance.

Figure 10-1:
A horse racing with blinkers on.

Photo by Skip Dickstein

Why and when blinkers are used

Horses have great peripheral vision and can literally see behind them. The main purpose of blinkers is to take away the horses' peripheral vision and keep them focused on the race ahead of him.

Why do horses have such great peripheral vision to start with? Horses are vegetarians, thus throughout history they've always been the hunted and not the hunters. Being able to see behind them is a great defense against the hated carnivores that prey on horses for their next meal. Maybe if the horses I bet on knew their jockeys were carnivores, they'd run a little faster.

Volponi, a famous blinker story

There are hundreds of stories about horses winning the first time they wear blinkers. But the most famous example in recent history is when Volponi won the $4 million Breeders' Cup Classic in 2002 at odds of 43/1.

Volponi was the biggest long shot in the Classic field and paid $89 for a $2 win bet. He not only won the race, but he also crushed the field by a winning margin of more than six lengths. What made the upset win by Volponi even more historic

is that without it, the perpetrators of the Pick Six fix (see Chapter 22) may have gotten away with cheating.

The horse's trainer, the late Phil "P.G." Johnson, said, "Volponi is a horse who always showed promise. The blinkers made him concentrate a little bit better."

The moral of the story is if you don't believe that blinkers help, think of Volponi.

Another reason for using blinkers is because lots of horses let their minds wander in a race. They look at other horses, the crowd, the trees, and the birds flying around. Blinkers keep them looking straight ahead and focused on the racetrack

In most cases, *maiden horses* (horses that have never won a race) run without blinkers until they prove they need them. The jockey may tell the trainer after a race that the horse is looking around and isn't interested in the race. The trainer typically tries blinkers on the horse in the morning during gallops and during a workout to see if they help. The exercise rider should be able to tell a difference. The *connections,* meaning the jockey and trainer, are looking for improved speed, agility, and, most importantly, focus.

A few trainers just throw the blinkers on for race day and see what happens. The riders of those horses require blind faith that the horses accept the blinkers kindly. Regardless, the trainer must get approval from the starter and the stewards whenever he wants to change whether the horse wears blinkers or not.

The *Daily Racing Form* lists a statistic that indicates when a blinker change occurs. Underneath the horse's past performances, you see a category that tells whether the horse has blinkers on or not and what the trainer's win percentage is for both scenarios.

Different cups

Blinkers have different kinds of *cups*. The cup is the curved part of the blinker that blocks the horse's peripheral vision. The size of the cup depends on the fullness needed to produce the desired focus from the racehorse. Following are the various types of cups:

- **Full-cup blinkers** are usually put on a horse that you want to send to the lead. The horse can hear the noise of the crowd or of the other horses and riders and may prick or pin its ears, but he goes on because he can't see exactly what's behind him.

- **Half-cup blinkers** help a horse that needs a bit more focus pay attention to the race and become more manageable. A lot of jockeys prefer horses to wear half-cup blinkers because the horses seem to respond a little better with them. The fullness of the cup allows the horse more peripheral vision than quarter-cup blinkers but less peripheral vision than full-cup blinkers.

- **Quarter-cup blinkers** give the racehorse even more vision than half-cup blinkers.

- **Cheater blinkers** are only about 1¼ inches long. Trainers use them to get the horses to stay focused, but the horses can see most everything around them.

How much cup to use on a blinker is partly trial and error. Horses react differently, and the trainer wants to find the right fullness of the cup to be effective.

A famous blinkers off story

The story I'm about to tell is actually a trick story, and I'm fessing up before I start. But it's a true story of a race on Oct. 30, 1988, at Hawthorne Race Course in Cicero, Illinois.

Roaring River was a 4-year-old colt belonging to the late Washington Redskins owner Jack Kent Cooke. Roaring River was winless in his first 18 career starts. The crowd wasn't deterred by that record of futility, though. He was the 4/5 odds favorite in a low priced maiden claiming race.

Soon after the start, the blinkers on Roaring River worked loose and were flapping around. Jockey Francisco Torres reached over the horse's neck, grabbed the loose blinkers with one hand, and yanked them off the horse's head. Torres then put the blinkers between his teeth so he could keep his hands free for riding. Roaring River went on to break his maiden by three lengths with his blinkers literally off.

Trainers have been known to get out their Swiss Army knives and carve the plastic cups to the exact measurement they want. Trainers have tried holes, slits, and you name it with the idea that whatever makes a horse run faster and straighter and keeps its mind on the race is worth it.

Why and when blinkers come off

A trainer takes the blinkers off of a horse when she thinks the blinkers don't help. She removes the blinkers and lets the horse see around itself and hopefully get more involved in the surroundings. By taking off the blinkers, she tries to get the horse to wake up and get more into the race. Removing them can sometimes make a positive difference, just like putting blinkers on can.

Bits of Helpful Information

From time-to-time, a long shot horse wakes up and runs an extraordinary race. This kind of horse is called a *form reversal* horse. Some sort of change to the horse causes the incredible race. One kind of change involves the *bit,* which is a metal bar in a horse's mouth that's attached to the reins the jockey uses to control the horse. Bits come in all shapes and sizes, and they're made of stainless steel, copper, rubber, brass, and sweet iron. There are literally dozens and dozens of different kinds of horse bits.

You don't need to be a horse-racing fan to know the meaning of the phrase "spit the bit." It's used in everyday conversation and in the media to describe someone or something that stops trying. A racehorse usually *spits the bit* — backs off the bit in its mouth and stops running into it — when fatigue sets in. But horses spit the bit for other reasons, such as when the bit itself is uncomfortable in a horse's mouth.

I've talked to trainers who have a complete veterinary examination done on a new horse that includes a close look at the horse's mouth and teeth. A big part of a racehorse's success comes from running relaxed. A tender mouth, overbite, or some other oral problem may cause the horse to have trouble with the bit in its mouth, and that alone can be a big reason for poor performance. By identifying such problems, the trainer can find the right bit to make the horse comfortable.

I won't get into too much detail about bits because, as a handicapper, your access to good information about this equipment is very limited. The *Daily Racing Form* reports nothing about bits, unless the information appears in a story or column. And unless you know the trainers and riders personally, that publication is your major source of news. Just understand that trainers try different bits in a horse's mouth for different reasons, and sometimes the equipment leads to seemingly improbable form reversals. Here's some information you may find useful:

✔ A lot of trainers who work mainly with claiming horses change the bit on older horses that have been mistreated around the mouth and head area. For example, a *rubber bit* may be used on a horse that just had dental work. A rubber bit is also good for a horse with a very soft mouth.

✔ A *snaffle bit* is broken in the middle and is one of the most commonly used mouthpieces. It has two rings, so when the rider pulls on the left rein, the left ring of the bit moves. And the same goes for the right side. Young horses respond favorably to this bit because understanding the rider's directions is simple for them.

✔ A *run out bit* has a big spur on the side of it. A horse uses this bit in his mouth if he's known to bolt on the turns. The key is a horse will run in the direction away from the spur, not into it. The jockey on this horse has his work cut out for him.

In conjunction with the bit, trainers use a cloth *tongue tie* around the horse's jaw. A horse has a tendency to flip his palate, meaning he accidentally gets his tongue stuck in the back of his mouth, which closes the air passage off so he can't breathe. Flipping the palate doesn't injure the horse, but it causes the horse to stop running, and the horseplayers then lose money if they bet this animal. Don't get upset if you see a horse's tongue tied down and the end of his tongue flapping around. This practice doesn't hurt the horse, and it prevents him from swallowing his tongue during the race.

That's a Wrap: Bandages

When you see a horse running with his feet covered in bandages, don't despair. More often than not, the bandages are being used to protect the horse's ankles and tendons, especially if the bandages are only used on the hind legs. However, if you see bandages on the horse's front legs, you should be a little leery.

Rear bandages

A very high percentage of horses wear rear bandages on their two hind legs during the race. Horses wear bandages because as they run, they may *run down,* meaning burn their heels on the sandy racetrack, as their *fetlocks* (ankles) hit the ground. The burning can literally take the hide off.

Rear bandages that have a big patch on the bottom are called *rundown bandages.* The patches are usually made of leather or polyurethane, and they don't hinder the horse's performance or stride. Horses with longer *pasterns* — the area of the foot between the fetlock and the coronet band — run down more than horses with short pasterns. Also, a sandy, real course (as in rough) racetrack can burn through the bandages, so the patches come in handy.

Rear bandages are good for added support. They give a horse more power and support for push-off. Horses that run without bandages are called *clean legged,* and the absence of bandages is usually a sign of a sound, well-made, racehorse.

Front bandages

When you see front bandages, you need to question whether they're a sign of problems. Sometimes, they're just for protection. But more often, the trainer is trying to hold an ankle together.

A comparison can be made to a prizefighter getting ready for the ring. His trainer tapes up his hands and knuckles before putting on his boxing gloves. The tape gives support so he doesn't break his hand or knuckles while punching his opponent. The protection is the same for the horse's ankles.

Trainers have been known to use front bandages to make other trainers leery about claiming their horse. The other trainer has to ask himself whether the horse is sound or not.

The *Daily Racing Form* past performances lists front bandages with a small "f." Rear bandages aren't marked.

"Fixing" a Horse's Chances

The castration of a horse, also known as *gelding,* is the ultimate equipment change — after it's done, it can't be reversed. (In case you weren't aware, castration is the removal of the testicles.) Gelding eliminates the reproductive potential, severely reduces the sex drive, and lowers the aggressiveness of the racehorse.

The gelding of a male horse is actually one of the strongest handicapping angles. A first-time gelding (after a male horse is gelded, he's known as a gelding) almost always improves after the procedure. In fact, some of the greatest racehorses ever, including Kelso, Forego, John Henry, and Funny Cide, have been geldings.

Although gelding a stallion racehorse may seem harsh, very logical reasons exist for doing so. Here are a few of the most common:

- **The horse is mean.** Training the horse effectively may be impossible, so castration will most likely remove a lot of that aggression.

- **Testicles are oversized.** If the testicles are too large, they may hurt the horse by literally slapping around while the horse is racing. He'll doubtfully ever reach his potential without being gelded.

- **The horse has an undescended testicle.** When this happens, the horse may be in real agony, and his performance on the racetrack may be affected, too.

- **The horse's pedigree is undesirable.** If the horse isn't a top-notch pedigree, his trainers geld him because he'll unlikely have a stallion career regardless. A stallion career awaits the very best male racehorses, because after they retire from racing, they're sent to stud.

- **The stallion is unfocused.** If the male horse doesn't stay focused when racing and is only interested in mares and other things going on, and if the pedigree is weak, he's gelded. The decision is economic because the horse has no stallion potential, so he must earn it on the racetrack. A horse with a very common pedigree is considered to have limited stallion potential.

The *Daily Racing Form* doesn't publish when a horse is gelded. The past performances only show whether the male is a gelding or not. The handicapping information would be extremely important if the *Daily Racing Form* and the racetracks could acquire the information for publication in a timely manner.

Lasix: Just Saying Yes to Drugs

Lasix is a human drug also known as furosemide. Lasix is a diuretic that decreases the amount of fluid in the body by increasing the amount of salt and water lost in the urine.

When given to racehorses, Lasix reduces, and in many cases, eliminates internal bleeding. I've found the most effective time to bet a horse is either first or second time out with Lasix. A big part of the reason is if a horse really is a bleeder, Lasix helps the horse a lot more the first and/or second time it's used, and then the benefits begin to plateau out.

Lasix is a hard drug, meaning it's very rough on your system (some of you may know from experience). Horses lose a lot of water weight racing on it, so trainers must be careful to pump the horses back up with electrolytes that get flushed out of their system. A Lasix shot must be administered four hours before the race by a licensed vet in accordance to horse-racing rules.

Getting Good Footing on the Importance of Horseshoes

People probably give no thought whatsoever to horseshoes when handicapping. And I can't blame them. Information about horseshoes is extremely hard to get a hold of at racetracks and simulcast facilities, and even then you need to understand the meaning of the information.

Racetracks announce what horseshoes horses are wearing on their back feet but never their front feet, because more than 80 percent of the horse's power comes from the back end. Here are some horseshoes I pay special attention to:

- **Mud calks or stickers:** These horseshoes have a block in the back, like a cleat, that helps the horse have more traction on the wet surface. I like to hear that certain horses are wearing these when it rains and the main track is sloppy or muddy. When a horse trainer puts mud calks on his horse, he's taking every legal advantage at his disposal as a horse trainer.

- **Bar shoes:** These horseshoes lend more support to the hoof but are a sure sign of foot problems. A horse may have a bruise or foot injury of some kind that needs the added protection. Bar shoes are definitely a negative signal.

A foot problem I want to know about is a *quarter crack*. A quarter crack is a vertical crack in the section of the hoof wall between the heel and toe. In human terms, it's like a split fingernail, which isn't a big deal, especially because you don't walk on your hands. For a horse, though, a quarter crack is a very big deal. Fortunately, new epoxy procedures can have it sealed up in no time. There's no mention of quarter cracks in the racetrack program or the *Daily Racing Form* past performances. However, sometimes they're mentioned in articles about the horses in the editorial coverage.

When you hear about a successful barn, you hear the usual accolades to the trainer, his assistants, and even the grooms and exercise rider. But one person who seldom hears thanks but can make or break a barn is a top-notch blacksmith, also known as a *farrier*. The person who shoes the horses is incredibly important, and a good farrier can give a barn a huge edge. For example, a racehorse needs to have good balance. A farrier is worth his weight in gold if he can shoe a horse to have that perfect balance for optimum performance.

Some of the hot products in racing include pads on the shoes to try and absorb some of the shock on the ankles and knees. I've been told there are more than 75 different styles of shoes in horse racing. And to think even Smarty Jones couldn't get a Nike contract.

Part III
Gaining and Keeping a Competitive Edge

The 5th Wave   By Rich Tennant

"It's a horse racing software program. It analyzes my betting history and makes suggestions. Right now it's suggesting I try betting on football."

In this part . . .

Handicapping horse races is part art and part science, but all brain power. If you think that picking winners is pure luck, think again. Handicapping is a brain game that requires skill and preparation. Your preparation begins with the *Daily Racing Form,* and in this part I show you how to read it and what information to look for. Good money management is essential to becoming a winning horseplayer, so I also go over planning your bets and managing your bankroll so that you can stay in action longer. Finally, every winning gambler must have discipline, and although I can't teach you that, I stress its value in this part.

Chapter 11

Starting with the Right Tools: The *Daily Racing Form* and More

● ●

In This Chapter

▶ Reading the past performances

▶ Studying Beyer Speed Figures

▶ Using statistical analysis to get ahead

▶ Looking to other resources

▶ Surfing the Web for advanced resources

● ●

The *Daily Racing Form* (*DRF* for short) is to horse racing what the *Wall Street Journal* is to the stock market. They're both must-reads every morning if you want to know what's going on in their respective areas of interest. And just like following the stock market on a daily basis is critical to investors, following horses racing from coast to coast is important to horseplayers.

Started in 1894, the *Daily Racing Form,* has seen more improvements since 1998 than in the 100 years previous. Before 1998, the editorial copy used to read like reworked track press releases. The racing industry, and in particular the racetracks, didn't mind because it was neutral promotion of the business. Nowadays, however, the *Daily Racing Form* not only provides thorough past performance information as the key handicapping tool in horse racing, but it also asks the hard questions that need to be asked of the racing industry.

In this chapter, I introduce you to the *Daily Racing Form* and show you how to comprehend the information it contains. I also clue you in on some other valuable tools, and if you're an advanced horseplayer, I point to a few additional resources you'll find handy.

Reading the DRF's Result Charts and Past Performances

You wouldn't dream of investing in the stock market without doing research. Well, the *Daily Racing Form* provides you, the horseplayer, with similar information daily on every horse entered in every race around the country. In this section, I show you how to read a result chart and a horse's past performances. I also give you tips on how I like to read the past performances.

Nuts and bolts: How all this information fits together

For newcomers, the *DRF* past performances and race results charts can look like Egyptian hieroglyphics. There's a method to the madness, though. Handicapping is based upon accessing information and analyzing statistical data. Call it number crunching, if you will. The amount of information and statistics squeezed into a past performance and result chart is truly remarkable. Figures 11-1 and 11-2 break down that information in graphical form.

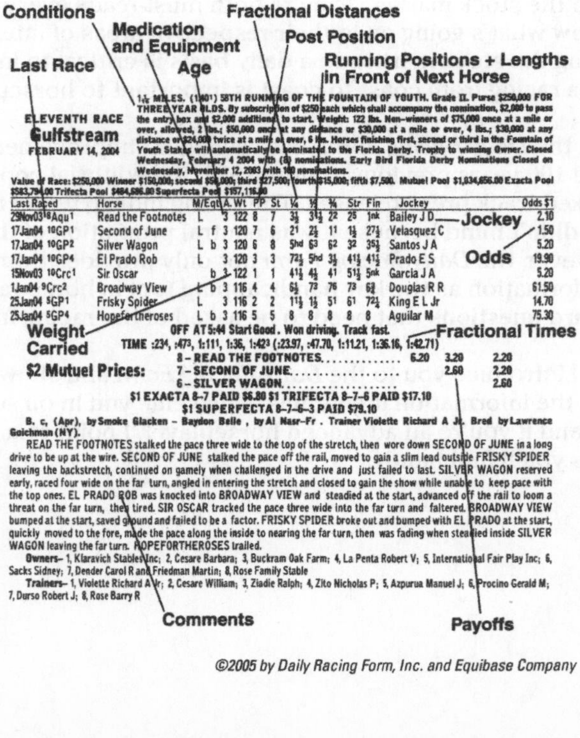

ELEVENTH RACE
Gulfstream
FEBRUARY 14, 2004

$1\frac{1}{16}$ MILES. (1:40[1]) 58TH RUNNING OF THE FOUNTAIN OF YOUTH. Grade II. Purse $250,000 FOR THREE YEAR OLDS. By subscription of $250 each which shall accompany the nomination, $2,000 to pass the entry box and $2,000 additional to start. Weight: 122 lbs. Non-winners of $75,000 once at a mile or over, allowed, 2 lbs.; $50,000 once at any distance or $30,000 at a mile or over, 4 lbs.; $30,000 at any distance or $24,000 twice at a mile or over, 6 lbs. Horses finishing first, second or third in the Fountain of Youth Stakes will automatically be nominated to the Florida Derby. Trophy to winning Owner. Closed Wednesday, February 4 2004 with (8) nominations. Early Bird Florida Derby Nominations Closed on Wednesday, November 12, 2003 with 180 nominations.

Value of Race: $250,000 Winner $150,000; second $50,000; third $27,500; fourth $15,000; fifth $7,500. Mutuel Pool $1,034,656.00 Exacta Pool $583,794.00 Trifecta Pool $484,686.00 Superfecta Pool $157,116.00

Last Raced	Horse	M/Eqt	A.	Wt	PP	St	¼	½	¾	Str	Fin	Jockey	Odds $1
29Nov03 ^{8}Aqu^{1}	Read the Footnotes	L	3	122	8	7	$3^{\frac{1}{2}}$	$3^{1\frac{1}{2}}$	2^{2}	2^{5}	1^{nk}	Bailey J D	2.10
17Jan04 ^{10}GP^{1}	Second of June	L f	3	120	7	6	2^{1}	$2^{\frac{1}{2}}$	1^{1}	$1^{\frac{1}{2}}$	$2^{7\frac{1}{2}}$	Velasquez C	1.50
17Jan04 ^{10}GP^{2}	Silver Wagon	L b	3	120	6	8	5^{hd}	6^{3}	6^{2}	3^{2}	$3^{5\frac{1}{2}}$	Santos J A	5.20
17Jan04 ^{10}GP^{4}	El Prado Rob	L	3	120	3	3	$7^{2\frac{1}{2}}$	5^{hd}	$3^{\frac{1}{2}}$	$4^{1\frac{1}{2}}$	$4^{1\frac{1}{2}}$	Prado E S	19.90
15Nov03 ^{10}Crc^{1}	Sir Oscar	b	3	122	1	1	$4^{1\frac{1}{2}}$	$4^{\frac{1}{2}}$	4^{1}	$5^{1\frac{1}{2}}$	5^{nk}	Garcia J A	5.20
1Jan04 ^{9}Crc^{2}	Broadway View	L b	3	116	4	4	$6^{\frac{1}{2}}$	7^{3}	7^{6}	7^{3}	$6^{\frac{3}{4}}$	Douglas R R	61.50
25Jan04 ^{5}GP^{1}	Frisky Spider	L	3	116	2	2	$1^{1\frac{1}{2}}$	$1^{\frac{1}{2}}$	5^{1}	6^{1}	$7^{2\frac{1}{4}}$	King E L Jr	14.70
25Jan04 ^{5}GP^{4}	Hopefortheroses	L b	3	116	5	5	8	8	8	8	8	Aguilar M	75.30

OFF AT 5:44 Start Good. Won driving. Track fast.

TIME :23^{4}, :47^{3}, 1:11^{1}, 1:36, 1:42^{3} (:23.97, :47.70, 1:11.21, 1:36.16, 1:42.71)

$2 Mutuel Prices:			
8 – READ THE FOOTNOTES	6.20	3.20	2.20
7 – SECOND OF JUNE		2.60	2.20
6 – SILVER WAGON			2.60

$1 EXACTA 8–7 PAID $6.80 $1 TRIFECTA 8–7–6 PAID $17.10
$1 SUPERFECTA 8–7–6–3 PAID $79.10

B. c, (Apr), by Smoke Glacken – Baydon Belle , by Al Nasr–Fr . Trainer Violette Richard A Jr. Bred by Lawrence Goichman (NY).

READ THE FOOTNOTES stalked the pace three wide to the top of the stretch, then wore down SECOND OF JUNE in a long drive to be up at the wire. SECOND OF JUNE stalked the pace off the rail, moved to gain a slim lead outside FRISKY SPIDER leaving the backstretch, continued on gamely when challenged in the drive and just failed to last. SILVER WAGON reserved early, raced four wide on the far turn, angled in entering the stretch and closed to gain the show while unable to keep pace with the top ones. EL PRADO ROB was knocked into BROADWAY VIEW and steadied at the start, advanced off the rail to loom a threat on the far turn, then tired. SIR OSCAR tracked the pace three wide into the far turn and faltered. BROADWAY VIEW bumped at the start, saved ground and failed to be a factor. FRISKY SPIDER broke out and bumped with EL PRADO at the start, quickly moved to the fore, made the pace along the inside to nearing the far turn, then was fading when steadied inside SILVER WAGON leaving the far turn. HOPEFORTHEROSES trailed.

Owners– 1, Klaravich Stables Inc; 2, Cesare Barbara; 3, Buckram Oak Farm; 4, La Penta Robert V; 5, International Fair Play Inc; 6, Sacks Sidney; 7, Dender Carol R and Friedman Martin; 8, Rose Family Stable

Trainers– 1, Violette Richard A Jr; 2, Cesare William; 3, Ziadie Ralph; 4, Zito Nicholas P; 5, Azpurua Manuel J; 6, Procino Gerald M; 7, Durso Robert J; 8, Rose Barry R

Figure 11-1: How to read the *Daily Racing Form* results chart.

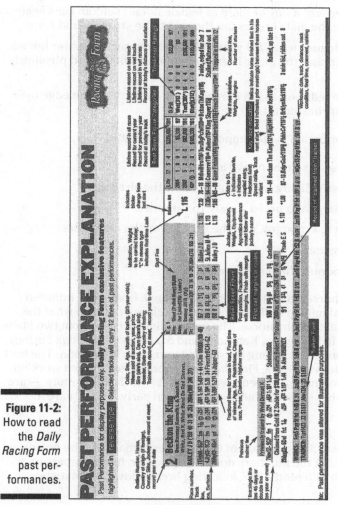

Figure 11-2:
How to read
the *Daily
Racing Form*
past per-
formances.

©2005 by Daily Racing Form, Inc. and Equibase Company

Horse information

Ninety percent of handicapping is the horse, so it's no surprise that the *DRF* past performances focus on the animal more than the jockey and trainer.

This chapter includes a sample past performance (see Figure 11-2) with a legend explaining what everything signifies. Every bit of information is important, and the savvy handicapper looks for small edges in a horse's resume.

The basic horse information begins with its name, color, sex, age, and month of birth, and some of this information if very helpful in handicapping:

✔ Sex matters because a *filly* or *mare* (a female horse) seldom runs against males, because the male horses are thought to be stronger and faster.

✔ Age matters because when a 3-year-old horse runs against older horses, (4-year-olds and up), the older horses are more mentally and physically mature.

✔ Common sense tells you that a horse born in January has an edge over one born in a spring month.

Horse pedigree information is also important and indicates

✔ Whether a horse is sold at public auction

✔ The *sire,* a horse's daddy, and the *grand sire,* the sire's sire

✔ The *stud fee* charged to breed a mare to the sire

✔ The *dam,* a horse's mommy, and the *grand dam,* the dam's sire

✔ The horse's breeder ·

✔ The state or country the horse was foaled in

The sale price of a horse bought at auction can range from a few hundred dollars up to several million dollars. The amount clues you in on what the trainer and owner think of the horse. The best pedigrees come from two horse sales — Keeneland in Lexington, Kentucky, and Saratoga in Saratoga Springs, New York. In these auctions, young horses undergo close inspection. The best 2-year-old horse sale is in Ocala, Florida. Young horses run a timed workout and can bring a lot of money. Expensive purchases — $75,000 or more — are the kind of horses that showed ability and may win early in their career.

Statistics

Statistics are the meat and potatoes of the past performances. The beauty of handicapping is that the numbers don't lie. However, handicappers interpret the information differently. The following breaks down the statistics even further:

✔ **Horse:** The *DRF* past performances list several *records* (the number of starts, wins, seconds, thirds, and purse money earned) for each horse:

• A lifetime record in all races, a record for the current year, and a record for the previous year.

• A record at today's racetrack.

The record at today's racetrack is where you find your *horse for course* angle. Horses often times prefer a particular dirt or turf track and excel over it.

• A record at today's race distance and surface.

• A lifetime record on a fast track, on a wet track, and in turf races.

• A Tomlinson rating for a wet track, turf race, and distance race.

The *Tomlinson rating* is an indicator of how a horse might handle a wet track, turf surface, or today's distance. The higher the number, the better the rating. A good rating is 300, and anything above 400 is outstanding.

✔ **Jockey:** Jockey information lists the name and race record for the year and for the meet. A *race record* includes the number of starts, wins, seconds, and thirds, and the win percentage. The better jockeys have a high win percentage of 20 percent or more. I like to see many more wins than seconds, because that statistic indicates that the rider has won more often with his best mounts.

✔ **Trainer:** Trainer information lists the name, race record for the year, and race record for the meet. The *DRF* past performances contain important trainer trends on the line labeled "Trainer." There are 34 categories, and are all worth noting.

✔ **Workouts:** Workouts are at the bottom of the *DRF* past performances on the "Works" line, just above the "Trainer" line. Workouts are broken down by date, where they're run, distance, track condition, and final time. This info also includes one letter denoting a comment from the clocker and a ranking comparing it to all same-distance workouts at that track that day.

The letters used by the clockers include *B* for breezing, *D* for driving, *(d)* for worked around *dogs* (orange cones placed off the inside rail), *g* for worked from the starting gate, *H* for handily, and *tr.t* for training track. A bullet denotes the best workout of the morning at the distance.

Past performance line (from left to right)

The *DRF* past performance line for a horse is jammed with information. Here are a few of the most important items in a past performance line:

✔ **Dates of the races:** A horse in good health and running well should start every three to six weeks.

✔ **Fractional times:** A quick look tells you how fast the pace was by the race's *internal fractions,* meaning the quarter-mile and half-mile time.

✔ **Type and class of the race:** This information tells you the class of horses this animal has been keeping company with.

✔ **Beyer Speed Figure:** Used correctly, this figure can shortcut your handicapping by eliminating horses too slow to win.

✔ **Running positions and lengths behind the lead horse:** This tells you immediately whether the horse is a speedball, pace horse, or closer.

✔ **Parimutuel odds:** These odds indicate whether the betting public liked the horse in prior races.

✔ **Who finished first, second, and third:** This information gives clues about the class of horses he has been running against.

✔ **Chart caller comment:** This information points out any trouble the horse incurred during the running of the race.

How I like to read the past performances

There's no best way to win at betting on horse racing. Horseplayers spend years refining a way of doing things in which they feel comfortable and are successful. In this section, I cover the way I read the past performances in the *Daily Racing Form*. The beauty of learning how to handicap is you can take this body of work, keep what you like, discard the rest, and come up with your own system of doing things. If you win, no one will second guess you.

Read from the bottom up

I suggest reading a horse's past performances from the bottom up because the horse's resumé was built the same way. For example, if you read the back of a baseball player's card, you start from the bottom, during his rookie season, and work up to the present. A baseball player develops from year to year, and a racehorse develops in a similar fashion from race to race, season to season.

Good and bad things happen to horses. For example, a horse may have started in a *maiden claiming race* (a maiden race in which anyone can buy him) but is now an *allowance* or a *stakes* type horse (meaning he's facing high caliber horses in classier races) — a good situation. Or the horse may have been fast early on, got hurt, and had to recuperate (you'll see a long time-gap between races in this case). If he returns to racing in a much lower class, that's bad.

Reading from the bottom up allows you to think like the horse's trainer, who usually has a game plan where each race builds upon the prior one. You may see changes where the trainer tries different tactics such as switching from dirt to turf, moving from sprints to *route races* (races one mile or longer in distance), dropping in first time for a *claiming price* (a race where the starters can be bought or claimed out of the race), and equipment or medication changes.

And if a horse is popular in the claim box — meaning other trainers have bought the horse out of a claiming race — you see who did it, how much they paid, and whether the horse improved or not. I see a horse claimed a lot by different trainers as a positive sign. If the horse has a physical problem, trainers would stay away from it like the plague.

Mark up the Daily Racing Form

A new *DRF* is a pristine newspaper with an attractive cherry red logo on top. Don't worry about keeping it that way. Even if you save your *DRFs* in stacks out in the garage, the idea is to handicap races well enough to make money.

Feel free to mark up the *DRF* from top to bottom — that's what I do. Make your notations where you can see them at a glance. Don't lose a bet because you overlooked something that you could've marked with an ink pen. No one grades for neatness. You're graded on how much money you win.

Mark any information you think is important. One category may be any changes you want to notice — for example, blinkers on or off, Lasix on, races over a wet racetrack, rider changes, and trouble comments. Typically, you review the field in a race multiple times, which is why you mark your *DRF.*

The worst thing to do is to make mental notes. You have too much information to digest in a short period of time, and you'll easily miss key changes if they're not marked.

Bringing In Beyer Speed Figures

Beyer Speed Figures, which are included in the *DRF's* past performances, are named after their developer, Andrew Beyer, the renowned horse racing columnist for the *Washington Post.* I won't get into how he makes his figures; just know that they're accurate and very helpful in flushing out winners.

The Beyers have had a big effect on horse race betting. Beyer Speed Figures accurately calibrate performance. For example, if one horse runs Beyers in the mid-70s, most likely he'll defeat another horse that runs Beyers in the mid-60s. Beyer Speed Figures also measure the quality of horses shipping in from other racetracks. In theory, a horse that runs Beyers in the 90s at Philadelphia Park should be equal to a horse that runs similar Beyers at Belmont Park.

Equibase takes over data collection for *DRF*

In 1998, the owner of the *Daily Racing Form,* Primedia, wanted to cut its losses and sell the horse racing newspaper. For years, the *DRF* was the official statistician for the sport. It collected the data necessary to publish horses' past performances and the official result charts.

In the early 1990s, the horse racing industry formed the Equibase company to collect its own data in competition with the *DRF.* Eventually, all North American racetracks had two teams of chart callers — one each from the *DRF* and Equibase. (*Chart callers* are the people who watch the races and chart the running positions of the horses during the race. This data enables chart callers to build running lines, where each horse was positioned during the race, for horses' past performances and to build a chart with an official order of finish and the lengths between horses.)

Steven Crist, former racing writer for the *New York Times* and publisher of the defunct *Racing Times,* headed a move by the Alpine Capital group to purchase the *DRF* from Primedia for more than $40 million.

What made the deal work was that the *DRF* and Equibase shook hands on a data contract. The *DRF* agreed to sell its vast database to Equibase and allow that company to become the sole data collector for the horse racing industry. The *DRF* in turn would pay Equibase a usage fee for the data. The deal saved the *DRF* a lot of money. No longer would it have to pay for chart caller teams out in the field. The new buyer, Alpine, could now focus its energy on rebuilding the brand, becoming a real newspaper, and developing new products and services to sell to horseplayers.

The *DRF* progressed so well that the Wicks Group of Companies, LLC purchased it in May 2004 for a reported $70 million. Alpine succeeded in rebuilding the *DRF* brand. Crist remains with the new *DRF* as chairman and publisher.

The higher the Beyer Speed Figure, the faster and classier the racehorse. The following ranges are general statements that may need adjustment depending on the quality of the racing at a particular track:

- ✔ Horses that run triple-digit Beyers are stakes horses.

Smarty Jones won the 2004 Kentucky Derby with a 107 Beyer. He won the Preakness with an exemplary 118 Beyer. But then in his upset loss in the Belmont Stakes, he slumped to a 100 Beyer. You can see the *DRF* past performances for Smarty Jones in Chapter 16.

- ✔ Horses that run between 85 and 99 Beyers are allowance and optional claiming horses that can win a stakes race under optimum conditions.

- ✔ Horses that run between 70 and 84 Beyers are mid- to high-priced claiming horses.

- ✔ Horses that run between 55 and 69 are low- to mid-level claiming horses.

- ✔ Horses that run below 54 are low claimers and are often maidens that can't run very fast.

- ✔ The lowest Beyer is zero, so the humiliation ends there.

My first Derby and my first *DRF*

There's something special to me about cracking open a fresh, new *Daily Racing Form*. The first one I ever read was on Saturday, May 5, 1973. I was attending my very first horse race, the 1973 Kentucky Derby at Churchill Downs in Louisville, Kentucky.

You always remember your first Kentucky Derby. I was a freshman at Xavier University in Cincinnati, Ohio. A dormitory buddy, Bruce Bailey, was from Cherry Hill, New Jersey. He was a big horse-racing fan because his family went to the races at Garden State Park in Cherry Hill.

Bruce and I hitchhiked from Cincinnati to Louisville. Admission to the Churchill Downs infield, which on Derby Day is a fenced in party for 50,000 people, cost $5. Bruce bought two *Daily Racing Forms* and said, "Let's go to work." I had no idea what to do. I didn't have the benefit of a

book like this one to help me. Bruce kindly explained a few things to me, a novice and a "dummy."

I made some bets and drank a few beverages, but I didn't cash a ticket. In the Derby, the race favorite was Secretariat. I saw he'd lost his last start finishing third in the Wood Memorial at Aqueduct. I decided to try and beat him (big mistake, it turns out). I bet two other horses to win — Sham and Forego. Both ran well but lost, finishing second and fourth, respectively. Meanwhile, Secretariat ran the fastest Kentucky Derby ever in 1:59⅖. After that race, he won the Preakness and Belmont Stakes also in track record times to become the first Triple Crown winner since Citation, 25 years earlier, in 1948. In hindsight, it was a pretty good first day at the races.

Beyer Speed Figures are great tools, but keep in mind that the horse that runs the fastest Beyers isn't always the winner. He may go off as the favorite, or he may be the classiest animal, but you may want to try to beat him, depending on many other circumstances.

Separating the contenders from the pretenders

My primary job is the turf editor and handicapper for the *Las Vegas Review-Journal*. I handicap the races every day from Santa Anita Park, Hollywood Park, and Del Mar.

The first thing I do when I handicap the races is separate the contenders from the pretenders, using the *Daily Racing Form*. I do this quickly, so I can focus on the most likely winners and who might be the possible upset horses. Here are three tactics I use to separate the real deals from the wannabes:

- ✔ **Look at the entire field and figure out the minimum Beyer Speed Figure for a horse to be competitive.** First I find a Beyer Speed Figure divisible by five. For example, let's make the cut-off point 70. I take a highlighter and mark the Beyer ratings 70 and up for every horse in the race. I'm interested in the minimum and am trying to eliminate two or three horses, at least. I begin to see a pattern develop in horses, and then I can move to the next steps. Figure 11-3 shows an extreme example of a horse that runs very slow Beyer Speed Figures. This horse runs mostly 0 Beyers, which won't win a race at any racetrack in North America.

  Within minutes, on an eight-race card of about 70 horses, I can eliminate 30 to 40 percent of the horses I think are too slow to win. I save time by eliminating the pretenders — even if a rare $60 horse sneaks below my radar screen. Even if I did handicap those eliminated horses with a fine tooth comb, I'd probably still miss that 30/1 horse that beats me. If I miss one or two *bombs* (racetrack jargon for a long shot winner) per month, I still end up picking many more logical, mid-priced, $12 to $15 winners instead, so eliminating the perceived slow horses is worth it.

- ✔ **Do a quick class analysis of the fields.** For a cheaper horse to win, he needs to be in peak condition to defeat classier animals. Defining class is easy if you're handicapping a claiming race. The claiming price is a clear indicator. Be careful if the horse is a shipper from another racetrack. A horse from a New York Racing Association track has lots of back class. A horse from Charles Town may not cut the mustard in a tougher circuit. I cover the class levels of race conditions in Chapter 2.

✔ **Find the horses that are running against the grain.** *Running against the grain* means they're doing something different for the first time, and I try to figure out why. The new tactic may be moving from turf to dirt (or vice versa); going from a sprint to a route race (or vice versa); or racing out of condition, which covers a lot of examples, such as a female horse running against males or a maiden running against winners.

Finding the horses that are running against the grain takes some experience because you need to know the trainer trends and tells. In Chapter 8, I cover how trainers develop tendencies to help them win races. Good trainers know their horses and make educated guesses that often turn out right. Bad trainers just fish for answers.

Figure 11-3:
An extreme
example of a
Beyer Speed
Figure.

©2005 by Daily Racing Form, Inc. and Equibase Company

Seeking positive and negative trends

Horses, like humans, are creatures of habit. After you identify things that they like to do, you can pretty much see a developing pattern. These trends can lead to powerful betting angles as you map out the race shape and focus on the strongest contenders. A horse's form is usually cyclical, so a handicapper must figure out whether a horse will improve, run the same, or regress.

Beyers accurately identify when a horse has delivered a peak performance. It's reflected in a very high Beyer rating. When a horse runs a high Beyer, different scenarios can happen next:

✔ If a horse runs an even higher Beyer next time, his following race is predicted to be a *bounce,* meaning the horse will react off the big efforts and run a slower race next time. (For more on predicting a bounce, see the section, "Knowing when horses will bounce," later in this chapter.)

✔ If the horse runs the same Beyer next time, it's called a *paired top,* meaning the horse runs two top efforts in a row. The horse has about a 50 percent chance he'll run a better Beyer and a 50 percent chance he'll regress.

✔ Very often the horse will run a slower Beyer off a top, which is a bounce or negative reaction.

In Figure 11-4, I use the career past performances of Devine Wind, because this horse exemplifies all three examples I've just given.

Devine Wind
Own: Englander Richard A

Dk. b or b. g. 8 (Mar)
Sire: American Chance (Cure the Blues) $7,500
Dam: Hail Babe (Within Hail)
Br: Paul Tackett & Clark Cleveland (Ky)
Tr: McLaughlin Kiaran P(0 0 0 0 .00) 2004:(353 65 .18)

	Life	42	10	7	4	$613,623	104	D.Fst	8	3	0	2	$86,700	102
	2004	5	2	1	0	$51,920	89	Wet(333)	1	0	0	0	$3,525	87
	2003	7	1	0	0	$29,265	93	Turf(235)	33	7	7	2	$523,398	104
	Aik	0	0	0	0	$0	–	Dst(333)	2	0	1	0	$16,550	99

Figure 11-4:
The career record for Devine Wind.

©2005 by Daily Racing Form, Inc. and Equibase Company

Devine Wind can affectionately be called an old "war horse." He's a *gelding,* meaning he's been castrated, so his career path is chosen for him. No stud duty for poor Devine Wind. (*Stud duty* or *stallion duty* is the future career of stakes horses in which they mate with females to produce fast babies and to improve the horse gene pool.) He has run 42 times and finished in the money in half his starts. His career purse earnings are more than $600,000.

Devine Wind is a good example of a cyclical, trending horse. Early in his career, he ran a string of climbing Beyers (67-69-75-92) that culminated with a 92 *top,* or peak race, on March 21, 1999. He wasn't fast enough to break his maiden that day, but he showed he had good ability.

Devine Wind was sidelined for 13 months from April 1999 until May 2000. He returned by breaking his maiden in a claiming race. He only ran an 80 Beyer that day. I would've loved to bet him the next time out. I like playing horses that win but have proven they can run even faster Beyers. He ran a 92 Beyer and an 82 Beyer the year before, so he had lots of room to improve.

Needless to say, Devine Wind ran an 87 Beyer and a career best 99 Beyer to win two more races at Hollywood Park in June and July of 2000. Devine Wind then showed another career trait by bouncing off his peak race to run a 91 the next time. This type of cycle proved typical of his career.

Andrew Beyer: Handicapping pioneer

Andrew Beyer is best known as an award-winning horse racing columnist for the *Washington Post*. He could've focused his career on any subject, but horse racing was his passion. Beyer would be too modest to admit it, but he'll go down as the Benjamin Franklin or Thomas Jefferson of horse race handicapping. As important as Franklin and Jefferson were to the development of the United States, Beyer has revolutionized Thoroughbred horse race handicapping.

Beyer has written many excellent handicapping books, including *My $50,000 Year at the Races* (Harcourt), *Picking Winners: A Horseplayer's Guide* (Houghton Mifflin), *Beyer on Speed: New Strategies for Racetrack Betting* (Houghton Mifflin), and *The Winning Horseplayer: A Revolutionary Approach to Thoroughbred Handicapping and Betting* (Houghton Mifflin). They all make for worthwhile reading as your horse racing education continues.

Beyer developed his own speed figures that enabled him to beat the races. His handicapping product came out in 1991. That's when the *Racing Times* was started to challenge the *Daily Racing Form* head on. *Racing Times* publisher Steven Crist made a revolutionary decision to add the Beyer Speed Figures onto a horse's past performance lines. Overnight, all horseplayers had accurate speed figures that only the wiseguys had before. The long shots that wiseguys used to uncover by themselves were now identified in the Beyers and were paying less money to win. Overall, more horseplayers became winners because they had more quality information.

The *Racing Times* eventually folded. But Beyer Speed Figures were soon incorporated into the *Daily Racing Form* past performances. I call Beyer a Benjamin Franklin or Thomas Jefferson of horse racing because, in his own way, Beyer empowered horseplayers by providing information that was previously held by a select few, and he revolutionized how horseplayers handicap.

High-class stakes races can earn a grade of 1, 2, or 3. In this case, the lower the number, the classier the race, so a grade 1 race is the pinnacle in horse racing. Devine Wind cycled forward (91-99-103) to win the grade 3 Bay Meadows Handicap on September 23, 2000. Then he regressed slightly but still ran a 101 to run second in the prestigious Knickerbocker Handicap at Aqueduct. He bounced again but then cycled forward (95-96-99) to run a strong second in the Turf Paradise Breeders' Cup Handicap on February 3, 2001. A little more than a year later, Devine Wind cycled forward (94-94-102-104) to run the best race of his life with a game second in the grade 2 American Handicap at Hollywood Park on July 4, 2002. He finished a neck behind a grade 1 winner, The Tin Man, who is a much more talented horse.

In 2003, as a 7-year-old, Devine Wind began running lower Beyer figures. It's called "losing a step" when old age starts catching up with a horse. He no longer could run triple-digit Beyers or even Beyers in the high 90s. Still, Devine Wind showed his heart and back class when he cycled forward

(69-84-87-91-92) to win a grass stakes at Suffolk Downs on June 21, 2003. By November 2004, as an 8-year-old, he ran five more times with a tight Beyer spread (85-89-86-89-87). His performance shows he's feeling pretty good and giving a strong effort in every race. He's just not as fast as he used to be.

If you were a horse owner, you wouldn't mind owning ten Devine Winds, because he's proven to be durable and he gives you an honest effort all the time. Here's hoping that when his racing days are over, the people he's been so good to take care of him in retirement.

Knowing when horses will bounce

When a horse runs a peak performance — which doesn't necessarily need to be a lifetime best race — he invariably *bounces* (runs a slower race) the next time out. The only way trainers can try to prevent a bounce is to give the horse enough time between starts to rest and regain his strength.

It takes about six weeks to recuperate, but every horse is different, so certain horses may need even longer. That's one reason why the Triple Crown has been so difficult to win. The Kentucky Derby, Preakness, and Belmont Stakes are run only five weeks apart, making the closely run series of races incredibly grueling. I cover the Triple Crown in more detail in Chapter 18.

Figure 11-5 shows the record of American Liberty, who switched to running on the main dirt track and ran very well before bouncing.

American Liberty was toiling on grass when he got another chance to run on dirt. He ran a creditable 80 Beyer at Golden Gate Fields on February 26, 2004. He started again on May 27, 2004, at Hollywood Park, where he ran a career best 93 Beyer and broke his maiden easily. The question on everyone's mind: Would he bounce off a career best race the next time out?

Figure 11-5:
American
Liberty's
record.

©2005 by Daily Racing Form, Inc. and Equibase Company

Twenty days later, American Liberty destroyed a strong first-level allowance field by more than 9-lengths. He ran another career best 100 Beyer. The race became a key race (see Chapter 16) when the second and third place finishers both came back to win in their next start. American Liberty again looked like a bounce candidate. However, the key race angle was strong, too, and his win was visually impressive in that he appeared to be running well within himself.

In this case, appearances were deceiving. American Liberty ran 17 days later against better horses and got destroyed as the 2/1 odds favorite. His Beyer rating was 60, a drop of 40 points. You won't see a clearer example of a horse bouncing than American Liberty.

Moving up and down: Form curves

Some horses seemingly train themselves, regardless of what their trainers try to do with them. The Beyers can tell an interesting tale. Some horses have a *form curve* (curving of Beyer numbers) that looks choppy because they constantly alternate between good races and bad races; others have a gradual curve they repeat over and over again.

Life Savior has a nearly flawless curving of her Beyer numbers spaced over a long period. In Figure 11-6, you see she has an exaggerated form curve going up, down, and then back up again. She broke her maiden in her second career start, running a 68 Beyer on November 9, 2002 at Churchill Downs. Then she bottomed out (68-34-38-26) to a very low 26 Beyer figure. She rounded back up to a winning race (26-52-69-78) at Churchill Downs on May 30, 2003.

Life Savior slid back down (78-41-38) to a snail-like 38 before, you guessed it, she rounded back up to a winning race (38-70-62-81) at Keeneland on October 18, 2003. At least when she won, she crushed her opponents winning by margins of 4½-lengths, 7-lengths, and 6-lengths.

Then came a crescent-like curve that was nearly perfect in its symmetry. It took Life Savior ten starts before she won again — by an open 4-lengths. Check Figure 11-6 and look at her Beyer curve (81-57-58-50-42-35-60-66-72-73-81) down and then up to a winning 81 at Churchill Downs on July 2, 2004.

```
Life Savior                Dk. b or b. f. 4 (Apr) KEESEP01 $2,700                     Life  25 5 3 5 $112,194 88 | D.Fst     24 5 2 5 $106,994 88
Own: Sunny Meadow Farm     Sire: Patton (Lord At War*Arg) $2,500                      2004  10 2 3 2  $63,820 88 | Wet(313)   1 0 1 0   $5,200 66
                           Dam: Full O Cherries (Full Out)                            2003  12 2 0 2  $36,114 81 | Turf(267)  0 0 0 0       $0  -
                           Br: Jane C. Hinkle & Samuel D. Hinkle IV (Ky)              Aik①   0 0 0 0       $0  - | Dst①(309)  0 0 0 0       $0  -
                           Tr: Friedman Mitchell E(0 0 0 0 .00) 2004:(71 3 .04)

23Sep04-2Bel fst 6f  :221 :453 :573 1:101 3+ⒻClm 50000(50-40)   78 5 2 43½ 31½ 32 21¾ Chavez J F  L120 b 2.85 86-13 Quppy1181¾ Life Savior120¾ Stacy's Squaw120no  Game finish outside 6
20Aug04-3Sar fst 6f  :224 :453 :574 1:102 3+ⒻClm c-(35-30)      88 3 3 1hd 1½ 1½ 12 Day P  L120 b 2.75 90-13 Life Savior1202 Lucky Paws1133¼ Drama Queen1201¾  Pace inside, clear 6
  Claimed from Landers, Steven J. and Arrington, James for $35,000, Vance David R Trainer 2004(as of 8/20): (175 21 13 30 0.12)
2Jly04-2CD fst 6f  :213 :45 :572 1:103 3+ⒻClm 25000(30-25)   81 8 1 2hd 11 13 14 Hernandez B J Jr5  L108 b 22.00 88-14 Life Savior1084 Blue Moon Rising123½ White Scarf117no  Hand urging,clear 9
23Jun04-5CD fst 6½f :23 :461 1:103 1:17 3+ⒻClm c-(20-17.5)   73 4 4 42¼ 41¾ 33 34 Shepherd J  L117 b 8.50 82-10 IWillSurvive1173¾ BoonesDiamond121nk LifeSavior1173½  5-6w late,no gain 8
  Claimed from Roemele, Fred L. and Holloway, David P. for $20,000, Connelly William R Trainer 2004(as of 6/23): (90 11 13 14 0.12)
3Jun04-6CD fst 7f  :23 :462 1:111 1:24 3+ⒻClm 20000(20-17.5)   72 1 6 74½ 32½ 22 24½ Shepherd J  L117 b 14.40 77-14 Smiling Sky1194½ Life Savior1171¾ Rubikisses117½  5w lane,2ndbest 8
15May04-5CD sly 6f  :214 :454 :59 1:121 3+ⒻClm 20000(20-17.5)   66 2 6 55½ 46½ 42½ 24 Shepherd J5  L112 b 12.80 76-17 BoonesDiamond1174 LifeSvior112no MinisterLdy1231½  Rallied 6-7w,all out 8
27Apr04-8CD fst 6½f :223 :461 1:113 1:182 3+ⒻClm 20000(20-17.5)   60 2 3 62¾ 51½ 34 36¾ Shepherd J5  L112 b 28.70 73-19 BlueMoonRising1172¾ BoonesDimond1173½ LifeSvior112½  No late response 9
25Mar04-7OP fst 1⅟16 :231 :471 1:122 1:452 4+ⒻClm 30000(35-30)   35 1 1½ 1hd 41½ 716 723¼ Shepherd J5  L111 b 30.40 60-16 TellerLine116hd AbovethHrbor1192¾ JoMthMony122½  Finished after a half 8
19Feb04-2OP fst 1⅟16 :232 :472 1:123 1:47 4+ⒻAlw 30000s   42 6 2hd 3½ 57½ 716 722¼ Shepherd J5  L110 b 22.50 53-25 Kylers Midge1222 Jiffy Wish1154½ Firecard118¾  Stopped 7
6Feb04-3OP fst 5½f :224 :473 1:002 1:071 4+ⒻClm 30000(30-25)   50 2 6 54½ 55 54¾ 57½ Shepherd J5  L113 b 8.80 74-27 PetiteDiablo1182¾ CandyHaze118no GottaJiboo1151  Tight start, no threat 7
4Dec03-6TP fst 6½f :223 :453 1:112 1:181 3+ⒻClm 25000(25-20)   58 3 3 2hd 1hd 35½ 68¾ Bejarano R  L118 b 3.80 77-14 Traci Girl116½ Savannah Hanna1164¼ Lady Justine111hd  Off inside, tired 9
11Nov03-8CD fst 1  :224 :453 1:104 1:373 3+ⒻClm 30000(30-25)   57 6 2½ 2½ 4¾ 44 410 Bejarano R  L115 b 2.30 69-27 Iffy114nk In Case of Wind113nk African Skyline1179½  Vied,inside,weakened 8
18Oct03-4Kee fst 7f  :224 :461 1:113 1:242 3+ⒻClm 25000   81 5 3 11½ 12½ 13 16 Bejarano R  L116 b 4.60 82-20 Life Savior1166 Traci Girl119¾ Glorado1192  Widened, hand urging 10
2Oct03-8TP fst 1⅟16 :24 :481 1:13 1:442 3+ⒻClm 30000(30-20)N3L   62 5 12 12 21 47½ 410 Butler D P  L113 b 5.90 80-17 Kissalyssa1195 Cheery One1163 Dream City1122  Drifted wide 1/4 pl 10
7Sep03-6TP fst 1  :23 :472 1:132 1:40 3+ⒻClm 30000(30-20)N3L   70 4 15 14 1hd 3½ 35¼ Butler D P  L112 b 5.70 69-28 Lady Lileah1094¼ Ummummgood116¾ Life Savior1121¾  Tired late 8
27Jly03-10EIP fst 1  :223 :452 1:11 1:383 3+ⒻAlw 30000N1X   38 1 11½ 1hd 22 611 726 Prescott R  L113 b 15.40 61-16 Del Rae1111¼ Donandru's Dream1104½ Dynasure11210½  Tired,far turn 8
2Jly03-3CD fst 6½f :224 :461 1:103 1:171 ⒻClm 45000(50-45)   41 8 1 54 66 712 719¾ Martinez W  L112 b 10.50 65-14 Semifinal1226 Gray Cache1163¾ Sinfulindulgence116hd  Tired 8
30May03-3CD fst 1  :224 :461 1:112 1:371 ⒻClm 30000(30-25)   78 3 11½ 11½ 11 14½ 17 Bejarano R  L116 b 6.50 81-17 LifeSvior1167 DylightRobbry116hd JoyousAppl1202  Drift out bad late,drv 5
7May03-6CD fst 6f  :211 :45 :574 1:114 ⒻClm 30000(30-25)   69 6 4 85¾ 74½ 53½ 42½ Bejarano R  L115 b 24.20 77-19 Hurry Home1151½ So Stated115no We'llsee Gold115¾  7w lane,mild gain 9
27Mar03-1TP fst 5½f :221 :453 :58 1:044 ⒻClm 30000(30-20)   52 2 2 22 21½ 23½ 36½ Lumpkins J  L116 b *1.20 86-14 Lilias Trotter1164¼ DaylightRobbery1152 LifeSavior1168¾  Off inside, tired 5
8Mar03-6TP fst 6f  :214 :46 :584 1:121 ⒻAlw 27845N1X   26 6 2 2½ 31 47 615¾ D'Amico A J  L116 b 19.20 65-18 Miss MaryApples1222½ SefapianosMiss1165 FlameinMyHeart1161½  Faded 7
8Feb03-7TP fst 6f  :213 :452 :582 1:114 ⒻAlw 25900N1X   38 4 3 12½ 2½ 56½ 710½ D'Amico A J  L116 b 4.80 72-18 PerfectAttitud1191 SfpinosMiss1162 WorthWinning1192¾  Inside, gave way 7
19Nov02-7CD fst 6f  :211 :452 :574 1:11 ⒻClm 50000(50-45)   34 3 4 69 810 615 618 Sellers S J  L116 5.60 65-18 Put Me In1165½ Paint It Black1161¾ ClassicMoment1182  Drift wide on turn 8
  Previously trained by Scherer Merrill R
9Nov02-2CD fst 6½f :222 :453 1:104 1:173 ⒻMd 30000(30-25)   68 6 1 2hd 11 12½ 14½ Sellers S J  L120 *2.50 83-16 Life Savior1204½ Cantilena1202½ Phillie City1205½  Press,mild urging 12
  Previously trained by Scherer Gary
18Oct02-1Hoo fst 5½f :22 :453 1:061 ⒻMd 15000   55 4 5 21½ 33 33 33 Long J S  B118 2.50 82-20 RightBackAtcha113¾ DoctorFree1182½ LifeSvior1184¾  Outside,no final bid 10
WORKS: ●Oct3 Hoo 4f fst :471 B 1/11  Sep26 Hoo 4f fst :493 B 12/23  Sep16 Bel 5f fst 1:004 H 6/15  Aug15 Sar tr.t 5f fst 1:02 B 3/12  Aug1 Sar 4f my :49 B(d) 5/8  Jly14 CD 4f my :482 B 2/15
```


Figure 11-6: Life Savior's Beyer numbers curve gradually.

Beyond the DRF: Other Important Tools

The *Daily Racing Form* is the bible of American racing because every serious handicapper uses it. However, other resources are available at the racetrack or at your local off-track betting parlor (OTB), and I recommend you use them.

The racetrack program

When you go to a baseball game, you can't tell the ballplayers apart without a program. The same goes for horse racing. Having a program in horse racing is even more important because you're betting real money, and the horses all look alike.

I suggest spending the $2 or $3 for a program. The cost is well worth it. Most racetracks include gobs of betting information, feature stories, and marketing information in their programs. And, of course, the programs include all the races that day with important late equipment changes. Check out Figure 11-7 to see what the program page for the 2004 Pennsylvania Derby looked like.

Figure 11-7:
The program page for the 2004 Pennsylvania Derby.

Handicapper's selections in the local newspaper

If there's a major racetrack near where you live, most likely the major local newspaper has a horse racing handicapper. If you're short on time, buy the newspaper to see who the public handicapper likes, it's 50¢ well spent.

Even though there's no live horse racing in Las Vegas, both the morning and afternoon newspapers — the *Las Vegas Review-Journal* and the *Las Vegas Sun*, respectively — have a turf editor and handicapper covering Southern California. The reason is that Las Vegas racebooks (I cover racebooks and Las Vegas in detail in Chapter 23) are full of horse racing fans most days of the week. Many moved here from other cities that have racetracks because of retirement or for work. So on any given day, there are probably more horseplayers in the Las Vegas race books combined than at any one racetrack around the country. Also, the Southern California racetracks attract the highest parimutuel handle in Las Vegas and thus spark the most interest.

A handicapper's selections in the sports section (see Figure 11-8) are another reason to buy the newspaper. The handicappers do their homework and have insights available to those who watch the races every day. On this day, November 20, 2003, I picked seven winners on top in the *Las Vegas Review-Journal*.

HORSE RACING

TODAY AT HOLLYWOOD PARK

By Richard Eng
Post Time 12:30 p.m.
Race 1 - 1 1/16th miles, Purse $28,000, Claiming $32,000, 3 and up
Proceed With Care - Logical chalk destroyed a similar group in last; claimed by Sadler who spots him to repeat.
Dixie Thrill - Has a fine record over Hollywood soil; P Val rides half of a hard-hitting O'Neill uncoupled entry.
Long Shot - **Pavlovsk**
Race 2 - 6 furlongs, Purse $12,000, Claiming $10,000, Cal-breds, Fillies and mares, 3 and up
Urgent Start - Third start off a 9-month hiatus; was razor sharp in victory last time and must repeat that effort.
Our Blazing Belle - Second start off a 1-year sabbatical; lost some ground at the start but ran well late.
Long Shot - **Granja Vivo**
Race 3 - 1 1/16th miles (turf, rail at 10 feet), Purse $41,000, Maiden special weights, Fillies, 2-year-olds
Shake Off - Second time out Baffert, many show big improvement off the first trial; blinkers off and saves ground.
Worksformoney - Stretches out and tries turf for the first time; her last race stunk so she may be some value today.
Long Shot - **Silver Hawk Lady**
Race 4 - 1 1/16th miles, Purse $28,000, Claiming $32,000, Fillies, 3-year-olds
The Borg Queen - Mullins filly drops down to a class she last won at; tactical speed for Espinoza to craft a trip.
Tracy's Tracton - Claimed by Mitchell so expect better he takes the blinkers off and legs up P Val, why not?
Long Shot - **Proud Nicole**
Race 5 - 5 1/2 furlongs (turf, rail at 10 feet), Purse $41,000, Allowance, Fillies and mares, 3 and up
Annabelly - Didn't run badly in her turf sprint debut; should improve more in third start off a 9-month sabbatical
Golden K K - Makes her turf debut in a sprint; turns back in distance but could be blasting fire in deep stretch.
Long Shot - **Place to Hide**
Race 6 - 6 furlongs, Purse $26,000, Maiden claiming $62,500, Fillies, 2-year-olds
Mizzen Lass - One of the cheaper Fulton buys but she could wake up here; she could show much more speed today.
Crafty Babe - Logical chalk off a nice debut; was well bet at 5/2 and a similar effort makes her the one to beat.
Long Shot - **Blazing Bartok**
Race 7 - 6 1/2 furlongs, Purse $41,000, Allowance, Fillies and mares, 3 and up
Hope Rises - Beat her uncoupled stablemate in debut like a bad stepchild; Flores still hasn't moved on her yet.
Lady Wildcat - OK effort after a sharp debut win; that little bit of experience can sometimes make a difference.
Long Shot - **Cat Fighter**
Race 8 - 6 1/2 furlongs, Purse $17,000, Maiden claiming $32,000, Cal-breds, Fillies and mares, 3 and up
Sweet Rhapsody - Baze exits others to ride this filly; she tried hard in last and figures to see another good trip.
Sky Reality - Dead late closer was smacked in the face late but there was no DQ; Espinoza got hit by the whip too.
Long Shot - **Light Up Your Life**
Best Bet - **Hope Rises** (race 7)
Hollywood Wednesday - Picks/Winners Mutuels, 16/6/$36.40; Long Shots, 7/1/$7.60; Best Bet, 1/1/$2.80
Hollywood Totals - 91/29/$173.20, Long Shots, 48/6/$59.20; Best Bets, 5/4/$13.60
Richard Eng recaps the day's contests and racing on the Race Day Las Vegas Wrap Up Show at 6 p.m. on KSHP-AM (1400)

Figure 11-8:
Handicapper selections for November 20, 2003 in the *Las Vegas Review-Journal.*

Daily Racing Form Simulcast Weekly

If you want to advance as a horseplayer, the *Daily Racing Form Simulcast Weekly* is an outstanding reference tool. It includes the result charts from all major racetracks, a bevy of statistics from those racetracks, and reports from on-site staff correspondents. Weekly columns focus on handicapping, pedigree analysis, the foreign market, handicapping tournaments, and more.

This publication is great to have around because from time to time, as you're handicapping, you'll want to pull up a result chart to see just how well that horse you like really ran.

Calling All Big Shots: Resources for Advanced Horseplayers

If you study the *Daily Racing Form* religiously, you qualify as an advanced horseplayer. If so, you may want to take advantage of other handicapping tools, which I briefly discuss in this section. You should also head to Chapters 12 and 16, where I take you deeper into sophisticated handicapping.

Brisnet

Brisnet stands for Bloodstock Research Information Service. The Broadbent family started the business in the 1970s in Lexington, Kentucky. The early years concentrated on bloodlines and pedigrees for breeders and owners, but it soon became apparent that horseplayers thirsted for more information to aid their handicapping and betting. Brisnet now offers the widest selection of handicapping products and services for the horseplayer. The Brisnet Web site (www.brisnet.com) is one of the most useful for horseplayers who bet from home and have access to a computer and Internet service.

Equiform

Cary Fotias used Ragozin sheets (see following section) for years and found them extremely helpful in making money betting on horses. But Fotias soon thought that a better product could be developed — one that didn't rely so much on final time numbers, but on pace numbers. *Pace numbers* judge the quality of the internal fractions that a horse runs. Fotias patented Equiform, which took in final time and pace numbers. His methodology has lead to new thinking in *form cycle analysis,* factoring in the current condition of the horse and how it's progressing. Visit Equiform's Web site at www.equiform.com for more information.

Ragozin Sheets

Len Ragozin is a revered figure in Thoroughbred handicapping. His pioneering of *The Sheets* developed a new way of handicapping and a new vocabulary to boot. Before The Sheets (www.thesheets.com), the *Daily Racing Form* was the only tool to handicap with. Ragozin invented a numerical rating based on final time that was incredibly accurate and pointed out live long shot horses to bet on. The horses' past performances were printed on half-page sheets, thus its name. Ragozin Sheets don't show running lines. Instead, you see dates when the horses raced and final time numbers rating the quality of the effort. Ragozin changed the way races are handicapped by taking into account factors like the wind, weight, and ground loss. He invented the term *bounce,* which is commonplace in horse racing.

Thoro Graph

Jerry Brown, president of Thoro Graph, used to work for Len Ragozin. In 1982, he branched out and refined his own handicapping product, calling it Thoro Graph. Brown calls his product a "proprietary formula," which in layman terms means he figures things out differently than Ragozin. It was feared his product would cannibalize the market; instead, the market for handicapping products has mushroomed. The seal of approval for Thoro Graph (and for The Sheets, too) is that trainers and owners use them religiously to handicap and learn about their own stable of horses. I stop by the Thoro Graph Web site (www.thorograph.com) to read the information in the "Red Board" room and download free stakes race of the week analysis. It's very good stuff.

Chapter 12

Trying Your Hand at Handicapping

O ne of the beauties of handicapping is it's an inexact science. For every proven handicapping principle, you still find a contrarian viewpoint somewhere else. You seemingly find as many betting systems and strategies as you do horseplayers.

Over the years, I've suffered many black and blue marks to my wallet and to my psyche that have prepared me to write this chapter. I want you to avoid the same pitfalls I've already experienced, so in addition to my own trial and error, I've researched lots of handicapping material to zero in on the best handicapping elements for you.

In this chapter, I lay out basic handicapping ideas and strategies. Consider this chapter to be a primer to advanced handicapping, which I cover in detail in Chapter 16. My goal is to shorten your horse racing learning curve. If reading this chapter helps you to win one more bet or to avoid a losing bet, then consider the monetary gain enough to buy a copy of *Betting on Horse Racing For Dummies* for a friend.

What Is Handicapping Anyway?

Handicapping, simply put, is studying all the different factors involved in trying to decipher the winner of a horse race. I explain those different factors in this chapter with more in Chapter 16 on sophisticated handicapping. The type of mind that does well handicapping excels at crossword puzzles, riddles, or problem solving. You use your mind in an analytical manner.

Handicapping horse races is a fun challenge because no two races are ever alike. In theory, you should be able to line up the same eight horses to run in two races a couple weeks apart and see the same result. In real life, races don't happen that way. The variables that can occur and affect a horse race are infinite. Horse racing is a puzzle in which the pieces change shape, and the assembly is different each time.

I'm convinced that older people who handicap the races stay mentally sharp because the activity is so intellectually stimulating. Your brain becomes a computer figuring out all the variables within a horse race. And when you're right with your selection and win, the feeling is terrific.

Good handicapping takes time. When I handicap the horse races for the *Las Vegas Review-Journal,* I spend on average of 10 to 15 minutes per race. Some days handicapping takes longer because of the degree of difficulty. It seldom takes less time.

Doing Your Prep Work

One day, years ago, I walked into the racetrack with a mentor friend of mine when we saw a line of horseplayers buying that day's *Daily Racing Form* (see the following section). "Suckers," he muttered under his breath. As a young pup, I was allowed to ask the wizened veteran the simple question, "Why are those people suckers?" He looked at me in disbelief and said, "It's 45 minutes to post for the first race. Those guys are just now getting the *Form.* Do you think they have as good a chance of winning money as somebody who studied the newspaper all night and did his homework?"

Many of you are either newcomers or casual fans of horse racing. What my friend told me 20 years ago shouldn't stop you from enjoying horse racing or going to the racetrack on the spur of the moment. Spontaneity has a place in our lives. And if you attend the races with friends to have fun and to win a few bets, go enjoy yourselves. (Just don't bet crazy or use the rent money as your bankroll.) But accept my friend's advice as a caveat. Horseplayers who handicap (see the next section) all night and use computers and systems to figure out good betting races for the next day are better prepared than you.

Daily Racing Form: Seat savers?

Live racetrack attendance used to be five to ten times what it is nowadays. Seating in the grandstand and part of the clubhouse was open to all patrons on a first come, first served basis.

The *Daily Racing Form* played a long forgotten secondary role in the storied history of horse racing. Go back 30 years or more, and the individual seats at racetracks used to be made of wood with slats on the seat part and the back rest part. Patrons took the outside pages of the *Daily Racing Form* and slipped them through the openings to cover a portion of the seat. In racetrack etiquette, covering part of the seat with *Daily Racing Form* pages meant that someone had saved that seat, and you'd better not sit there.

Today, if you work for a newspaper, someone may say your newspaper is only good enough for bird cages — meaning only good enough to line the bottom of the bird cage to catch the bird droppings. Well, critics used to say that the articles in the *Daily Racing Form* were only good enough to save seats. You can't say that anymore, because the journalistic integrity of the articles is excellent, and you no longer have to save seats.

Bottom line, if you have the time, doing some prep work the night before is a good habit. If you don't have the time to handicap, you can access many good sources of handicapping material. Many newspapers, like the *Las Vegas Review-Journal,* publish handicapping of a major racing circuit. I handicap the races from Southern California (Santa Anita, Hollywood Park, and Del Mar). Most newspapers have Web sites, and the horse racing selections are in the sports section.

Buying the Daily Racing Form

The *Daily Racing Form* is called "the bible of horse racing" for good reasons. Other publishers have tried to compete against it, replace it, and build a better mousetrap. But no publication has succeeded. Above the front page logo for the *Daily Racing Form* is the slogan, "America's Turf Authority since 1894." (To find out more details about the *Daily Racing Form,* turn to Chapter 11.)

The first thing I do when I buy the *Daily Racing Form* is read the articles on the front pages. Correspondents from most major racetracks write the articles. For details about what goes on at smaller racetracks, the *Daily Racing Form* has a wrap-up section called "Around the Ovals." These stories, from large and small racetracks, include interesting bits of information that can be useful now or later. The correspondents report on racetrack news involving the horses, jockeys, trainers, and the racetrack in general.

Racetrack touts and tip sheets

When I first began going to the horse races, I quickly found out about racetrack *touts*. A tout is a person who gives or sells betting information. I was at Aqueduct when a stranger came up to me and started talking about a long shot horse in an upcoming race. I must have been wearing an invisible sign on my back that read "chump."

The stranger suggested we each bet $20 to win on a particular horse. Then he said he had to go back to his seat, and he'd be right back with his money. In others words, he wanted me to put up the whole $40. I was confused but actually thought about placing the bet. Fortunately, another horseplayer overheard our conversation and told me not to make the bet. He said, "That guy's a tout. You won't see him again unless the horse wins. Then he'll demand his $20 win bet."

The tout went from person to person and asked them to make a sizable win bet on a horse. The kicker is he gave each person a different horse. If he snookered enough gullible rubes, odds were he'd hit upon the winner and then go back to collect his money. The lesson I learned, and you should too, is don't give money to strangers at the racetrack or make bets for them.

In the same period of time that the tout tried to make me his mark, *tip sheets* (race selections sold by handicappers at the racetrack) were hawked near the racetrack entrance by *tipsters*. These colorful men yelled and screamed at horseplayers to buy their handicapping sheets, because, as they said, "I got all the winners right here!" Their antics made for a pretty rowdy scene. After the races were over, you could stop by the tipsters' selling booths and see how they did that day. Invariably, nearly every race had the winner circled, and the prices of the winner, daily doubles (winners of two consecutive races on one bet), and exactas (first and second place finishers in a race in exact order on one bet) were written down in thick magic marker. Little did I know at the time that the tipsters reworked their sheets during the races and then reprinted new sheets for horseplayers to pick up for free on the way out.

Today, tip sheets are available at racetracks where you buy the *Daily Racing Form* and the racetrack's program. Despite their shady past, the handicappers who put the tip sheets out nowadays honestly try to do a good job.

The main reason horseplayers buy the *Daily Racing Form,* however, is for the past performance records of the racehorses running that day. That's where all the handicapping takes place. If you read the *Daily Racing Form* from cover to cover, you'll understand why it's considered the horse racing industry's *Wall Street Journal.*

Say the *Daily Racing From* reports that a certain horse ran poorly last time due to health reasons, but the trainer now says the horse is in perfect health and is training well. I file that information away for the next time he runs. If you don't have a photographic memory, computer Web sites can help you set up a file to make a *horses to watch* list. (I cover a horses to watch list in more detail in Chapter 16.)

The *Daily Racing Form* has a handicapper at each racetrack. I like to read the handicappers' comments in the *Form* to pick up any new information. After all, they watch all the races and have access to excellent research information, so it makes sense that they have worthwhile commentary.

Getting the morning line

The *morning line* is a prediction of how the public will bet a horse race. Each horse is assigned win odds. For example, if a horse is assigned win odds of 4/1, that means a $2 bettor would receive four-times his money ($8) plus his original $2 wager.

An employee of the racetrack makes the official racetrack morning line. The line maker can be a person in the publicity department, the racing office, or sometimes the mutuel department. The mutuel department includes all the employees involved in the processing of horse bets at the racetrack.

The morning line is *not* the same as the handicapper's selections. To this day, that misconception plagues veteran horseplayers as well as newcomers to racing. For example, a long shot horse wins a race at 20/1 odds, and the morning line maker assigned the horse a 20/1 odds morning line. In this case, the line maker did a perfect job. He accurately predicted how the public would bet the race, and he was right. It's the betting public that determines the final win odds on horses by who they wager upon in the win pool (see Chapter 3 for more on parimutuel wagering). I've heard people say, using this example, that the line maker did a lousy job since he assigned the winner 20/1 odds, meaning he didn't like the horse's chances to win. However, the line maker's job isn't to handicap the winner of the race. His job is to handicap the bettors and predict how he thinks the public will wager.

A good morning line is very helpful in your handicapping. It quickly points out who the logical race choices are without you doing any handicapping. If, after handicapping a race, you like a horse with higher win odds, you've come across a scenario where your opinion is opposite the public's. Your situation is fine, because that's the essence of handicapping: finding a value horse (called an *overlay*) to like that the public doesn't like.

The morning line in the *Daily Racing Form* is okay to look at, but it's not the best. The *Form* makes its odds 48 hours in advance of the race and doesn't take into account late scratches (see "Changing your strategy for scratches," later in the chapter) and rider changes. I prefer to use the racetrack's morning line, which is available on the Internet. To find it, you can go to a Web site like Equibase.com (`www.equibase.com`) or to the individual racetrack Web sites.

In Las Vegas, where a menu of racetrack satellite signals is transmitted daily into the race books for horseplayers to wager upon, you find a one-page overnight sheet for each of those racetracks (see Figure 12-1 for an example). The overnight lists the field for each race with the betting numbers of the horses in post position order (see "The Importance of Post Positions," later in the chapter), the assigned weight that each horse has to carry, the jockeys, and the racetrack's morning line. Horseplayers use these overnights in lieu of a racetrack's program (see Chapter 5), which isn't available in Las Vegas.

Figure 12-1:
An overnight from a Las Vegas race book.

The Orleans Hotel & Casino

RACE 1 POST 12:30

Race 1   7 1/2FUR F&M 3YO&UP MDN CLM
1	NO MORE BLUES	121	J VALDIVIA	5/2
2	NOBLE PLAN	123	T BAZE	4
3	HOLLYWOODSETRIGHT	117	D FLORES	7/2
4	PATRIOTIC DIVA	123	R DOUGLAS	3
5	SUNNY STREET	121	K DESORMEAU	2

WIN PLC SHW EXA QUIN DBL PICK 3 PICK 4 PICK 8

Race 2   6 1/2FUR FIL 2YO ALW
1	BAR LITE	118	F MARTINEZ	3
2	CRISANE	118	T BAZE	9/5
3	MOUNTAIN MEETING	118	A DELGADILL	20
4	COSMIC LADY	118	V ESPINOZA	5/2
5	NETTY'S KNOCKOUT	120	C NAKATANI	2

WIN PLC SHW EXA QUIN DBL PICK 3

Race 3   1 1/16M TURF FIL 2YO MDN
1	JUBILEE	120	V ESPINOZA	6/5
2	GOOSE AT FIFTY		o vergara	20
3	FIGUERAS	120	F MARTINEZ	5/2 L1
4	CALIFORNIA THUNDER	120	A BISONO	3
5	STORM WALKING	120	T BAZE	3
6	CROW AUTUMN	113	D COHEN	20

WIN PLC SHW EXA QUIN TRI DBL PICK 3 PICK 6

Race 4   6FUR 3YO CLM
1	JOHN THE MAIL MAN	118	F MARTINEZ	5/2
2	TRISH'S DIAMOND	111	D COHEN	8
3	SKIPPY'S GOLDENBOY	118	V ESPINOZA	3
4	BLAIRS ROARIN STAR	122	T BAZE	2
5	HICKORY PETE	118	G GOMEZ	7/2
6	NEVER SURRENDER	118	J COURT	12

WIN PLC SHW EXA QUIN TRI DBL PICK 3

Race 5   1M TURF F&M 3YO&UP STR ALW
1	MERCEDES DANCER	116	M SMITH	7/5
2	FREETOUCH	116	A CEDENO	15
3	BAJA DANCER	119	J ALFEREZ	20
4	RASPBERRY BBRET	116	D SORENSON	8
5	LUNAR DREAMS	116	J COURT	6
6	FREE RENT	116	G STEVENS	8/5
7	MYSTERIOUS PEACE	116	F MARTINEZ	8

WIN PLC SHW EXA QUIN TRI DBL PICK 4

Race 6   6FUR 3YO CLM
1	YOUARETHEMAN	118	d flores	6
2	FISHERMAN'S FRIEND	118	J COURT	5
3	YODELTILYOURBLUE	109	D COHEN	4
4	DONTCALLMEFRISCO	118	V ESPINOZA	7/2
5	BLACK BUTTE	118	C DEALBA	20
6	CARRY JIG	118	L JAUREGUI	12
7	IRON CITY JACK	118	F MARTINEZ	20
8	LEGENDARY TRAITORS	118	I ENRIQUEZ	15
9	TIZALYIN	118	G GOMEZ	3
10	CHIKENDINNERWINNER	118	R DOUGLAS	12

WIN PLC SHW EXA QUIN TRI SUPER DBL PICK 3

Race 7   1 1/16M 3YO&UP OPT CLM/ALW
1	OUTTA HERE	119	R DOUGLAS	4
2	PRIMERICA	119	G GOMEZ	6
3	SAINT BUDDY	119	T BAZE	9/5
4	CAPITANO	116	D FLORES	7/2
5	FORTY SUERTUDO	121	G STEVENS	2

WIN PLC SHW EXA QUIN DBL

Race 8   7FUR F&M 3YO&UP MDN CLM
1	C'EST LULU	123	A CASTANON	4
2	CHASENTHEBLUESAWAY	121	C FUSILIER	5/2
3	ALSYSTEMSGOHOUSTON	121	A CEDENO	20
4	BERRY SOUTHERN	121	M LINARES	15
5	LOU'S REALITY	114	K KAENEL	5
6	MYSTERIOUS PHOENIX	121	M BAZE	5
7	FOREVER AND A DAY	121	A BISONO	10
8	TALAVERA GAL	119	F MARTINEZ	3

WIN PLC SHW EXA QUIN TRI SUPER

PICK 6 CARRYOVER $87,783.44

Developing the Race Shape

As I stated earlier in this chapter, seemingly as many betting systems and strategies exist as horseplayers do. I've defined my own systems and strategies through trial and error and research. In this section, I outline some factors that I look for in breaking down a race. Then I piece the factors back together to form a clearer snapshot of how a race will be run. I call it "developing the race shape."

Separating the running styles

Horses, over time, develop a signature style of running. You can either argue that a trainer creates a horse's running style or that a horse shows the trainer how it wants to run. Regardless, a pattern emerges, and the handicapper's job is to see how the pattern fits into the overall race shape. I separate horses into three basic running styles: speed horses, pace horses, and closers.

Speed horses

In the *Daily Racing Form* past performances, which is a resume of a horse's racing record, *speed horses* (also known as *pacesetters* or *speedballs*), have mostly ones and twos in the early part of the horse's running lines. (In Chapter 11, you can find a legend outlining how to read the past performances.)

Top Shoter, whose past performances are shown in Figure 12-2, is a good example of a one-dimensional speed horse. The ones to the left of his past performance runnings lines signify that as soon as the race starts, Top Shoter leaves the starting gate fast and assumes the lead. If another speed horse also wants the lead, Top Shoter will fight him for it. This sets up what's called a *speed duel,* when two or more horses fight for the lead.

Figure 12-2:
Past performances for Top Shoter, a speed horse.

©2005 by Daily Racing Form, Inc. and Equibase Company

In developing the race shape, the first thing to look for is *lone speed,* which means that a speed horse has no challengers in the field to fight him for the early lead. When a speed horse like Top Shoter has no early challengers, he has an easier time dictating the pace of the race. Notice the running lines when Top Shoter has been able to gain a one, two, or three length early lead; he's been able to relax on the lead and last all the way to the finish, called winning *wire to wire.*

A lone speed horse is the best bet in horse racing. When a horse is in front by himself, any chances of getting into traffic trouble are eliminated, because no other horse is out there with him. In this situation, the importance of the jockey is also lessened. As I cover in Chapter 7, even a bad jockey on a speed horse is less likely to make mistakes, as long as he leaves the starting gate in good order.

Pace horses

Pace horses, also known as *stalkers,* prefer to run a few lengths off the pace set by the speed horses. In past performance lines, a pace horse has mostly threes and fours in the horse's early running positions.

Afleet Alex, whose past performances appear in Figure 12-3, has developed a natural running style as a pace horse. When the race starts, Afleet Alex is allowed to settle in third or fourth position, a few lengths off the lead horse. About midway through the race, Afleet Alex is asked to go after the leaders. In the middle of the stretch run, Afleet Alex makes his best move, which has won him four of six starts so far in his career.

Figure 12-3:
Past performance for Afleet Alex, a pace horse.

Afleet Alex						
Own: Cash is King LLC						

©2005 by Daily Racing Form, Inc. and Equibase Company

Stalkers are dangerous horses in any pace scenario. If the early pace is fast, he sits in perfect position for when the speed horses get tired. If the early pace is slow, the jockey has tactical speed to jump into the race sooner and not allow the speed horse to steal the race.

Closers

Late-running horses are called *closers* because their jockeys wait until the top of the stretch before asking for the horse's best run. (The configuration of a racetrack is covered in Chapter 5.) At the top of the stretch is a pole that marks a quarter-mile left to go in the race. Logically enough, this pole is called the *quarter-pole.*

For most of the race, closers sit in the back half of the field biding their time until the quarter-pole. Then their jockeys commence a late rally, attempting to overtake the speed horses and stalkers before the finish line.

Hangers (not the clothes type)

As you're handicapping or watching a horse race, you may come across the term *hang* or a derivative of the word. A horse hangs when he rallies up to the lead horse and then refuses to go by him. His effort looks gallant, but it's not. As the horse keeps appearing in more races, his *Daily Racing Form* past performances may show a number of finishes where he appears on the verge of victory but doesn't go past the final horse to seal the deal. Horseplayers call that kind of horse a hanger.

Amorama, whose past performances appear in Figure 12-4, is a good example of a dead late closer. In nearly all her career starts, she's either been in last place early or far back in the field. Even in the middle of the stretch, she's been well behind before closing fast.

Figure 12-4:
Past performance for Amorama, a closer horse.

Amorama (Fr)	

©2005 by Daily Racing Form, Inc. and Equibase Company

Horseplayers love betting closers because they're the most exciting horses to watch. However, they're also the toughest horses to bet because they must pass most of the field to win. In doing so, closers often run into traffic problems caused by other horses that impede their progress. Also, closers are at the mercy of the pace of the race. Closers like a fast, early pace that tires out the front runners, because their chances of rallying past these animals are improved. If the early pace is slow, a closer's rally can be ineffective because the front horses still have energy to keep going.

Considering the track surface

I cover the differences between dirt and turf surfaces in Chapter 9. But in this section, I discuss the differences that exist between the ways races are run on the two track surfaces.

TRACK TALES

Silky Sullivan: The most famous closer of them all

Silky Sullivan is the most famous closer (see "Separating the running styles") of all-time in thoroughbred racing. Even today, his name is used ("We pulled off a Silky Sullivan") when someone or something comes from far behind to win. The most famous races in his career came in the spring of 1958 when he was a 3-year-old.

On Feb. 25, 1958, Silky Sullivan won a 6½ furlong sprint race at Santa Anita Park. A furlong is an eighth of a mile, so the race wasn't that long. But the way he won the race is what cemented his popularity among racing fans. With a half-mile left in the race, Silky Sullivan was 41 lengths behind the leader, Fire Alarm, and 35 lengths behind the second to last horse, Brown Drake. He made a bold run around the far turn and into the stretch, but by the eighth pole, Silky Sullivan was still 13 lengths off the lead in seventh place. In big, powerful strides, he surged to the front to win by a half-length.

In the 1958 Santa Anita Derby, Silky Sullivan trailed by nearly 30 lengths before unleashing his famous half-mile rally. By the final 50 yards, he gained the lead and won by 3½ lengths.

Silky Sullivan was shipped to Churchill Downs in Louisville, Kentucky to run in the 1958 Kentucky Derby. He ran in a 7 furlong prep race called the Steppingstone Purse, also at Churchill. As usual, he trailed the field by more than 30 lengths before commencing his rally. Silky Sullivan came up short but was beaten by only 2½ lengths.

In the Derby, Silky Sullivan was bet down to second choice at 2/1 odds. Again, Silky Sullivan was in last place, a distant 32 lengths behind the leaders. Jockey Bill Shoemaker shook the reins at the half-mile pole, and Silky Sullivan made a brief and ineffectual rally, losing by 20 lengths.

The Derby was a major disappointment, but Silky Sullivan remained a matinee idol and one of the most famous race horses of his era.

Dirt surfaces

About 75 percent of the races in the U.S. are run on the dirt surface, also called the *main track*. Dirt tracks can withstand the daily pounding that comes from year-round racing and the variable weather conditions that occur, especially during the winter.

American racing on the main track favors speed. The bloodlines of modern race horses are very much slanted towards speed, sometimes at the sacrifice of stamina. American jockeys place a premium on putting their horses *into the race,* meaning they like to position their horses on the lead or close to it.

The way jockeys ride on dirt surfaces is also an indicator of the way American trainers train for speed. When handicapping a dirt race, three or four horses wanting to race on the lead isn't unusual. The horses put early pace pressure on one another, invariably tiring each other out. As a handicapper, you must anticipate how the race will be run, and this is just one possible scenario.

Saving ground, meaning racing close to the inside rail to run the least amount of distance, is usually a good idea. But on the main track in particular, many riders don't mind racing wide. Some riders, even while in front, race in the two- or three-path. (A *path* is the width of a horse. So the horse closest to the rail is in the one-path, outside him is the two-path, and so on.) Following are some reasons riders may race wide on dirt surfaces:

- **To avoid being hit by clods of dirt being kicked back by the front horses as they run.** Depending on the track condition, these clods can be the size of baseballs, can be hard, and can strike the horses running right behind.

- **To stay out of traffic trouble.** As the front horses begin to tire and slow down, they can literally back up right into the horses behind them.

- **To relax the horse.** In the morning training hours, when horses are asked for speed, they're usually positioned near the rail. When horses are galloped for exercise or to relax, they're typically taken wide into the four- or five-path, at least. Horses, like people, are creatures of habit. So when a rider races him wide while on the lead, the horse has a tendency to relax a bit.

Turf surfaces

In turf racing, the principles are the reverse of dirt racing. You see jockeys from the start pulling their horses back towards the rear of the pack. They're avoiding the lead like the plague. Being on the lead, more often than not, is a bad position to be in on turf.

American turf racing mirrors European grass racing, where jockeys ride *covered up,* meaning they tuck their horses inside towards the rail behind other horses. Not only is this a drafting technique, cutting down on wind resistance, but also most horses relax while running behind other horses. This is a part of the *herd mentality* theory. Herd mentality describes the way horses run in the wild. Usually, a horse leads, and the rest of the pack runs together behind the lead horse.

Turf racing is very exciting because the finishes look like a cavalry charge to the finish line. The lead horses have slowed the early pace down as much as possible. The stalkers and closers (see "Separating the running styles," earlier in the chapter) sit patiently waiting for the right time to move and for room to maneuver. By the top of the stretch, a turf race can explode with action because all the riders ask their horses to run their best to the wire. Closers sometimes must angle out very wide to find a *clear lane* (a path in the stretch run where no other horse is in front of them) to run.

Turf racing lends itself to close, exciting finishes, called *blanket finishes.* Sometimes the runners finish so close together, you can throw a blanket over the top finishers and cover them all.

Turf racing, unlike dirt racing, can be affected by the placement of a tempo-rary inside rail. Most racetracks have only one turf course. If every grass race were run with the permanent rail in place, the paths closest to the rail would be torn up by the horse's hooves to the point that the course would be ruined. To avoid that scenario, tracks have multiple positions for temporary rails on their turf courses. Depending on the width of the turf course, two, three, and even four temporary rail positions may be in place. As the course gets used, the track superintendent moves the rail out to allow the inner paths to recover and grow new grass. He moves the rail on a consistent basis to spread the usage out evenly among the various temporary rail positions.

Studies have shown that the farther out the temporary rail is from the permanent rail, the more the speed horses are helped. This rule is true at all racetracks without exceptions.

Changing your strategy for scratches

One thing that can throw a monkey wrench into your prep work the night before are *late scratches*. A *scratch* is when a horse is withdrawn from a race. A *late scratch* happens on the actual day of the race. A late scratch can occur right up until *post time,* the time the race is to start. For example, while being loaded into the starting gate, if a horse acts up, breaks through the front of the gate, throws his rider, and runs off, the track stewards will likely scratch that animal from the race. The scratch can change the entire complexion of a race.

Picture this: The night before a race you handicap a race with two speed horses dueling each other into exhaustion. You look at the stalkers and closers and have a good idea which horses you like. You go to the racetrack, get all settled down, and find out that one of the speed horses is scratched. That scratch changes the whole pace scenario. Now you have lone speed (see "Separating the running styles," earlier in the chapter) — the best bet in horse racing. So, you've gone from liking the stalkers and closers the night before to betting on a lone speed horse. You have to be flexible.

Getting the day's scratches and changes is really important for a lot of rea-sons. Sometimes a top jockey gets injured or sick and cancels off all his mounts. You want to know the replacement riders. And as I just mentioned, the late scratch of a horse from the field can change the entire race shape.

One angle I pay close attention to is when scratches allow a horse from the also eligible list to draw into the main body of a race. The *body* of a race is the maximum number of starters that can run in a race. If more horses are entered than can be drawn into the body, the racing office makes up an *also eligible list*. When a horse scratches out of the body of a race, and an eligible horse draws in, the also eligible horse is worth keeping an eye on. Many times, handicappers completely overlook the also eligible horse because it starts from the widest post.

An extension of the also eligible list is when a turf race has a list for *main track only* horses. Main track only horses draw into the race and run only if there's a surface switch from turf to dirt. For example, at Saratoga, where a thunderstorm can hit at a moment's notice, they draw turf races with an also eligible list of main track only horses. If the rain comes, and the turf race is transferred to the main track, lots of turf horses scratch, allowing the main track only horses to draw in and run. They now become the horses you need to focus upon. The racing secretary uses this maneuver to ensure full fields for horseplayers to bet on.

Finding Value in the Odds

The secret to betting on horse racing is to beat the race favorites with overlays, meaning horses going off at higher win odds then their perceived chances of winning. Professional handicappers have the expertise and take the time to make their own morning line. The pros are placing an odds value on each horse, which enables them to identify overlays.

I don't expect newcomers to make their own morning line. However, the oddsmaker at the racetrack makes a morning line for every race. In theory, his morning line (see the section, "Getting the morning line," earlier in the chapter) is slightly different from a professional's. The racetrack oddsmaker is making a prediction of how the public will bet a horse race. The morning line doesn't reflect an oddsmaker's own selections. Still, the morning line is very useful for you to determine overlays.

Most morning line makers are pretty good, especially at the big racing circuits like New York and Southern California. I don't hesitate using their morning line for comparisons when I do my handicapping for the *Las Vegas Review-Journal* or when I'm betting in a race book.

Looking for overlays

Something I recommend to newcomers is to compare a horse's morning line odds versus what the betting public is making the horse so that they can readily find overlays. If the betting public allows a horse to go off at much higher odds than the morning line, bet a couple dollars to win on the horse. It's a no-brainer system.

For example, in Figures 12-5 and 12-6, Run Thru the Sun was made 6/1 odds in the morning line for race 8 at Del Mar on August 25, 2004. He was ignored by the betting public and allowed to go off at 27/1 odds, meaning he was an overlay. (Overlays are horses going off at higher odds than their actual chance of winning.) Look at the result chart. Run Thru the Sun won by two-lengths and paid $57.60 for each $2 win bet. My only caveat is to apply the system to the major racetracks where the oddsmaker is much more reliable.

```
RACE–8 POST                    OFF
SC# DMR 6FUR 2YO MDN CLM
#1    MI ESTILO          30    A DELGADILL  120
█████████████████***LATE SCRATCH***███████████
#3    TIME TO SING       9/2   K JOHN       120
#4    CHARADE EVENT      6     M PEDROZA    120
#5    TIZ BUENO          15    A BISONO     115LI
#6    BEAT THE CHALK     8     V ESPINOZA   120
#7    YAK THE DESERT RAT 8     D FLORES     120
#8    RUN THRUTHE SUN    6     J COURT      120
#9    C R POWER          5/2   T BAZE       120
#10   MAGO ILUSION       8     O FIGUEROA   120
█████████████████***LATE SCRATCH***███████████
#12   RUNN'N WILD        20    J LEYVA      120
#13   PROUD RINGER       20    O VERGARA    120
```

Figure 12-5:
An overnight
of race 8 at
Del Mar on
August 25,
2004.

Del Mar - August 25th, 2004 - Race 8
Maiden Claiming - For Thoroughbred Two Year Old (S) Six Furlongs On The Dirt
Purse: $24,000
Plus: $2,400 (Other sources)
Available Money: $26,400
Value of Race: $26,400, 1st $14,400, 2nd $4,800, 3rd $2,880, 5th $480, 4th $1,440, 6th
$400, 7th $400, 8th $400, 9th $400, 10th $400, 11th $400
Weather: Clear   **Track:** Fast
Off at: 5:35   **Start:** Good for all but 4

Pgm	HorseName (Jockey)	Wgt	M/E	PP	SP	1/4	1/2	Str	Fin	Odds
8	Run Thruthe Sun (Court, J.K.)	120	B	7	3	1-Head	1-Head	1-2 1/2	1-2	27.80
6	Beat the Chalk (Espinoza, V.)	120	BL b	5	9	9-6	8-1 1/2	5-1 1/2	2-1	15.10
7	Yak the Sesert Rat (Flores, D.R.)	120	BL b	6	10	10-2 1/2	11	9-3 1/2	3-3/4	8.80
3	DQ-Time to Sing (John, K.)	120	BL b	2	7	5-Head	5-Head	4-1	4-1	2.90
4	Charade Event (Nakatani, C.S.)	120	BL f	3	11	11	10-1 1/2	8-1/2	5-1/2	7.70
13	Proud Ringer (Vergara, O.)	120	BL	11	1	3-Head	3-1/2	2-1	6-Neck	6.60
9	C R Power (Baze, T.)	120	BL b	8	5	6-1/2	6-1	3-Head	7-7	2.60*
10	Mago Ilusion (Figueroa, O.)	120	BL	9	6	7-1 1/2	7-2 1/2	10-Head	8-1/2	14.80
5	Tiz Bueno (Bisono, A)	115	BL b	4	4	4-1	4-1 1/2	7-Head	9-Nose	7.10
12	Runn'n Wild (Leyva, J.C.)	120	BL b	10	2	2-1 1/2	2-1 1/2	6-Head	10-1/2	77.50
1	Mi Estilo (Delgadillo, A.)	120	BL b	1	8	8-2 1/2	9-2 1/2	11	11	85.20

Figure 12-6:
The *Daily
Racing Form*
result chart
of race 8 at
Del Mar on
August 25,
2004.

You hear over and over again in this book that the secret to making money at the racetrack is betting overlays. Run Thru the Sun at Del Mar is a simple and obvious example of an overlay. His odds of winning were 6/1, and he went off at post time at 27/1. However, the process of finding overlays isn't always so black and white. I mention that professional horseplayers make their own morning line.

After a morning line is completed, a horseplayer can then discern for himself whether a horse is an overlay or not, but horseplayers can and do disagree on this. For example, if a horse is going off at high odds, like Run Thru the Sun, some horseplayers use the term *dead on the board* to describe that horse. *Board* refers to the tote board where you look at the win odds, and *dead* means that the public isn't betting the horse because it doesn't like its chances of winning. So what happens here is one horseplayer's overlay is a dead on the board horse to another handicapper.

Handicapping the races is very subjective and open to interpretation. That's one reason why the learning curve to this sport is so great.

Knowing when to beat 'em and when to join 'em

The betting public establishes the race favorite. After the first bet is made on a horse race, whom the morning line maker made the favorite no longer matters. The public votes for which horse will be favored with its own betting dollars.

No matter how you slice it, the favorite wins one out of three races. No ifs, ands, or buts. One thing you can decide is when the race has a good favorite or a bad or beatable favorite.

Good favorites have all the handicapping elements you want in a winner: speed, class, pedigree, conditioning, a good jockey, a good trainer, and a race shape that's to his advantage. Good favorites are horses you want to *key,* meaning to put in the win position in exotic wagers, which I cover in Chapter 15. A well-deserved favorite is called a "free bingo square." Like the center square in bingo, a good favorite should look like a universal winning number. You can try to beat good favorites, but going with the flow and letting them make money for you is usually better.

Bad favorites are the horses you try to beat every time. They create tremendous betting opportunities. Bad favorites have what are called *holes* in them, meaning they lack one or more of the primary things that good favorites possess: speed, class, pedigree, conditioning, a good jockey, a good trainer, and a race shape that's to his advantage. If a favorite looks like Swiss cheese, that's a good time to jump into the betting pool and bet against him.

Wata Sunrise is an example of a bad betting favorite. In six of ten starts on her *Daily Racing Form* past performances (shown in Figure 12-7), Wata Sunrise was the race favorite. The favorite is denoted by an asterisk next to the horse's win odds. She won one time, on October 26 at 1/2 odds, meaning she paid $3 to win. Even though she won on October 26, she was a terrible favorite that day because her odds were underlaid. The betting public is enamored with horses like Wata Sunrise, and she's the type of favorite that you can make money on trying to beat her.

Figure 12-7:
Past performances for Wata Sunrise, a bad betting favorite.

©2005 by Daily Racing Form, Inc. and Equibase Company

The Importance of Post Positions

The shortest distance between the starting gate and the finish line is following the one-path along the rail (see "Considering the track surface" earlier in the chapter). If horse racing strategy were that simple, every horse in every race would be clamoring for that spot.

The first strategic decision begins for the jockey when post positions are drawn. Post positions are drawn at random for each race in the racing secretary's office. A numbered pill is pulled for every horse in a race until they all have an assigned post position. Post position numbers begin with the inside rail (number 1 post) and extend to post number 14.

As a general rule, speed horses like to break from inside posts, because these posts puts them closest to the rail to begin with. Stalkers prefer the middle posts, because a good position for them is to sit just off the right flank of a speed horse or two. Closers shouldn't really care where their posts are. They have no early speed, so the field outruns them, and they get to tuck in behind horses wherever they want.

Because the world isn't perfect, the post position draw can work against the horses. A speed horse drawn in post 12 may have to really hustle to get to the lead. The extra energy needed to get to the lead can cost a victory in the end. A stalker from post 1 may have to move a bit sooner to hold his position; otherwise, he could get shuffled back by horses to his outside. (*Shuffled back* means that other horses run past him early and move in front of him, possibly forcing the rider to take back further than he'd like.)

When I'm handicapping, I look at the post positions for obvious problems. In the long run, though, post position analysis is not my number one priority. Jockeys are paid good money to make decisions that win and lose races. I let them handle problems that come with a bad post draw.

Post positions in sprints and routes

Different distances and racetrack configurations can make post positions extremely important. This is especially true in route races. Route races are considered races 1 mile and longer in distance. For example, most 1-mile races start near the finish line, which is close to the first turn. In this type of race, the inside posts have a big advantage because the start of the first turn comes up very quickly. If an outside horse doesn't have much speed, he can be fanned out very wide into the first turn. That creates a tremendous amount of ground loss, meaning the horse has to run wide and is forced to go extra distance of ground.

A 6 furlong race is the most common distance in horse racing. Remember that a furlong is ⅛ mile, so 6 furlongs is ¾ mile. That distance fits perfectly on a racetrack 1 mile in circumference. Some racetracks like to schedule one-turn races at longer distances, such as 6½ furlongs, 7 furlongs, 7½ furlongs, and up to 1 mile. The racetrack builds a chute, which is an extension of the backstretch, to accommodate these distances. When races begin from a chute, the inside posts can be deeper, so those horses can be at a disadvantage. Also, when horses leave the chute and enter the main part of the racetrack, a white temporary rail is placed to guide horses down the straightaway. Horses in the past have spooked from this temporary rail, which can hurt their chances of winning. When races start from a chute, I prefer the horses with middle to outside post positions.

The best example of how post positions can affect a race is the 1-mile start at Ellis Park in Henderson, KY. The mile chute is on the first turn, not the backstretch, so horses go straight when they begin and then make a severe left turn as they enter the backstretch. Horses from the inside posts have a distinct advantage. Horses from posts 6 through 10 have to be the best to win, considering all the extra yardage they have to run.

Post positions in turf racing

Because saving ground is considerably more important in turf racing than dirt racing, inside posts are beneficial. (I touch on saving ground and some turf handicapping angles in "Considering the track surfaces," earlier in the chapter.)

Every track in North America, except for Woodbine near Toronto, Ontario, Canada, has its turf course inside the main dirt track. Most main tracks are 1 mile in circumference. To fit a turf course inside, the circumference of the oval must be ⅞ mile or less. Therefore, turf races have some awkward starting points.

Many tracks build a chute that cuts across the infield and joins the main turf course in the middle of the stretch. The horse is forced to run straight down the chute and then make a sharp left onto the main turf course. The inside post positions have an advantage because they don't have to run as hard to maintain their positions.

Santa Anita has a unique turf run called the Hillside turf course. It's the only turf course in the U.S. with a right-hand turn. The Hillside turf course races are 6½ furlongs. The start is literally down a slope. The horses turn right and then back to the left. They run across the main dirt track and back onto the main turf course for the stretch run. The shape is like a question mark. The course is difficult to ride and takes some getting used to. Horses and riders often can't navigate the part right before they cross onto the main track. Horses often drift far to the right and sometimes take themselves out of contention. I prefer horses with outside posts on the Hillside turf course.

Weight Matters (or Does It?)

The racetrack axiom "Weight can stop a freight train" is pooh-poohed by some horsemen and handicappers and is a religion among others. I subscribe to the theory that the spread in the weight is what really matters. For example, if every horse in the field carries 122 pounds, than there's no spread. But, if one horse carries 122 pounds and another horse carries 115 pounds, the 7-pound spread in the weights, to me, makes a difference.

Forego: The greatest weight carrier of all

I was very lucky that I got interested in horse racing during the career of Forego. The great gelding was Horse of the Year in 1974, 1975, and 1976. Forego is considered the greatest handicap horse of all-time because he carried very high weight to victory against the best horses of his generation. Back then, racing secretaries assigned huge weight on the back of Forego. But rather than complain, trainer Frank Whiteley took on all comers.

My best memory of Forego came in the 1976 Marlboro Cup Handicap at Belmont Park. Forego was packing 137 pounds, including the diminutive jockey Bill Shoemaker. I sat in a chilly grandstand at Belmont under dreary, gray skies. It had rained earlier and the track was sloppy, a surface Forego

didn't care for. He ran anyway, conceding up to 27 pounds to his lightest rival. Turning for home, Forego was six-wide entering the home stretch and not gaining on the leader, Honest Pleasure. At the eighth-pole, Forego was still four-lengths behind and running closer to the hot dog vendors in the grandstand than he was the inside rail.

Then in the last 100 yards, Forego made a miraculous rally, Shoemaker urging him on with every stride. Forego ate up long shot Father Hogan and then in a last gasp lunged at Honest Pleasure. The photo showed he won by a head. What a victory! Honest Pleasure, a grade one winner in his own right, carried 119 pounds, 18 pounds less than the great Forego.

You often hear trainers complain about their star handicap horses having to carry high weight in a stakes race. High weight is whatever the racing secretary assigned to the star horse — 126 pounds, 124 pounds, maybe as low as 122 pounds. On the surface, the complaint is ridiculous. In the Breeders' Cup Juvenile, 2-year-old colts carry 122 pounds. During the Triple Crown in the spring, 3-year-old colts carry 126 pounds. So for a mature 4- or 5-year-old horse to carry 126 or 124 pounds in a stakes race should be no big deal.

An example where the argument may carry weight (no pun intended) is if horse A carries 122 pounds and horse B carries 116 pounds, and both horses are of equal ability. The trainer of horse A then has a point.

I look at the spread of weights in all the races I handicap. As a handicapper, you're always looking for an edge, and sometimes weight is a subtle edge that gets overlooked.

Trite, But True, Clichés

Horse racing is full of axioms and clichés, and I love every one of them. While some are considered trite, many remain true to this day. When you hear them, think about their meaning and how they can help you become a better horse-player in today's modern age.

You can beat a race, but you can't beat the races

I've heard different interpretations of this cliché. One says, "You can't beat a race, but you can beat the races." I know for a fact you can beat a race, or else people would quit playing horses all together. The person who said you can't beat a race, but you can beat the races, told me you can lose a race due to bad luck. But if you bet the horses correctly over the long run, you'll win money. I'd like to start a cliché that says, "You can't beat the races if you try to beat every race." You have to pick and choose your spots and find money-making opportunities.

The speed of the speed

This is a simple line, but you need to think about it. When a race is loaded with speedball horses, is a stalker or closer automatically going to win? The answer is no.

Sometimes you see *the speed of the speed* emerge from a race full of front runners. One horse bolts to the front and takes all the heart out of the other front runners. For that speed horse to win, he has to *bottom out the field,* meaning he goes so fast early that he takes all the starch out of the rest of the field too.

Pace makes the race

You hear this phrase a thousand times at the racetrack, OTB (off-track betting) parlor, or Las Vegas race book. To me, this saying is another way of defining the race shape. If the pace is slow, the speed horses hold on. If the pace is fair, the race is anyone's. If the pace is very fast, stalkers and closers have an edge. Bottom line, you must anticipate how the pace will go, and then you can define the shape of the race.

Horses for courses

Thank the *Daily Racing Form* for making this cliché easy to follow. In its past performances, you see a breakdown of a horse's record on dirt, on turf, at today's distance, and at a particular racetrack. This breakdown profiles a horse's preference for a surface, distance, or racetrack.

When you see a record where a horse does particularly well, you have your horse for course. Before the *Daily Racing Form* published this information, wiseguy horseplayers kept the information among themselves. Now you're able to share in the secret too.

Sightseek is a perfect horse for course example (see Figure 12-8). The filly raced six times at Belmont Park in Elmont, New York, and won all six races. Five of the six wins came in grade 1 stakes races, meaning against the highest caliber of competition. So, Sightseek really proved she loved the main track at Belmont Park.

Sightseek
Own: Juddmonte Farms Inc

Ch. m. 5 (Feb)
Sire: Distant View (Mr. Prospector) $15,000
Dam: Viviana (Nureyev)
Br: Juddmonte Farms, Inc. (Ky)
Tr: Frankel Robert J(0 0 0 0 .00) 2004:(461 130 .28)

Life	20	12	5	0	$2,445,216	115	D.Fst	17	11	4	0	$2,239,266	115
2004	7	4	1	0	$1,011,350	112	Wet(372)	2	1	0	0	$196,350	110
2003	8	4	3	0	$1,171,888	115	Turf(327)	1	0	1	0	$9,600	85
Bel	6	6	0	0	$1,468,800	112	Dst(0)	0	0	0	0	$0	–

9Oct04-9Bel	fst	1⅛		:48^2	1:12^4	1:36^4	1:49^3	3↑ⒻBeldame-G1	101	1	1^{hd}	1^1	1^{½}	1^6	1^{2¾}	Castellano J J	L123	*.30	83-20	Sghtsk123^{2¾} SoctySlctn120^{1¼} StrmFlgFlyng123^{¾}	In command from start	5	
19Sep04-9Bel	fst	1 1/16		:23^3	:46^1	1:10^3	1:41^2	3↑ⒻRuffianH-G1	112	3	3^{½}	3^{½}	1^{½}	1^8	1^{11¼}	Velazquez J R	L122	*.25	93-25	*Sightseek*122^{11¼} Pocus Hocus114^{2½} MissLoren117^{¾}	3 wide move, hand ride	5	
1Aug04-9Sar	fst	1⅛		:47^3	1:10^4	1:35	1:47^4	3↑ⒻGoFWandH-G1	103	4	2^{1½}	2^{½}	2^{½}	2^{hd}	2^{1¾}	Bailey J D	L122	*.75	94-14	Azeri120^{1¾} *Sightseek*122^2 *Storm Flag Flying*117^7	Tried winner 1/4 pole	5	
19Jun04-9Bel	fst	1 1/16		:23^1	:45^3	1:10	1:41^2	3↑ⒻOPhippsH-G1	99	3	2^{½}	2^{hd}	1^{½}	1^6	1^{3¼}	Bailey J D	L120	2.35	93-20	Sightseek120^{3¼} StormFlagFlying117^{6½} PassingShot116^2	Wrapped up late	4	
30Apr04-8CD	sly	1 1/16		:24^1	:47^4	1:12^3	1:44^1	3↑ⒻLouvlBCH-G2	87	2	3^{1½}	2^{1½}	2^{½}	4^{3½}	4^7	Bailey J D	L122	*.40	80-17	Lead Story116^{¾} Yell114^3 Cat Fighter116^{3¼}	Led for stride,tired	6	
14Mar04-6GP	fst	1⅛		:48^2	1:11^4	1:37^2	1:51	3↑ⒻRampartH-G2	101	3	2^{1½}	2^1	2^{hd}	1^6	1^{7½}	Bailey J D	L121	*.50	84-27	Sightseek121^{7½} Redoubled Miss113^2 *Lead Story*117^9	Drew off, easily	4	
25Jan04-8SA	fst	7f		:21^4	:44	1:08^2	1:21^1	4↑ⒻSntMncaH-G1	93	2	3	5^{4½}	5^4	4^{2½}	4^{4¾}	Bailey J D	LB122	*1.20	94-08	IslndFshion120^{¾} Buffythcntrfold114^{½} GotKoko119^{3½}	Stalked pace, no bid	6	
25Oct03-2SA	fst	1⅛		:47	1:11	1:35^4	1:49	3↑ⒻBCDistaf-G1	84	5	6^{2¾}	6^4	6^{2¾}	5^{6½}	4^{10½}	Bailey J D	LB123	*.60	78-07	Adoration123^{4½} Elloluv119^{2½} Got Koko123^{3½}	Bit crowded start	7	
4Oct03-9Bel	fst	1⅛		:47^4	1:12^2	1:36^3	1:49^1	3↑ⒻBeldame-G1	107	2	5^{1½}	5^3	3^{nk}	1^{2½}	1^{4½}	Bailey J D	L123	*.30	84-26	Sightseek123^{4½} Bird Town120^{4¾} Buy the Sport120^{¾}	When asked, in hand	7	
27Jly03-9Sar	fst	1⅛		:49^1	1:13^2	1:38	1:50^4	3↑ⒻGoFWandH-G1	115	5	3^{1½}	2^{1½}	2^{½}	1^8	1^{11½}	Bailey J D	L121	*.15	81-27	*Sightseek*121^{11½} *ShesGotthBt*112^5 NonsuchBy113^4	When ready, ridden out	6	
21Jun03-9Bel	sly	1 1/16		:22^2	:45^1	1:09^1	1:40^4	3↑ⒻOPhippsH-G1	110	2	2^{½}	2^{½}	2^{hd}	1^{1½}	1^5	Bailey J D	L118	*1.05	96-18	*Sightseek*118^5 TkeChrgeLdy119^5 MndysGold118^{1¾}	Drew clear under drive	5	
3May03-8CD	fst	7f		:22^2	:45^2	1:10	1:22	4↑ⒻHmnaDstH-G1	107	2	5	5^{1¼}	5^{1½}	1^{1½}	1^{4½}	Bailey J D	L116	*.80	92-08	*Sightseek*116^{4½} Gold Mover119^{hd} Miss Lodi114^{2¼}	Split foes,3w,driving	8	
9Mar03-8SA	fst	1⅛		:47	1:10^3	1:35^3	1:48^1	4↑ⒻSMrgrtaH-G1	108	4	1^1	1^1	1^{1½}	2^{hd}	2^2	Valdivia J Jr	LB116	2.50	91-16	Starrer121^2 *Sightseek*116^3 Bella Bellucci116^5	Inside, 2nd best	5	
8Feb03-6SA	fst	1⅛		:46^3	1:10^4	1:35^3	1:48^2	ⒻLaCanada-G2	105	1	1^{½}	1^{hd}	1^{hd}	1^{½}	2^{¾}	Valenzuela P A	LB118	*.90	91-11	Got Koko121^{¾} Sightseek118^{1½} Bella Bellucci118^3	Bit off rail,worn down	5	
25Jan03-8SA	fst	7f		:22	:44^3	1:09^2	1:22	4↑ⒻSntMncaH-G1	101	5	6	4^{1½}	3^{nk}	1^1	2^{½}	Bailey J D	LB115	*.70	95-07	Affluent119^{½} Sightseek115^{1½} Secret of Mecca110^3	Bid 3wd,led,willingly	7	
29Nov02-9Aqu	fst	1		:23	:45	1:09^3	1:35^2	3↑ⒻTopFlgtH-G2	100	7	2^{½}	4^{1½}	2^{½}	2^{½}	1^{1¾}	Bailey J D	L113	*1.40	89-19	Sightseek113^{1¾} *Zonk*116^{¾} Nasty Storm116^{5½}	Stalked wide, clear	9	
9Oct02-8Kee	fst	7f		:22^3	:45^4	1:11^2	1:23^4	ⒻRavenRun-G3	98	7	11	5^{2¼}	4^{1¾}	2^1	1^{3¼}	Bailey J D	L117	*.90	85-23	*Sightseek*117^{3¼} Miss Lodi123^{hd} Respectful117^{6½}	Slow start,between,drv	12	
20Sep02-2Bel	fst	1 1/16		:23^1	:46^1	1:10^4	1:41^1	3↑ⒻAlw 48000n1x	99	1	2^1	1^{½}	1^{hd}	1^8	1^{12}	Bailey J D	L117	*.35	94-11	*Sightseek*117^{12} ClerDestiny117^{1½} *TresureBech*119^2	When asked, ridden out	7	
14Aug02-7Sar	fm	1	Ⓣ	:23^1	:46^1	1:11	1:35^4	3↑ⒻAlw 48000n2L	85	1	2^3	2^8	2^{½}	2^{½}	2^{¾}	Bailey J D	L117	*.85	88-11	Title Nine119^{¾} *Sightseek*117^{1¼} Marquet Rent117^{5¼}	Dug in gamely inside	6	
28Jly02-2Sar	fst	6f		:22^2	:46	:58^2	1:11	3↑ⒻMd Sp Wt 45k	89	7	6	5^{1½}	3^1	1^{1½}	1^{7¾}	Bailey J D	L118	1.70	87-14	Sightseek118^{7¾} Truly a Legend118^{1½} Adversity118^{2¾}	Going away, driving	7	

Figure 12-8: Past performances for Sightseek, a horse for course.

Chapter 13

Planning Your Wagers

• •

In This Chapter

▶ Thinking like a winner

▶ Creating a plan of attack

▶ Identifying your winning pattern

• •

he sizzle in horse race betting focuses on the beginning and end of the process and hardly ever on the middle. The front part is the handicapping involved in searching for contenders, picking winners, and eliminating losers. The back end pertains to watching the races, making trip notes, and learning from what you just saw.

What gets short shrift is the middle part that I call *planning your wagers*. Focusing on this part is critical if you want to become a winning horseplayer. Finding the right horses to bet isn't enough. You need to plan how you want to invest in the straight pools and exotic wagers (see Chapter 15). You need to allow yourself a chance to almost be right and still win money. All the components of planning your wagers go part and parcel into becoming a winning horseplayer, and this aspect of horse race betting may be the most difficult to master.

A Winning Strategy: What's the Big Deal?

Here's a classic example of the modern day horseplayer: You looked at the races in the *Daily Racing Form* (covered in Chapter 11) the night before, but your main handicapping occurs this afternoon, going track to track, race to race. Now you find a race you really like. You spend a whole eight minutes handicapping it. You look up and see that *post time* — when the race starts — is in three minutes.

Getting shut out — No sweat

Getting *shut out* (running out of time and not getting your bet in) is common. It may happen on your first visit to the racetrack. Getting shut out is no big deal, but a lot of horseplayers make a federal case out of it.

A few reasons horseplayers lose track of time and get shut out include

✔ Getting into a conversation

✔ Becoming engrossed in handicapping multiple races

✔ Standing in a betting line behind some very slow horseplayers

Here's the skinny on getting shut out: In the long run, you save money. Remember that a majority of the bets you make are losers. You seldom get shut out of a bet that would've made you a big score. And you know what? If the bet was that important, you should've gotten in the betting line sooner. The only person to blame is yourself, regardless of all the excuses or circumstances.

You run up to the betting windows but have to wait in line behind a couple horseplayers. In your mind, you try to figure out how to play the race: exactas, trifectas, daily doubles, pick 3s (exotic wagers are covered in Chapter 15). You get up to the *mutuel clerk* (the person at the betting window who punches out your wagers) as the horses are loading into the starting gate. You call out bet types and numbers (see Chapter 4 for details about the betting process). A few tickets are punched out. The bell goes off, and betting ends for the race. You're not sure what you actually bet, but you do have action on the race.

Is this betting scenario a winner's profile? I don't think so. You may win some and lose some betting this way. But in the long run, it's a loser's profile. Figuring out the betting strategies, meaning which types of bets you want to use and how you're going to use the horses you like, is just as important as handicapping the races.

A horseplayer is not going to divide his time 50/50 between handicapping and strategizing his wagers. But if you plan for at least a two-to-one split — five minutes of bet planning for every ten minutes of handicapping — you have a fighting chance instead of helter-skelter wagering.

Getting To and From the Betting Window with Your Game Plan Intact

When you wager, you want to be organized and orderly. Writing down your bets and checking your tickets for mistakes are two simple ways to make sure your game plan is in tact. Remember: You're betting hard earned money, so you want to do it right.

Writing down your bets

If you make a straight bet (win, place, or show bets are covered in Chapter 4), writing your bets down isn't important. Your short-term memory can handle that. But in the case of exotic wagers, writing them down is a good idea for two reasons:

 ✔ You want to ensure your bets cover the horse or horses you like the most. If those horses run well, you want to maximize your profits.

 ✔ You don't want to be hemming and hawing at the mutuel window.

If you're not sure what bet you want to make, you have no business being in the betting line. Also, you may leave out a bet that covers one of your key horses. To think you've won a race and then look at your tickets and discover that your betting was flawed is a bad feeling.

If you have your plan laid out and your bets written down, you don't have to worry about making any mistakes when you reach the mutuel window. This extra step can save you money and heartache down the road.

Checking your tickets for mistakes

Even though you're less susceptible to mistakes when you have your bets written down, mistakes still happen. Some occur because of the noise pollution at the betting windows.

Maintaining your composure

Bet enough horse races, and some bad things happen along with the good. Here's a litany of things that may very likely happen to you:

 ✔ You get shut out, and the bet would've won.

 ✔ You think you've won and find out your ticket was punched wrong.

 ✔ You won the race, but the stewards disqualify your horse, making your tickets worthless.

Though your reasons for being upset are valid, getting mad doesn't do any good. Gambling endeavors like betting on horse races can cause incredible mood swings. You're king of the world one minute and the lowest of the low later on. Regardless of the situation, you have to keep your composure. (I realize this is easier said that done.) Allow yourself to vent a little bit, but remember that a temper tantrum doesn't get your money back. Levelheaded thinking might. There's an old cliché horseplayers use: "Just turn the page," meaning move on to the next race.

Mistakes can happen if the mutuel teller can't hear you and punches your ticket wrong. Whose fault the error is doesn't matter. What's important is to get the bets correct.

Take a few seconds to scan your tickets before you leave, and you can rest assured that your bets were placed correctly. If there's a mistake, show the mutuel clerk. He'll cancel that ticket and punch out a new one for you.

Developing a Winning Pattern of Wagering

At some point in your horse racing growth, you evolve from the novice/newcomer level to the casual fan. From there, you move into weekend warrior status and then graduate into a regular horseplayer. Your experiences range from the sublime, when everything you do turns out roses, to the ridiculous, when you lose every photo finish, get disqualified out of winners, and make every wagering mistake known to man.

You can control some of the circumstances in horse race betting — namely, your handicapping and wagering. But for those circumstances you can't control, just forget about them. Luck, in the long run, is supposed to even out.

Figuring out what kind of horseplayer you are

Your pattern of wagering starts with knowing your own personality. Have you ever taken a personality test at your workplace? You know — the kind where a person falls into categories like introvert versus extrovert. Can handle criticism or can't handle it. Sees the glass half-full or half-empty.

Horseplayers should be required to take a similar personality test. I think you'd find some horseplayers are risk takers, while others prefer playing close to the vest. Some are *chalk players* (see the sidebar, "The chalk"), while others like long shots. Some are win bettors, while others like the pick 4 or pick 6. (I cover exotic wagers like the pick 4 and pick 6 in Chapter 15.)

I believe your personality helps shape the type of horseplayer you become. Some handicapping books subscribe to a heavy-handed theory of betting — my way or the highway. Although the end goal of making money is the same, individual horseplayers find the methods that suit them best for winning at the races. The way to discover the best method for you is to know your personality and to be honest about your limitations. If you can't stand losing, make higher percentage plays like straight bets. If you're a risk taker that can withstand long losing streaks before cashing a big ticket, then you're fine playing exotic wagers like the pick 4, pick 6, and superfecta. Playing the ponies is supposed to be fun and profitable at the same time.

Keeping track of your bets

Discipline is a word you hear a lot in any form of gambling. Losers are undisciplined. They keep betting until every dollar in their pockets is gone. They bet when they have no edge or advantage, and simply put, they take the worst of the odds in betting when they shouldn't.

Winners are disciplined, or at least disciplined enough, to make good betting choices. To find out where your strengths and weaknesses are as a bettor, try keeping a diary of your bets. Writing down your bets is tedious work, but by doing so, you create a history of your actions to learn from. Table 13-1 illustrates a simple log for keeping track of your bets.

Table 13-1				A Simple Betting Log			
Date of Race	Racetrack	Horses, Odds	Race Type	Bet Amounts	Bet Types	Results	Notes
July 4	Churchill Downs	Perfect Drift, 5/2	Stephen Foster Handicap	$10	Win and place	Won, $7.20 and $3.80 +$35	
July 4	Churchill Downs	Perfect Drift, 5/2 Roses In May, 4/1	Stephen Foster Handicap	$2	Exacta box	Won, $19.40 +$15.40	

The chalk

Chalk is part of the colorful phraseology used in horse racing. Its origin comes from the old book-maker days of the sport. Before modern technology, the races were written in chalk on black boards. As the odds of the horses changed according to the betting, the writer erased the old odds and wrote in the new odds. As you can figure, the favorites' odds changed more often than the long shots' odds. Because the writer had to keep erasing and writing the ever-changing odds in chalk, the race favorites became known as the *chalk*.

When you keep track of your bets, you discover a pattern of wagering that wins for you. Perhaps you consistently win on the same type of races and lose on others. Find your strengths, wherever they are, and minimize your weaknesses.

Allowing yourself to almost be right and still win money

Allowing yourself to almost be right and still win money is a method of wagering in which you don't put all your eggs in one basket. Think of this method as diversifying your portfolio; only instead of your investment portfolio, I'm talking about your betting portfolio.

For example, you handicap a race and find two contenders you really like. How do you bet to maximize your winnings? Depending on the win odds, you may bet both horses to win, which is known as *dutching* (betting more than one horse to win a race). The win odds should be high, 8/1 or more. If you make $2 win bets on two horses at 8/1 odds, you get back at least $18 if one wins — pretty good for a $4 investment. If the horses are among the favorites, the bet is poor. If you make $2 win bets on two horses at 3/1 odds and one wins, you get back at least $8, which, considering the risk, is a poor return on your $4.

Chapter 14

Making the Most of Your Bankroll

Making the most of your betting bankroll is an overlooked part of gambling. I dedicated a chapter to the topic because it's that important. Lots of pitfalls can occur — like betting with your heart and not your head or losing your discipline when something bad happens — and I've suffered most of them myself. The discipline needed to win will make sense to you in the long run.

For the purposes of this chapter, a *bankroll* is a $100 one-day limit as your betting nest egg for the afternoon. Keep in mind that a bankroll also refers long-term to the amount you've set aside as gambling money. Most experts recommend that your gambling bankroll be separate from the household account, so you aren't guilty of dipping into the rent or grocery money to gamble on. You should never gamble with money you can't afford to lose.

Knowing Your Own Personality and Temperament

I hate losing money, and you should too. Knowing this about myself, I try to break up bad betting cycles by being extra careful with my prime plays or by abstaining from betting for a while to freshen up mentally.

In my job as a public handicapper for the *Las Vegas Review-Journal,* a lot of racing fans follow my picks for the Southern California racetracks (Del Mar, Hollywood Park, Santa Anita Park). Losing my own money is bad enough, but I feel worse if I'm losing other people's money when I'm in a slump.

How do your personality and temperament fit with your betting style? If you're a conservative person, you may not be well suited for betting *exotic wagers* (see Chapter 15) like the *pick 4* or *pick 6,* in which you must select four straight or six straight winners, respectively. With these wagers, losing a long string of bets before winning one is common. A conservative person may need to concentrate on *straight bets* (win, place, and show) or *exacta wagers* (see Chapter 4) to keep your equilibrium, and maybe even your sanity.

Many horseplayers find a steady diet of straight bets too boring. If you like to fire it up and go for a big score, then who am I to dampen your enthusiasm? That type of personality, which I call a risk taker mentality, is better suited to handling a long losing streak before the whopper bet comes in.

Knowing yourself shapes the type of horseplayer you become. Just promise me that if you're a risky bettor, you have some checks and balances on your bankroll. Exhausting your bankroll way too soon is no fun.

Keeping Your Emotions in Check

Regardless of your job, outside interests, or family and friends, emotion plays a big part in your life. However, when you gamble, your emotions need to be held in check. Gambling takes focus, skill, knowledge, and intestinal fortitude. To be a winning gambler, you want to be analytical, not emotional.

Oh, there's a time to cut loose, like on the verge of a big win. Andy Beyer, an award-winning horse racing columnist for the *Washington Post,* wrote in his book, *Picking Winners: A Horseplayer's Guide* (Houghton Mifflin), that it's not appropriate to root in the press box for a big score unless it's worth at least a good portion of your yearly income.

Playing horses is a cerebral activity. You go through all the preparation of handicapping the races (see Chapter 12 and 16), planning your wagers (see Chapter 13), and getting the bets on time (see Chapter 13). When it's *post time* (scheduled start time of a race), and the horses start running, rooting on your horse or horses is a release of your emotions. But before the bell rings and the race starts, you need to be as focused as possible. You need to be calculating and cunning in playing the races.

Parimutuel wagering (see Chapter 3) means you bet against all the other horseplayers, whether they're at the racetrack or at simulcast (see Chapter 21) locations around the country. You're playing to have fun, but you're also playing to win money. Believe me when I say that having fun and winning money go hand in hand.

Making Your First Bet of the Day a Winning One

In 1986, I'd just taken a job as the public relations director at Turfway Park in Florence, Kentucky. I met Rick Cushing, the horse racing handicapper for the *Louisville Courier-Journal,* who first told me the line, "Make your first bet of the day a winning one." What Cushing meant was to take the necessary steps to make your first bet a solid play with an excellent chance of winning.

Too often, horseplayers rush to get into action by placing their first bet of the day before getting fully organized. This means you haven't gotten all the scratches and changes for the tracks you want to bet on, and you haven't looked at your handicapping notes from the night before. Planning your first bet and making the first bet a winning one put you in the right frame of mind for the day.

Preparation is vital to improving your chances of winning at the races. Buying the *Daily Racing Form* (see Chapter 11) minutes before the first race guarantees that your preparation is minimal, at best. Doing this doesn't mean you won't win, but you face an uphill climb betting against other horseplayers who did their homework the night before, or at least earlier that morning.

If you were to build a checklist of what you need to do to win the first bet, it would include the following:

✔ Buy and read the *Daily Racing Form* early — preferably the night before, but no later than breakfast time.

✔ Download pertinent handicapping material off the Internet.

✔ Give yourself a quiet period to handicap the races. Make your notes in the *Daily Racing Form.* Compare your notes with the handicapping material you downloaded off the Internet.

✔ Arrive at the racetrack, Las Vegas race book (see Chapter 23), or OTB (off-track betting parlor) early enough to get set-up. Take time to get the *scratches* (horses taken out of the races) and jockey and equipment changes, because they may affect your decision making.

✔ Rate the races so you know your strongest plays of the day, your action bets (see following section), and the races you want to skip entirely.

If you perform these tasks before you decide on your first horse bet of the day, you give yourself an excellent shot of winning the wager and getting the day off to a good start. Like a starting pitcher striking out the first batter on three pitches or a quarterback completing his first pass for a first down, winning your first bet is inherently positive.

Differentiating Your Bets: Action, Prime, and Going for the Score

Professional handicappers use their personal parameters for deciding which wagers are action, prime, or going for the score bets. An *action bet* is a small wager to have something to root for in a race. A *prime bet* should be one of your best bets of the day. And *going for the score* are bets like the pick 6, pick 4, or superfecta (see Chapter 15) that can make you a lot of money.

A term that you'll hear at the races is *finding value*. Finding value means betting overlays in the win odds and overlaid prices in exotic pools. If you can extract good value out of a race or races, then the likelihood of a bet increases. And the type of wager — action, prime, or going for the score — sometimes defines itself.

You should differentiate your bets, because doing so determines how you play your bankroll. If you bet half your bankroll going for a score, you stand an excellent chance of losing it all, because those are high risk, high reward bets.

Getting in on the action

Many authors of handicapping books suggest you should focus on your *primary bets,* meaning your best bets of the day, and wait for opportunities to emerge. That style is fine if you can sit like a monk and let many races pass without betting. Most horseplayers have more passion, however, and need to let their adrenaline flow a few times during the day. As a newcomer, I don't expect you to go to the racetrack and make only two or three primary bets.

My definition of an action bet is that it's a minor percentage of your bankroll. If your one-day bankroll is $100, an action bet is $2, $4, or $6 — a small percentage of your bankroll.

An action bet can be a 12/1 long shot you like, but not enough to make it a prime wager. An action bet for a novice bettor could be $2 to win. It may be a $2 across the board wager — meaning to win, place, and show — or a $1 exacta box (see Chapter 4) using other horses with your long shot.

If you win an action bet on a long shot horse, the bet can turn into a random score, meaning you may turn $2 into $30 or more. One of the beauties about betting on horse racing is that you can bet a little to win a lot.

Picking a prime bet

Prime bets are your strongest plays of the day. Prime bets are a function of your own ability to handicap, study the odds, and recognize value. You bet a higher percentage of your bankroll on prime bets.

I lump bets I call "bankroll builders" into the prime category. I consider a typical bankroll builder as a win bet on a 4/1 odds horse. Nothing fancy, but it sure helps your bankroll if you win $10 for every $2 you wagered.

A prime bet for a $100 one-day bankroll is between $12 and $15 a shot — allowing you to budget for four prime bets in a day. This strategy lets you gamble about half the money you brought to the racetrack on horses and race scenarios that you really like. You can then budget the other half of your one-day bankroll for action bets and a couple of going for the score wagers.

A prime bet can be as simple as betting a sharp 4/1 odds horse to win or to win and place, meaning to finish second. Or you can place a prime bet by using the horse you like in a *quinella* or *exacta box,* meaning you're betting on two horses to finish first and second. A prime bet may involve a *daily double,* where you like a couple horses in both legs and bet them accordingly.

Prime bets don't need to involve large long shots. If you make four prime bets in one day and win with two, you should finish close to even for the day and maybe turn a profit. If all four prime bets lose, at least you got beat betting on the horses you liked best. If all four prime bets win, you'll be eating steak for dinner instead of something off the 99¢ menu at the local fast food joint.

Going for the score

The definition of a *score* depends on the kind of horseplayer you are and how much you bet. As a beginning horseplayer, you can consider making a $50 to $100 profit on a small bet to be a *score.* For example, if you bet $15 and win $100, you're doubling your bankroll. Not bad. For a big bettor, a score may be a profit of $1,000, $10,000, or $100,000, depending on how much was wagered. So, as you can see, what a score constitutes is a personal measure.

With a $100 daily bankroll, you want to find situations where you can bet a little to win a lot. Certain types of wagers can produce big payoffs without you having to bet a lot of money or use huge long shots. Wagers that can produce big payoffs include the pick 3, pick 4, trifecta, and superfecta (see Chapter 15 on exotic wagers). With these bets, you try to link multiple horses and/or multiple races in a vertical or horizontal manner. *Vertical* means horses finish in the up and down positions of first, second, third, and even fourth place. *Horizontal* means to link sideways more than one race in a wager, such as the daily double, pick 3, pick, 4, and pick 6. The best way to get bigger payoffs is to beat favorites. Most bettors use the favorite, so if you can beat the favorite, the payoff on a winning ticket jumps up considerably.

A race favorite that looks unbeatable is called a *free bingo square* in horse racing. In bingo, the center square on a bingo card is a free square. Horse-players look at the most likely race winner the same way. The way to make money with a free bingo square is to play exotic wagers. In a vertical wager, you use some long shot horses underneath the surest winner to try and win an exacta, trifecta, or superfecta. In a horizontal wager, you use some long shot horses to try and win the daily double, pick 3, pick 4, and pick 6.

Of course, using lots of long shot horses potentially could lead to a big payoff. The expectancy is many of these bets will lose. One nice win, though, can make your day, week, and maybe even month.

Don't tie up a lot of money going for scores, unless you can stomach a lot of losses before hitting a home run. You need an iron constitution, the right mentality, and a sizable overall bankroll to handle day after day of losing.

Wagering a Little to Win a Lot

It's easy to get frustrated while betting the horses. Betting on horse races isn't like having a compound interest bank account that's FDIC insured. Your bankroll goes through rolling peaks and valleys. The winning streaks are a great ride. Inevitably, though, come the losing streaks when you can't even pick the winner of a one-horse race.

A tendency is to bet more money when you're losing to try and get even for the losses. That's a definite no-no.

Instead, you want to follow the racetrack axiom, *Bet a little to win a lot.* Horse race betting is a game of odds and trying to get the best return possible for your betting dollars. The system is perfectly set up for you to bet a few dollars, and if you're right, win enough money to sign an IRS form (see Chapter 3 to find out when the IRS form comes into play).

Bankroll builder plays

If you read the accompanying chapter, you can tell I really believe in bankroll builder bets, because I mention them more than once. Bankroll bets are an extension of prime plays (see "Picking a prime bet," earlier in the chapter). You're confident that your bet is going to win.

I use the bankroll builder strategy in real life and in tournament play. (In Chapter 18, I cover big money handicapping tournaments.) In the spring of 2003, my partner, Lou Filoso, and I won The Championship at The Orleans Handicapping Tournament in Las Vegas. We shared the first prize of $111,680. Our style of tournament play is different than most. Most tournament players don't bet a horse unless he has 10/1 odds or higher. Lou and I think differently.

Early in a tournament, we'll accept surest type winners at acceptable odds. Acceptable odds can be as low as 3/1, but the horse must look excellent on paper. We'll still make bets on long shots that are 10/1 odds and up. In essence, we're bankroll building within tournament competition.

In a big money handicapping tournament, it's not unusual for a champion horseplayer to score zero points for the week. That happens when you play 10/1 long shots and higher all week long. At those odds, you can lose 45 straight win bets in a handicapping tournament. In real life betting with your own money, if you lose 45 straight bets, your bankroll would be in woeful condition.

This approach is different from betting on sports or gambling at the casino. For example, football bettors need a big bankroll to last the whole season. Betting on a team to win yields 11/10 odds, meaning you bet $11 dollars to win $10. The bet has a huge house advantage of 10 percent, which is called the *vigorish*. In essence, vigorish in sports betting is the same as takeout in horse race betting. It's a tax the player pays for the privilege of wagering.

At the casinos, the most popular games are slot machines and video poker. The machines are calculated for a percentage of payout by the casino. By law, the casinos supply that information to the state gaming control board so the gambling is highly regulated, just like horse race betting is. Bottom line: In the long run, the casinos can't lose, but the slot players can. In horse racing, bettors have more control than slot machine players on how much they bet and who they bet their money on. That's why in my opinion, horse racing is a much better gambling proposition than slot machines are for the gambler.

In horse race betting, you can wager small amounts of money and win a lot because of the odds. This form of gambling is preferable because your skill can turn the odds in your favor. (Refer to Chapter 12 on handicapping.) For example, using exotic wagers like the exacta, trifecta, and daily double, you can bet a few dollars and win big. You use your handicapping skills to find long shot horses and beat the favorite, thus creating the value you're looking for.

Betting Favorites to Avoid Losing Streaks

A favorite, also called *chalk,* is a nasty word to a lot of horseplayers. Horseplayers who play chalk are frowned upon by their brethrens because they consider betting the favorites an almost wimpy thing to do. In Chapter 12, I cover how beating favorites is essential to creating *overlays,* meaning win odds higher than a horse's probability of winning the race. But, conversely, betting on favorites can also work to your advantage.

Finding beatable favorites is one of the first things you look for in handicapping. As you handicap, you find some chalks that are very strong — the most likely winners. Betting money to try to beat very strong favorites can be a fruitless pursuit. Instead, either pass the race (that's not a crime), or use the favorite as a single or key in an exotic wager (see Chapter 15).

A good time to use a strong chalk horse is when you want to break a losing streak. If the favorite is a free bingo square (see "Going for the score," earlier in the chapter), you can build a bet around that horse with the belief that it has a very high probability of winning.

Using Percentage Wagering over Same-Size Wagering

I want to shed light on an age-old handicapping discussion: percentage wagering versus same-size wagering. *Percentage wagering* means betting a percentage of your bankroll as the overall total moves up and down. Depending on the initial size of your bankroll, the percentage may be as small as 1 percent.

Say you begin with a $1,000 bankroll for the season. If you wager 2 percent of the bankroll, your first bet is $20. If the bet loses, the bankroll is reduced to $980. The second bet is another $20. If that loses too, the bankroll drops to $960. The next bet theoretically is $19, if you round to the nearest dollar.

If you're unlucky enough to lose ten straight bets, your bankroll shrinks to $816, and your most recent bet is $17.

Bottom line, the idea is to bet more money when you're winning and less money when you're losing. This premise is good, because in a long losing streak, the size of your wagers get smaller as your bankroll diminishes.

Same-size wagering means you wager the same size bet every time, regardless of whether you're winning or losing. The idea of same-size wagering is a reaction to differing amounts wagered on action and prime bets (see "Differentiating Your Bets: Action, Prime, or Going for the Score," earlier in the chapter). I believe action bets should be small with more money invested in prime plays.

Other horseplayers don't like to differentiate between action and prime bets. To them, a bet worth making is a bet worth winning.

Compare the following example with percentage wagers earlier in this section. Starting with a $1,000 bankroll, $20 wagers, and ten straight losing bets, the bankroll drops to $800. After ten losing bets, the bankroll difference is $16, between $816 and $800. Ten bets is a tiny bet sample. Run out the numbers over hundreds and even thousands of wagers, and the difference is huge. What's more, when you're winning, the percentage bankroll increases faster than the same-size bankroll, because the bet size is mushrooming.

Whatever you do, practice discipline with your bankroll. If you bring $100 to bet for a day at the racetrack, and you bet $20 to win and place as your first bet, you stand a good chance of *tapping out* quickly, meaning you lose your stake or bankroll. Using 40 percent of your bankroll for one play is too much.

Chasing Your Losses: Don't Do It

Comedian Tim Conway uses this joke in his comedy routine: "For the last 30 years, I've been chasing the first $5 bet I ever made on a horse race."

It's funny but true. Chasing your losses in horse racing can be like a dog chasing its tail. Human emotion in gambling has to be kept in check (see "Keeping Your Emotions in Check," earlier in the chapter). If you're having a losing day, human nature is to try and win the money back quickly.

I can tell you from personal experience that trying to win the money back quickly seldom works out. Why do you think racetracks and casinos have bank ATM machines in all the right places? You lose your gambling stake for the day, so you reach into your wallet for your ATM or credit card and withdraw more money to chase. Once in a while you break even for the day or perhaps win some money. But most of the time your losses multiply.

So what should you do? Cut your losses for the day, and stop betting. It's easier said than done, but your bankroll ran out because the prime bets (see "Picking a prime bet," earlier in the chapter) didn't win, and the action bets (see "Getting in on the action," earlier in the chapter) were, well, just action bets. Trying to force the issue when you're under pressure is not a good response.

When you try to chase your losses, your state of mind changes. You force your plays, placing prime bets on marginal horses. Using a sports analogy, betting this way is like a football player trying to score a 14-point touchdown or a baseball batter trying to hit a 6-run homer. The advantages you've built into your prior bets, solid handicapping, betting overlays, and positive expectancy all go out the window. Basically, you're betting more money on a horse or horses that you don't like a whole lot.

Staying Within Your Means: Scared Money Never Wins

Your betting bankroll should be separate from your household account. You've heard of the phrase "betting the rent money," which in the movies is an edgy thing to do. In real life, betting the rent money is stupid, but it happens. There are professional gamblers who make a living at it, but only a select few succeed. And when they go bad, they don't bet their mortgage.

Making a living at gambling takes a disciplined mind. It's very difficult. I live in Las Vegas where professional gamblers chase the dream. Even the good ones *tap out* from time to time, meaning they lose their stake or bankroll.

For those of you who bet on horse racing for fun and entertainment, the rules are different. If you bring $200 to the racetrack — half to bet with and half to entertain with — it's discretionary income. You can take the profits and go to Disneyland with the family or take your wife or husband to a Broadway show. The beauty of horse racing is it's part sport, part entertainment, and part gambling, and you can have fun trying to win your expenses back, and then some.

If you bring household money to the casino or racetrack, that money is called *scared money* in the gambling business. And the axiom is that "scared money never wins." You have so much pressure on you to win and not lose that thinking clearly is next to impossible. Exhibiting discipline is a key to winning, and betting with the rent money is not showing any discipline at all.

If you only bet the amount of money you can afford to lose, you aren't any worse off at the end of the day, and you may just get lucky and take home a little more.

Part IV

Risky Business: Tackling More Advanced Bets

In this part . . .

Now you're ready to kick your handicapping into high gear. You want to earn your summa cum laude in picking the ponies, and you find out in this part that one of the best ways to advance in your betting is to start using handicapping tools that take in factors like feet per second, wind velocity, and deceleration. They give you a tremendous edge playing the horses, but they also come at a price.

You also find out about exotic wagers like the pick 6, pick 4, and superfectas that pay off regularly in the five- and six-figure range. I show you how handicapping tournaments are a way to turn an investment of a few hundred dollars into $100,000 or more. Then I get into the Triple Crown — the Kentucky Derby, Preakness, and Belmont Stakes — and explain why picking the Derby winner early isn't just for bragging rights but can make you a lot of money too.

Chapter 15

Betting Exotic Wagers

. . . .

In This Chapter

▶ Seeing the value in exotic wagering

▶ Placing bets on multiple horses

▶ Betting on more than one race

▶ Developing a style of betting

. . . .

At various points in this book I compare betting on horse racing to playing the stock market to describe the levels of play as far as risk versus reward goes. Some market plays are much riskier than others, but you can make more money. Your decisions depend on your bankroll and your personality. Comparing risk and reward correlates well into horse race betting.

This chapter covers exotic wagers, which include multiple horse and multiple race wagers. You can choose inexpensive ways to play, but then your margin of error becomes very small. The more bankroll you have, the more horses you can include on your tickets. Exotic wagering is a fun way to bet the horses, because with a relatively small outlay, you can win more money — maybe even enough to have to sign an IRS form.

Getting Value from an Exotic Wager

When betting on horse races, you constantly hear the axiom "trying to bet a little to win a lot." In *straight betting* — betting to win, place, and show (see Chapter 4) — sometimes making a worthwhile play takes too much money out of your bankroll. Also, grinding out profits using just straight betting is very difficult in the long run because of the *takeout,* which I discuss in more detail in Chapter 3.

Every one of us, unless you're Donald Trump or Steve Wynn, is gambling with a finite bankroll. From time to time, it's worth taking a calculated risk to go for a *score* — cashing a big payoff by playing *exotic wagers* that entail multiple horses, multiple races, and often times a combination of the two. Keep in mind, though, that exotic wagering is risky business. Most of the horseplayers I know use a strategy of combining straight wagering and exotic play to maximize their profit potential.

A common betting error is to make all exotic wagers and forsake a win bet on a horse you like. For example, an improbable horse messes up your exotic wagers, but your key horse wins, and you don't have so much as $2 to win. Even a small win bet on your key horse can cover your investment and maybe generate a small profit, regardless of the outcome of your exotic wagers.

The number one thing to remember in making an exotic wager is this: *In order to get a lot of value, you must beat the race favorite.* Even if you can win with the second or third choice in the wagering, your advantage is multiplied. A $10 winner may not sound like much. But if you defeat a 7/5 favorite, you've separated yourself from a lot of chalk players. (*Chalk* is a horse racing term for the race favorite.) Singling a strong favorite makes sense at times, but another horse or two in the vertical or horizontal bet must be a long shot to make the play worthwhile. (Exotic wagers are bet either vertically — up and down — within a race, like the exacta, quinella, trifecta, and superfecta, or horizontally — sideways — using multiple races like the daily double, pick 3, pick 4, pick 6, and place pick all.)

You'll hear the phrase *the power of the mid-priced horse* as you move on in handicapping. I define *the mid-priced horse* as a winner in the $10 to $15 range. Horses in this range aren't *pure long shots,* which are classically defined as 10/1 odds or more. But if you have a string of mid-priced horses that are 4/1, 9/2, 5/1, and 6/1 in your exotic wagers, you'll be handsomely rewarded. Horses at those prices are much easier to come by than 20/1 bombs. So a steady diet of mid-priced winners is good for your bankroll.

Making Multiple-Horse Bets

Multiple-horse bets like the *exacta* (first two finishers in order), *trifecta* (first three finishers), and *superfecta* (first four finishers) are tricky bets for newcomers but are major weapons in the betting arsenal of veteran horseplayers.

When dealing with multiple horse bets, you lose many more bets than if you just wager to win, place, and show. But if you want to cash a *signer* (any winning ticket large enough that by law you must complete an IRS form before the racetrack can pay you), placing multiple-horse bets is a path you need to take at some point.

TIP

Beating the tax man

In the business of betting on horse races, cashing *signers* (large winning tickets that require you to complete an IRS form before the racetrack can pay you) is a wonderful feeling. But wait a minute! What if I told you there's a legal loophole that allows you to win a big bet and not have to fill out an IRS form?

When you make an exotic wager using multiple horses and/or multiple races, always use a $1 bet unit as long as it's available. The IRS taxes your race winnings at 300/1 odds or higher for a $2 bet. However, when you make the same type of bet using a $1 unit, you don't start paying the IRS until

your race winnings are at 600/1 odds or higher. You save time because you don't have to fill out an IRS 1099 gambling earnings form, and you save money because the IRS takes 28 percent of your winnings. Winning more than $5,000 is when they take money off the top, and winning less than $5000 is just reported as income.

If you itemize your tax return each year, you can deduct gambling losses up to the amount of your IRS declared winnings. So you get that 28 percent back, but you have to wait a long time to get it. Why let Uncle Sam hold onto your money when you can use it right now?

Exacta

The most common multiple horse wager is the *exacta* (see Figure 15-1), which is when you wager on the first two finishers in exact order. In some horse racing venues it's called a *perfecta* or *exactor,* but you get the idea.

Figure 15-1:
A mutuel ticket of a 3-horse, $1 exacta box.

```
    SUNSET STATION

      89524-0D8F-6B70

  Race  5    26-Dec-03 186
              FAIRGROUND

   $1  EXA BOX          $6
      1,2,8

    6 BETS. TOTAL        $6

  59534   W:005909        10896
  26Dec03             12:20:38
      89524-0D8F-6B70
```

Courtesy of Station Casinos

The mutuel ticket in Figure 15-1 clearly shows that three different horses have been selected to use in the exacta bet. To *box* means you've used all three horses in both the win and place position. To win this particular exacta box, two of your three horses must finish first and second.

I like to mix horses of contrasting running styles and at least one good long shot to give the ticket value. For example, if the best horse looks like a speedball, I look for stalkers and closers to finish with him.

If you put an exacta ticket together with three speed horses, chances are good that not all three will last to the finish because they'll kill each other off. If a closer looks like the best horse, and you box a closer with two other closers, odds are good that all three of them won't get there either.

Quinella

In *quinella* wagering, you must have the first two finishers, in either order, to win the bet. All racetracks offer exacta wagering, but quinellas aren't universally offered. Some racetrack executives believe that the quinella pool cannibalizes the exacta pool. The term *cannibalizing* means that the quinella pool eats away at the exacta pool rather than creates any additional betting.

That way of thinking is foolhardy! The advantage of betting a quinella instead of an exacta comes when the horses you like are roughly the same odds. In this case, you're maximizing your investment. A quinella's advantages especially come into play when you like two favorites.

If one of the horses you like is a nice long shot, I recommend an exacta box instead of a quinella bet. If your long shot wins, your exacta explodes in value. Meanwhile, the quinella pays the same whether your horses came in 1/2 or 2/1, and it results in a significant loss of parimutuel value.

Trifecta

As the prefix *tri* suggests, you need to have the first three finishers in exact order (first, second, third) in a *trifecta*. Connecting two horses and hitting an exacta is much easier than hitting a trifecta. But the chances of making a score on a trifecta increase if you can make a long shot horse finish *in the money* — meaning first, second, or third — and God forbid, get two long shot horses to finish in the money.

Betting trifectas in a way that allows you a good shot of winning may eat into your bankroll rather quickly. But some races may lend themselves to trifecta wagering, especially if the favorite looks pretty weak and you really like a particular long shot.

One way to lower the cost of the ticket is to take a stand on the win end. For example, if you think the number seven horse is the most likely winner, you key that horse to win the race on top of the trifecta and put the other horses underneath it (see "Keying a horse," later in the chapter). Figure 15-2 shows an example of a $1 trifecta keying a horse to win over three other horses.

Figure 15-2:
A mutuel ticket of a $1 trifecta keying one horse over three others.

```
SUNSET STATION
    D5023-3FE3-6B52
Race  9   26-Nov-03 279
          AQUEDUCT
$1  TRIFECTA          $6
  7 with 2, 8, 11 with 2, 8, 11
  6 BETS. TOTAL       $6
59537   W: 005902        9044
26Nov03              13:11:20
      D5023-3FE3-6B52
```

Courtesy of Station Casinos

Here are the costs of some basic $1 trifecta plays:

- 3 horse box (6 combinations): $6

- 4 horse box (24 combinations): $24

- Trifecta key over 3 horses (6 combinations): $6

- Trifecta key over 4 horses (12 combinations): $12

- Trifecta key over 5 horses (20 combinations): $20

Superfecta

If you take a winning trifecta and handicap the fourth place finisher too, you have yourself a *superfecta*. The superfecta horseplayers I know have a much larger bankroll than I have. They can afford investing a lot of capital chasing a big payoff with the knowledge that losing 10 to 12 superfecta bets in a row isn't just bad luck, but it's also extremely possible. In any horse race on any given day, any long shot in the field can run fourth.

The best advice I've gotten on superfecta wagering is to bet all the horses in the fourth spot. Doing so allows the random finish of a race to take over. For example, a long shot speed horse may hang on, or a long shot closer may pass enough tiring horses to finish fourth. But then, in trying to keep the cost of the ticket affordable, tough decisions need to be made on how many horses can be put in the first, second, and third positions.

The superfecta is for a seasoned professional, but if you want to dabble, I won't stop you. Just know that this bet is in the high risk category.

Here are the costs of some basic $1 superfecta plays. I've taken the liberty to use letters rather than horse numbers so you can follow along easier:

- Superfecta key over four horses (24 combinations): $24

- A / BC / BCDEF / BCDEF (24 combinations) $24

- AB / ABC / ABCD / ABCDE (16 combinations): $16

- AB / ABC / ABCD / ABCDEF (24 combinations): $24

- AB / ABC / ABCD / ABCDEFG (32 combinations): $32

- ABC / ABC / ABCDE / ABCDE (36 combinations): $36

The cost of the ticket grows or contracts exponentially with each horse you add or subtract. For example, in the last $1 superfecta that costs $36, the formula of ABC/ABC/ABCDE/ABCDE yields 36 possible four-horse combinations. If you eliminate the C horse from the win position only — AB/ABC/ABCDE/ABCDE — the cost drops to $24 because there are 12 fewer four-horse combinations. If you add an F horse to the fourth position only — ABC/ABC/ABCDE/ABCDEF — the ticket explodes upwards to $54 because 54 four-horse combinations are now possible.

Placing Wagers on Multiple Races

The birth of *multiple race wagers* came about as racetrack managers were trying to invent bets that would lead to larger payoffs. They began linking races together starting with the two-race daily double and continued linking more races together until they came up with the place pick all, which includes every race on the card. In this section, I discuss each of the multiple race wagers and look at some of their pros and cons.

With every chance of a higher reward in the form of a big payout, there's added risk in betting your money.

Daily double

The *daily double* was the first exotic wager at the racetrack. Horseplayers were challenged with betting on the winners of two consecutive races on one bet. The first daily double bet was made on the first two races on the card as a marketing tool to ensure that racing fans would arrive at the racetrack early.

Over the years, horseplayers shortened its name to "The Double," and it still remains one of the best bets on the wagering menu. Nowadays, some tracks offer a rolling daily double on every race from start to finish. Figure 15-3 shows an example of a $2 daily double using two horses in each race.

You'll find two big advantages for betting the double:

✔ You can see the win odds of the horses in the first race of the double. If you think the favorite is very beatable, the double payoff will normally exceed the parlay. A *parlay* means taking your winnings from one horse and betting it all on the next horse.

✔ You can see the probable payoffs for the double on the TV screens. Thus, you can accurately measure your risk versus reward.

Figure 15-3:
A mutuel ticket of a $2 daily double using two horses in each race.

Courtesy of Station Casinos

Pick 3

The *pick 3* entails picking the winners of three races in a row. For example, the California racetracks offer a "rolling pick 3," linking races 1–3, 2–4, 3–5, and so on through the end of the card.

The pick 3 is a very popular wager for two reasons:

- ✓ In the realm of risk versus reward, the pick 3 is pretty hittable, even for the weekend horseplayer.
- ✓ Nearly all tracks offer the pick 3 for a minimum $1 betting unit, making it a very affordable wager — even for those horseplayers with smaller bankrolls.

Figure 15-4 shows an example of a $1 pick 3 using three horses in each race.

Here are the costs of some basic $1 pick 3 plays (I use a letter to signify a horse):

- ✓ AB / AB / AB (8 combinations): $8
- ✓ ABC / ABC / ABC (27 combinations): $27
- ✓ A / ABCD / ABCD (16 combinations): $16
- ✓ AB / AB / ABCDEFGH (32 combinations): $32
- ✓ AB / ABC / ABCD (16 combination): $24

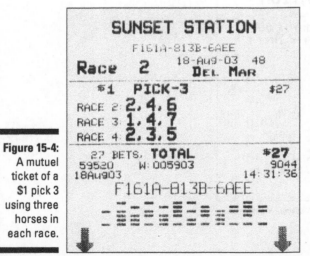

Figure 15-4: A mutuel ticket of a $1 pick 3 using three horses in each race.

Courtesy of Station Casinos

The cost is fairly affordable in using multiple horses in each race of the pick 3. In the example of using two horses in every race — AB/AB/AB — the cost is only $8 because you have only eight possible winning combinations (A/A/A, A/A/B, A/B/B, A/B/A, B/A/A, B/A/B, B/B/A, B/B/B). As long as the A or B horse wins each of the three races, you win the pick 3 bet.

Pick 4

In simplest terms, take a pick 3 and extend it out one more race and you have a *pick 4*. Picking four race winners in a row isn't easy, but you're handsomely rewarded if you can.

Like the pick 3, the pick 4 should always be bet for a minimum $1 betting unit. If you hit, why pay Uncle Sam a 28 percent tax on your winnings, when you can keep it all for yourself? (See the sidebar, "Beating the tax man," earlier in the chapter.)

Most racetracks card one pick 4 a day. In multi-race wagers, racetrack managers have the idea that if you stay alive on your ticket, you'll sit on your bet and not make any additional wagers. The smart ones will card two pick 4s, because horseplayers know it's one of the best bets in horse racing. Figure 15-5 shows an example of a pick 4 wager.

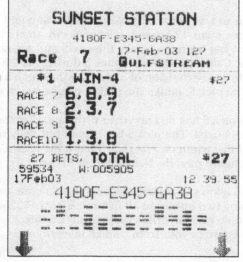

Figure 15-5: A mutuel ticket of a $1 pick 4 singling one horse and using three horses in each of the other three races.

Courtesy of Station Casinos

Here are the costs of some basic $1 pick 4 plays (I use a letter to signify a horse):

- AB / AB / AB / AB (16 combinations): $16
- A / ABC / ABC / ABC (27 combinations): $27
- A / AB / ABCD / ABCD (32 combinations): $32
- A / AB / ABC / ABCDE (30 combinations): $30
- AB / AB / ABC / ABC (36 combinations): $36

The additional fourth race in a pick 4 adds more cost to the wager compared to a pick 3. In the above example, I use two horses in each race. In the pick 3, the ticket costs $8, but in the pick 4, it costs $16. You now have 16 possible winning combinations for your bet.

For the biggest payoffs in your multiple race wagers, the most important favorite to beat is in the first leg, and here's why: The first leg is the only race where horseplayers can see the actual win odds. The public typically over-bets favorites, creating value for you. Beating the first favorite almost always creates an *overlay* price. An overlay is a horse or a payoff going off at much higher odds than warranted in comparison to its real chances of winning.

Pick 5

The first *pick 5* that I know of was started by Magna Entertainment Corp., Inc. in the spring of 2004. Magna owns 12 horse tracks in North America. Magna linked five races in a pick 5 bet from the tracks they own and operate. Later on, Santa Anita in Arcadia, California offered a pick 5 during the 2004 Oak Tree meet. The rules made it an extension of a pick 4 rather than a wager comparable to a pick 6. The pick 5, unlike the pick 6, can be bet in a $1 unit.

Also unlike the pick 6, the pick 5 has no carryover provision (see the following section) if no perfect tickets exist. The pick 5 bet is paid out daily regardless of whether anyone has all five winners. The pick 5 has a big future, because it has already produced six-figure payoffs. Not bad for a $1 bet.

The economy of the pick 5 allows small bettors to go for a score on a small bankroll. For example, using two horses in all five races costs $32 when bet in a $1 unit. If you beat a couple race favorites on your pick 5 ticket, you could easily cash a four- or five-figure payout from a small investment.

Pick 6

This bet is capable of changing your life. The *pick 6* is the one horse-racing bet that has paid out in the millions of dollars. And often times it pays hundreds of thousands of dollars. But the reason it pays out so much money is because picking six straight winners on one wager is awfully difficult.

Another factor in the high payout is cost. The pick 6 is a $2 minimum unit at most racetracks, which makes the cost of the wager pricey — too pricey for a lot of horseplayers and expensive even to those willing to jump into the pool.

My recommendation is to stay away from the pick 6 unless you think your handicapping skill level has advanced enough, and your bankroll is big enough to wager with the knowledge that your bet is most likely going to lose.

Here's why the pick 6 costs a lot (I use a letter to signify a horse):

AB / AB / AB / AB / AB / AB (64 combinations): $128

The pick 6 is the epitome of a multi-horse, multi-race, big-time exotic wager. You use multiple horses in races to increase your chances of winning each race. For example, if you use only one horse in each leg of the bet, your chances of losing are excellent. Using two horses in every race improves your chances, but winning the pick 6 is still a huge long shot.

If you don't have unlimited funds to invest in a big pick 6 ticket, you can do what lots of successful bettors do — find partners. Finding partners to share horse racing bets is easier than you think. There's power in having a larger bankroll to play with, so partnering up on bets is very logical.

If your partners aren't really friends but are more like business associates, then the sharing is called a *syndicate.* You may think a syndicate has mob connotations, but it's nothing of the sort. In a syndicate, a primary handicapper is in charge of organizing the pick 6 ticket and makes final decisions on which horses to play. Then after figuring out the cost of the pick 6, this person sells percentages to friends and acquaintances that want a piece of the action. Having more horses on a pick 6 ticket logically increases your chances of winning. I figure having a small piece of something is better than a whole lot of nothing.

The best time to play the pick 6 is when no one has hit it the day before, creating a *carryover pool.* A carryover pool is the money left from the pick 6 pool after the takeout is deducted and the *consolation tickets* have been paid. A consolation payout goes to those bettors with the most winners in the pick 6 races, which typically is five. In Southern California, a one-day carryover can be $75,000 or more, and in New York, it can be more than $30,000.

The carryover amount is added onto the next day's pick 6 pool, so if people win the pick 6 the next day, they're paid the natural payoff of the mutuel pool and a lot more money because of the carryover. Carryovers create a *positive expectancy* in the pool, which means even more to you if you didn't bet the pick 6 the day before. In other words, you aren't chasing your own money in the carryover pool; you're trying to win someone else's losing wagers.

Place pick all

The only state to offer the *place pick all* is California. To win a place pick all, you must select a horse to finish first or second in all races on the bet. That rule is constant, but the number of races can change. Usually the number of races on a card is eight, but it can be as many as nine or ten.

The bet is fun to play and cheap because you can buy in at a $1 unit. For example, my typical ticket consists of a single horse in four races and two horses in four races — costing me $16. If the ticket wins, it'll pay hundreds and even thousands of dollars. And because my horses only have to finish second and don't have to win, I'm rewarded sometimes for being almost right.

The greatest pick 6 win of all time

I witnessed the greatest pick 6 win of all time at the 1999 Breeders' Cup at Gulfstream Park in Hallandale, Florida. A group of my friends and co-workers, headed up by G. D. Hieronymus, were the only winners of the $5 million Ultra Pick Six offered on that year's Breeders' Cup races. After taxes, the winnings amounted to $3,058,138.

Many of us had worked together year after year on the Breeders' Cup Newsfeed. And each year, Hieronymus organized a pick 6 ticket and invited everyone to invest in it. That year, the ticket cost $192 and was shaped 2x3x2x2x2x2, or in other words, two horses in five of the races and three horses in leg two of the pick 6.

As each winner came in and the ticket remained alive race after race, the budding excitement was mind-boggling. In the Juvenile, a giant long shot named Anees won and paid $62.60. Horses like Anees that win are called *separators* because they eliminate a lot of live tickets.

The last leg of the pick 6 was the Breeders' Cup Classic. The Newsfeed ticket had the race favorite Behrens and a 19/1 long shot named Cat Thief from Hall of Fame trainer D. Wayne Lukas. At the top of the stretch, Behrens was nowhere in sight, but Cat Thief was gaining and then battling two other long shots — Budroyale and Golden Missile — for a quarter-mile before pulling away in the last 100 yards. Cat Thief paid $41.20 to win.

One of the Newsfeed workers asked me what I thought the winning ticket might pay. I guessed $300,000 or $400,000, figuring there'd be between five and ten winning tickets. When the mutuel prices went up, the track announcer said that the Ultra Pick 6 had one winning ticket. The Newsfeed crew had won more than $3 million! I had friends who bought new homes, financed college educations for their children, and funded their IRA. It changed people's lives and epitomized the meaning of going after a big score.

The place pick all has no carryover rule, so it's paid out at the end of the racing day to whoever selects the most races. Figure 15-6 shows an example of a place pick all.

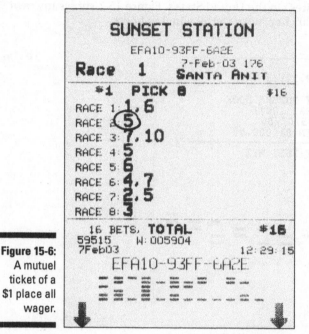

```
      SUNSET STATION
       EFA10-93FF-6A2E

Race   1      7-Feb-03 176
              SANTA ANIT

   $1  PICK 8           $16
RACE 1: 1,6
RACE 2: (5)
RACE 3: 7,10
RACE 4: 5
RACE 5: 6
RACE 6: 4,7
RACE 7: 2,5
RACE 8: 3

   16 BETS, TOTAL       $16
59515    W:005904
7Feb03                12:29:15

    EFA10-93FF-6A2E
```

Figure 15-6: A mutuel ticket of a $1 place all wager.

Courtesy of Station Casinos

Future bet

The name *future bet* defines exactly what it is: You're trying to pick the winner of a race or event to be held weeks or even months from now. A future bet is a house or book bet available primarily in Las Vegas.

Future bets aren't easy to handicap, even using a Ouija board. What makes future betting so enticing is getting high odds on a horse you like a lot. I wouldn't settle for anything lower than 50/1 odds. Believe me, it's 50/1 odds just to get to the race. Get 100/1 odds or more, and its time to get into the action. Comparing risk versus reward — figuring out whether you'll get enough value —should be the deciding factor in whether you make the wager.

Over the past few years, Churchill Downs in Louisville, Kentucky, has been offering a parimutuel Future Wager on its marquee races — the Kentucky Derby and Kentucky Oaks. Churchill Downs offers its Future Wager three times each during the months leading up to the Kentucky Derby and Oaks.

The Derby is always run on the first Saturday in May, and the Oaks is run on the Friday before the Derby. The Future Wager is a parimutuel pool, so you don't know your final odds until the pool closes on the Sunday of the weekend it's offered. Future Wager betting outlets include nearly all racetracks and OTBs (off-track betting sites) in the United States. Figure 15-7 shows my own future book bet on the 2005 Kentucky Derby winning horse.

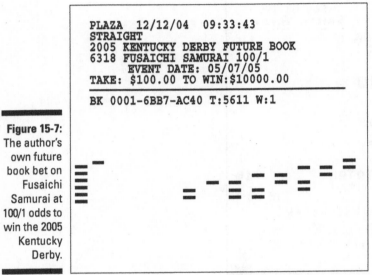

```
PLAZA  12/12/04  09:33:43
STRAIGHT
2005 KENTUCKY DERBY FUTURE BOOK
6318 FUSAICHI SAMURAI 100/1
        EVENT DATE: 05/07/05
TAKE: $100.00 TO WIN:$10000.00

BK 0001-6BB7-AC40 T:5611 W:1
```

Figure 15-7: The author's own future book bet on Fusaichi Samurai at 100/1 odds to win the 2005 Kentucky Derby.

Courtesy of Plaza Hotel and Casino

Betting Styles

I've said before — if I had to choose between being a good handicapper or a good bettor, I'd rather be a good bettor. Some horseplayers I know manage to put together beautifully constructed winning tickets, time and again. The thought process you want to implement is to allow yourself to be almost right and still win. In this section, I cover some styles of betting and define the terms. These betting styles are used when making exotic wagers.

Keying a horse

One of the most common betting styles is *keying* a horse. Most horses are keyed in the win position, meaning you're confident the horse will win the race, so you key the horse to win in a vertical exotic wager and use other horses in the second, third, and fourth spots underneath. For example, you may key a horse to win in the exacta and then put some horses in the place hole.

This style of betting is referred to as taking a stand — which may sound like a macho thing to do, but if you have a strong opinion, you should bet it accordingly.

The variables are endless when keying a horse. You want the key horse to run well and surround it with some long shot horses that create value. You're trying to play smart with your bankroll and are practicing good money management. (I cover money management in more detail in Chapter 13.)

On occasion, keying a horse in the place position makes sense, especially if it's a long shot. If you key a long shot on two tickets — one of them to win and the other to place — you can make a nice score if the long shot runs well.

Saving money with part-wheels

When you build a ticket to bet a multiple horse or multiple race wager, your bankroll determines how much money you can afford to invest. If the ticket needs to be cost-effective, most horseplayers use a *part-wheel*. A part-wheel is a way to be creative and economical using multiple horses in vertical and horizontal exotic wagers.

Your handicapping has narrowed down which horses you like. If money is no object, then you box (see "Boxing," later in the chapter) all the horses in a vertical exotic wager. A five-horse $1 trifecta box costs $60, and a five-horse $1 superfecta box costs $120. I don't know about you, but my bankroll can't afford that, and I consider it wasteful. This is where the part-wheel comes in.

Within your handicapping, you need to pare down which horses realistically can win. For example, if you bet a $1 trifecta part-wheel 2x5x5 — meaning two horses keyed to win with five horses in the place and show spot — the cost of the trifecta is reduced to $24. To reduce the cost from a $60 box to a $24 part-wheel, you need to take a stand on two horses to win the race.

Another $1 trifecta part-wheel example is a 3x4x5 — meaning three horses to win, four horses in the place spot, and five horses to show. That ticket cost $27 and gives you tremendous coverage of the five horses you like at less than half the $60 cost of a box.

Part-wheels come into play constantly in the daily double, pick 3, pick 4, and pick 6 wagers. Using numerous horses in each leg of these horizontal exotic wagers is too expensive. For example, a $1 pick 4 part-wheel 3x3x3x3 costs $81. If you have a $100 betting bankroll for the day, spending 81 percent of it on one wager is too much.

Exotic wagers were created to give horseplayers chances to bet a little money to make a lot. Good handicapping is necessary to come up with *live horses* (horses that have a good chance of winning), and you need creativity in betting the race. When you build a multi-race or multi-horse exotic wager, every horse you add to the ticket increases the cost. So, you must factor in the odds of winning the bet and how much you can win against how much the bet is going to cost. Using part-wheels keeps the cost of the ticket affordable.

Figure 15-8 shows an example of a $1 pick 3 part-wheel.

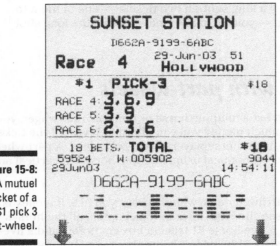

Figure 15-8:
A mutuel ticket of a $1 pick 3 part-wheel.

Courtesy of Station Casinos

Using the all button

One sure way to cover yourself in a position or in a race is to do a *wheel* or bet on all horses. In horse racing, it's called using the *all button*. Using the all button in a race or in the win, place, show, or fourth position is the only way to guarantee you won't miss a thing. But the downside is the increased cost of the ticket.

The all button helps by allowing randomness to work for you. I believe that in a trifecta or superfecta, almost anyone in the field can run third or fourth. Horses *outrun their odds,* meaning they run much better than their win odds on the tote board, all the time. Figure 15-9 shows an example of using the all button. I used every horse in race 8 of this pick 3.

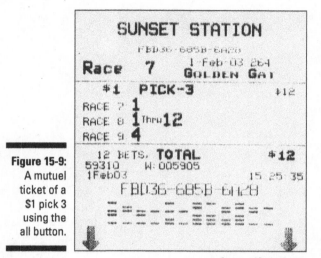

SUNSET STATION

Race 7   1·Feb·03 264
               Golden Gat

#1 PICK-3   #12
RACE 7 1
RACE 8 1 Thru 12
RACE 9 4

12 BETS TOTAL   #12
59310   W:005905
1Feb03   15 25 35

FB036-685B-6H28

Figure 15-9: A mutuel ticket of a $1 pick 3 using the all button.

Courtesy of Station Casinos

Boxing

Boxing, or using multiple horses in all positions of a wager, is done with vertical bets like the exacta, trifecta, and superfecta. For example, a three-horse $1 exacta box costs $6 (see Table 15-1 for more). To win, two of the three horses must run first and second.

Table 15-1	**Cost of a $1 Exacta Box, Trifecta, &**		
	Superfecta — Multiple Horses		
Type of wager	*3-horse box*	*4-horse box*	*5-horse box*
$1 Exacta	$6	$12	$20
$1 Trifecta	$6	$24	$60
$1 Superfecta	N/A	$24	$120

Your final handicapping (covered in Chapters 11, 12, and 16) of the race and how much money you want to spend determine whether to use a box or a part-wheel. You may like a few horses equally and some at high odds. So, if you box them, you're betting that you isolated the live contenders and then let randomness play out how they finish.

Chapter 16

Getting Into Sophisticated Handicapping

* * *

In This Chapter

▶ Utilizing advanced handicapping resources

▶ Putting your finger on class

▶ Understanding trip handicapping

▶ Handicapping guidelines that really work

* * *

*1*n any form of gambling, it seems like the people who win are luckier than those who lose. I believe in the adage, "Luck is the residue of design." Those gamblers who prepare diligently by doing their homework are luckier by design.

This chapter helps you become a so-called luckier horseplayer by taking your handicapping to the next level. The first half of this chapter introduces many sophisticated handicapping tools, which take a scientific approach to handicapping and are readily available to you. If you want to bet big money in the world of betting on horse races, you can't go out there armed with only a sharp stick. However, plenty of proficient handicappers make money relying on the *Daily Racing Form* past performances and good money management, as well as on their own eyes, ears, brains, and wits.

The rest of this chapter looks at situations you come across again and again. I see them every day during my handicapping work for *the Las Vegas Review-Journal*. I go over class comparisons, trip handicapping, and some common handicapping guidelines to improve your learning curve.

Taking a Scientific Approach: Advanced Handicapping Resources

Chances are if you're betting on horse races, you also like betting on sports like basketball and football. If you bet sports, I hope you don't handicap by picking up the morning newspaper, looking at the two teams' won-lost records, and choosing a side. To win betting on sports, you need to be a student of the game. The same goes in betting on horse racing.

In horse racing, the premise that the fastest horse wins the race isn't always true. The horse that gets to the finish line first wins the race — and that horse isn't necessarily the fastest. But it's important to know who the fastest horses are, so you can plot how a race will be run — something I call *developing the race shape*. Horse racing naturally lends itself to intense statistical analysis. Here are some of the factors that get analyzed:

- **Time:** Horse races are timed to a fifth of a second with fractional timing at various intervals.

- **Post position:** Horses leave from a starting gate where they're assigned different post position stalls. Quite naturally, horses with outside post positions have to travel a farther distance.

- **Length of trip:** A horse's trip is measured by the path of the racetrack a horse runs and whether it encounters any traffic trouble.

- **Weight carried:** Horses carry different assigned weights.

- **Energy:** Horses have a finite amount of energy to use during a race.

- **Wind speed:** The speed of the wind and whether the horses are running with the wind or into it make a huge difference.

- **Track variants:** Variants include whether the racetrack is fast, slow, or on par on a given day.

The list of variables within a horse race is a long one. Mathematicians and statisticians have developed handicapping products that horseplayers can use to decipher many variables that went into a horse race and use this information to project what will happen in future races. When a horse's performances can be boiled down into accurate numbers, these numbers become very valuable handicapping tools.

Beyer Speed Figures

Andrew Beyer, a horse racing writer for the *Washington Post,* created the *Beyer Speed Figures* — an important part of the horse racing lexicon. Beyer Speed Figures accurately measure the quality of a race run by a horse. Before

Beyers were first published in *The Racing Times* in 1991, the few handicappers who devised their own speed figures had a huge handicapping edge over the general betting public.

Beyers take into account the final time of the race and the inherent speed of the racing surface. The speed of the racing surface is different from day to day and from racetrack to racetrack. Weather and track maintenance are two big factors that come into play.

The ability to place an accurate numerical value on a horse's performance is an important handicapping tool. I've heard handicappers say they don't look at the Beyers or that Beyers are an inaccurate measure. I think those people do themselves a disservice. Beyers *tilt the tote board,* meaning that horses that run higher Beyers get bet by the public. And if more favorites are winning nowadays, Beyers must deserve some of the credit.

I cover Beyers Speed Figures in more detail in Chapter 11 and discuss many handicapping angles that utilize the Beyers — the most useful of which is eliminating horses that can't win. By using a safe sampling of Beyers numbers, you can reject horses that run too slow to win the race. If you don't purchase some of the speed figure products that I cover in the following sections, the Beyers in the *Daily Racing Form* provide a reliable measure that can supplement your own handicapping.

Formulator 4.0

The *Daily Racing Form* past performances are the cornerstone of any handicapper's work. Regardless of the supplemental materials a horseplayer purchases, you still refer to the *DRF* for putting your work together.

In April 2000, the *DRF* released a new kind of past performance computer program called *Formulator 1.0,* which gave the horseplayer creative freedom to manipulate past performance data and customize information to one's own handicapping style — all on a personal home computer.

The *Daily Racing Form* has introduced new product lines since then. In October 2000, *Formulator 2.0* brought on many more filtering elements. *Formulator 3.0* introduced the ability to access the lifetime past performances for every horse on the race card. *FormNotes* enabled users to insert their own personal comments into the past performances rather than rely on abbreviated chart comments.

In April 2004, *Formulator 4.0* was released with even more sophistication and information at your fingertips. The two biggest improvements are *Trainer Form* and *Full Chart Navigation.* You can click on tabs and see important trainer variables and full result charts from previous racing days.

In *Trainer Form,* you can click on the trainer's name in the past performance view and access queries within the enormous *DRF* database. There are 18 category analyses within *Trainer Form:* age, blinkers, class, class move, distance, jockey, Lasix, maidens, odds, purse, recency, sex, shipper, starts, surface, track circuit, trainer change, and winners.

For example, if trainer Todd Pletcher is running a maiden for the first time on the grass at Belmont Park with four weeks between starts, you can enter this information into *Formulator 4.0 Trainer Form.* The requested variables will be filtered through Pletcher's history to list detailed results of all Pletcher starters that fit that profile. That, my friends, is revolutionary stuff.

In *Full Chart Navigation,* you can click on a running line and produce a full *DRF* result chart instantaneously. You can also look at all the charts on that race card, the last three race charts in a horse's past performances, and the lifetime past performances for every horse listed in that one specific chart.

For more information about *Formulator 4.0* go to www.drf.com.

Ragozin Sheets

The way Andrew Beyer affected horse racing with his Beyer Speed Figures in 1991, Len Ragozin did ten-fold beginning in the late 1960s. Ragozin's father, Harry, was the one who actually started crunching numbers in the late 1940s to try to find the Holy Grail of handicapping — good *speed figures.* Eventually, Harry began producing his own speed figures that helped him win huge sums of money betting at the New York racetracks.

In 1962, Len Ragozin took his father's research and improved upon it. He began plotting the speed figures of horses on half-page sheets. *The Sheets,* as they're still called today, have a horse's racing history on them. Ragozin soon realized that horses don't run speed figures in straight lines, but in peaks and valleys with discernible patterns. Ragozin invented the term *bounce* to describe a horse that runs an extraordinarily fast race and regresses the next time out.

Ragozin's first clients were huge bettors that paid for his services and gave him a piece of their betting action. Eventually, he looked to expand and started producing The Sheets commercially out of his Greenwich Village office. The seal of approval that The Sheets had reached mainstream was when owners and trainers began using them to buy and race their horses. Today, The Sheets cost $35 per track per day and are mailed coast to coast to clients everywhere.

The Sheets give a rating for each race a horse runs. The rating signifies how much quality the horse shows that day. To come up with a rating, Ragozin examines these factors:

- ✔ Speed
- ✔ Weight
- ✔ Allowance for unusual track condition
- ✔ Racing wide or saving ground
- ✔ Headwinds or tailwinds
- ✔ Peculiarities of track construction, such as downhill areas

The lower the rating, the better the race. It's possible for a winning horse to earn a higher rating than a horse that finished behind him. In this case, the losing horse had a very difficult trip and the winner had a very easy one. For example, the winner may have run close to the rail the whole race and set very slow fractions — basically an easy trip. The loser may have run in the 5-path all the way around, lost a lot of ground, and had to check hard behind a tiring horse in the stretch, all pointing to a tough trip.

For more information about The Sheets, go to www.thesheets.com.

Thoro-Graph

Jerry Brown, president of Thoro-Graph, used to work for Len Ragozin in Greenwich Village producing The Sheets (see preceding section). In 1982, Brown branched off to form his own company, and the rest — as they say — is history. Thoro-Graph is a parallel product and is known for producing speed *figs,* which is short for figures.

The equation for making Thoro-Graph figs is listed on its Web site as "the time of the race, beaten lengths (a proprietary formula different than generally used), ground lost or saved, weight carried, and the effect wind may or may not have had on the time of the race." The final figure is tweaked manually to take into account a "carefully crafted track variant." Like The Sheets, the lower the number, the better the rating.

I'm not sure which product sells more — Thoro-Graph figs or Ragozin Sheets — but I know that Brown created new customers for the industry instead of cannibalizing existing customers away from The Sheets. Thoro-Graph figs cost $25 per track per day.

Both products have a lengthy client base among horsemen, although Brown earned more publicity in 1998 when he recommended the purchase of Victory Gallop as a 2-year-old. The Preston brothers bought Victory Gallop and saw him go on to win the Belmont Stakes.

For more information about Thoro-Graph, go to www.thorograph.com.

The Xtras on Equiform

I mention more than once in this book that I compare horse race handicapping and betting to playing the stock market. Cary Fotias, president of Equiform, is living proof that the comparison is valid. Equiform is another company that produces speed figure sheets, but the product is different from The Ragozin Sheets and Thoro-Graph.

Fotias had a natural affinity for games of chance and mathematical probabilities. He graduated from the University of Michigan and earned an MBA from Indiana University. He worked for eight years on Wall Street trading foreign currency. But horse racing was his calling, and he was a student of the game. He read all the handicapping books and used The Sheets for a period of time with success. Still, he believed something was missing, and he began tinkering with his own formulas.

Fotias was able to come up with his own product, which he called The Xtras. Some of what he puts into The Xtras include conditioning factors, pace, deceleration, velocity, feet per second, and ground loss.

Fotias, like Ragozin before him, saw that horses' performances don't improve and regress in a straight line. Fotias calls the improvement and regression a *form cycle*. Fotias's Xtras stress conditioning in a form cycle analysis with a New Pace Top. Other handicapping variables to look for in the Xtras are a Cyclical Pace Top and Delayed Pace Top. He has put all the information in his book, *Blinkers Off: New Frontiers in Form Cycle Analysis* (United Book Press, Inc.).

The Xtras cost $20 and $15 per track per day. For more information about The Xtras, go to www.equiform.com.

Brisnet

Brisnet stands for Bloodstock Research Information Services. Formed by the Broadbent family in the early 1970s in Lexington, Kentucky, Bloodstock Research has developed a wide array of excellent handicapping products for all levels of horseplayers.

For handicappers who want a horse's past performances with bells and whistles, Brisnet offers *Premium Past Performances* and *Ultimate Past Performances*. Premium Past Performances include extra features like par times, pedigree ratings, pace ratings, prime power, detailed trainer statistics, and comprehensive workouts. Pace ratings are extremely important because knowing who the likely pacesetters are going to be can firm up the race shape. Brisnet *Ultimate Past Performances* include additional comprehensive jockey and trainer statistics, prime power, pedigree ratings, and pedigree statistics.

Brisnet also offers *Winner's Choice* — a one-page racetrack overnight for simulcast horseplayers. Each sheet has numerous angles for each racetrack, including speed, class and pace ratings, best bets, lists for hot trainers/jockey combos, trainer angle plays, distance specialists, and a clocker's special workout report.

My tournament handicapping partner, Lou Filoso, likes using Brisnet's *Ultimate Race Summary,* which isn't to be confused with *Ultimate Past Performances.* The *Ultimate Race Summary* lists pace, speed, and final time figures; pedigree stats for dirt, turf, and mud; and the average winning distance for the sire's and the dam's offspring. It's all tremendously useful handicapping information.

On CD-ROM, Brisnet offers the *American Produce Record, European Produce Record, Maiden Stats, Sire Stats Book,* and much more. The CD-ROM products are just the tip of the iceberg of the Brisnet handicapping products. If you want a taste of being a sophisticated handicapper, go to www.brisnet.com and peruse the product line.

Pace numbers

The speed figures generated by the Beyers and Ragozin Sheets are based upon final times of the races. A different kind of handicapper develops *pace numbers,* which take into account the internal fractions of a race, meaning the first quarter-mile, half-mile, and so on.

Good pace numbers can help determine the race shape. For example, a race may have three horses that want the early lead. The casual fan may have no idea which of the three horses is fastest. But the horseplayer with good pace numbers knows. His pace numbers may tell him that horse A is much faster early on that horses B and C. Thus, the pace numbers determine that horse A is the speed of the speed and will outrun the other two.

In 1975, Dr. Howard Sartin, a clinical psychologist from Beaumont, California, set course on research that would mushroom into the *Sartin Methodology.* In typical horse racing lore, his discoveries came about when he was assigned to treat a group of truck drivers who were compulsive gamblers.

Sartin reasoned that the problem wasn't their gambling; it was their losing. So he set about finding a way for the truck drivers to become winning horse-players. Sartin assigned tasks within the group to analyze positive influences on the horses from more than 18,000 horse races. After hours upon hours of crunching numbers, the number one factor was *second call velocity* — better known as *Early Pace.*

Without getting overly technical, a couple keys of the Sartin Methodology for making pace numbers include identifying a paceline representative of what the horse could be expected to do in its current condition and a feet-per-second calculations for each horse.

Sartin Methodology was alien to horseplayers in 1975. Two books that take the study to new levels include Tom Hambleton's *Pace Makes the Race: An Introduction to the Sartin Methodology* (Henry House Publishers) and Tom Brohamer's *Modern Pace Handicapping* (Daily Racing Form Press). Brohamer is considered the leading expert on the original Sartin Methodology.

In all honesty, for those of you interested in following up on the Sartin Methodology, it's considered doctorate level material for the most sophisticated handicapper — which is why I include it in this chapter. You can find out more about pace numbers from a number of racing authors such as Steve Davidowitz, author of *Betting Thoroughbreds: A Professional's Guide for the Horseplayer* (Plume Books); Andrew Beyer, who has written numerous handicapping titles; as well as Dr. William Quirin, Tom Hambleton, James Quinn, Huey Mahl, Ray Taulbot, and Dick Mitchell, among others.

Sample pages

Here are samples of the *Daily Racing Form* and Brisnet past performances, Ragozin Sheets, Thoro-Graph figs, and Equiform Xtras for 2004 3-year-old Eclipse Champion Smarty Jones, winner of the Kentucky Derby and the Preakness.

I put all his past performance files together so you can make easy comparisons race-by-race among each of the handicapping products. For example, most experts consider Smarty Jones's best career race his win in the 2004 Preakness Stakes at Pimlico in Baltimore, Maryland. Smarty Jones's *Daily Racing Form* Beyer rating for the May 15, 2004 race was an outstanding 118 (see Figure 16-1). Compare the four other products in Figures 16-2, 16-3, 16-4, and 16-5 to see if they too gave Smarty Jones a career best speed figure.

Figure 16-1:
Daily Racing Form past performances for the career of Smarty Jones.

©2005 by Daily Racing Form, Inc. and Equibase Company

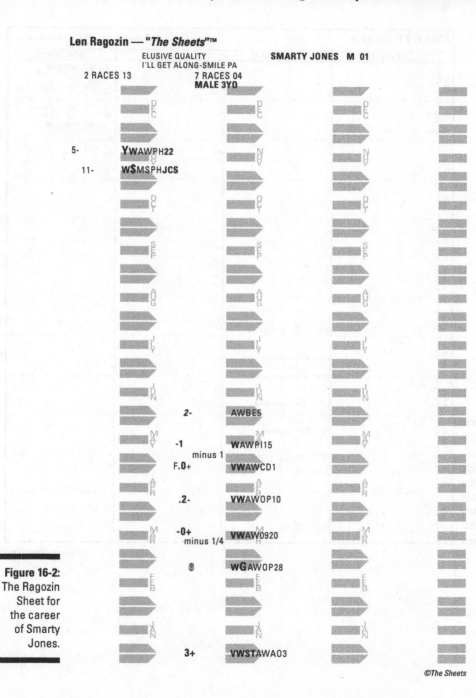

Len Ragozin — "*The Sheets*"™

ELUSIVE QUALITY
I'LL GET ALONG-SMILE PA
SMARTY JONES   M 01

2 RACES 13   7 RACES 04
                    MALE 3YO

5-   **Y**WAWP**H22**
11-   **W$M**SPH**JCS**

                    2-   AWBE5
                    -1   WAWP**I15**
                         minus 1
                    F.**0**+   **VW**AWCD**1**
                    .2-   **VW**AWOP**10**
                    -**0**+   **VW**AW09**20**
                         minus 1/4
                    ⑥   w**G**AWOP**28**
                    3+   **VW**STAWA**03**

©*The Sheets*

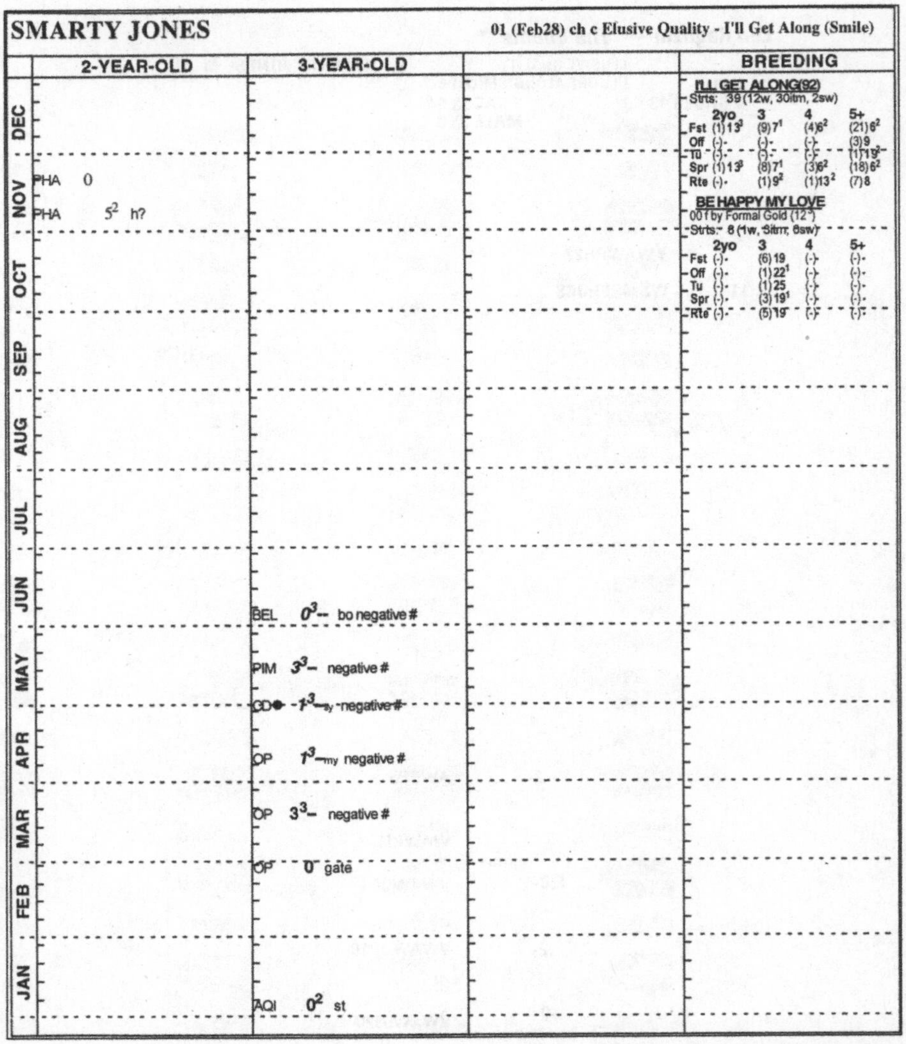

Figure 16-3: The Thoro-Graph Figs for the career of Smarty Jones.

Courtesy of Thoro-Graph

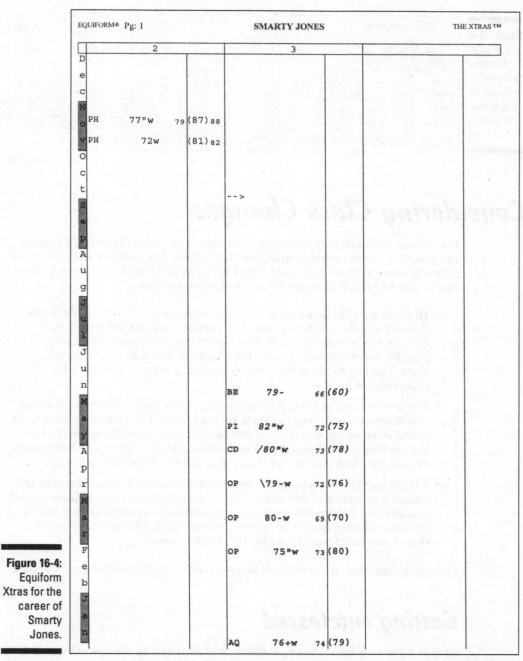

Figure 16-4:
Equiform Xtras for the career of Smarty Jones.

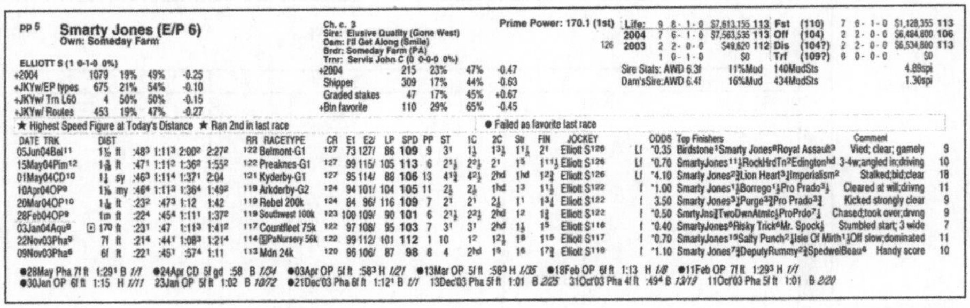

Figure 16-5:
The Brisnet *Ultimate Past Performances* for the career of Smarty Jones.

Courtesy of Brisnet

Considering Class Changes

Every year, about 35,000 Thoroughbred horses are *foaled* (born). I'd love to tell you that all are created equal, but they're not. The number one thing that differentiates racehorses is *class*. Class isn't easily defined, but when a horse has it, you know it. Following are some signs to look for:

✔ The first sign of class comes from the *pedigree* — who the horse's *sire* (father) and *dam* (mother) are. The classier animals have sires that cost a lot of money to breed. The idea is that a classy stallion will pass on his talent and class to his offspring. The same goes for the mare. You like to know that she was a stakes winner and has a lot of class to pass on.

✔ The second sign of class emerges when young horses start the training that leads up to the start of their racing career. The classier horses work faster, learn faster, and want to compete against other horses in the morning workouts. Word about special horses spreads fast — another reason to read the *Daily Racing Form* for news tidbits about young horses.

✔ A third sign of class appears when the horses start racing. The classier horses win early and win often. When challenged in a race, a classy animal accepts and defeats his rivals. You can measure a racehorse's class by the other horses he or she keeps company with. Classy horses run in stakes and handicaps races for rich purse money.

Understanding class in racehorses is a big part of sophisticated handicapping.

Getting outclassed

Horses have a certain amount of talent, and as they win their way through their conditions, they look better and better on paper. But at some point — earlier for some horses than others — horses get outclassed. I compare it to the Peter Principle with humans, in which workers get promoted until they eventually reach their level of incompetence and remain there. Racehorses move upwards in class levels until they reach a point where they can't win anymore, and it's the best they can do.

When you watch stakes races during the year, you notice some long shot horses acting up at the starting gate. I believe that those animals know they're outclassed and don't belong in the same race with the other animals.

Look at the past performances for Saratoga Sugar in Figure 16-6. She was meant to be a good racehorse sired by Gone West, a son of Mr. Prospector, who stands for a robust stud fee of $150,000. Her workouts before her debut on April 9, 2004, must have been impressive. At Keeneland, she went off at 2/1 odds and attracted Hall of Fame jockey Jerry Bailey to ride. After running well for a half-mile, she completely *spit the bit,* meaning she stopped running. One key that she was going nowhere was in her next start on April 18, 2004, when she went off at 13/1 odds. Her high odds are what's called being *dead* on the tote board.

Saratoga Sugar
Own: Manganaro Frank

B. f. 3 (Apr)
Sire: Gone West (Mr. Prospector) $150,000
Dam: Connecting Link (Linkage)
Br: F.J.F.M., LLC (Ky)
Tr: Biancone Patrick L(0 0 0 0 .00) 2004:(102 26 .25)

Life	5	M	1	0	$14,810	75	
2004	5	M	1	0	$14,810	75	
2003	0	M	0	0	$0	-	
Aik Ⓣ	0	0	0	0	$0	-	

D.Fst	2	0	0	0	$1,230	67
Wet(345)	0	0	0	0	$0	-
Turf(304)	3	0	1	0	$13,580	75
DstⓉ(367)	0	0	0	0	$0	-

12Sep04-9Bel	gd	1 1/8	Ⓣ	$:49^3$	$1:13^4$	$1:37^2$	$1:48^4$	ⒻGrdCyBCH-G1	62	7	$1^{1\frac{1}{2}}$	1^1	2^{hd}	7^{13}	$7^{17\frac{1}{4}}$	Farina T	116	4.30e	69– 16	Lucifer's Stone118 1 1/4 Barancella116 3/4 Noahs Ark116nk Set pace, gave way 7
25Aug04-4Sar	fm	1 3/8	Ⓣ	$:49^1$	$1:14^4$	$1:39^4$	$2:16^3$	3↑ⒻMd Sp Wt 46k	75	2	$5^{1\frac{1}{4}}$	3^2	$2^{1\frac{1}{2}}$	$2^{\frac{1}{2}}$	2^5	Prado E S	118	7.30	81– 13	ChristmasCard118 5 SartogSugr118 1 1/4 SpringStroll118 1/2 Led between calls 9
9Aug04-9Sar	fm	1 3/16	Ⓣ	:48	$1:12^2$	$1:37^1$	$1:55^4$	3↑ⒻMd Sp Wt 46k	73	5	$2^{\frac{1}{2}}$	2^{hd}	3^{nk}	$6^{2\frac{3}{4}}$	$5^{4\frac{3}{4}}$	Blanc B	118	14.20	81– 14	PrdingTomisue118 1/2 ShsStrling118 2 3/4 ThnkthAcdmy118 1 Vied inside, tired 12
18Apr04-5Kee	fst	1 1/16		$:47^3$	$1:12^2$	$1:38^4$	$1:52^1$	ⒻMd Sp Wt 50k	67	8	$9^{7\frac{1}{4}}$	9^9	$10^{8\frac{1}{2}}$	9^{10}	$8^{14\frac{1}{4}}$	Sellers S J	119	13.00	66– 19	*Adventure*119 2 1/4 *FlyAwayAngel*114 3 *TooMuchClass*119 3 1/4 Bmp start,no factor 11
9Apr04-5Kee	fst	*7f		$:22^3$	$:45^4$	$1:11^4$	$1:28^3$	ⒻMd Sp Wt 49k	41	3	7	2^1	$2^{\frac{1}{2}}$	$5^{8\frac{1}{2}}$	$5^{16\frac{1}{4}}$	Bailey J D	119	*2.20	67– 09	The K O Touch119 2 3/4 Aurelia119 1 1/4 Susan's Angel119 7 3/4 Between, faltered 9

WORKS: Sep8 Sar tr.tⓉ 4f fm :48 B *2/2* Aug18 Sar tr.tⓉ 5f sf 1:03 B(d) *7/17* Aug6 Sar tr.tⓉ 4f fm :48 B(d) *2/20* ● Jly21 Sar tr.tⓉ 5f gd 1:01 B(d) *1/20* Jly14 Sar tr.tⓉ 4f fm $:48^2$ B(d) *3/23*

Figure 16-6: *Daily Racing Form* past performances for Saratoga Sugar.

Saratoga Sugar was supposed to be a classy animal, but she didn't live up to her early promise. The stock of Saratoga Sugar sunk so low that even though she was a *maiden,* having never won a race, trainer Patrick Biancone used her as a *rabbit* (to sacrifice a horse's performance by setting a fast early pace) for stablemate Mambo Slew in the Garden City Breeders' Cup Handicap. Biancone is a top of the line conditioner, and he can tell a sow's ear from a silk purse.

Moving way down in class

Owners spend a lot of money buying racehorses with the hopes that some of them will develop into stakes winners and even future champions. A few horses pan out, but most don't. Even though a vast majority of horses disappoint their owners and trainers, as long as the horses pay their way, these horsemen will hold onto them. They're not in the business of giving horses away.

Owners and trainers are in the business to make money, and they do that primarily by winning races to earn the purse money. When a horse is at a class level where he can't win, to improve his chances of winning, he'll be dropped down in class to face weaker opponents.

WARNING!

As a handicapper, when you see a top trainer double and triple drop a seemingly useful racehorse, that should be a glaring red flag to you. There's no charity among the horsemen in buying and selling racehorses. If you had the money to claim that horse and wouldn't buy it, why should you even consider betting on it?

Take the case of Commercant Vic, whose past performances are shown in Figure 16-7. At Del Mar, on Aug. 19, 2004, top trainer Jeff Mullins dropped the horse in class from a claiming $40,000 race to a claiming $10,000 race. Clearly Mullins wanted to get rid of the animal. Another trainer claimed Commercant Vic for $10,000 and ran him back in a much tougher Fairplex starter handicap $25,000 race on September 26, 2004, in which he was never competitive. This trainer ran Commercant Vic 24 days later at Santa Anita in a claiming $25,000 race. The horse broke down early in the second turn. On August 19, Mullins won a purse and salvaged $10,000 for Commercant Vic, while the other trainer claimed a bad-legged animal that broke down two races later. This is a perfect example why you as a horseplayer should be wary of betting your money on drop down horses.

Figure 16-7:
Daily Racing Form past performances for Commercant Vic.

Graduating from maiden races to facing winners

Within the normal scope of racing a horse through its conditions, the biggest class rise is when a maiden graduate moves up and races winners for the first time. In a maiden special weight race, a talented horse may race against only a few legitimate contenders, if that many. When the horse faces winners for the first time, obviously the entire field has already won, so there's no telling at this stage how many real tigers there are in the field.

REMEMBER

The betting public has a tendency to overbet a convincing maiden special weight winner. That, of course, creates overlays on other horses that have a good chance of winning.

Say Hey Willie (see Figure 16-8 for this horse's past performances) was a sharp maiden special weight winner at Saratoga on August 8, 2004. Saratoga is where owners and trainers love to win with maidens to show off their racing stock. Say Hey Willie was a betting man's horse, because her odds were a generous 11/1 in her debut, and she won like she was a 2/1 favorite.

Figure 16-8:
Daily Racing Form past performances for Say Hey Willie.

Say Hey Willie	B. f. 3 (Apr)	Life	2 1 1 0	$33,200	66	D.Fst	2 1 1 0	$33,200	66
Own: Paraneck Stable	Sire: Artax (Marquetry) $10,000	2004	2 1 1 0	$33,200	66	Wet(291)	0 0 0 0	$0	–
	Dam: See Me Willie B. (Dr. Blum)	2003	0 M 0 0	$0	–	Turf(243°)	0 0 0 0	$0	–
	Br: Mia Gallo & Paraneck Stable (NY)	Alk ①	0 0 0 0	$0	–	Dst①(336)	0 0 0 0	$0	–
	Tr: Pedersen Jennifer(0 0 0 .00) 2004:(308 27 .09)								

22Aug04- 7Sar fst 6f .221 .454 .58 1:111 3↑⑤Alw 43000n1x   66 7 3 2½ 3ns 23½ 23   Chavez J F   L119 b 1.60 83– 09 Dinner Date116³ Say Hey Willie119² Quiet Rose120no   3 wide, second best   7
6Aug04- 1Sar fst 6f .221 .459 .58² 1:11² 3↑⑥Md Sp Wt 41k   63 4 13 33½ 42 1½ 11³ Chavez J F   L118 b 11.90 85– 10 SayHeyWillie118¹³ MsWillWy122nk TownChrmer118² Off slowly, clear late 13
WORKS: Aug20 Aqu① 4f fst :47¹ H 1/1 Aug5 Aqu① 4f fst :49¹ Bg 6/7 Jly30 Aqu① 5f fst 1:01 H 2/3 Jly21 Aqu① 5f fst 1:00¹ H 3/6 ●Jly14 Aqu 4f fst :47³ H 1/7

Say Hey Willie's natural progression was into a first level allowance race for New York-breds on August 22, 2004. Even though Say Hey Willie wasn't favored, she was a strong second choice at 8/5 odds. In fact, only two horses took betting money — Say Hey Willie and the even money favorite, Funny Honey. The third choice was a filly named Dinner Date who finished 12th and last in the $250,000 New York Stallion Stakes 17days earlier at Saratoga. Dinner Date ran a quintessential "pop and stop" race, dueling hard for the early lead and fading badly in the stretch. On August 22, against heavy favorites Funny Honey and Say Hey Willie, Dinner Date, a big overlay at 7/1 odds, stalked the pace and won with authority by three lengths. She paid $17.80 to win. Say Hey Willie ran gamely for second. The moral of the story is that Dinner Date, coming out of a stakes race, had more than enough class to beat two more highly regarded young fillies.

Say Hey Willie is a typical example of the public overbetting a horse that just won her first race. At 8/5 odds, she was no value because she faced a much stronger field made up of winners. This scenario occurs quite often in handicapping. You should look to beat the overbet maiden winner by looking at the other horses in the field.

Dropping from maiden special weight to maiden claiming

I've long maintained that dropping down in class from maiden special weight to maiden claiming is the biggest class drop in racing. In a maiden special weight race, the horses are protected — meaning not for sale. When the owner and trainer finally drop their horse down for a claiming price, they do so reluctantly in search of a win.

Most of the horses stuck in the maiden claiming ranks have already proven that they can't run very fast or have little class or heart when it counts. I'd take my chances any day on an unproven horse running for a claiming price for the first time than on those horses that are fast becoming professional maidens.

Freefall is a good example of an unproven horse running in a maiden claiming race for the first time (see Figure 16-9). He was far back in his debut, beaten by 13-lengths, on May 6, 2004. However, the *Daily Racing Form* chart explains that "Freefall, a bit slow to begin, steadied when green between and behind rivals early, raced outside on the turn and into the stretch and was not a threat." After reading that, although the race wasn't very good, I liked the fact that the horse was kept outside on the turn and into the stretch. When a trainer wants to teach a horse something in a race, often times he instructs the jockey to stay wide and out of trouble. When next entered in a maiden claiming $40,000 race on May 26, 2004, Freefall popped the gate, showed high speed throughout, and won ridden out at 9/2 odds. I'd take that win price any day on an 8-length winner.

Figure 16-9:
Daily Racing Form past performance for Freefall.

Moving between open company and restricted state-bred races

The vast majority of races in the United States are for *open company,* meaning a horse born in any state or country can enter and run. Nowadays, most racing states have restricted races for only horses bred in that state to promote in-state breeding programs. The races are restricted because the horses are considered lower in class than in the open company races.

You see restricted state-bred races with New York-breds, California-breds, Ohio-breds, and so on. The two state breeding programs that don't practice a protectionist policy are Kentucky and Florida, because the best racehorses in the world come from those two states.

In New York, the purses and incentives for state-breds are outstanding, and the quality of state-breds is improving yearly. In fact, 2003 Kentucky Derby winner Funny Cide is a New York-bred gelding. However, for many runners, the jump up in class from state-bred to open company isn't a step but a launch.

For example, West Virginia (see Figure 16-10) is a New York-bred and a good one. I'd love to own ten racehorses like him. However, the three times he's tried an open company stakes race — on November 29, 2003, February 21, 2004, and September 18, 2004 — he's had his head handed to him. I have no doubt he'll eventually win in open company, but it may take a less ambitious race.

When a horse that was running mainly in restricted state-breds races moves up in class to face open company, he needs to be held to a higher standard. He's been facing weaker competition, so the open company race is a solid class rise for him. Take that into account in your handicapping.

Figure 16-10:
Daily Racing Form past performances for West Virginia.

West Virginia	Dk. b or b. c. 3 (Apr)		Life 11 5 1 1 $424,750 95	D.Fst 7 3 1 1 $344,845 95

West Virginia Daily Racing Form past performances chart.

Entering a claimer in a non-selling race

You hear the term _hard-knocking claimer_ as a compliment for a horse that runs for a claiming price but runs hard and wins races regardless of the competition.

As a handicapper, you shouldn't summarily dismiss a hard-knocking claimer when entered in a non-selling race like an allowance or optional claiming. The animal is doing so well that the trainer believes the time is right to step up and run for a bigger purse, even though he'll be running against superior stock. You should consider horses that like to win races, like a hard-knocking claimer, when you handicap a race.

Take the case of Infinite Glory, whose past performances are shown in Figure 16-11. He was claimed out of a win in a claiming $35,000 race on August 15, 2004. The horse had won a claiming $18,000 race on July 17, 2004 before then. Obviously, the horse was doing very well.

The new trainer understood that Infinite Glory had won only claiming races, thus the horse was still eligible for all of his allowance conditions. He was entered September 15, 2004 in a first level allowance for non-winners of a race other than maiden, claiming, or starter. Infinite Glory had already won four career races and was now facing other allowance horses that had only broken their maiden. Despite the public's perception of him as a modest animal, Infinite Glory already qualified to be a hard-knocking claimer. He won the race by a neck and paid $8.70 to win. In his next start only four days later against allowance horses in a non-winners of two races other than maiden, claiming, or starter, Infinite Glory lost by a head at 6/1 odds.

Infinite Glory
Own: Sullivan Lane Stable and L Hollow Far
Gr/ro. g. 3 (Mar)
Sire: Hennessy (Storm Cat) $35,000
Dam: Brandy Rose (Distinctive Pro)
Br: Henry G. Steinbrenner & Kinsman Farm (Fla)
Tr: Dutrow R E Jr(0 0 0 0 .00) 2004:(463 126 .27)

Life	14	5	1	1	$106,784	99	D.Fst	13	5	1	1	$106,554 99
2004	7	3	1	0	$71,894	99	Wet(352)	0	0	0	0	$0 -
2003	7	2	0	1	$34,890	83	Turf(288)	1	0	0	0	$230 30
Aik Ⓣ	0	0	0	0	$0	-	DstⓉ(335)	0	0	0	0	$0 -

19Sep04-6Bel	fst	1	:241 :473 1:113 1:362	3↑ Alw 50000n2x	99	3	51½	52	51¼	3½	2hd	Prado E S	L120 b	6.30	79-25	BrodwyVw116hd InfntGlory120no ThundrTouch1181¼	Game finish outside	6
15Sep04-3Bel	fst	1 1/16	:231 :454 1:094 1:423	3↑ Alw 48000n1x	94	7	63	63¾	62¾	41½	1nk	Velasquez C	L116 b	3.35	87-15	InfiniteGlory116nk *GoNow*116nk GrncntrlPkwy1161¼	Prevailed under drive	7
15Aug04-6Sar	fst	7f	:221 :45 1:10 1:224	Clm c-(35-30)	95	6	4	34	36	2hd	1¾	Sellers S J	L120 fb	11.80	90-12	*InfiniteGlory*120¾ *OneToughDud*1206 FittingTribut1162	Inside move, scored	9
Claimed from Harrell Georgann for $35,000, Domino Carl J Trainer 2004(as of 8/15): (30 3 4 5 0.10)																		
17Jly04-2Bel	fst	6f	:222 :46 :581 1:103	Clm 18000(18-16)	80	5	6	63¾	2½	1hd	12¼	Santos J A	L120 fb	11.50	86-14	*InfinitGlory*1202¼ FttngTrbut12010¼ FnnCntwntgn120nk	4 wide run, scored	7
3Jly04-1Bel	fst	7f	:223 :451 1:091 1:221	Clm 40000(40-30)	56	7	3	41	52¾	610	712¾	Santos J A	L120 fb	40.00	76-08	*Lucky Guy*1201½ *Diligent Gambler*1204¾ Talkin Tough120¾	4 wide trip, tired	8
Previously trained by Warren Fred G																		
11May04-5Crc	fm	1 1/16 Ⓣ	:233 :474 1:112 1:424	Clm 40000(40-35)	30	5	31	65½	79	715	622¾	Monterrey P Jr10	L108 b	25.10	62-15	ForgiveblSin1171¼ OnlySon1221½ HloforMry1172¼	Checked, bumped turn	7
1May04-11Crc	fst	6f	:212 :443 :572 1:112	Alw 26000n1x	47	3	6	109¾	1011	914	815¼	Garcia J A	L119 fb	14.30	77-13	*Sami's Majic*1194¾ Economist At Last1142 Black Raptor1191	Showed little	10
Previously trained by Delk Danny																		
3Nov03-9Crc	fst	1	:234 :473 1:13 1:394	Alw 24000n1x	17	5	75¾	76	78¼	716	738¼	Boulanger G	L117 b	6.30	43-24	*Second of June*1174¾ Mr. Willie Joe117¾ Moon Warrior1208	Trailed	7
11Oct03-6Crc	fst	6f	:212 :443 :572 1:11	Birdonwire75k	50	2	9	86	107½	1011	917¾	Rivera J A II	L115 b	23.60	71-16	Wynn Dot Comma1194 Twice as Bad117hd Super Cherokee1155¼	Outrun	10
25Sep03-6Crc	fst	5½f	:221 :462 :591 1:06	Clm c-(50-45)	83	4	5	43	32	31½	1hd	Garcia J A	L117 b	*1.30	91-17	Infinite Glory117hd Alyazuli1173½ Song of America1171½	3 wide, just up	6
Claimed from Kinsman Stable for $50,000, Tortora Emanuel Trainer 2003(as of 9/25): (315 47 48 43 0.15)																		
30Aug03-2Crc	fst	6f	:222 :461 :59 1:123	Md 32000(32-30)	82	11	1	3nk	3nk	11½	15¾	Garcia J A	L118 b	*.90	81-19	*Infinite Glory*1185¾ *Sir Louie*1181¾ Plantation Acres1131¾	3 wide, drew away	12
19Jly03-10Crc	fst	7f	:231 :471 1:131 1:263	Md Sp Wt 28k	47	4	3	21	2½	21	34¾	Toscano P R	L118 b	4.30	76-14	Skip Past1133 Western Man1181¾ *Infinite Glory*1183	Off rail, weakened	8
4Jly03-1Crc	fst	6f	:224 :471 1:001 1:134	Md 50000(50-45)	60	1	4	32	63½	54	41	Boulanger G	L118	4.50	74-20	Wander Time118no *Skip Past*113nk FourthofJuly110¾	Angled wide, gaining	7
14Jun03-10Crc	fst	5½f	:223 :471 1:001 1:071	Md Sp Wt 28k	35	5	4	55	53	66½	69¼	Homeister R B Jr	L118	2.60	76-14	Double K118hd Western Man118hd Blaine's Storm1187¼	4 wide, faltered	8

WORKS: Oct4 Aqu 5f fst 1:021 B 1/3 Sep11 Aqu Ⓣ 5f fst 1:02 B 5/15 Sep4 Aqu Ⓣ 5f fst 1:021 B 4/5 ●Aug29 Aqu Ⓣ 5f fst 1:011 H 1/7 Jly31 Bel 5f fst 1:002 H 2/21

Figure 16-11: *Daily Racing Form* past performances for Infinite Glory.

Respecting a key race

A *key race* is where at least two horses in the field win in their next start, thus signifying that the class of the key race is very good and that other horses coming out of the key race must be respected the next time they start. Here I go in-depth into a result chart and explain what happens when you see a key race explode like this result chart shows.

The tenth race at Ellis Park on July 24, 2004 (see Figure 16-12) looks like a million result charts before it and a million more races that'll come after. It's a first level allowance race on turf for "3-year-olds and upward which have never won a race other than maiden, claiming, or starter, or which have never won two races."

The winner, Sell to Survive, made a five-wide rally in the stretch to win in the final strides. As can happen in turf racing, the race was what I call a cavalry charge to the wire. The first nine horses were separated by about four lengths. Gamble Monger, the last place horse, was practically eased, finishing another eight lengths behind the ninth place horse.

Now take a look at each horse and see how it ran the next time out. They all made their next start at Ellis Park:

- **Gamble Monger** returned on August 4 and ran second at 7/1 odds. That finish tells me something about the quality of the field, if the last place finisher ran very well the next time out.
- **Jamian** returned on August 7 and won a turf race at 8/1 odds. He paid $18.80 to win.
- **Manaus** returned on August 7 and finished seventh behind Jamian.
- **Charmer Jim** returned on August 9 and won a turf race at 9/2 odds. He paid $11.60 to win.
- **Really Bad News** returned on August 9 and finished seventh behind Charmer Jim.

- **Sure Prize** returned on August 13 and ran second at 6/1 odds. He lost by a neck in a very game effort — what I call a tough beat.
- **Good Job** returned on August 20 and won a turf race at 4/5 odds. He paid $3.60 to win. Good Job is now the third winner to exit this key race.
- **Sell to Survive** returned on August 27 and won a turf race at 12/1 odds. He paid $26.20 to win.
- **Intemperate** returned on August 29 and won a turf race at 4/5 odds. He paid $3.80 to win.
- **Skiding** has yet to run back.

TENTH RACE
Ellis Park
JULY 24, 2004

$1\frac{1}{16}$ MILES. (Turf) (1.38^{4}) ALLOWANCE . Purse $27,500 (includes $8,500 KTDF – KY TB Devt Fund) FOR THREE YEAR OLDS AND UPWARD WHICH HAVE NEVER WON A RACE OTHER THAN MAIDEN, CLAIMING, OR STARTER OR WHICH HAVE NEVER WON TWO RACES. Three Year Olds, 117 lbs.; Older, 123 lbs. Non-winners Of A Race At A Mile Or Over Since June 24 Allowed 2 lbs. Such A Race Since May 24 Allowed 4 lbs. Such A Race Since April 24 Allowed 6 lbs. (Races Where Entered For $20,000 Or Less Not Considered) (Preference To Horses That Have Not Started For $20,000 Or Less In Last 5 Starts). (If deemed inadvisable by management to run this race over the turf course, it will be run on the main track at One mile out of the chute.). (Rail at 24 feet).

Value of Race: $27,500 Winner $17,115; second $5,500; third $2,750; fourth $1,375; fifth $190; sixth $190; seventh $190; eighth $190. Mutuel Pool $164,783.00 Exacta Pool $134,767.00 Trifecta Pool $122,124.00 Superfecta Pool $52,156.00

Last Raced	Horse	M/Eqt.	A.	Wt	PP	St	¼	½	¾	Str	Fin	Jockey	Odds $1
26Jun04 ^{7}CD^{2}	Sell to Survive	L	4	117	6	3	$5\frac{1}{2}$	5^{hd}	5^{1}	$4^{2\frac{1}{2}}$	1^{nk}	Castanon J L	4.80
2Jly04 ^{5}CD^{1}	Good Job	L	3	117	5	1	$1^{1\frac{1}{2}}$	1^{hd}	1^{hd}	$3\frac{1}{2}$	$2\frac{1}{2}$	Day P	2.10
8Jly04 ^{7}ElP^{4}	Jamian	L b	3	113	2	7	6^{hd}	$7\frac{1}{2}$	8^{2}	$5\frac{1}{2}$	3no	Prescott R	26.20
20Jun04 ^{7}CD^{3}	Sure Prize	L b	3	111	10	5	3^{hd}	$3\frac{1}{2}$	$3\frac{1}{2}$	2^{hd}	4^{nk}	Martinez W	2.30
5Jun04 ^{9}CD^{5}	Manaus	L b	4	117	9	6	7^{4}	6^{2}	4^{2}	1^{hd}	5^{2}	McKee J	11.90
26Jun04 ^{7}CD^{4}	Skiding	L	4	121	4	8	$8^{2\frac{1}{2}}$	8^{2}	7^{2}	6^{2}	$6\frac{1}{2}$	Troilo W D	15.40
7Jly04 ^{6}Mth^{5}	Intemperate	L	4	117	3	10	10	10	10	9^{3}	$7\frac{3}{4}$	Melancon L	5.00
5Jun04 ^{9}FP^{3}	Really Bad News	L b	4	117	8	9	9^{2}	9^{2}	$9\frac{1}{2}$	7^{hd}	8^{nk}	Kurek G	68.90
8Jly04 ^{7}ElP^{7}	Charmer Jim	L	3	113	1	4	$4^{1\frac{1}{2}}$	$4\frac{1}{2}$	6^{hd}	8^{hd}	9^{8}	Stokes J	67.30
9Jly04 ^{5}ElP^{1}	Gamble Monger	L b	3	113	7	2	$2^{1\frac{1}{2}}$	$2^{1\frac{1}{2}}$	2^{hd}	10	10	Coa D	15.40

OFF AT 5:09 Start Good . Won driving. Course good.

TIME :24^{2}, :49^{1}, 1:14^{3}, 1:39^{1}, 1:45^{2} (:24.50, :49.33, 1:14.66, 1:39.35, 1:45.40)

$2 Mutuel Prices:

6 – SELL TO SURVIVE	11.60	4.40	3.40
5 – GOOD JOB		3.80	3.40
2 – JAMIAN			7.80

$2 EXACTA 6–5 PAID $23.90 $2 TRIFECTA 6–5–2 PAID $666.00
$2 SUPERFECTA 6–5–2–3 PAID $2,199.00

B. c, (Mar), by Patton – Mama Hawk , by Silver Hawk . Trainer Morse Randy L. Bred by Brereton C Jones (Ky).

SELL TO SURVIVE settled in behind horses early, advanced five wide entering the stretch and was hard ridden to prevail. GOOD JOB gained the lead early, raced near the inside, lost the advantage at the furlong grounds, then dug in gamely and was coming back at the end. JAMIAN, bumped at the start and unhurried, swung out seven wide leaving the far turn and was gaining late. SURE PRIZE, rated along four wide, made a bold bid entering the upper stretch, gained even terms for the lead but couldn't sustain the needed momentum. MANAUS, never far back and five wide, gained a slight edge nearing the final furlong and weakened soon after. SKIDING failed to rally. INTEMPERATE broke slow and awkward, was outrun for six furlongs, circled horses eight wide and failed to rally. REALLY BAD NEWS failed to menace. CHARMER JIM came out at the start bumping JAMIAN, raced in contention inside for six furlongs and tired. GAMBLE MONGER pressed front-running GOOD JOB four wide to the stretch and gave way.

Owners– 1, Langford Michael; 2, Klein Richard Bertram and Elaine; 3, Ducharme Stables; 4, Myers Keith N; 5, Two Bucks Farm; 6, Hunter Barbara; 7, Kinsman Stable; 8, Stiritz William; 9, Hines James T Jr; 10, Thornton Eric

Trainers– 1, Morse Randy L; 2, Flint Steve; 3, Pate David E; 4, Booker John A Jr; 5, Bowman Carl; 6, Casey Stephen E; 7, Mott William I; 8, Zook Jimmy; 9, Nesbitt Kim; 10, Thornton Eric

Scratched– Skip Vigorously (03Jul04 ^{10}AP ^{2}) , Dandy Gentleman (07Jul04 ^{9}ElP^{5})

$2 Daily Double (3–6) Paid $65.00 ; Daily Double Pool $39,927 .
$1 Pick Three (3–3–6) Paid $119.70 ; Pick Three Pool $16,890 .
$2 Pick Four (1–3/6–3–6) Paid $1,106.40 ; Pick Four Pool $29,082 .
$2 Pick Six (1–1/7/12–1–3/6–3–6) 5 Correct Paid $781.00 ; Pick Six Pool $4,006 ; Carryover Pool $3,155.

Ellis Park Attendance: 4,203 Mutuel Pool: $337,567.00 ITW Mutuel Pool: $339,950.00 ISW Mutuel Pool: $3,327,279.00

Figure 16-12: *Daily Racing Form* result chart for race 10, Ellis Park, July 24, 2004.

After seeing Gamble Monger and Jamian's strong finishes, I knew to keep an eye on this result chart, because two horses have run very well out of the July 24th race. The July 24th race officially became a key race when Charmer Jim won, because he was the second horse to win the next time out (Jamian was the first).

Because the race had been identified as a key race, I kept a close eye on the others horses from the field. Sure Prize returned on August 13 and lost by a neck at 6/1 odds — a tough beat. Good Job became the third next-out winner from the key race when he won on August 20, verifying that this key race had a very classy field. Then, Sell to Survive, the horse that actually beat all the other horses, ran on August 27. The betting public dismissed his chances at 12/1 win odds, which I consider tremendous value on the win price. Sell to Survive won and paid $26.20 — incredible. By then, everyone in the grandstand knew about the key race. Intemperate ran back on August 29 and was an underlaid heavy favorite at 4/5 odds. He won easily and paid $3.80.

When I read a result chart, I mark down horses that either won or ran second in their next start. That way, the strength of the field jumps out at you without you having to rely upon your memory.

All key races aren't as strong as this one or plot as well. But I handicap for a living, and races such as this one prove to me that if you do your homework, you can make money betting on horse racing. Having five winners and two seconds from nine comeback starters is as strong of a key race as you'll find.

Staying at the bottom

The class levels of horses at the racetrack go up and down like a ladder. One constant that holds true is that the bottom rung — the very worst horses at the racetrack — is the bottom no matter where the horse races. To identify the bottom class, you really need to see the condition book (see Chapter 2) from the racetrack. Without the condition book, you need to look at one week's worth of result charts from the *Daily Racing Form Simulcast Weekly* (see Chapter 11). You'll be able to identify the bottom class level by looking at the claiming prices of the races.

Whether they're maidens or winners, you should avoid the bottom horses except for in one scenario. If a horse drops down and runs at the bottom level for the first time, it may be worth a bet at the right odds. The other horses have proven that they don't want to win another race. Thus, the drop down horse is actually a classier animal than those mired at the bottom rung.

When a bottom level horse ships in from a major circuit to a smaller racetrack, the tendency is for the public to overbet the supposedly classier animal. I consider this bet a trap, because I believe that the bottom is the bottom no matter where you go. So if the worst maiden or claiming horse on the grounds of Santa Anita is shipped to Charles Town or Mountaineer Park, I won't bet on it.

Trip Handicapping

Trip handicapping is part art, part science. Anyone can do it by just watching and learning enough about the horse races. _Trip handicapping_ means to watch for horses that get into trouble at some point during the race. The best trouble notes to make are the ones that aren't so obvious. The obvious trip horses are those that get in trouble during the stretch run. The hidden trip horses are those that have trouble leaving the starting gate, get bothered while running down the backside, or run into traffic around the far turn.

I think trip handicapping is a lost art that's returning to popularity for a couple reasons:

- Professional handicappers have access to accurate pace numbers and speed figures (see "Taking a Scientific Approach: Advanced Handicapping Resources," earlier in this chapter). So to find good value horses, you need to discover live horses that aren't so obvious. Trip handicapping is one way to do that.

- Not a lot of horseplayers bother to study trips. It's a lot of work and is very time consuming. Not only does studying trips entail watching the live races closely, but many trip handicappers I know watch races on television, order tapes from racetracks, and watch races on the Internet. The handicappers make notations and enter the trip horses into a horses to watch list so they know when the horse is making its next start. If you're willing to take the time, though, you'll have important information that's in the hands of very few horseplayers.

Paying attention to the horses to watch list

Luckily you don't have to build your own database on your home computer and keep track of a horses to watch list. Brisnet, Equibase, and the _Daily Racing Form_ (to name a few) offer excellent free service to horseplayers on their Web sites that are simple to use (see "Taking a Scientific Approach: Advanced Handicapping Resources," earlier in this chapter). To set up a free account, you just type in the names of the trip horses and your own trip notes. The service needs your e-mail address, because it e-mails you alerts so you can keep track of workouts, when horses are entered, and when the horses are scheduled to run.

WARNING!

The worst thing you can do is work hard at paying attention to the horses to watch list and then miss the horse's next start, especially if it wins at a square price.

Watching the replays

In the *Daily Racing Form* result charts, the chart-callers do a fine job of describing what happened to each horse in a race. You can read the comments and have a good idea, but remember that the chart-callers aren't perfect. The commentary is subjective, so a bad trouble trip in the eyes of one handicapper, may not be to another. Watching race replays is where you can gain an edge over other horseplayers.

So, get your pen and paper ready to write some trip handicapping notes while watching race replays. Here are a few clues for trying to extract the most information from watching a race:

- **Pay close attention to the start.** More horse races are won and lost in the first few strides out of the starting gate. The racetrack typically shows you see two angles of the start: the *pan camera,* meaning the side view, and the *head-on shot,* which is actually a steward's camera view. In the head-on shot, the horses leave the starting gate and run directly towards you.

  Some trip notes to look for are obvious. Horses can stumble upon leaving the starting gate. There's a lot of contact among the horses banging into one another before they get into stride. Horses can duck in or out causing them to lose momentum or delay getting into stride. Anything out of the ordinary can qualify as a trip note.

- **The straightaways before a turn are extremely important.** If the race is a sprint, pay attention to the backside. If it's a route race, be concerned with the two straightaways. The straightaways are what I call "the race within a race." The jockeys are trying to maneuver their horses into good position for the turns and for the stretch run. Some trip notes to look for are horses that get checked, steadied, and bothered by other horses. At times, you can literally see a jockey have to take up his mount or even stand straight up to keep his mount from clipping the heels of the horses in front of him. Clipping heels is enough to make a horse and rider fall, which you never want to see.

  Just imagine you're in rush hour traffic and you have cars all around you. Another car cuts you off, and you slam on your brakes. That's what happens in a horse race. When the horses are bunched up, one horse changes paths and forces another horse or two to react.

- **The action in the stretch is in full view of everyone.** I minimize stretch trouble because it's usually so obvious. A horse that gets checked in the stretch will reflect that trouble in the win odds for its next start. Although getting checked may have cost the horse the race or a position, the win odds are usually undervalued.

After you finish watching the race replays and making your trip notes, go to your computer and enter the horses' names and trip notes into a horses to watch list on the Internet.

Common Sense Guidelines

In this section, I list some common sense guidelines you should keep track of while handicapping. Some will save you time, some will save you money, and some will hopefully make you money.

Eliminate losers

Most handicappers go through the *Daily Racing Form* and try to pick winners. What I do to save a lot of time is try to eliminate losers — the horses that have no chance of winning. I use Beyer Speed Figures (see "Beyer Speed Figures," earlier in the chapter) as a barometer, and I pay attention to horses I think are outclassed (see "Getting outclassed," earlier in the chapter).

Eliminating losers doesn't mean I won't use one of these horses in a vertical exotic bet like an exacta, trifecta, or superfecta (see Chapter 15). I just won't use the losers on top of the ticket to win the race. However, the race shape may force me to use horses I don't think can win in the second, third, or fourth positions underneath the winner.

Bet a horse that bounces back

Racehorses aren't machines. They can run well one time and horribly the next. I like to find horses that have a chance to bounce back off a poor performance.

Taint So is one example of a bounce back horse (see Figure 16-13). He won his debut on May 5, 2004 in a maiden special weight race at 47/1 odds. He ran a very creditable 81 Beyer. His next time out on June 5, he broke slowly, showed no speed, and eased up in the late stages. Also note, the race was a key race (see "Respecting a key race," earlier in the chapter), because both Country Judge and Thunder Touch won the next time out. The *Daily Racing Form* uses italics to denote a next start winner.

Figure 16-13:
Daily Racing Form past performances for Taint So.

Taint So was laid up nearly three months before returning at Saratoga on August 21. His trainer put the horse on Lasix (see "Look for Lasix," later in the chapter), which tells me the gelding may have bled the last time out. The jockey who won on him the first time returned to the saddle, and Taint So dropped in class. In the race condition, a "non-winners of two races lifetime" is a lower class level than a "non-winners of a race other than maiden, claiming, or starter" race.

These three positives — adding Lasix, returning jockey, and dropping in class — catch my eye, and at 8/1 odds in a seven-horse field, he represented value, too. Taint So bounced back to earn an 89 Beyer and won the race by two-lengths. Taint So represents the kind of long shots you can find during a weekday simulcast.

Decipher hidden middle moves

When you're looking for betting angles that aren't so obvious to the general public, the *hidden middle move* is maybe as good as it gets. Handicappers have a tendency to look for horses that show high early speed or rally fast in the late stages. A hidden middle move in the central part of a race indicates that a horse's physical form is improving. The animal may not have enough conditioning yet to sustain the move, but it's a very positive sign.

Generalist is an example of a hidden middle move (see Figure 16-14). In his career debut on May 20, 2004, he was bet down to 4/1 odds in a nine-horse field — a sure sign his connections liked him a lot. He ran an even fourth, and he didn't start again until July 21.

Generalist
Own: Malmuth Marvin and Sonya and McCay, N

Dk. b or b. c. 2 (Feb)
Sire: General Meeting (Seattle Slew) $10,000
Dam: Good Faith Woman (Syncopate)
Br: Marvin Malmuth (Cal)
Tr: Garcia Juan J(0 0 0 0 .00) 2004:(220 16 .07)

Life	5	1	1	0	$54,755	81	D.Fst	5	1	1	0	$54,755 81
2004	5	1	1	0	$54,755	81	Wet(309)	0	0	0	0	$0 -
2003	0	M	0	0	$0	-	Turf(327)	0	0	0	0	$0 -
Aik ①	0	0	0	0	$0	-	Dst①(336)	0	0	0	0	$0 -

30Sep04-2SA	fst	7f	:22^3	:45	1:10	1:23	[S]Cavonnier77k	71	3	4	2^1	3$^{1/2}$	2^2	2^5	Smith M E	LB118 b	3.90	85-10	SwissLd118^5 Generlist118$^{4\frac{1}{2}}$ JohnnyHighBrite118^{11}	Bid 3wd turn,2nd best	4
6Sep04-1Dmr	fst	6f	:22^2	:45^3	:57^2	1:09^1	[S]ImSmokin98k	81	4	2	3^1	3^1	4^3	4^4	Smith M E	LB117 b	4.30	89-06	Top Money116^3 Fallfree119$^{1/2}$ Proud Tower Too117$^{1/2}$	3wd turn,outfinished	4
22Aug04-5Dmr	fst	5½f	:22^1	:45^2	:57^4	1:04^2	[S]Md Sp Wt 51k	78	6	8	2^{hd}	2^{hd}	1$^{2\frac{1}{2}}$	1$^{5\frac{1}{2}}$	Smith M E	LB119 b	13.70	93-09	Generalist119$^{5\frac{1}{2}}$ [DH]Orbits World119 [DH]New Cloud119^2	3wd to turn,clear	12
21Jly04-5Dmr	fst	5½f	:22^2	:46^2	:58^4	1:05^1	[S]Md Sp Wt 51k	60	4	11	9^7	7$^{3\frac{1}{2}}$	5$^{2\frac{3}{4}}$	5$^{4\frac{3}{4}}$	Flores D R	LB118 b	13.50	84-14	RomnJke118^{nk} *ProudTowerToo*118no Trritoril118^3	Bumped,squeezed start	12
20May04-8Hol	fst	4½f	:22^2	:45^3		:52^1	[S]Md Sp Wt 43k	56	1	9	6$^{9\frac{1}{2}}$		4$^{5\frac{3}{4}}$	4$^{3\frac{3}{4}}$	Espinoza V	LB119 b	4.20	91-11	Mr. Fondue119^2 Oly's Oak119^1 Beau119$^{3/4}$	Came out str,mild bid	9

WORKS: Sep24 SA 6f fst 1:12^2 H *4/26* Sep18 SA 5f fst 1:02^4 H *37/39* Sep1 Dmr 3f fst :37 H *6/8* Aug18 Dmr 3f fst :38^2 H *24/27* Aug11 Dmr 5f fst 1:00^1 H *18/44* Jly31 Dmr 5f fst 1:01^2 H *47/63*

Figure 16-14: *Daily Racing Form* past performances for Generalist.

Generalist broke slowly and was seven lengths behind at the first call. He gained nearly four lengths and then gained another length to the stretch call before tiring.

That improvement isn't easy to spot, even for trip handicappers. But this is the beauty of a hidden middle move. Even Generalist's Beyer Speed Figure improved some from 56 to 60. Generalist was sent off again at 13/1 odds on August 22, where he broke like a rocket from the gate, fought for the lead, and never looked back — winning for 5½ lengths. His class was exemplified later by two starts in stakes races. To find live long shots like Generalist at juicy 13/1 odds, don't be a master of the obvious. Look for angles like the hidden middle move.

Forgive a horse that doesn't finish the last start

Some good handicappers look long and hard at a horse that's either eased, lost rider, fell, or that just didn't finish the last start.

The betting public shies away from horses that don't finish the last start, for whatever reason. If you can forgive the horrible last running line for any legitimate excuse, you'll get tremendous value on the animal. Look for positive signs like returning to normal workouts, coming back to the races within 60 days or less, and having a jockey that's named a top ten rider in the jockey standings.

Chispazo was eased in a race at Gulfstream Park on March 7, 2004 (see Figure 16-15). He went off at 9/1 odds in a maiden claiming $45,000 race. He returned in seven weeks on April 26 with a top ten rider in Manuel Aguilar. The race was at Calder, another south Florida racetrack, at a much lower class, maiden claiming $25,000. I don't know for sure why Chispazo was eased in his race on March 7. But you like to see changes, and in this case, Chispazo had his blinkers taken off. The combination of factors would normally depress his odds much lower than the 9/1 he went off at last time. At 7/1 odds with a big class drop and racing at Calder instead of Gulfstream, Chispazo was playable under the circumstances.

Figure 16-15:
Daily Racing Form past performances for Chispazo.

Look for Lasix

Lasix is a human drug — a diuretic — that when taken by horses, prevents bleeding internally in the breathing passages. Lasix isn't some magic potion that makes horses run incredibly faster. It helps horses run to their ability.

When a trainer puts his horse on Lasix, this change is positive and is a sign that he's giving his runner a better chance to win.

Beachblanket Bingo ran for the first time on Lasix on September 8, 2004 and won at 5/1 odds, as shown in Figure 16-16.

Also note the filly was dropping in class from maiden claiming $15,000 to maiden claiming $7,500. The more positive handicapping angles you can find to build your case for a horse, the more confident you can be in your betting.

Figure 16-16:
Daily Racing Form past performances for Beachblanket Bingo.

1 Beachblanket Bingo

B. f. 2 (Apr)
Sire: Count the Time (Regal Search) $1,500
Dam: Jazz the Glass (Apalachee)
Br: Dr Jeff Allen (Ky)
Tr: Habeeb Donald Jr(2 0 0 1 .00) 2004:(55 4 .07)

Spot a sprinter stretching out

A sprinter stretching out in distance for the first time is a very strong handicapping angle in American horse racing. American horses and racetracks are designed for speed. You'll hear the phrase "getting into the race," meaning the jockeys know that to improve their chances of winning, they must place their horse close to the early pacesetters.

You can't get into the race any faster than by being in front from the start. In this handicapping angle, you want a sprinter with early speed, not a sprinter that comes from behind. You want the horse to be leading from the start and to be able to relax on a slow, early pace.

On July 10, 2004, Littlebitofzip showed a ton of early speed at 5½ furlongs. He ran what I call a "pop and stop" race, meaning he popped right to the lead and then stopped running fast at the end. On August 25, Littlebitofzip was stretched out in distance to a two-turn, 1-mile race. Littlebitofzip went to the front, as expected.

Compare the early fractions of the turf sprint against the turf route. In the first quarter mile, instead of 21⅘ seconds, he ran a much slower 22⅖ seconds. At the half-mile pole, instead of 45⅖ seconds, he was galloping along in 46⅗ seconds. Is it any surprise that Littlebitofzip had lots of energy in reserve to win, going away at 15/1 odds? This was a dream handicapping scenario. Check out Figure 16-17 for the details.

Littlebitofzip
Own: Peacock Cecil H

Dk. b or b. c. 2 (Mar) BARMAR04 $30,000
Sire: Littlebitlively (Lively One) $3,500
Dam: Kafaf (Zilzal)
Br: John Franks (Fla)
Tr: Hendricks Dan L(0 0 0 0 .00) 2004:(125 13 .10)

Life	5	1	0	1	$55,860	67	D.Fst	3	0	0	1	$24,400	55
2004	5	1	0	1	$55,860	67	Wet(282*)	0	0	0	0	$0	-
2003	0	M	0	0	$0	-	Turf(235*)	2	1	0	0	$31,460	67
Aik ①	0	0	0	0	$0	-	Dst①(300*)	0	0	0	0	$0	-

3Oct04-7SA	fst	$1\frac{1}{16}$		:23	:46	$1{:}10^3$	$1{:}44^1$	Norfolk-G2	55	3	1^1	1^1	1^{hd}	$3^{6\frac{1}{2}}$	$3^{17\frac{1}{2}}$	Flores D R	LB120 b	7.70	66- 17	RomnRulr$120^{4\frac{1}{2}}$ BostonGlory120^{13} Litllbitofzip120^2	Speed,inside,wkened	4
25Aug04-4Dmr	fm	1	①	$:22^2$	$:46^3$	1:11	$1{:}36^1$	Md Sp Wt 56k	67	1	$1^{1\frac{1}{2}}$	$1^{2\frac{1}{2}}$	1^2	1^3	1^4	Bisono A5	LB113 b	15.30	80- 10	Littlbitofzip113^4 *ThisWizrdRocks*118^3 WhosAlyn118^1	Speed,inside,driving	10
10Jly04-6Hol	fm	$5\frac{1}{2}$f	①	$:21^4$	$:45^2$	:58	$1{:}04^3$	Md Sp Wt 45k	53	9	1	1^{hd}	$2^{\frac{1}{2}}$	$3^{2\frac{1}{2}}$	5^6	Baze T C	LB119 b	16.20	76- 18	MircleMker$119^{1\frac{1}{2}}$ CshintheBnk$119^{2\frac{1}{2}}$ ChntforGold119^1	Dueled, weakened	10
30May04-2Hol	fst	5f		$:21^3$	$:44^1$		$:56^1$	Md Sp Wt 46k	39	9	7	$7^{6\frac{1}{2}}$	8^{11}	10^{12}	$10^{19\frac{1}{2}}$	Solis A	LB119	29.70	83- 10	DlgntProspct$119^{3\frac{1}{2}}$ IllPryforYo$119^{1\frac{1}{2}}$ *SwssSlvr*$119^{2\frac{1}{2}}$	Btwn to turn,wkened	10
8Apr04-1SA	fst	2f		$:11^1$			$:21^3$	Md Sp Wt 39k	–	1	5			$4^{1\frac{3}{4}}$	6^4	Jauregui L H	LB118	44.80	93- 13	CptMcCriger$121^{1\frac{1}{2}}$ SemiQueen118^{no} Shrmnthlnk118^{no}	Inside, no late bid	9

WORKS: Sep27 SA 6f fst 1:12 H *3/7* Sep20 SA 6f fst $1{:}13^2$ H *4/15* Sep14 SA 5f fst $:58^3$ H *2/34* Sep6 Dmr 4f fst $:48^3$ H *15/39* Aug19 Dmr 6f fst 1:13 H *5/28* Aug7 Dmr 5f fst $:59^4$ H *9/50*

Figure 16-17: *Daily Racing Form* past performances for Littlebitofzip.

Watch for winners that run a low Beyer

This handicapping angle points to horses that may get overlooked coming off a win. When a horse wins a race — any race — you can assume the animal is in good physical condition. As a handicapper, you're trying to make a judgment of whether a horse will bounce the next time out because it exerted so much energy in winning.

Beyer Speed Figures are a barometer of the quality of the races a horse runs. So, if a horse usually runs Beyers in the 70s and explodes to 95 and wins, there's a good chance the animal will bounce back down in the next start. Conversely, I like to see horses winning in slower Beyer times with a chance of running even faster the next time out.

A subtle example of this handicapping angle is Wild Senorita, whose past performances are shown in Figure 16-18. Beginning on May 6, 2004, this filly ran a 68, 67, and 69 Beyer without winning. On July 26, she won a mile race for claiming $20,000 with a 64 Beyer at 9/5 odds. The 64 Beyer told me she could run a little bit faster in her next start. On August 26, in the exact same condition, claiming $20,000 going one mile, she went off at higher odds of 5/2. Wild Senorita ran a career best 74 Beyer, won by a nose, and paid $7.60 to win. This scenario happens a lot, and often times at much higher odds than 5/2.

```
Wild Senorita                                   Dk. b or b. f. 3 (Mar)                          Life 10 3 1 2 $66,605 74 | D.Fst     9 3 1 2 $64,730 74
Own: Baneth Phil, Goldstein, Sy and Sherma      Sire: Wild Event (Wild Again) $7,500            2004  8 2 1 2 $47,225 74 | Wet(367)  0 0 0 0      $0  -
                                                Dam: Senority (Jolie's Halo)                    2003  2 1 0 0 $19,380 50 | Turf(248) 1 0 0 0  $1,875 58
                                                Br: Tommy Town Thoroughbreds, LLC (Cal)         Alk   0 0 0 0      $0  - | Dst(357)  0 0 0 0      $0  -
                                                Tr: Sherman Art(0 0 0 0 .00) 2004:(474 114 .24)

30Sep04-7BM fm 1 :232 :481 1:13 1:384 ⒻClm 25000(25-22.5) 58 6 44 43 54 56½ 48 Lumpkins J LB116 b *2.10 71-21 Tavern OnRush116½ SkyDreams1161 StrongFaith1166½ 3w 2nd turn, no bid 6
26Aug04-6Dmr fst 1 :221 :461 1:111 1:382 ⒻClm c-(20-18) 74 7 42½ 53½ 53½ 21½ 1no Pedroza M A LB120 b 2.80 82-22 WildSnorit120no CorporlGrinr1201 CmpDlMrRuls1132 Carried out,up late 8
  Claimed from Sprague, Sprague and Winters for $20,000, Carava Jack Trainer 2004(as of 8/26): (216 31 28 31 0.14)
26Jly04-5Dmr fst 1 :214 :454 1:114 1:391 ⒻClm c-(20-18) 64 2 59 56 55 32½ 13 Baze T C LB118 b 1.80 78-14 WildSenorita1183 DncingEvent1182½ IceltHoney116½ Came out str,rallied 8
  Claimed from Brocoff, Brian, S T D Racing Stable and Wood, Jason for $20,000, O'Neill Doug Trainer 2004(as of 7/26): (523 89 77 70 0.17)
1Jly04-6Hol fst 6f :214 :45 :571 1:102 ⒻClm 32000(32-28) 69 3 7 74 65 47 35 Baze T C LB118 b 8.00 80-17 AwsomLdy1185 HighlyArrognt120hd WildSnort1182 3wd into str,missed 2d 8
3Jun04-2Hol fst 6f :22 :454 :581 1:111 ⒻClm c-(16-14) 67 3 3 52½ 41½ 31½ 3½ Cohen D10 LB108 fb 1.60 80-13 Smokegetnyourys111hd AndrsAngl115½ WildSnorit1085 3wd,4wd,willingly 6
  Claimed from 5C Racing Stable LLC for $16,000, Gutierrez Jorge Trainer 2004(as of 6/3): (26 0 4 3 0.00)
6May04-1Hol fst 7½f :223 :453 1:111 1:293 ⒻClm c-(12.5-10.5) 68 6 2 1hd 1hd 1hd 2no Enriquez I D LB118 b *1.00 87-10 TlegdeOro118no WildSenorit11810½ Pulchritude118½ Vied,clear 1/4,gamely 6
  Claimed from Tommy Town Thoroughbreds LLC for $12,500, Cardenas Ruben Trainer 2004(as of 5/6): (65 7 9 10 0.11)
25Mar04-2SA fst 1 1/16 :232 :472 1:121 1:462 ⒻAlw 40000s 63 6 51¼ 63 54½ 55½ 56 Valdivia J Jr LB118 b 9.30 67-27 ShrpenedCopy1201 SilentKingdom1203½ Missice118½ 3-4wd to lane, no bid 7
5Mar04-4GG fst 1 :232 :472 1:122 1:372 ⒻAlw 40000s 65 6 79 78 65¼ 44 45½ Baze R A LB117 b 3.50 76-18 Lost Bride1173 SlewsinDemand1171 TerraFirma1171½ Off poorly, 3w 2nd trn 7
  Previously trained by Casse Mark
26Nov03-3WO fst 1 1/16 :232 :48 1:14 1:473 ⒻMd 25000(25-22) 50 3 21½ 32½ 1½ 13 16½ Husbands P L119 b *2.00 68-23 Wild Senorita1196½ Mentow1172 Raven's End1101½ Stalk rail, drew off 12
31Oct03-5WO fst 6f :223 :461 :582 1:111 ⒻMd 40000(40-35) 43 4 5 31 55 69½ 69¾ Husbands P 119 6.65 78-13 ThtctsOfdnc1196½ EchLbdAnl1151 Spltthdffrnc115hd Stalk 3w, no factor 12
WORKS: Sep26 BM 4f fst :524 H 25/28 Sep19 BM 4f fst :511 H 24/29 Sep12 BM 4f fst :512 H 30/32 Aug20 Dmr 4f fst :483 H 16/47 Aug11 Dmr 4f fst :49 H 39/60
```

Figure 16-18: *Daily Racing Form* past performances for Wild Senorita.

Try a horse that turns back in distance

Horses that run a shorter distance in their next start tend to show more energy in the latter stages of the race. If a horse runs six furlongs instead of seven, common sense tells you that the horse's energy is condensed within a shorter span.

A good example is Jersey Giant (see Figure 16-19). On October 11, 2002, Jersey Giant won going 1 mile and 70 yards. When turned back to a mile race, he won again. He ended his season going a mile and a furlong on December 7, 2002. He returned six months later and rallied strongly to win a six-furlong, New Jersey-bred sprint stakes. His trainer followed the same pattern again on June 12, 2003, winning at 1 mile and 70 yards. Jersey Giant was turned back to 1 mile on July 4 and won yet another race.

```
1   Jersey Giant                                  Dk. b or br g. 5 (Apr)                                  Life 26 9 3 4 $320,729 108 | D.Fst     21 7 3 3 $253,637 108
Red Own: Kilgman Joel A                           Sire: Evening Kris (Kris S.) $3,000                     2004  2 0 0 0  $10,500  87 | Wet(351)   4 2 0 1  $66,782  90
    Turquoise, Black Diamond Frame, Two           Dam: Sporty Card (On to Glory)                    L 120 2003  7 4 1 1 $160,600 108 | Turf(150)  1 0 0 0     $310  43
PIMENTEL J (1 0 0 0 .00) 2004: (681 111 .16)      Br: Joel Kilgman (NJ)                                   Aqu   1 0 0 0       $0  65 | Dst(332)   4 2 1 1  $74,007 101
                                                  Tr: Ryerson James T(3 0 0 1 .00) 2004:(176 24 .14)

22Apr04-8Kee sly 1⅛ :462 1:102 1:344 1:463 4↑BenAli-G3 83 3 33 37½ 47½ 513 424 Bailey J D L116 b 11.00 84 - Midway Road11611¼ Evening Attire116½ Sir Cherokee12012½ Tired, 4w 5
27Mar04-11GP fst 7f :221 :444 1:08 1:22 3↑ArtaxH100k 87 7 7 75½ 77½ 58 58¾ Velasquez C L116 b 9.50 83-16 Speightstown1164½ Pretty Wild111no Wacky for Love1153¼ Saved ground 9
3Oct03-8Med fst 1⅛ :464 1:10 1:341 1:464 3↑MedBC-G2 85 6 42 31½ 63½ 58½ 614 Pimentel J L119 b 11.60 84-08 BowmnsBnd1191¾ Dynvr1203 DUnfrgttblMx116nk Outside,mid track turn 6
13Sep03-3Mth fst 1 1/16 :234 :471 1:102 1:41 3↑SkipTrial57k 101 2 42 32 31½ 21 1hd Pimentel J L119 b *.90 106-04 Jersey Giant119hd Abreeze11910¾ SeattleGlory11315 Bid 3 wide, long drive 4
23Aug03-10Mth fst 1⅛ :48 1:121 1:372 1:501 3↑IselnBCH-G3 108 7 51½ 31 3½ 2½ 31 Pimentel J L115 b 14.70 89-27 Tenpins1191 Aeneas114no Jersey Giant1152¼ Close duel,missed 2nd 9
26Jly03-9Mth fst 1 :234 :471 1:111 1:354 3↑SalvtrMH-G3 97 1 33½ 32 31 22 2¾ Pimentel J L117 b 2.80 97-02 Vinemeister114¾ JrsyGint1172 HighwyProspctor113½ Close,eased out,game 6
4Jly03-8Mth fst 1 :233 :471 1:12 1:371 3↑SkipAway60k 101 3 2hd 31½ 31 1hd 1½ Pimentel J L116 b 2.90 91-14 JerseyGint116½ SeofTrnquility1149¾ BwrAvlnch1131 Aggressive hand ride 6
12Jun03-8Mth fst 170 :231 :464 1:113 1:413 3↑OC 40k/n3x-N 101 1 42½ 43 41½ 21 11¾ Pimentel J L121 b 1.90 95-19 JerseyGint1211¾ LstIntention1216½ StreetLif1191 Long drive,edged ahead 6
24May03-8Mth sly 6f :213 :444 :573 1:103 3↑SJJReillyH50k 90 7 2 610 66½ 33 1¾ Pimentel J L115 b 6.70 86-13 JerseyGiant115¾ BeknowntoMe115nk OurWildcat1194 Steadied 3/16,up late 7
7Dec02-6Aqu fst 1⅛ :50 1:143 1:393 1:52 3↑Alw 44000n1x 87 1 62½ 62¾ 31½ 22½ 24 Pimentel J L119 b 7.00 73-20 Short Hair1194 Jersey Giant1191¾ If He Hollers1171½ Second best 11
8Nov02-8Med fst 1 :233 :463 1:112 1:363 3↑OC 100k/n2x 90 2 32 32½ 2hd 1hd 11 Pimentel J L117 b 2.90 89-22 Jersey Giant1171 Babson1177½ Matzsayo1152½ Lead 1/8,steady drive 6
11Oct02-2Med sly 170 :241 :48 1:122 1:422 3↑SAlw 41250n3x 82 5 43 32 31 31½ 11 Pimentel J L116 b 3.50 83-19 JrsyGint1161 PrfysLgcy114½ TwilightIntrvw1173¾ Momentum lane,clr late 6
WORKS: Nov6 Mth 6f fst 1:14 B 1/1 Oct29 Mth 5f fst 1:01 B 2/18 Oct23 Mth 5f fst 1:01 B 6/39 Oct15 Mth 4f fst :51 B 18/26 Oct9 Mth 4f fst :503 B 34/57 Oct2 Mth 4f fst :514 B 66/76
TRAINER: +180Days(9 .11 $1.40) Dirt(325 .16 $1.55) Routes(167 .14 $1.27) Alw(61 .13 $2.08)
```

Figure 16-19: *Daily Racing Form* past performances for Jersey Giant.

Jersey Giant is a talented gelding and was in good condition, but to see him win over and over again is more than coincidence. Jersey Giant moved up in class with each win. On August 23, 2004, he ran a spirited third in the Iselin Handicap, going a mile and a furlong. Then on September 13, in the shorter 1 1/16-mile Skip Trial, Jersey Giant shortened up to win once more.

Alas, his streak was broken in his return to the races on March 27, 2004. His previous race was 6 months earlier going a mile and a furlong in the Meadowlands Cup. He was soundly beaten in the Artax Handicap at seven furlongs. The quality of the Artax field was excellent. Speightstown and Pretty Wild are both graded stakes winners. In fact, Speightstown won the 2004 Breeders' Cup Sprint at Lone Star Park, so losing to him is no shame.

Keep an eye out for surface changes

In handicapping, you should always pay attention to change. When a trainer changes something, she's trying to find a winning strategy. Switching from dirt to turf or turf to dirt is a very basic change that most horses try at some point in their career.

I'm not sure if one angle is more powerful than the other. But one thing you must consider is the pedigree of the animal, particularly when it comes to grass racing. If a horse considered to have strong turf pedigree runs on grass for the first time, look out for a possible big effort.

Tight Spin is a good example of a horse with hidden turf pedigree (check out Figure 16-20). Her first three races were on dirt, and she was a beaten favorite twice. Notice her very low Beyer numbers: 51, 46, and 54. With Beyers that low, there's nothing to lose trying her on grass. In her first grass race on July 2, 2004, she exploded to an 81 Beyer and broke her maiden by six lengths. Every grass race since, she's been either first or second sprinting, and her grass Beyer numbers remain much higher than her dirt Beyers.

3 Tight Spin
Own: William S Farish
Blue Green, Gold Chevrons, Gold Band On Green
FOGELSONGER R (246 58 25 39 .24) 2004: (927 192 .21)

Dk. b or br f. 4 (Jan)
Sire: Favorite Trick (Phone Trick) $7,500
Dam: Special Moves (Forty Niner)
Br: W S Farish W S Kilroy & Eugene E Weymouth (Ky)
Tr: Weymouth Eugene E(1 1 0 0 1.00) 2004:(120 23 .19)

L 124

Life	9	4	4	0	$107,930	91	D.Fst	3	0	2	0	$8,740	54
2004	9	4	4	0	$107,930	91	Wet(316)	0	0	0	0	$0	-
2003	0	M	0	0	$0	-	Turf(256)	6	4	2	0	$99,190	91
Pim	0	0	0	0	$0	-	Dst(376)	0	0	0	0	$0	-

30Oct04-9Med	gd	5f	Ⓣ	:214	:45		:571	3+ⒻWitchesBrw60k	91	2	7	41½	53½	32	2no	Santagata N	L119	3.60	91- 09	KissMKti116no TightSpin1192½ AmbitionUnbridld115nk	Inside, just missed 12
9Oct04-9Med	fm	5f	Ⓣ	:213	:442		:562	3+ⒻIncrblRvng60k	86	10	2	42	42	41	1nk	Santagata N	L115	5.20	95- 05	TightSpin115nk MelodyofColors1191 TheRodoExprss115nk	3 wide, driving 10
27Sep04-7Del	fm	*5f	Ⓣ	:223	:453		:57	3+ⒻAlw 38900n2x	85	5	2	31½	31½	1hd	13	Santagata N	L119	*1.10	100 -	*Tight Spin*1193 Party Pirate1171¼ Kallie Bird1223¾	Bid 1/8 out, drew off 8
7Sep04-8Del	fm	5f	Ⓣ	:221	:45		:57	3+ⒻAlw 39500n2x	79	8	3	61¾	72¼	64	21	Alvarado R Jr	L122	*1.20	94- 05	Fashion Idol1121 *Tight Spin*122¾ ⒹParty Pirate117½	Looped,up for 2nd 10
18Aug04-2Pen	fm	5f	Ⓣ	:221	:45		:563	3+ⒻAlw 12900n1x	82	5	6	42¼	3½	31	15	Santagata N	L116	*.70	90- 10	Tight Spin1165 *Texasquickstepper*1171¾ Mexican Riviera1162¼	Driving 12
2Jly04-4Col	fm	5f	Ⓣ	:221	:45		:564	3+ⒻMd Sp Wt 27k	81	3	3	1½	11	14½	16¼	Fogelsonger R	L124	*1.90	95- 07	*Tight Spin*1246¼ Debbie Sue1174½ Cavallo Grigio124hd	Driving 9
8Jun04-10Pha	fst	6½f		:214	:45	1:113	1:183	3+ⒻMd Sp Wt 24k	54	3	4	1½	1½	3½	42½	Molina V H	L122	*.80	79- 19	Star of Sahm117nk *Nash's Valay*1121¼ *Power Tower*1121	Faded late 10
17May04-6Pha	fst	7f		:223	:454	1:114	1:263	3+ⒻMd Sp Wt 19k	46	3	4	1hd	1hd	2hd	2¾	Molina V H	L123	*1.20	75- 15	AlrmngFntsy117¾ TghtSpn1234½ RynsWtAngl1173½	Dueled inside, gamely 6
10Apr04-7Pha	fst	5½f		:222	:464	:593	1:061	4+ⒻMd Sp Wt 23k	51	6	3	44	42½	22	23½	Molina V H	L122	4.30	79- 17	Best Issue1223½ Tight Spin1224¾ Mint' Luck1222¼	Wide, tired late 8

TRAINER: Turf/Dirt(20 .20 $1.37) Dirt(182 .18 $1.37) Sprint(66 .20 $1.44) Stakes(7 .14 $1.77)

Figure 16-20: *Daily Racing Form* past performances for Tight Spin.

Remember horses for courses

Horses for courses is a horse racing cliché you hear a lot because it's true. Horses do prefer certain courses, and with the information provided by the *Daily Racing Form,* their preferences are much easier to spot.

A horse that perfectly exemplifies horses for courses is Sightseek (see Chapter 12). She has run from coast-to-coast, but what jumps off her past performances is that she's undefeated in six starts on the Belmont Park main track. Conversely, she has never won in five starts at Santa Anita. I'm not assuming she likes Belmont and dislikes Santa Anita. Her history tells me so in black and white.

Chapter 17

Taking On Handicapping Tournaments

. . . .

In This Chapter

▶ Getting acquainted with tournament rules

▶ Creating a winning game plan

▶ Playing in the big-money Las Vegas tournaments

. . . .

Horse racing doesn't take a back seat to poker when it comes to big-money tournaments. Although the poker craze has led to an expanded World Series of Poker and The World Poker Tour worth millions of dollars, horse racing has its own tournament schedule that can turn your head in no time with illusions of grandeur.

Currently, horseplayers can participate in two end-of-season, rich handicapping tournaments: the *Daily Racing Form*/National Thoroughbred Racing Association National Handicapping Championship and the Horseplayer World Series. Horseplayers play in satellite tournaments all over the country year-round to try to qualify for one or both of these events.

The growing popularity of handicapping tournaments is due mainly to prize money. Handicapping tournaments give you, the horseplayer, a chance to put up $400 or $500 in an entry fee with a chance to win $75,000, $100,000, or more. And there are plenty of smaller tournaments with lower entry fees but still generous prize money available. You're capable of winning a tournament if you know how to handicap and can make smart decisions based upon your knowledge and understanding of the tournament rules.

Knowing the Rules and Requirements

Before you enter a tournament, take time to read the rules and the format of the tournament. If you don't think the tournament set-up fits your style of handicapping, you don't have to play. There's no crime in passing, because there are plenty of other handicapping tournaments. For example, if you like win betting, why enter a tournament that allows exactas and trifectas? If your focus is primarily on New York and Southern California racing, do you want to be forced into playing races from Delta Downs and Sam Houston? Read the rules, read the format, and make a decision that's right for you.

Tournament format

A correlation exists between tournament format and your chances of doing well. If you understand your own strengths and weaknesses, you'll know which tournaments are best suited for you.

For example, a basic thing you need to know is whether a tournament is held over one, two, or three days. I can tell you that a three-day tournament takes a large amount of stamina to get through. By the third day, your brain is turning into mush. Regardless of how many days the tournament is, if the only races you're handicapping are the live races at that racetrack, the tournament is less taxing. You're handicapping between 10 and 30 races maximum. However, a multiple-day tournament with as many as eight simulcasts (the satellite signals from other racetracks), and you're looking at 220 races in three days. That'll take the starch out of the strongest horseplayer.

Some tournaments require you to play mandatory races. Mandatory races are races that everyone in the tournament must play. In mandatory races, you have a tough decision to make. Should you play a long shot with a chance to win, or should you bet one of the logical favorites? Remember, if you pass on an $8 winner to bet a 12/1 long shot that loses, you've conceded ground to many competitors. If the 12/1 horse wins, you've blown past a lot of handicappers.

To make a good decision, you need to know the situation you're in. Where are you on the leader board? If you're far behind, the decision is easy — play the long shot. If you're in the hunt, a surest winner makes sense. Do you have enough races left to catch up, or do you need a big long shots right now?

One of the newest tournament formats is bracketing, like you see with the NCAA basketball tournament. Horseplayers are bracketed to face one another in a head-to-head face-off. If you win, you move on to the next bracket. The Turf-Vivor tournament at Gulfstream Park in Hallandale, Florida and the Brawl in the Fall at the Reno Hilton in Nevada use this format.

Another format is using real money for betting and scoring in a live bankroll tournament. The advantage is two-fold. When you make real live bets for tournament scoring, if you win, not only does your score go up, but you also get to keep the profits because the bankroll is live, meaning it's really your money. The host racetrack or casino is happy too, because a live bankroll tournament guarantees more parimutuel handle from the tournament players.

Scoring

If you brought together the most diabolical minds in horse racing and asked them to concoct dozens of different ways to score a tournament, you'd be shocked at the mish-mash of different rules they'd come up with. Even something as basic as the dollar unit for scoring isn't uniform in horse racing tournaments. Some venues use $2, some $20, some $100, and some $200. Some venues even use no dollar unit at all because they're reality-based live bankroll tournaments (see preceding section).

The types of wagers also differ. Some venues have just win betting, others win and place betting, and still more across the board — meaning to win, place, and show (see Chapter 4 on straight bets). Some venues allow exotic wagering like exactas, trifectas, and superfectas (see Chapter 15). Although I've seen tournaments use multi-horse wagers, I've yet to see multi-race wagers (see Chapter 15) allowed. Thank goodness.

Why payoffs are capped

Caps, meaning a limit on the parimutuel prices, are necessary to maintain the integrity of a handicapping tournament. Otherwise, the handicappers turn into indiscriminate dart throwers. Nowadays, all tournaments have caps, except for real live bankroll tournaments (see the section, "Tournament format," earlier in the chapter). Why? Well, here's a little story.

In 1997, when Don Barberino organized the first Sports Haven Handicapping Challenge in New Haven, Connecticut, he thought he had all his bases covered. He had a sold out tournament, fine hospitality in place for all the players, and a leader board to keep track of the action. What could possibly go wrong?

Back then, most handicapping tournaments didn't have caps on parimutuel prices. So on day one, when Criminal Suit won at Gulfstream Park and paid $110.80, the leader board exploded. Those handicappers who had Criminal Suit were so far ahead of the rest that the other handicappers needed another $100-horse just to catch up.

On the second and final day of the tournament, players were reduced to stabbing at the longest-price horses they could find that had some glimmer of hope. One of the final tournament races was the Hutcheson Stakes at Gulfstream Park, the same racetrack that produced Criminal Suit.

In the Hutcheson field was Frisk Me Now, at 20/1 on the morning line, who went off at 99/1 odds on the tote board. He was a closer in a field packed with speed, and under the circumstances, he was worth playing. Barberino watched in disbelief as Frisk Me Now rallied down the center of the track and passed the favorite, Confide, in the final strides to win the Hutcheson.

Frisk Me Now paid an incredible $213.80 to win. He was a 105/1 long shot. In the tournament, 19 players bet on Frisk Me Now and those 19 zoomed into the top of the leader board.

Most tournament win caps are 20/1 on the win price, meaning a maximum $42 payout for a $2 win bet. So under today's win cap rules, Frisk Me Now would've paid $42 in a tournament, not $213.80.

Unless you're an indiscriminate horseplayer, the scoring system should mean a lot to you. The purest form of handicapping is *win-only scoring*. If your horse finishes first, you win. If you suffer a tough beat, too bad, you lose. When allowed, *place scoring* or *place and show scoring* is more soothing to the psyche. Place and show scoring rewards big long shots that run second and/or third but don't win. Generous place and show prices on long shots can add up fast. But I've found that even in win and place or win, place, and show scoring, you still need to pick mostly winners to be successful.

When exotic wagers are allowed, it turns handicapping tournaments into wagering tournaments. Although you may like this style of tournament, I have a problem with it, because the advantage goes to players who are good bettors and not necessarily good handicappers.

Bottom line: Read the scoring rules first. Know your own strengths and weaknesses as a horseplayer. To get your money's worth, enter the tournaments that are right for you.

Entry fees

Although you'll find some free handicapping tournaments out there, most tournaments have an entry fee. Even a minimum entry fee weeds out a lot of so-called horseplayers. The entry fees I've seen range from $5 to $5,000.

I handicap horse races for the *Las Vegas Review-Journal* and get criticism from time to time. (It goes with the territory.) But critics who thought I couldn't pick a one-horse race were astounded after I won the 2003 Championship at the Orleans Handicapping Tournament. First prize was $111,680. The entry fee was $500, but anybody can join in, including you.

One way you can look at entry fees is to consider what you get for your money. Some tournaments give away gifts and feed you all week. You get free *Daily Racing Forms,* programs, and other handicapping tools. If you play real money, you build *comps,* which are points that lead to other perks. Most tournaments pay smaller prize money to the top finishers. If you're one of the top finishers, in essence, you receive your entry fee back plus any additional prize money. Of course, you can bet real money out of your pocket and win, even if you don't win a cash prize in the tournament. If you play a lot of tournaments and do well, the entry fee is a tax write-off if you itemize your IRS return (see Chapter 3).

Some venues include added money for prizes on top of returning all the entry fees. The hosts of the tournaments are in it to make a profit, but returning all the entry fees as prize money is very equitable to all the contestants. The added money also creates a positive expectancy, somewhat like a carryover in a pick 6 pool. It puts extra money into the pot for you to win.

If you want to go to Las Vegas in January to play in either the *Daily Racing Form*/National Thoroughbred Racing Association National Handicapping Championship or the Horseplayer World Series (see "Headin' to Vegas: Big-Money Tournaments," later in the chapter), you need to qualify, and paying entry fees is part of the cost of doing business.

Strategizing for Success

A football coach wouldn't go into the Super Bowl without a strong game plan to win. For you to win a big-money handicapping tournament, you need the same mentality. When my partner, Lou Filoso, and I won the 2003 Championship at the Orleans Tournament, we had a game plan going into it. But we learned some valuable lessons over the 3-day tournament that I'm happy to share with you. This is friendly advice that you can choose to use or not use.

Tournament horseplayers make up one of the friendliest fraternities you'll find. People are willing to share ideas and insights with one another, and you should listen. I have and will continue to learn from other tournament players, because they know tricks of the trade that can really help you in the long run.

Play to a number

Of all the tips I've been given, *playing to a number* may be the most basic and the most important. By playing to a number, you find out the past winning scores for the tournament you're involved in. Unless the rules have changed at some point, you should see a trend. Most tournament directors supply you with this information in a handout.

What I do is find a score that would put me in the top-ten nearly every year. Whatever the number is, that's the score I shoot for. If you reach that number on the final day of the tournament, you should be in a position to win it all. At worst, you'll probably cash for good prize money.

If you're in a two-day tournament, you divide the final score by two to create your daily goals. If you're in a three-day tournament, you divide by three for your daily goals.

If on day one, a player records a colossal score, don't lose sleep over it. History tells you that the horseplayer will finish with a final score close to the trend you've researched for the tournament. It's nearly impossible for a horseplayer to have two fantastic days, much less three, in a row.

Handicap the races early

You absolutely can't win a tournament without studying the races the night before and again in the morning. Although no law restricts you from enjoying yourself at a handicapping tournament, the main reason you pay a big entry fee is to win. These tournaments require work.

When you study the races ahead of time, you find unplayable races to throw out. You familiarize yourself with races that are prime betting opportunities. As the scratches and changes come in during the day, you're flexible enough to make necessary adjustments.

After your game plan is in place, you give yourself chances to make changes on the fly, be flexible, and really focus on what you need to do to win.

Maintain your focus

Keeping your focus in a tournament atmosphere is very hard. You may sit at a table with a bunch of talkative horseplayers. You may have friends stop by to chat. You may handicap real bets and not focus on tournament plays. Or you may be preoccupied with fuming over a tough beat.

Bottom line: Try not to get distracted. The next bet may be the one that wins the tournament for you. If you suffer a bad beat, you have to act like a pitcher who just gave up a home run. Shake it off and pitch a good game the rest of the way.

Sitting with people you know and get along with is important. For example, if you sit with someone who's a chatterbox or who smokes (and you don't), you'll be distracted all day long.

Arrive at acceptable odds

Early in a tournament, I don't mind playing lower odds horses because I want to post a score on day one. This style of betting is where I deviate from many professional tournament players. In win, place, and show betting tournaments, common advice is for you to play horses only 10/1 odds or higher. That advice makes sense because you really need to find long shot plays to score well. However, I'll play a $10 or $12 horse that I feel very strongly about. My reasoning is that on the first day, I want to establish a good score and not *zero out* (lose every bet and have a zero score).

This strategy of playing lower odds horses on day one does two things:

- ✔ It takes the pressure off of day two if you've posted a good number.
- ✔ It affords you breathing room, depending on the prices of the winners from day one.

When Lou Filoso and I won the 2003 Orleans Tournament, scores were very low on day one because very few long shot horses won. The favorites did well at the contest tracks. Our score ended up in the top-20 because we accepted some surest type winners. Taking the points early on placed us in a position to win the whole tournament on day three.

Many veteran tournament players aren't afraid to lose lots of bets playing 10/1 odds horses and higher. Their strategy is different than mine. However, it's possible for all of their long shots to lose. If you have a cast iron stomach that can handle losing and the tough beats that go along with playing all long shots, then long shots is a good proven formula for you. You just need to know ahead of time that playing all long shot horses can be feast or famine.

Save some bullets for the end

A *bullet* is the term used for a tournament bet. Saving bullets for the end is comparable to a football coach saving his time outs for the end of the game. Saving bullets is sound strategic maneuvering, because you may need your bets at the end of the tournament. In any tournament, you have a finite number of plays, so each one is precious.

If you play in a venue that has a leader board, you know exactly how to play the final races to try to win. Without a leader board, you still can make an educated guess.

In the 2003 Orleans Tournament, my partner liked a horse at Santa Anita in the final race on day three of the tournament. He had me save our last bullet for a turf maiden named Royal Fan. Royal Fan won at 9/1 odds and paid $21.60. That win catapulted us from 12th place all the way to 1st. In fact, the 60¢ parimutuel price was the winning margin over the second place finisher. A 12th place finish would've won us $3,490. Instead, we won $111,680. Now that's an expensive bullet.

Play multiple entries

Many tournament professionals play more than one entry or ticket, and here's why: They spread out a series of long shot horses over two, three, or even more tickets. Their hope is that some of the long shots will win and will be fortunate enough to be aligned on the same entry.

If that's the case, the horseplayers have at least one entry with a gigantic score. That entry becomes the main ticket going into day two, while the others become back-up tickets. The formula is proven successful, but you need a lot of moolah upfront to pay for all the entry fees.

Betting more than one horse in a race often comes into play. If you identify a weak favorite and narrow down a play to three or four long shot horses, you'll spread the three or four long shot horses out and hope to win with one of the long shot horses at 20/1 odds, 30/1 odds, or more.

The frustrating part of playing multiple entries is winning with a few nice long shots and not having more than one long shot come in on any one ticket. That's unlucky. The strategy is to align two or three of the long shot winners on one ticket to create a very high score, but that requires some luck.

Be careful of cap horses

Here's where reading the rules of the tournament becomes very important: If there's a cap on the win price — in most cases, 20/1 odds — playing horses with higher odds doesn't make sense unless you really like the animal. Usually, there's a good reason why horses are 30/1, 50/1, or higher odds.

Some tournaments allow for a full win price for part of the bet and a cap on the remainder. If so, then a horse like Frisk Me Now that wins and pays $213.80 may be a good play (see the sidebar, "Why payoffs are capped," earlier in the chapter for more on this horse). In essence, you have a partial win cap because part of your bet is eligible for the full value of the win price. Most tournaments nowadays have a cap at 20/1, so restricting your plays to 20/1 horses and less is the way to go.

Pray for luck

Any horseplayer who wins a big money handicapping tournament and says she wasn't lucky isn't telling you the truth. A lot of skill is required to handicap the races and decipher horses that have a good chance at acceptable odds. But luck is a huge variable when most of your horses run so well that you collect enough points to get into position to win a tournament.

Luck enters the picture when you win a lot of photo finishes. Or when a horse is disqualified, and you benefit when your horse gets placed first. So, if you have a lucky pair of socks, a medallion from your mom, or anything that brings you good luck, take it with you to the tournament.

Headin' to Vegas: Big-Money Tournaments

For horseplayers, the pot of gold at the end of the rainbow is winning either the *Daily Racing Form*/National Thoroughbred Racing Association National Handicapping Championship or the Horseplayer World Series. Of course, you might win both, but first read the preceding section about luck.

If you think you'll qualify to play in both tournaments, plan on spending two weeks in Nevada. (Can I interest you in a great time-share condo opportunity? Just kidding.) Both championships are held in Sin City (also known as Las Vegas) in January.

A yearlong series of qualifying tournaments is held throughout the United States at racetracks and OTBs (off-track betting sites) for horseplayers to earn their way to Las Vegas in January. Horseplayers are willing to fly to out-of-town tournaments until they qualify. Because there's a limited number of qualifying positions each year, every seat at the proverbial poker table has tremendous value. For tournament schedules, check the *Daily Racing Form, Horseplayer Magazine,* or some handicapping Web sites for more details.

The Daily Racing Form/National Thoroughbred Racing Association National Handicapping Championship

Steven Crist, chairman and publisher of the *Daily Racing Form,* is a Harvard graduate who loves playing the ponies and understands the Thoroughbred horseplayer. As the saying goes, it takes one to know one. For years, he covered horse racing for the *New York Times.* During that time, Crist became known as one of the best pick 6 players on the East Coast. He'd construct a pick 6 ticket and then sell shares to friends and acquaintances in the press box. For many, buying a share from Crist was a worthwhile leap of faith.

 In 1998, Crist led a group that purchased the *Daily Racing Form,* the publication known as "America's Turf Authority since 1894." He brought scores of new ideas to the horse racing daily, many of which he'd incorporated into the now defunct *Racing Times* newspaper. (In the early 1990s, Crist began the *Racing Times* as a direct competitor to the *Daily Racing Form.* How ironic that today Crist is chairman of the *DRF.*)

Crist developed one of his new ideas with then National Thoroughbred Racing Association commissioner, Tim Smith. They came up with a plan for their two organizations to sponsor a year-end handicapping tournament to crown a Horseplayer of the Year at the Eclipse Awards, horse racing's equivalent to the Oscars for movies or Emmys for television. Thus was born the *Daily Racing Form*/National Thoroughbred Racing Association National Handicapping Championship (*DRF*/NTRA NHC).

The format of the championship is simple. Contestants make 15 $2 win and place bets each day of the two-day tournament — that's 30 bets overall. Eight races each day are mandatory, meaning everyone plays the same races. The remaining seven races each day are optional. Participants track the proceedings by watching the leader board. But as I discuss earlier in this chapter (in "Play to a number"), the key is to play to a number and not let the leader board sway you until you get to the very end of the tournament.

The first *DRF*/NTRA NHC in January 2000 paid out $200,000 with $100,000 going to the winner. By January 2005, the money had doubled to $400,000 total and $200,000 to the winner.

If you're not quite ready to play in the tournament, plans are in place to televise the championship, which is played at Bally's in Las Vegas, on a tape-delayed basis. The show format will look a lot like ESPN's coverage of the World Series of Poker at the Horseshoe in Las Vegas.

The Horseplayer World Series

The $1 million Horseplayer World Series — the newest, richest tournament on the block — is hosted by one of the most respected race book (see Chapter 23) proprietors in the country, the Coast Resorts properties of Las Vegas.

The first annual tournament was held January 27 through 29, 2005. At first glance, some people viewed it as a competitor to the *DRF*/NTRA NHC (see the preceding section). But if you ask the big horseplayers, they'll tell you the Horseplayer World Series is an opportunity, not a competitor. And no tournament is quite like this one on the tournament landscape: The $500,000 first prize is bigger than the total purse of any other handicapping tournament.

One major difference between the Horseplayer World Series and the *DRF*/NTRA NHC is that if you don't qualify, you can still buy in to the Horseplayer World Series for a $1,000 entry fee. That makes entering a lot like the World Series of Poker. If you have the cash, you can try your hand against the best. After all, taking on the best handicappers in the business isn't all about the money; it's also about the thrill of playing and possibly beating the pros at their own game.

Qualifying for the Horseplayer World Series is done in a similar manner to the *DRF*/NTRA NHC — at racetracks and OTB satellite handicapping tournaments throughout the calendar year. The Horseplayer World Series tournament rules call for 11 bets a day each of three days. Every play is a mythical $200 win and place bet. The first $10 win and place payoffs are at full track prices. The remaining $190 win and place prices are capped at 14/1 odds for win and 6/1 odds for place.

It'll be interesting to see how the Horseplayer World Series evolves in the future. The first time out of the box is always a little trial and error. But one good thing about horseplayers is that if you treat them right, they'll be back.

Other Las Vegas tournaments

Penn National may have hosted the first handicapping tournament, but Las Vegas is where the genre evolved into what it is today.

Today, Las Vegas is the home to many big money handicapping tournaments throughout the year. Many horseplayers think nothing about flying in for a long weekend from anywhere in the country. Table 17-1 lists some of the major tournaments in town. Please contact the host casino for more information.

Table 17-1	Big-Money Las Vegas Tournaments	
Tournament	*Host Casino*	*Month*
Win a Place to the Big Show	Bally's	January
Daily Racing Form/National Thoroughbred Racing Association National Handicapping Championship	Bally's	January
Suncoast, Barbary Coast Last Chance Shoot Out	Barbary Coast and Suncoast	January
Horseplayer World Series	The Orleans	January
Championship at The Orleans	The Orleans	March
Bally's Moolah	Bally's	April
Gold Coast, Suncoast, The Orleans Derby Shoot Out	Gold Coast, Suncoast, and The Orleans	May, week of the Kentucky Derby

(continued)

Table 17-1 *(continued)*

Tournament	Host Casino	Month
Pick the Ponies Invitational	Las Vegas Hilton	May, week of the Kentucky Derby
Gold Coast Summer Classic	Gold Coast	July
Summer Stakes	Bally's	August
Fall Classic at The Orleans	The Orleans	October
Pick the Ponies Invitational	Las Vegas Hilton	October, week of the Breeders' Cup
Gold Coast, Suncoast Breeders' Cup Shoot Out	Gold Coast and Suncoast	October, week of the Breeders' Cup

* Denotes that horseplayer must qualify for tournament

Chapter 18

The Race for the Triple Crown: Picking a Kentucky Derby Winner and More

- -

In This Chapter

▶ Getting the quick facts about the Derby

▶ Knowing why 2-year-old races are important

▶ Being leery of the jinx of the Breeders' Cup Juvenile winner

▶ Following the results of the spring 3-year-old Derby prep races

▶ Zeroing in on the primary contenders

▶ Understanding why post positions are critical

▶ Picking winners for the Preakness and Belmont

- -

*T*he Kentucky Derby is the world's most famous horse race. On the first Saturday in May, everyone in the United States and many people outside of the country become horse racing fans. Well, at least for the two plus minutes the 1¼ mile race takes.

The Kentucky Derby, however, is only the first leg of horse racing's *Triple Crown,* which includes the Preakness at Pimlico (Baltimore, Maryland) and the Belmont Stakes at Belmont Park (Elmont, New York). Winning the elusive Triple Crown is among the most difficult feats in all of sports. Only 11 horses have won the Triple Crown, but none since Affirmed in 1978.

In this chapter, I give some must-know info about the Kentucky Derby, and I talk about what a horse has to do to make it to the Derby and the other Triple Crown events. I also clue you in on handicapping tips for picking the primary contenders for the Derby, the Preakness, and the Belmont Stakes.

Derby 101: What You Need to Know

If you're a newcomer to horse racing, you want to know enough about the Kentucky Derby to be able to talk about it around the water cooler at least. Here's a list of some pertinent details about this famous race:

- ✔ **Purse:** $2 million
- ✔ **Horses:** 3-year-olds
- ✔ **Distance:** 1¼ miles
- ✔ **Racetrack:** Churchill Downs
- ✔ **Where:** Louisville, Kentucky
- ✔ **When:** First Saturday in May
- ✔ **Surface:** Main dirt track
- ✔ **Starters:** Limited to 20 horses
- ✔ **Average attendance:** 145,000
- ✔ **First time run:** 1875
- ✔ **Traditional drink:** Mint julep

  The mint julep has been the traditional drink of the Kentucky Derby since the early 1900s. A quintessential southern drink, a mint julep is made by mixing 2 cups sugar, 2 cups water, sprigs of fresh mint, crushed ice, and Kentucky whiskey.

- ✔ **Nickname:** The Run for the Roses

The Not-So-Terrible Twos: Why 2-Year-Old Horses Should Race

The first Kentucky Derby was run in 1875. In all the years since, only one colt went on to win the Kentucky Derby without racing as a 2-year-old — Apollo in 1882.

Gaining racing experience as a 2-year-old is very important. Trainers have made this human comparison to the development of a racehorse:

  ✔ **The 2-year-old season is considered grade school.** Some kids grow up faster than others do. The physically mature kids excel early in sports, while many of the other kids are gangly or uncoordinated and need more time to develop. Horses are the same way. Some horses are precocious and run fast early, while some horses are gangly and need more time to grow into themselves. The 2-year-old horses that run fast early aren't necessarily good long-term Kentucky Derby prospects. The Derby distance separates those horses that are sprinters and milers from the true-distance horses that can last the grueling 1¼ miles. So, a horse's 2-year-old season is very important. A trainer not only teaches a horse good habits, but he learns about the horse's ability and personality — information that can help him maximize the potential of the animal.

✔ **The 3-year-old season is comparable to high school.** In high school, many of the precocious grade schools kids have stopped growing. No longer are they the biggest and fastest athletes. Some of the slow developers had major growth spurts and are now the star athletes. In horse racing in the spring, 3-year-old horses develop quickly, and the good ones show improvement with every start. You find that the horses that were fast 2-year-olds can't win as 3-year-olds when the distance of the races grows longer. Watch the Derby prep races closely and study which horses are improving and which horses run poorly and fall by the way-side on the road to the Kentucky Derby.

✔ **The 4-year-old year season is like college and graduate school.** Physical maturity peaks, and the mental part isn't far behind. This time is when a horse should be running some of the best races of his career. The Triple Crown is for 3-year-old horses, but a lot of those talented horses run even better the following season.

All Thoroughbreds have the same birthday — January 1 — even if they have different birthdates, called *foal dates* in horse racing. The January 1 birthday provides continuity to the sport in regards to the ages of the horses. That means some 2-year-old horses are a few months older than others, depending on their foal dates.

Beware the Breeders' Cup Juvenile Jinx

The winner of the Breeders' Cup Juvenile is usually named the champion 2-year-old colt. The Breeders' Cup races are usually held in late October or early November. The Breeders' Cup Juvenile winner becomes one of the early favorites for the following spring's Kentucky Derby.

However, the cold hard fact is that since the Breeders' Cup World Thoroughbred Championships started in 1984, no Breeders' Cup Juvenile winner has gone on to capture the Kentucky Derby. That's right — zero. In fact, only three horses that even ran in the Breeders' Cup Juvenile have gone on to win the Kentucky Derby — Spend a Buck in 1984, Alysheba in 1986, and Sea Hero in 1992.

In theory, you'd think that the best 2-year-olds in training run in the prestigious Breeders' Cup Juvenile and that the top Kentucky Derby contenders come out of that field. History, however, has proven otherwise.

In fact, the jinx has begun to affect many trainers who think about the long-term implications of running their 2-year-olds in the Breeders' Cup Juvenile. For instance, in 2003, trainer Nick Zito, who has won two Kentucky Derbies with Strike the Gold (1991) and Go For Gin (1994), had three top 2-year-olds (Birdstone, Eurosilver, The Cliff's Edge) and passed on the Breeders' Cup Juvenile for all three. I'm sure the jinx entered into Zito's mindset.

Theories about the jinx abound, but the one that makes sense to me is that although a trainer wants her 2-year-old colt to gain racing experience, running in a few stakes races and then the Breeders' Cup Juvenile may be too stressful for the horse. Year after year, the number of colts that run in the Breeders' Cup Juvenile and make the Kentucky Derby field the following spring is fewer and fewer. Another theory is that the colts that excel in their 2-year-old season may be early bloomers that over time don't develop into top 3-year-olds. I cover the physical and mental maturity factor earlier in the chapter in "The Not-So-Terrible Twos: Why 2-Year-Olds Should Race."

In handicapping the Kentucky Derby winner, especially if you're looking to make a future book wager (see Chapter 23 on Las Vegas), don't rely on the Breeders' Cup Juvenile to help you with your predictions (except for maybe some horses to avoid).

Watching the Kentucky Derby Prep Races

Horses just don't magically appear on the first Saturday in May and win the Kentucky Derby. Hollywood scripts may take creative license, but in real life, Kentucky Derby contenders run in a gauntlet of grueling prep races beforehand.

The Triple Crown season begins on January 1 — the official birthday of all racehorses. Over the next four months, the trainer of a Kentucky Derby hopeful plans a three-race schedule to prove two things: one, that her horse is talented enough to be competitive, and two, that the horse is peaking to run his best race on the first Saturday in May.

The Derby prep races have gained so much recognition, and the purses are so rich that Churchill Downs in 2005 decided to double the purse of the Kentucky Derby to $2 million. Winning money is one thing, but winning the Kentucky Derby gains a place in history, and all the prestige that goes along with it, for the winning horse, jockey, trainer, and owner.

Table 18-1 shows some of the major Kentucky Derby prep races, where they're run, and when they're usually run.

Table 18-1	Major Prep Races for the Kentucky Derby	
Name of Prep Race	*Racetrack*	*Number of Weeks before the Kentucky Derby*
Lexington	Keeneland	2
Arkansas Derby	Oaklawn Park	3
Blue Grass Stakes	Keeneland	3
Wood Memorial	Aqueduct	4
Santa Anita Derby	Santa Anita Park	4
Illinois Derby	Hawthorne	4
Florida Derby	Gulfstream Park	5
Lane's End	Turfway Park	6
Gotham	Aqueduct	6
Rebel	Oaklawn Park	7
San Felipe	Santa Anita Park	7
Tampa Bay Derby	Tampa Bay Downs	7
Louisiana Derby	Fair Grounds	9
San Rafael	Santa Anita Park	9
Fountain of Youth	Gulfstream Park	9
Holy Bull	Gulfstream Park	13

My advice to you in watching the Kentucky Derby prep races is to avoid the obvious. Anyone can see who the winner is and that he ran well. The secret is watching the remainder of the field in these prep races, because you'll find the Kentucky Derby long shots here. You're looking for horses getting into traffic trouble, a veteran trainer using a prep race for conditioning off of a long layoff, or a race shape that makes the race difficult for certain types of runners.

A racing term you don't want to be called as a horseplayer is a *MOTO,* which stands for *master of the obvious.* The Kentucky Derby is the type of race where the public overbets the obvious horses. The betting favorite lost the Kentucky Derby every year between 1980 and 1999.

Future wager for the Kentucky Derby

There's one parimutuel source of a future bet on the Derby, and it's the *Kentucky Derby Future Wager*. Churchill Downs offers this bet during three betting periods each spring. Logically, they're called pool one, pool two, and pool three. Because the future bet is a parimutuel bet, your final odds on a Kentucky Derby hopeful won't be determined until the pool closes. I cover future book wagers on the Kentucky Derby and other special event horse races in detail in Chapter 23.

Following (or Not) the Buzz on Public Horses

In the weeks leading up to the Kentucky Derby, daily reports come out covering each of the contenders. If a horse has a flaw, or if some horse is looking great and is working exceptionally well, the press magnifies the issue.

A fine line exists between media hype and a colt's real progress. The public, probably influenced by the media, are like sheep looking for and following the hot horse, or what I call the "public horse." In every Kentucky Derby, at least one or two horses' chances get blown out of proportion. The bettors back the public horse heavily at the betting window and then watch him run nowhere.

The public horse isn't the favorite but rather a horse whose odds are well below its real chances of winning. The real odds should be 12/1 and higher. Some of the recent public horses are listed in Table 18-2.

Table 18-2	Public Horse Results of Recent Years		
Year	**Horse**	**Derby Odds**	**Derby Finish**
2004	Tapit	$6.40-1	9th
2003	Ten Cents A Shine	$6.60-1	8th
2002	Saarland	$6.90-1	10th
2001	Dollar Bill	$6.60-1	15th
2000	Captain Steve	$8.10-1	8th
1999	Vicar	$8.20-1	18th
1998	Favorite Trick	$4.40-1	8th
1997	Concerto	$10.80-1	9th

The reason a horse becomes a public horse may be because of its well-respected trainer, as was the case with Tapit (Michael Dickinson), Saarland (Shug McGaughey), and Captain Steve (Bob Baffert). Or perhaps the horse has a famous owner, like Concerto's George Steinbrenner, who also owns the New York Yankees. Or, maybe a horse got into obvious trouble during a prep race, like Dollar Bill or Ten Cents A Shine did.

You're looking for a good reason to bet a nice long shot. But in the case of the public horse, the attention on the horse has taken all the parimutuel win value out of the play, and the horse ran out of the money. A public horse is not a good bet, because it's now a big underlay.

Getting into Place: The Importance of Post Position

You'd think that a quick statistical study of Kentucky Derby post positions would tell the tale. Most Derby winners — 12 — have come out of post positions one and five. So those two are the best post draws for the race, right? Not necessarily.

No horse has won from post one since Ferdinand in 1986. If you saw that Derby, you can recall that Hall of Fame jockey Bill Shoemaker had a miracle trip in one of his greatest rides ever, weaving through small openings and eventually working his way to the front.

A more telling statistic about post one is that since 1964, Ferdinand is the only winner from the one post. The logical reason for this drought is that the size of the Kentucky Derby fields had gotten bigger and bigger, to the point that a rule was implemented restricting the field to a maximum of 20 starters. The 1974 Derby, which had 23 starters and was a very roughly run race, helped instigate the new rule.

So, although post one can be an advantage in a 6-, 8-, or 10-horse field, it's at a distinct disadvantage in a 16- to 20-horse field. Too much pressure comes from the outside horses, forcing the jockey in the one post to do something he may not want to do, such as move prematurely to maintain his position or take way back to avoid getting jammed by outside horses.

At the Kentucky Derby draw for post positions, where the horse's owners and trainers take turns picking their posts, the posts that are taken first are 6, 7, 8, and 9 because they're the middle posts in a 14-horse starting gate. When the Kentucky Derby has more than 14 starters, an auxiliary gate is used for horses post 15 and out.

The recent en vogue posts to grab are 13, 14, 15, and 16 because of the big gap between post 14 (the end of the main starting gate) and post 15 (the start of the auxiliary gate). The space is about the width of two stalls. The horses in posts 14 and 15 invariably break towards the space to avoid bumping with other horses. Horses 13 and 16 benefit because they have less pressure from that one side.

The Kentucky Derby is a 1¼ mile race. The race starts from a chute extending well past the top of the stretch. Even though there's a long run until the first turn, getting a clean start remains very important to Derby success. It may be a coincidence, but in the ten Derbies run between 1995 and 2004, six winners have come from posts 13 through 16. That's why the post position in the Kentucky Derby is more important than in any horse race run all year long.

Going for It All: What Happens after the Kentucky Derby

The Kentucky Derby may be the world's most famous horse race, but it's only the first leg of horse racing's Triple Crown. A horse hasn't won The Triple Crown since Affirmed in 1978. Many colts have won the Kentucky Derby and Preakness, only to get tripped up in the Belmont Stakes. And others have missed the honor by not winning either the Kentucky Derby or the Preakness.

What makes the Triple Crown so difficult to win is that after a grueling spring running in prep races all over the country, young 3-year-old colts and geldings must win three more races at three different racetracks within a five-week period. It turns into a survivor series more than anything else.

Picking a Preakness winner

The Preakness is the shortest race in the Triple Crown at 1³⁄₁₆ miles. The perception of handicappers is that Pimlico, the racetrack where the Preakness is run, is a speed-favoring oval because of tight, egg-shaped turns. But year after year, the race proves to be a fair test with no discernable track bias. In fact, the Preakness is the most formful race in the Triple Crown series, because more than 50 percent of the betting favorites have won the race since 1873.

Another perception is that the fresh horses that bypass the Kentucky Derby are the ones to fear in the Preakness. The idea is that these colts are well-rested and primed to take on tired horses. The opposite is true.

A majority of the recent Preakness winners are horses that ran in the Kentucky Derby. The reason for that is the best colts from the spring prep races, barring injury, make the Kentucky Derby field. So it makes sense that those who move on from Churchill Downs to Pimlico are the better horses in training at that moment in time. A typical Preakness field has about one-third of the Kentucky Derby starters in it. One of those six or seven horses is most likely the Preakness winner.

From time to time, a local Maryland horse jumps up and runs a big race. These local hoses seldom win, but they can make your exotic wagers explode at large odds (refer to Chapter 15 for more on exotic wagers).

Betting on the Belmont Stakes

The Belmont Stakes is the oldest of the Triple Crown races. It was first run in 1867. It's also the longest at 1½ miles — a grueling distance that earned the race the nickname, "The Test of the Champion."

The Belmont Stakes has gained even more notoriety since 1997. A six-pack of horses — Silver Charm (1997), Real Quiet (1998), Charismatic (1999), War Emblem (2002), Funny Cide (2003), and Smarty Jones (2004) — have had a chance to become horse racing's 12th Triple Crown champion but lost in the Belmont Stakes. Four of those horses — Silver Charm, Real Quiet, Charismatic, and Smarty Jones — had the lead in the middle of the stretch run but couldn't hold on to the lead.

Every one of these six horses was heavily favored and lost. Should they've been favored? For sure. Were they *underlays,* meaning bet down to odds lower than their actual chance of winning? Most likely.

All the media hype and the fact that the last Triple Crown champion was in 1978 contributed to each horse becoming a strong sentimental choice. People became so excited about these horses that souvenir hunters purchased thousands of $2 win tickets to be used as collectibles after the horses won the Belmont Stakes. It's a classic case of betting with your heart, and not your head, in wanting to see a Triple Crown champion.

As a smart and emotionally detached bettor, you have to keep in mind that the Belmont Stakes is such a difficult race to win because of the distance and because it comes at the end of a tortuous Triple Crown campaign. Horses are being asked to do something they've never done before — race 1½ miles. The wear and tear on the still developing 3-year-olds take their toll. In fact, two of the six horses listed earlier — Charismatic and Smarty Jones — retired after their Belmont Stakes and never raced again.

In future Belmont Stakes, what should you look for in handicapping the race? Here are some tips to keep in mind:

- **Horses who win the Belmont often skip the Preakness.** The last four upsetters of Triple Crown hopefuls in the Belmont Stakes (Lemon Drop Kid, 1999; Sarava, 2002; Empire Maker, 2003; and Birdstone, 2004) all skipped the Preakness, choosing instead to train or to run in a different prep race. Sometimes running in an easy race instead of the Preakness sets a horse up perfectly for a peak performance in the Belmont Stakes.

- **Gallopers do well in the Belmont.** Conditioning seems to be a key element in the Belmont Stakes. This race has been called a galloper's race, meaning that horses rarely win with a big burst of energy but rather gallop along at a steady, fast clip, quarter-mile after quarter-mile. *Tactical speed* is a positive running style contributing to the galloper's theory. Jockeys don't want their horses to go too fast too soon, and they don't want to rally from far back either.

- **Post position is a non-factor.** The Belmont Park oval is 1½ miles around. Horses win regularly with wide trips, so saving ground, meaning running closest to the rail, isn't a big advantage.

Part V
Playing Different Ponies and Different Venues

The 5th Wave   By Rich Tennant

GIL NEVER LOST MONEY BETTING ON THE QUARTER HORSES

25¢

In this part . . .

Until the early 1980s, the racetrack was where you went to play the horse races. Then new technologies kicked in — like satellite transmissions, computers, the Internet, fax machines, and cell phones to name a few. Now, you can bet at off-track betting parlors — some with luxurious amenities — all over the country. Betting in your own home is available with horse racing networks like TVG and HRTV broadcasting over cable and satellite television. Telephone account wagering is also a big, booming business. And finally, you have Las Vegas, which set the bar for the entire off-track wagering industry. In this part, I show how the horse racing industry has expanded the marketplace and handles wagers away from the racetrack.

Also, I look at two different horse racing breeds, harness and Quarter Horse, that have a smaller (but devoted) fan base than Thoroughbred racing.

Chapter 19

Harness Racing: It'll Drive You Wild

. . . .

. . . .

*I*n the early 1900s, *harness racing* was more popular than Thoroughbred racing in the United States. Americans first embraced harness racing because of their dependence upon the horse, long before the automobile was invented. The first races were literally horse and buggy challenges of "my horse is faster than your horse" along city streets and country roads. Later, actual harness races were featured in county fairs.

Harness racing is a unique form of racing, because the horse pulls a cart, called a sulky, in which a driver sits and steers. Harness racing is conducted on racetracks as small as a half-mile circumference. The race strategy is in the driver's control, because he positions the horse and sulky.

These days, harness racing may play second fiddle to Thoroughbred racing, but it's still quite popular at county fairs and racetracks across the country, such as The Meadowlands in East Rutherford, New Jersey, and the Delaware Country Fair in Delaware, Ohio. If you've never seen (or bet on) a harness race, I suggest you try it sometime. It's a completely different form of racing that's every bit as exciting as Thoroughbred racing.

In this chapter, I fill you in on the key differences between harness racing and Thoroughbred horse racing. I also give you plenty of handicapping pointers for harness races, as well as a list of lingo that's unique to the sport.

Harness Racing Equipment

The first difference you notice between Thoroughbred horse racing and Standardbred harness racing is the human element. In Thoroughbred horse racing, the jockey sits atop the horse in a saddle. In Standardbred harness racing, the horse pulls a cart called a *sulky* that the driver sits in and steers. Check out Figure 19-1 for a picture of a harness horse pulling a sulky and driver during a race.

Figure 19-1: Harness horse pulling a sulky and driver during a race.

Photo courtesy of Ed Keys, United States Trotting Association

Harness horses are called *Standardbreds* because the early trotters — en vogue long before pacers (see the next section for more on trotters and pacers) — were required to race a mile in a standard time before they were registered as part of the breed. Standardbreds have developed shorter legs and longer bodies than Thoroughbreds. They're much more docile than Thoroughbreds, which at times are very high-strung.

Harness horses require a lot of equipment, because the drivers need to have as much control as possible. See Figure 19-2.

Figure 19-2:
Harness
horses
decked
out in
equipment
and racing
to the finish.

Photo by Lisa Photo

Some common equipment that a harness horse wears includes

- ✔ **Bit:** A metal bar that fits into a horse's mouth and is attached to the bridle and reins giving a driver control of the horse

- ✔ **Blinkers:** Worn around a horse's head to restrict its vision and keep it focused straight ahead

- ✔ **Bridle:** Worn around the horse's head to give the driver control

- ✔ **Buxton martingale:** A leather strap connecting the girth and noseband that prevents a horse from throwing its head back

- ✔ **Harness:** The gear used to attach the sulky and the hobbles to the horse

- ✔ **Head pole:** Used to keep a horse's head in position

- ✔ **Hobbles:** Straps attached to the legs on the same side of a horse that help maintain stride and keep balance

- ✔ **Knee boots:** Worn to protect a horse from hitting itself while pacing or trotting

- ✔ **Overcheck:** A strap that holds the bit in place

- ✔ **Reins:** Long leather straps attached to each side of a bit on the horse's bridle that give the driver control of the horse

- ✔ **Shadow roll:** A wool roll worn above the horse's nostril to prevent it from looking down and seeing shadows on the racetrack

Dan Patch: The most famous harness horse of all-time

Dan Patch was one of the most famous harness horses of all-time. He grew so famous that he had his own brand of smoking and chewing tobacco. In addition, a brand of washing machines and a dance were named after him. Try the Dan Patch Two Step next time you get busy on the dance floor!

Dan Patch had modest beginnings. He was born in 1896 in Indiana and was owned by Dan Messner, Jr. Dan Patch's first race was on August 30, 1900. He was successful but was sold in March 1902 for $20,000 to M. E. Sturgis from Buffalo, New York.

Racing in Dan Patch's time was done in heats, meaning that horses ran in the first heat to qualify for the next heat. They didn't have to win the first heat; they just had to finish among the top horses. Sometimes even a third heat, on the same day, was needed to decide the winner. Dan Patch made 56 starts in 1902 and lost only two heats. He set a pacer mark (see "Comparing Pacers and Trotters" in this chapter) of 1:55½ for

a mile in 1905, and the record stood for an incredible 32 years. Dan Patch was nearly invincible, and he was becoming a legend.

In December 1902, Sturgis decided to sell high, or so he thought, and he sold Dan Patch for $60,000 to M.W. Savage of Minneapolis, Minnesota. Little did Sturgis know that Dan Patch had only scratched the surface of his future popularity. Savage ran Dan Patch in time trials against the clock rather than against other opponents. The exhibitions drew huge crowds, and Dan Patch continued to break world records.

Savage earned an estimated $3 million from Dan Patch for exhibitions, public appearances, and product marketing. The horse lived in a spacious barn rather than a stall like most horses live in. And when he traveled, he had his own private railway car. Ironically, when Dan Patch died on July 11, 1916, Savage died the following morning.

Because of the sulky and all the equipment, the racing strategy is a lot different in harness racing than in Thoroughbred racing. In turn, your handicapping and betting strategy is different, too. See the section, "Handicapping Harness Race-Style," later in this chapter for more.

Comparing Pacers and Trotters

When I started working as a harness racing publicist, the idea that a horse can have two kinds of gaits — pacing and trotting — was as foreign to me as speaking Russian or Latin as a second language. But after I became more familiar with the different gait styles, I realized they're not that difficult to figure out.

Pacers

Pacers move in a lateral gait, meaning they move both legs on the same side of their body forward in unison. For example, the left front leg and the left rear leg stride forward at the same time, and the right front leg and the right rear leg take the next stride.

Pacers wear *hobbles* to assist their controlled movement (see Figure 19-3). Hobbles are leather straps that connect the front and rear legs on the same side of a horse. Pacers rarely break stride, making them more dependable to bet on.

Because of its stride, a pacer's body leans left and then right, as it shifts its weight back and forth. This unique action lends to the nickname "side-wheelers."

When you go to a harness racetrack or bet them at simulcasts (see Chapter 21 on off-track betting), a majority of races are for pacers. Approximately 80 percent of harness races are pacing, while 20 percent are trotting.

Figure 19-3:
A pacer wearing hobbles.

Photo courtesy of Ed Keys, United States Trotting Association

Trotters

Trotters move in a diagonal gait (see Figure 19-4), meaning the left front leg and the right rear leg move forward simultaneously, and the right front leg and the left rear leg move forward together. Trotting is a natural gait for a horse, but to maintain that gait at high racing speed takes a lot of skill from the horse's trainer.

Figure 19-4:
A trotter has a diagonal gait.

Photo by Lisa Photo

A horse that *breaks* (loses stride and starts cantering or galloping during a race) must be pulled back by the driver until he can correct the horse's gait. If he doesn't lose ground before regaining its stride, the horse can be disqualified. Trotters break more often than pacers, only adding to the million ways a horse can lose a horse race.

Although pacers race faster than trotters, this factor means little in helping you win money. Of the two gaits, trotters are more formful to bet on, even factoring in the instances that trotters break stride.

Defining the Lingo of Harness Racing

You'd think that if you understand Thoroughbred horse racing, you know harness racing too. Well, it's not that simple. You have a horse and a small man controlling the horse, and they race around an oval counterclockwise. But the similarities end there.

In this section, I define some harness racing terminology and how it relates to your handicapping and betting of the sport. (For definitions of specific pieces of equipment, see "Harness Racing Equipment" earlier in the chapter.):

- **Boxed in:** When a horse is racing on the rails, or fence, and is surrounded by other horses in front, to the outside, and behind it. A horse that's boxed in is held up and unable to gain a clear passage.

- **Break:** To start galloping and lose natural trotting or pacing rhythm. Breaking occurs more with trotters than pacers.

- **Catch driver:** A driver that doesn't train her own horses. She's engaged by other trainers and owners to drive their horses in races.

- **Colors:** The special colorful jacket worn by drivers during a race. Drivers register their own colors and wear them every time they race, unlike in Thoroughbred racing, where the owners register their own colored silks that the jockeys wear in a race.

- **Conditioned race:** A race where eligibility is based on age, sex, money won, or races won. For example, "3-year-old fillies, non-winners of $10,000 or 4 races."

- **Cover:** When a horse races with another horse in front of him. Racing with cover is good, because the leading horse cuts the wind resistance.

- **Death hole:** The position third in line behind the lead horse.

- **Driver:** The person holding a license permitting him to drive a harness horse in a parimutuel race (see Chapter 3 on parimutuel wagering). Different types of licenses correspond to differing levels of experience.

- **Early/late closer:** A race requiring payments that start much closer to the actual race date than a stakes race. "Early" and "late" involve specified periods of time.

- **First-over:** The first horse to make a move on the leader in a race, moving up on the outside.

- **Free legged:** A pacer that races without wearing hobbles.

- **Garden trip:** The position directly behind the lead horse. Also called the garden spot.

- **Invitational:** A race for the top horses in the area that's also known as an Open or Free-For-All.

- **Jog cart:** A cart pulled by the horse that's attached to the harness and carries the trainer. This cart is used when horses are training or warming up for a race. It's larger, longer, and heavier than a sulky.

- **Mark:** A horse's fastest winning time at a particular distance.

- **Parked:** A horse racing on the outside, with at least one horse between it and the inside rail.

✔ **Pocket:** A horse unable to obtain a clear run because of other runners situated in front, behind, and to the side of it.

✔ **Qualifier:** A non-betting race in which a horse must go a mile faster than a minimum established time (as in a mile race faster than two minutes) to prove itself capable of competing in a parimutuel horse race.

✔ **Sire stake:** Stakes race designed to promote Standardbred breeding and racing within a state. Different states have different rules regulating eligibility for its sire stakes program.

✔ **Sulky:** A two-wheeled cart attached to the harness and pulled by the horse that carries the driver. A sulky is lighter and more streamlined that a jog cart, normally weighing about 40 pounds.

✔ **Time trial:** An attempt to have a horse beat its own best time in a non-competitive event. A time trial isn't a race. Galloping horses hitched to sulkies, called *prompters,* are used to push a horse to its best effort. Most prompters are actually Thoroughbred horses that gallop alongside.

Handicapping Harness Race-Style

Harness racing presents a new set of dynamics for you, the handicapper, compared to Thoroughbred (see Chapters 12 and 16) or Quarter Horse (see Chapter 20) racing. The driver in harness racing is a bigger part of the winning formula than a jockey in Thoroughbred racing. The driver has more control over the horse and the strategy during the race. Handicappers should watch harness races closely and make trip handicapping notes on any horses that get into trouble. Some trip handicapping notes can be found in the past performance comment line. Look for running lines for horses that were forced to race *first over,* meaning to race outside of the pacesetter with no *cover,* or no horse in front to block the wind, or horses that were boxed in or pocketed.

Sizing up the racetrack

One of the first things you notice in harness racing is that the racing surface is cinder rather than dirt as in Thoroughbred and Quarter Horse racing. The track is hard, because the horses pull a sulky with two wheels that need to be able to roll, even in rainy weather. Because of the sulky, horses race in single-file, meaning one behind another in a line. When a driver is ready to advance on the leaders, he tips his horse out, meaning he starts a second file of horses and gains on the outside. One of the best spots to be is the second horse over, getting live cover from the horse in front of him (the horse in front blocks the wind). The driver can then move freely around the horse in front of him in the stretch to begin his late rally.

A major difference in the styles of harness racing is that the size of the racetrack varies between a half-mile and 1-mile oval. The size of the racetrack affects the way races are run. On a half-miler, the driver needs to move sooner, because the four turns make gaining ground hard. Also, the *stretch run*, meaning the straightaway from the end of the final turn to the finish line, is short, so closers are at a great disadvantage. In half-mile racing, a second tier of horses lines up two paths (the width of two horses) off the inside rail.

A big change to harness racing at half-mile and five-eighth mile racetracks was the invention of the *passing lane*. The passing lane debuted at Maywood Park in Melrose Park, Illinois in 1994. The passing lane is an additional inside lane created for use only in the final stretch run. It can't be used during the early part of the race. This lane allows horses that are boxed in along the rail and trapped behind the lead horse an inside lane to rally during the stretch run. By rule, the lead horse entering the stretch run must maintain its path and isn't allowed to move over to the left into the passing lane. The passing lane gives more horses a chance to win and creates even more exciting finishes.

On a mile racetrack, the strategy of patience is a virtue. The stretch run is long, and horses fan out sometimes five- or six-wide to begin their rally. You see very exciting finishes at a mile track too.

Considering the driver's importance

The driver is more important to the outcome of a harness race than a jockey is to a Thoroughbred race. Some of the maneuvers I mention in this section can greatly improve the chances of an inferior horse winning if he gets a perfect trip. The trip is dependent on where the driver places his horse during the race and when he decides to make his best move. Getting a good trip is what makes the better drivers great. I describe good and bad trips in this section.

Harness horses don't leave from a starting gate like Thoroughbreds do. In harness racing, the starting gate is attached to the back of a high-powered car. The car moves slowly on the track with the gate open, allowing the racehorses to jog up behind their assigned post positions. As the car nears the starting point, it speeds up, leaving the horses behind it to begin racing. In the early part of the race, you'll see the drivers maneuver for position. The better drivers seem to make the right move every time, getting the spot they want and staying out of trouble.

When the driver is ready to pass, he'll *tip out* his horse, forming a second line of horses two paths off the rail. The horse leading the second line is called the *first one over,* which is the poorest position to try and win from. Like the leading horse, he's cutting the wind resistance for the horse behind him, and he's racing wide.

A driver's preference is to race *covered up,* meaning to have a horse in front blocking the wind while she drafts behind him. The time for a driver to give up his cover is in the stretch run when he needs clear sailing to the finish.

The best harness drivers rarely get caught out of position. They let another driver race first one over and block the wind while they tuck in behind them. If a good driver must move early, he'll tip out his horse into the two-path and quickly rush to the lead so they don't get stuck racing wide the whole race. When you watch a harness race, study the best drivers even if you didn't bet on them. The best drivers give their horses a chance to win every race, even if the horse isn't the most talented.

A really clever maneuver is when a driver from the rear of the field tips his horse out first one over. As he advances, invariably other horses from the rear get in behind him. At this point, he's providing the other horses with live cover. But he doesn't want to get stuck out there the whole way around. As the train of horses advances, the smart driver hesitates before getting to the leaders. She's trying to *flush out cover,* meaning to entice another driver to tip out in front of her. The most logical horse to flush out is the third horse on the rail behind the leader (in the spot called the *death hole*). If the third horse doesn't tip out to be first one over, then he gets passed and shuffled far back as the train of horses moves by. If the third horse doesn't tip out at that moment, he's conceding any chance of winning the race. Watching a harness race is like a chess game — the good drivers are thinking two or three moves ahead like a chess master.

Paying attention to past performances

Harness racetracks produce their own daily past performance program for the Standardbreds. The information is similar to what the *Daily Racing Form* (see Chapter 11 on the *DRF*) does for Thoroughbreds. Figure 19-5 shows a sample past performance for 1995-96 champion harness horse Jenna's Beach Boy with a legend breaking everything down for you.

Getting a grip on trip handicapping

In addition to checking out past performances (see the preceding section), *trip handicapping* is extremely effective in harness racing. I discuss how the better drivers give their horses good trips in "Considering the driver's importance," earlier in the chapter.

How to Read the Meadowlands Past Performances

① ⑥ ⑦ ⑨ b h 4 Beach Towel-Five O'clock Cindy-Cam Fella   ⑫ Tr.-Joe Holloway (48-16-10-3-.458)
4-5
PP2 ② **JENNA'S BEACH BOY (L)** ⑩ L&L Devisser Partnership, Holland, Mich.   ⑬ M1   1:47³ 1996   10   6   1   1 $264,800
2• $1,777,877 - 4, 1:47³ 1 ⑧   ⑪ Driver-WILLIAM FAHY (170) (5/28/54) br-or (640-63-76-72-.202)   Lex1   1:48¹ 1995   16   14   2   0 $1,031,793
④   ⑭ BREEDER - L&L DEVISSER PARTNERSHIP

BLUE **⑤**

1. Morning Line Odds
2. Post Position (Starting Position)
3. Today's class versus previous start:
   ▲ Stays in same class
   ▲ Moves up in class
   ▼ Moves down in class
4. Wagering Number
5. Saddle Pad Color
6. Name of Horse
7. (L)-Lasix

8. Lifetime Earnings - Lifetime Mark (Age, Time, Track Size)
9. Breeding – Color (b-bay; br-brown; blk-black; ch-chestnut; r-roan, gr-gray)
   Sex (c-colt; h-horse; g-gelding; r-ridgling; f-filly; m-mare)
   Age of horse as of January 1 of current year
   Sire-Dam-Maternal Grandsire
10. Name of Owner
11. Name of Driver (weight) (birthdate) (colors) (starts at current meet-wins-seconds-thirds-UDR average)
12. Name of Trainer (starts at current meet-wins-seconds-thirds-UTR average)
13. Two year summary showing best time, starts wins, seconds, thirds, and earnings
14. Name of Breeder

6-22⁹⁶ M¹ 7 200000 gd FFA Stk 1 26¹ 53⁴ 120² 147³   2 2ⁿᵈ 2ⁿᵈ 2¹⁴ 2¹⁴ 1¹ 26⁴ 147³ *.80 L WFahy world record -10 JnasBachBoy,Ryadh,TrmpCasno 75-0

6-22⁹⁶
DATE OF RACE: This race was run on June 22, 1996.

6-22⁹⁶ **M¹ 7**
TRACK AND RACE NUMBER: This was the seventh race (7) at the Meadowlands (M), a one mile (1) track.

6-22⁹⁶ M¹ 7 **200000**
PURSE: The purse for this race was $200,000. "D" indicates the horse participated in pre-race quarantine barn prior to the race.

6-22⁹⁶ M¹ 7 200000 **gd**
TRACK CONDITION: The track condition was good ("gd"); "ft" would mean the track was fast; "sy" would denote a sloppy track.

6-22⁹⁶ M¹ 7 200000 gd **FFA Stk**
RACE CONDITIONS: Describes what caliber and type of horse which contested this event. This race was a free for all stake.

6-22⁹⁶ M¹ 7 200000 gd FFA Stk **1**
DISTANCE: The race was at one mile. The majority of harness races are at a distance of one mile.

6-22⁹⁶ M¹ 7 200000 gd FFA Stk 1 **26¹ 53⁴ 120²** 147³
FRACTIONAL TIMES: Shows the times of the lead horse after a quarter, half mile, and three-quarters of a mile.

6-22⁹⁶ M¹ 7 200000 gd FFA Stk 1 26¹ 53⁴ 120² **147³**
FINAL TIME: This is the final time of the winner of the race.

6-22⁹⁶ M¹ 7 200000 gd FFA Stk 1 26¹ 53⁴ 120² 147³ **2**
POST POSITION: The position behind the gate from which this horse started.

6-22⁹⁶ M¹ 7 200000 gd FFA Stk 1 26¹ 53⁴ 120² 147³ 2 **2ⁿᵈ 2ⁿᵈ 2¹⁴ 2¹⁴**
POINTS OF CALL: Where this horse was at the 1/4 mile, 1/2 mile, 3/4 mile and stretch points of call. For example, he was 2ⁿᵈ at the 1/4, a head behind the leader. A raised ⁰ means the horse was parked out.

6-22⁹⁶ M¹ 7 200000 gd FFA Stk 1 26¹ 53⁴ 120² 147³ 2 2ⁿᵈ 2ⁿᵈ 2¹⁴ 2¹⁴ **1¹**
FINISH: The horse won, finishing a length ahead of the second horse. If he was 3⁵, that would mean he was third, five lengths behind the winner.

6-22⁹⁶ M¹ 7 200000 gd FFA Stk 1 26¹ 53⁴ 120² 147³ 2 2ⁿᵈ 2ⁿᵈ 2¹⁴ 2¹⁴ 1¹ **26⁴ 147³**
FINAL QUARTER/FINAL TIME: Shows the time it took this specific horse to run his final quarter mile (26 & 4/5ᵗʰˢ seconds) and the entire race (1 minute, 47 & 3/5ᵗʰˢ seconds).

6-22⁹⁶ M¹ 7 200000 gd FFA Stk 1 26¹ 53⁴ 120² 147³ 2 2ⁿᵈ 2ⁿᵈ 2¹⁴ 2¹⁴ 1¹ 26⁴ 147³ ***.80**
ODDS: This horse's odds were 80 cents on the dollar (which is 4-5). The *signifies that the horse was favored. An "e" means the horse was part of a betting entry while "f" means the horse was part of the mutuel field.

6-22⁹⁶ M¹ 7 200000 gd FFA Stk 1 26¹ 53⁴ 120² 147³ 2 2ⁿᵈ 2ⁿᵈ 2¹⁴ 2¹⁴ 1¹ 26⁴ 147³ *.80 **L**
MEDICATION: This horse raced on Lasix (L), a medication permitted in the State of New Jersey.

6-22⁹⁶ M¹ 7 200000 gd FFA Stk 1 26¹ 53⁴ 120² 147³ 2 2ⁿᵈ 2ⁿᵈ 2¹⁴ 2¹⁴ 1¹ 26⁴ 147³ *.80 L **WFahy**
DRIVER: The driver was William Fahy.

6-22⁹⁶ M¹ 7 200000 gd FFA Stk 1 26¹ 53⁴ 1:20² 147³ 2 2ⁿᵈ 2ⁿᵈ 2¹⁴ 2¹⁴ 1¹ 26⁴ 147³ *.80 L WFahy **world record**
COMMENT: A brief description of the horse's performance.

6-22⁹⁶ M¹ 7 200000 gd FFA Stk 1 26¹ 53⁴ 120² 147³ 2 2ⁿᵈ 2ⁿᵈ 2¹⁴ 2¹⁴ 1¹ 26⁴ 147³ *.80 L WFahy world record **-10**
NUMBER OF STARTERS: Ten (10) horses competed in this race.

6-22⁹⁶ M¹ 7 200000 gd FFA Stk 1 26¹ 53⁴ 120² 147³ 2 2ⁿᵈ 2ⁿᵈ 2¹⁴ 2¹⁴ 1¹ 26⁴ 147³ *.80 L WFahy world record -10 **JnasBachBoy,Ryadh,TrmpCasno**
FIRST THREE FINISHERS: The names of the first three finishers.

6-22⁹⁶ M¹ 7 200000 gd FFA Stk 1 26¹ 53⁴ 120² 147³ 2 2ⁿᵈ 2ⁿᵈ 2¹⁴ 2¹⁴ 1¹ 26⁴ 147³ *.80 L WFahy world record -10 JnasBachBoy,Ryadh,TrmpCasno **75-0**
TEMPERATURE/TRACK VARIANT: The temperature was 75 degrees and no time allowance for the track condition or weather was granted (0). A time allowance indicates how many seconds slower the track was that night versus a normal night.

Classification of Races

The following are commonly used abbreviations for classifications of races run at the Meadowlands Racetrack:

Qua	qualifying (non-betting) race	OPEN	open race
Qua-t-p	qualifying race involving trotters and pacers	INV	invitational race
50000CL	claiming race with horse entered for $50,000	HCP	handicap (post position drawn to class)
50000CLCD	claiming race with additional conditions for eligibility attached	FFA	free for all
50000CLz	horse was claimed in that race for $50,000	STK	stake race
50000CL.HC	claiming race with post position drawn according to price entered	LC	late closing series
NW2CD	non-winners of two pari-mutuel races lifetime	EC	early closing stakes
NW7500L6	non-winner of $7,500 in last six starts		

Figure 19-5:
A sample past performance for a harness horse.

The idea of trip handicapping began in harness racing. Thoroughbred handicappers use the same principles when they watch horse races and make notes when horses get in trouble. Most harness horses run once a week. So by the nature of the sport, if a horse gets a bad trip one week, you only have to wait seven days before you get another chance to race. That's how a lot of winning harness bettors make money.

If a harness horse in great condition gets a bad trip, he's usually an outstanding wager next time.

A bad trip can occur because of many reasons, including the following:

✔ **Racing luck:** The number one reason for a bad trip is racing luck. Sometimes bad trips are preordained after the draw for post positions. For example, a speed horse draws an outside post. The driver may try his best to get to the front or at least to a forward spot. If he fails, he may get forced to the back and not get the trip he needs to win. Mark him down for next week.

✔ **Dead cover:** Your horse may be getting cover, but if it's *dead cover* (meaning the horse in front doesn't have the speed, talent, or conditioning to get into the race), you're in trouble. Imagine being pocketed on the highway behind a car going 55 miles per hour. If you're in a hurry, that's real life dead cover.

✔ **Gapping:** *Gapping* is when a horse can't keep up with the horse in front of him. Getting shuffled back happens a lot, and many times the driver can't do anything about it. A driver can get shuffled more than one way. Her horse may be third in line on the rail. If the horse in front of her can't keep up with the leader, she gets shuffled back until she can move around him.

Sharp harness handicappers watch all the races looking for trouble trips. They're easier to spot than in Thoroughbred racing. So even if you don't place a bet, watch the race anyway, and you may find a good bet for next week.

Championship Races

Like Thoroughbred racing, which has the Triple Crown (see Chapters 2 and 18) and the Breeders' Cup World Thoroughbred Championship (see Chapter 2), harness racing has its own championship events. The Triple Crown for 3-year-old pacers is held during the fall, usually in September and October. Table 19-1 shows the three races that make up the pacers' Triple Crown.

Table 19-1	Races in the Pacers' Triple Crown		
Race	*Racetrack*	*Location*	*Size of the Racetrack*
Cane Pace	Freehold Raceway	Freehold, New Jersey	Half-mile
Little Brown Jug	Delaware County Fairgrounds	Delaware, Ohio	Half-mile
Messenger Stakes	The Meadows	Meadow Lands, Pennsylvania	⅝-mile

A Triple Crown for 3-year-old trotters is held in late summer during August and September. You can see a description of the three races in Table 19-2.

Table 19-2	Races in the Trotters' Triple Crown		
Race	*Racetrack*	*Location*	*Size of the Racetrack*
Hambletonian	The Meadowlands	East Rutherford, New Jersey	1 mile
Yonkers Trot	Yonkers Raceway	Yonkers, New York	Half-mile
Kentucky Futurity	The Red Mile	Lexington, Kentucky	1 mile

Finally, the Breeders' Crown series consists of 11 divisions for trotters and pacers of all ages and sexes. The series is run usually during the fall.

Chapter 20

American Quarter Horse Racing: Don't Blink or You'll Miss It

*I*f you like your horse racing fast and furious, Quarter Horse racing is for you. Quarter Horse races are short in distance, ranging from 220 yards up to 870 yards. The shorter Quarter Horse races begin from a chute at the top of the stretch and are a straight run to the finish line. In the longer Quarter Horse races, horses start on the backside and have to turn left around the far turn.

Thoroughbred and harness racing may get more publicity, but the followers of Quarter Horse racing are a hardy, loyal bunch. People in the business call the Quarter Horse "America's Fastest Athlete." The fans of Quarter Horse racing are mainly in the southwestern and western states like Texas, Oklahoma, Arizona, New Mexico, Colorado, and California. Quarter Horse fans will tell you that handicapping their races is more true to form than handicapping Thoroughbred and harness races. They have a point, which I explain later in this chapter.

Despite the differences among the races and horses, what's similar among all three sports is the betting. So, you can go elsewhere in the book for tips on parimutuel wagering (Chapter 3) and how to bet (Chapters 4 and 15). In this chapter, I focus on some different handicapping angles that can help you become a winning Quarter Horse bettor.

Horse Racing That's Short and Sweet

Quarter Horse racing is a very exciting sport to watch. In theory, shorter races involve less strategy and more hustling on the part of the jockeys, which lead to one close finish after another.

The start is extremely important in Quarter Horse racing. Unlike a Thoroughbred race where a good horse can overcome a slow start, in Quarter Horse racing, a horse has little time to recover from a tardy beginning. After a quick burst of energy from the starting gate, the jockeys whip their horses from the get-go for even more speed.

This kind of aggressive activity lends itself to roughly run races. The jockeys get so preoccupied with getting speed out of their mounts that the horses have a tendency to drift left or right as they shy away from the whip. Horses bouncing off one another are part of trip handicapping for these Quarter Horses. *Trip handicapping* entails watching the races and making notes when a horse or horses get into trouble. The information is useful the next time the horse runs.

Interested in checking out some Quarter Horse racing? Table 20-1 shows the leading Quarter Horse racetracks in North America and where they're located.

Table 20-1	Leading Quarter Horse Racetracks in North America	
Racetrack	*Location*	*Live Racing Dates*
Arapahoe Park	Aurora, Colorado	June - August
Assiniboia Downs	Winnipeg, Manitoba, Canada	July - August
Blue Ribbon Downs	Sallisaw, Oklahoma	February - November
Canterbury Park	Shakopee, Minnesota	May - September
Delta Downs	Vinton, Louisiana	January - March
Downs at Albuquerque	Albuquerque, New Mexico	March - June
Eureka Downs	Eureka, Kansas	May - July
Evangeline Downs	Lafayette, Louisiana	September - October
Evergreen Park	Grande Prairie, Alberta, Canada	July - August
Fair Meadows	Tulsa, Oklahoma	June - July
Grants Pass Downs	Grants Pass, Oregon	May - July
Fairplex Park	Pomona, California	September
Hipodromo de las Americas	Mexico City, Mexico	January - December
Les Bois Park	Boise, Idaho	May - August
Los Alamitos Race Course	Los Alamitos, California	Year round

Racetrack	Location	Live Racing Dates
Louisiana Downs	Bossier City, Louisiana	November - December
Marquis Downs	Saskatoon, Saskatchewan, Canada	May - September
Mt. Pleasant Meadows	Mt. Pleasant, Michigan	May - September
New Mexico State Fair	Albuquerque, New Mexico	September
North Dakota Horse Park	Fargo, North Dakota	July - September
Picov Downs	Ajax, Ontario, Canada	May - October
Portland Meadows	Portland, Oregon	January - April & October - December
Prairie Meadows	Des Moines, Iowa	April - June & July - September
Remington Park	Oklahoma City, Oklahoma	June - November
Ruidoso Downs	Ruidoso, New Mexico	May - September
Sagebrush Downs	Kamloops, British Columbia, Canada	May - September
Sam Houston Race Park	Houston, Texas	January - March & October - December
Sun Downs	Kennewick, Washington	April - May
Sunland Park	Sunland Park, New Mexico	January - April & November - December
Sunray Park	Farmington, New Mexico	August - November
The Woodlands	Kansas City, Kansas	September - October
Turf Paradise	Phoenix, Arizona	January - May
Rocky Mountain Turf Club (Whoop Up Downs)	Lethbridge, Alberta, Canada	June - November
Will Rogers Down	Claremore, Oklahoma	November
Wyoming Downs	Evanston, Wyoming	June - August
Yavapai Downs	Prescott, Arizona	May - September

Most racetracks run mixed bred meets including Thoroughbred, Appaloosa, Paint, and Arabian races

Handicapping Factors in Quarter Horse Racing

One of the key factors that makes handicapping Quarter Horse racing easier is the lack of what I call the *race shape*. Race shape means analyzing the running styles of the horses and predicting how the race will be run. In Thoroughbred racing, you have *speed horses* that want to be on the lead, *stalkers* that prefer to settle a few lengths off the lead horses, and *closers* that rally late from far back.

In Quarter Horse racing, the distances are so short that you don't need to worry about race shape. All the horses exert an all out burst of speed after the starting gate opens. Jockeys don't take back and save energy for a late run but rather break on top and improve their position from there.

Distance

The distance in Quarter Horse races ranges from 220 yards to 870 yards. Following are the different types of races and their coinciding distances:

- **Sprint races:** 220, 250, 300, 330, and 350 yards
- **Long sprints or middle distance races:** 400, 440, 550, and 660 yards
- **Distance races:** 770 and 870 yards.

When handicapping, you must be aware of the circumference of the racetrack oval. *Straightaway races,* which begin from a chute at the top of the stretch and are a straight run to the finish line, are distinctly different than *hook races,* which are longer races that start on the backside and include a left turn around the far turn. In hook races, the outside horses are at a disadvantage because they're forced to race wide around the far turn.

The distances in Quarter Horse racing are just as important as they are in Thoroughbred racing. For example, instances occur when a Thoroughbred can win at six furlongs (a *furlong* is one-eighth of a mile) but not at seven, even though the race is just one furlong longer. Or, a horse continually wins one-mile races but can't shorten up to seven furlongs and succeed. Some Quarter Horses excel at 350 yards but are lost at 400 yards. And some can win at 870 yards, but their trainers dare not shorten their race. You can see these trends develop by looking at a horse's past performance record in the track program.

AQHA speed indexes

In Quarter Horse racing, the AQHA produces a *speed index* for each horse, which is the average of the horse's three fastest winning times run each year for the immediate past three years at each distance at each racetrack. The higher the speed index, the faster the horse.

In some ways, the speed index is more precise than Beyers are. AQHA speed indexes are pure mathematical calculations based upon horses' final racing times, which are an exact measure in Quarter Horse racing. Quarter Horse races are timed from the moment the starting gate opens until the horses cross the finish line. Each horse is timed individually, and the time is recorded down to 1⁄₁₀₀ of a second.

Class

Jockeys don't need to make a lot of decisions in Quarter Horse racing because the horse does most of the work. With less emphasis placed on the rider and more on the horse, class becomes an important element.

Class basically comes from pedigree. In judging *pedigree* (the horse's mother and father), you want to find what's called *black type*, meaning stakes wins on both sides of the bloodlines — the sire's side and the dam's side.

The speed index is also an important class measure, which I cover in the sidebar, "AQHA speed indexes."

 You won't find the stakes history of the sire and dam in past performance records. The best place to find their stakes history is at the American Quarter Horse Association (AQHA) Web site (www.aqha.com). The AQHA Web site has great information on pedigrees and stallions. They also have a section specifically devoted to handicapping Quarter Horse races. To increase your knowledge of the sport, AQHA also has publications you can subscribe to.

Post position

In straightaway races, post position isn't a big deal unless a track bias is apparent. A *track bias* means that a certain part of the racetrack lends itself to horses getting better footing and running faster times.

Sometimes jockeys like outside post positions in a straightaway race because they prefer to run on the *crown* of the racetrack, which is the outer part of the track that's slightly higher than the inside part. (The track superintendent creates the crown on purpose to help with drainage whenever it rains. Water seeps towards the inner rail where the drainage ditches are located.) Horses running on the outside of the track are nearer to the top of the crown, thus they get the feeling of running slightly downhill. So for the handicapper, there's a small advantage to the outside posts in a straightway race.

Post position is a big deal in hook races, where the horses go around a turn. An outside post is a disadvantage unless the horse has a lot of early speed and breaks well. Thus, a speed horse with an inside post is a good bet if the horse is classy enough.

If the outside horse has just average early speed, he's forced wide on the turn. He runs a farther distance than the inside horses, thus losing ground. Also, Quarter Horses run full speed all the time, so the chances of getting *floated* (forced wide) on the far turn are much greater.

Post position can also be a factor on certain sizes of racetrack ovals. Los Alamitos Race Course in suburban Los Angeles is a ⅝-mile racetrack. An 870-yard race has a long run to the turn, minimizing the disadvantage of the outside posts somewhat. At a 1-mile oval such as at Lone Star Park or Sam Houston Race Park in Texas, however, an 870-yard race has a short run into the turn, which factors greatly into the inside versus outside post position advantages.

The break

I can't stress enough that the *break* (start) of a Quarter Horse race is extremely important. If the distance of the race is only 220 or 350 yards, a tardy beginning practically eliminates a horse's chances of winning.

The comment line in a horse's past performances, which appear in the race-track program, usually mentions a poor start. One or two bad starts can happen to any Quarter Horse. You're looking for a horse that consistently gets banged around early, because he may be a problem animal that you should probably avoid betting on.

A good betting angle is to find a quality horse sandwiched by two bad starters. If the quality horse gets off to his usual good start and is flanked by two slow starters, his odds of getting bumped off stride early are minimized.

The gallop out

Watching the horses gallop out past the finish line is definitely a part of race watching that's identical in both Quarter Horse racing and Thoroughbred racing.

Look for a horse that keeps running strongly past the finish line. Where the horse officially finishes in the race doesn't matter. But if he gallops out with energy, he's finishing with a lot left in the tank and is a horse to watch the next time out.

Chapter 21

Visiting Your Local OTB: Off-Track Betting

*B*efore 1971, the only way to make legal wagers on horse races was at the racetrack. Back then, there was very little gambling competition throughout the United States. Horseplayers were content with betting on a single card at their local racetrack with nine or ten races spaced approximately 30 minutes apart.

But that all changed in 1971 with the birth of New York City Off-Track Betting (OTB).

In this chapter, I give you the history of OTBs and describe the renaissance that transformed OTBs into first class facilities. I tell you how to locate the closest OTB and clue you in on what amenities you should expect to find when you go there.

In the Beginning: New York City OTB

The origin of *off-track betting* (OTB), meaning betting on horse races at a facility away from the racetrack, began in New York City, where the first OTB opened in 1971. Over the years, state racing commissions have sent personnel to study the New York model to avoid the mistakes made there.

Getting the idea off the ground

A brand-spanking new Belmont Park opened on May 20, 1968. The facility in Elmont, New York cost $30.7 million to build, and many people considered it the greatest racetrack in the world. Unfortunately, this great racetrack didn't compensate for the fact that New York City was going broke, so Mayor John V. Lindsey came up with a very simple idea to raise a lot of money for the city to further help New York racing maintain its position as the best horse racing in the country.

Mayor Lindsey recognized the fact that when horseplayers couldn't go to the racetrack, many bet illegally with bookmakers. Bookies were easy enough to find and convenient, too. They offered credit and were available most of the day to get bets down on horses and sports.

In 1969, Mayor Lindsey proposed to the executives of the New York Racing Association (NYRA) the idea of establishing OTB parlors, modeled after the English bookmakers — a legal and respected business — in New York City. At these OTBs, horseplayers could legally bet on New York racing when they couldn't get to the racetrack. NYRA would operate the parlors for the City and receive a percentage of the handle, which could be used to increase purses, improve track facilities, and so on. Mayor Lindsey's idea was brilliant. Why let bookies make money on horse racing when the NYRA and the City could do it legally and share in the profits?

In a decision that has haunted the horse racing industry to this very day, the NYRA declined. Their reasons carried some logic at the time. Because no OTBs existed in the United States, the concept was frightfully new. The NYRA had just spent $30.7 million building Belmont Park, which could easily accommodate 100,000 fans. They wanted people to come to their racetracks, not stay away and bet. Although the NYRA Board of Trustees was made up of successful businessman, its goal was to run horse racing as a sport, not to get involved in what was considered legalized bookmaking.

So, Mayor Lindsey proceeded without the NYRA as a partner. He formed a governmental agency, the New York City OTB Corporation, and the first two parlors — one in Queens and the other in Grand Central Terminal in Manhattan —opened for business on April 8, 1971. Mayor Lindsey placed the first wager — a $2 win bet on a horse named Moneywise.

Starting off on the wrong foot

If the three letters "OTB" make a horseplayer squeamish, the New York experience is to blame. The early parlors had absolutely no amenities — no food, no beverages, very little seating, and no restrooms (which would've promoted loitering).

The mutuel clerks were protected behind bulletproof glass. On the *overnight sheet* (a sheet which lists the day's races) for each racetrack, the horses weren't even numbered like they are in the racetrack program. They were lettered. It was very impersonal and unorthodox to order a bet like this: "$2 exacta box A, D, and F."

I can remember going with my family on trips to Chinatown in lower Manhattan. We'd walk by the OTB parlor, and the place was always jammed with Chinese workers betting on the horses. The parlor was the size of a snack bar. In 1979, I got a job with the NYRA. I asked one of the track executives about the Chinatown OTB, and he told me it handled the most money of any parlor in New York City. And the place was a dump.

Fortunately, many OTBs are different today than they were back then. In fact, some of the nicest OTBs are now in New York City. Who says you can't teach an old dog new tricks? (To find out more about the positive changes made to OTBs, turn to "A New Era for OTBs" later in this chapter.)

Studying OTB's effects on New York racetracks

The main effect of NYC OTB has been the erosion of the fan base at NYRA racetracks. For example, in 1971, the first year of New York OTB, the daily average attendance for the Belmont Park fall meet was 27,425. In 2003, the average attendance figure had dropped to 5,930 per day. Although the NYRA executives were correct that OTB would hurt on-track attendance, they turned down an opportunity to control their own destiny. For example, NYRA could've received a bigger share of the betting profits, and they could've controlled where the OTBs were located. Currently a huge OTB parlor is just a couple blocks away from the stable gate entrance to Belmont Park.

In 1975, because of another fiscal crisis for New York City, a 5 percent surcharge was placed on all New York City OTB wagers. That means that horseplayers in the city receive a 5 percent lower payoff than on-track NYRA customers. That onerous surcharge has yet to be rescinded.

Eventually, regional OTBs started popping up throughout New York state, which in turn has created a large government bureaucracy and layers of political patronage jobs with expenses that eat away at the bottom line. In a 1992 audit, the New York State Finance Committee found that 75 percent of New York OTB expenses were labor costs. The ratio of managers to employees was a shocking 1/3, compared to a norm of 1/7 in the private sector. OTB employees are nearly impossible to fire due to a strong union, so downsizing the number of employees isn't an option to reduce costs.

A New Era for OTBs

The stigma that the original NYC OTBs created has been difficult to overcome. But believe me when I say that the OTBs I've been to throughout the country, for the most part, have been very presentable. The OTB industry got off on the wrong foot but has made great strides ever since.

The starting point of a new era for OTBs came out of Connecticut in the late 1970s. The first OTB parlors in the state were very similar to what was the norm in New York City. Then an idea was born that combined the experiences of being at the racetrack with the betting going on at an OTB.

The idea was Teletrack — the world's first "Theater of Racing." The huge facility, opened in October 1979, was the first of its kind in the world. Teletrack cost $8 million to build and was situated on a 10.8-acre site in New Haven's Long Wharf harbor area. Just like a racetrack, it had a grandstand with seating for 1,800 and a clubhouse for 500 more patrons. The main viewing area was a big 24-foot by 32-foot projection screen in the front of the theater. The amenities included 29 betting windows in the grandstand and 9 in the clubhouse. The grandstand had a food court offering typical sporting event food, and the clubhouse had a sit-down restaurant serving lunch and dinner fare. Both areas had bar service. Four VIP suites were built on the top level with a capacity of 32 people per suite. Teletrack showed racing industry leaders that OTBs could be a lot more than just faceless betting parlors.

Then by the early 1990s, Connecticut OTB and Teletrack were aging, and profits were dwindling. Autotote stepped in and purchased the franchise from the state for $20 million, so now it was privately owned. The privatization brought fresh capital for improvement and renovations. Autotote was able to cut costs, bring in dozens more simulcast signals, and invest $20 million to upgrade the facilities.

Teletrack reopened in April 1995 as Sports Haven, as shown in Figure 21-1. The main floor was transformed into a humongous Las Vegas style *race book* (a fancy area in Las Vegas casinos where horseplayers bet on the races), where each customer had a personal TV. New restaurants and a sports bar were built, and in the center of the building was a spectacular 2,800-gallon aquarium known as the "Shark Tank" because of its exotic sharks. Four movie-sized screens were added, as were scores of TV monitors. Sports Haven reopened as the best simulcast facility in the country.

Sports Haven began to market itself, too, with its main thrust being the $100,000 Sports Haven Handicapping Challenge — making it one of the biggest horse handicapping tournaments (see Chapter 17 on big money handicapping tournaments) in the U.S.

Figure 21-1:
Sports
Haven in
Connecticut.

Photo courtesy of Autotote

Finding an OTB Nearby

Off-track betting in the United States is still an underutilized industry. And
although many state governments openly embrace casino expansion — be it
private operators or Indian tribal gaming — they're still a bit standoffish when
it comes to racetracks and expansion.

The easiest way to find a nearby OTB is to visit the Web site of the National
Thoroughbred Racing Association (NTRA). They have a "simulcast facility
locator" search engine to find the closest OTBs to where you are. Also, the
local racetracks in your state should promote on their Web sites a listing of
any off-track sites that they control. If the off-track wagering system is separate from the racetrack, you need to do an Internet search of OTBs. Make
your search location-specific for your state.

Visiting an OTB isn't the same as going to live racing, but you can't beat the
convenience.

What to Look For in an OTB

After you know where the OTBs are, you need to figure out which ones are worth going to.

A well-run OTB should offer you a lot more attraction that just a convenient location. To win at betting on horse racing, you need the tools to succeed.

When NYC OTB built its first parlors, they were stark, bare bone rooms. It took a while before someone figured out that copying Las Vegas style race books was the way to go. State racing commissions sent people to New York to study how not to do things and to Las Vegas to find out how to run a successful race book. If imitation is the highest form of flattery, then Las Vegas should be blushing.

In this section, I tell you what to look for in an OTB, based on my own experiences.

Televisions

The best choice is to have an individual TV at your seat so that you can listen to the *simulcast* (satellite feed) of the horse racing from each of the racetracks. The simulcast presentation may have a good commentator worth his salt if the information he gives helps you win money. Also, you can switch the TV channels from racetrack to racetrack as you need to. However, if individual TVs aren't available, a generous bank of TVs will suffice. (If you're going to bet more than one simulcast signal, you need access to them.)

Because you're not at the racetrack, the TV is your main source of information about a simulcast. If you can't hear the track announcer or the simulcast commentator, then the racetrack must provide excellent graphics and an information crawl along the bottom of the screen. Information concerning such basics as scratches, jockey and equipment changes, and track conditions is very important for you to obtain. The OTBs should have lots of TVs so you have every chance to see the simulcast signals that you want to bet on.

A simulcast signal needs to pass what I call "the bar test" to be any good. I got the idea a long time ago from watching NFL games on Sunday at a local sports bar. A sports bar is so noisy that often times you can't hear the game announcers. So, to know what's going on, the graphics on the television screen need to show the score, down and yardage, game clock, and so on. And that's how a good horse racing simulcast signal needs to broadcast: If you can't hear the sound, you should still be able to get the information you need to make betting decisions and to know what's going on in the race.

Lots of betting windows or machines

You want enough betting windows that you don't get shut out from a bet. Some facilities have *self-automated mutuels,* or SAMs, which are bet machine kiosks where you insert money, punch in your own bets, and cash out getting a voucher and whatever tickets you purchased.

Some of the modern OTBs now even have a personal betting terminal at your seat. You set up a betting account for the day, deposit money, and make bets off of it. At the end of the day, you settle up — hopefully on the plus side.

Freebies (or at least low prices)

Racetracks and OTBs can't rival Las Vegas race books for cost. Everything in Las Vegas is literally free — right down to the drinks. A fairer cost comparison is one between a racetrack and an OTB.

A well-run OTB should be able to offer some free services that the racetracks charge for, such as free parking, seating, and overnights. The cost of doing business at an OTB should be much lower than at a racetrack, which pays expenses for putting on the show.

In Las Vegas, the casinos earn a lower percentage of its overall profits from gambling, and they do so for a reason. Casinos have built a variety of nice restaurants and shopping malls on-site, and they have shows and attractions — all things that generate revenue by themselves without the support of gambling dollars. Maybe racetracks and OTBs need to modernize and think the same way as Las Vegas casinos.

Food and beverage

Many OTBs nowadays include restaurants and bar service. In fact, some of the biggest strides forward have been made by the folks at NYC OTB. Just in Manhattan alone, they've developed four themed restaurants that are very nice OTBs and teletheaters similar to the Sports Haven model: The Yankee Clipper on Water Street, The Inside Track on 53rd Street, The Winner's Circle on 38th Street, and The Playwright Restaurant on 35th Street between 5th and 6th Avenues.

Philadelphia Park has built six *turf clubs* — hybrid OTB/restaurant/ teletheaters — that are good, fan-friendly models to emulate. You can dine in the turf club restaurant as if you were in a nice restaurant in the city. The turf clubs are located throughout the Delaware Valley in Center City, Upper Darby, South Philly, Valley Forge, Brandywine, and Northeast.

Spacious seating — and plenty of it

You definitely want a place to sit at an OTB, and you need space to spread out your *Daily Racing Forms* and programs. If your priority is to make money, be very picky about where you sit. However, if going to the local OTB is a night out with your spouse or date for entertainment, you don't have to be as choosy because you're not on a hardcore gambling excursion.

Hopefully, the days are long gone when a stark OTB parlor offers only a handful of seats, little counter space, and few televisions.

Chapter 22

Betting from Home

• •

In This Chapter

▶ Getting all the handicapping information you need without leaving the house

▶ Wagering over the telephone and the Internet

▶ Watching the horse races on your own TV

• •

*N*ot long ago, going to work meant you'd get up in the morning, shave, shower, dress, have breakfast, and drive to the job. Things have changed dramatically in our society. Now, going to work for millions of Americans means getting up, brushing your teeth, grabbing a cup of coffee, and going downstairs to your home office.

The same changes are happening in horse race betting. A horseplayer used to spend endless hours at the races betting on one racetrack card. He'd fight the traffic getting there and back, pay all the expenses associated with attending the races, and put up with the negative aspects of the races (smoke, noise, too cold or hot, and so on) to focus in on the task at hand. Nowadays, though, life for the horseplayer is as good as ever. Because of the modern technologies of fax machines, cell phones, personal computers, overnight couriers, and the Internet, a horseplayer literally doesn't have to leave her house to bet on the horse races unless she wants to.

The horse racing industry was a little slow to accept the new wave of technology. But now that it has, it's jumping in with both feet to make betting on horse racing more convenient for its legion of fans.

Doing Your Research

Researching and handicapping (see Chapters 12 and 16 on handicapping) are just as important when you're betting from home as when you're at the track. Fortunately, not only can you bet from home, but you can handicap, too.

Here's a list of some handicapping products that are readily available over the Internet and how they arrive at your house. The services, for the most part, charge a fee:

✔ **Daily news:** Many services provide a fax or e-mail to you of the horse racing news of the day. It's kind of like starting off your morning by reading your own horse racing *Wall Street Journal.*

✔ **Workouts:** Private clockers, not employed by the racetrack, time the horses' morning workouts and sell their reports to professional handicappers. These reports cover the major horse racing circuits and can be faxed or e-mailed to you. Many professional handicappers subscribe to a clocker service, because it's invaluable inside information that separates them from most other horseplayers who don't buy these services.

✔ **Sheets:** *Speed figure sheets,* produced by such companies as Brisnet, Equiform, Ragozin, and Thoro Graph (see Chapter 16 on advanced handicapping), are available through a variety of means. Some use overnight courier services to provide you with a hard copy of the sheets for the racetracks you request. You can download them off the Internet, but make sure you have lots of copy paper. Even with two horses per sheet, you'll use up many reams of paper.

✔ **Ratings:** These are different than sheets because they don't break down each individual horse in past performance style. This service provides ratings of horses or *pace numbers,* and you draw your own conclusions, using them in conjunction with the *Daily Racing Form.* These are usually Internet items.

✔ **Selections:** You can purchase a handicapping selection service that faxes, e-mails, or allows you to download its files off the Internet. These services hire professional handicappers who do the work for you, but you're on your own betting-wise.

✔ **The Daily Racing Form:** Most handicappers are familiar with the newsstand print version, but now, you can download the *Daily Racing Form* (see Chapter 11) off the Internet. You can pick and choose among the racetracks you want to handicap that day. The Web site is www.drf.com.

✔ **Horses to watch:** There are services, such as clocker reports, that sell a horses to watch list. Some free services let you set up your own account. Log in your information of horses to watch. When activity occurs such as a workout, an entry into a race, or a result, you're sent an e-mail.

All these handicapping products are easily obtained via the Internet. A search engine can find the various services for you. Which ones you should buy depends on how much money you're willing to spend, what level of handicapper you are, how much time you commit to handicapping and horse racing, and how much money you bet. I don't recommend these services if you bet $2 a race or if you bet on horse racing once a month. But these services are very helpful for the weekend horseplayer on up to the everyday professional horseplayer.

Wagering by Telephone

It's an exciting time to be a risk taker and to be technologically savvy, because lots of gambling options are available over the telephone and Internet.

Considering your options

Many services from coast-to-coast offer horse racing account wagering via the telephone. Be advised that there are rules concerning the eligibility of residents from one state signing up with a betting service located out of state. Before you sign up, the service should tell you if you're within its legal jurisdiction.

I've listed *legal* betting services available within the U.S. and have intentionally ignored off-shore services that, in some cases, circumvent American laws. In writing this book, I wouldn't intentionally promote anything deemed unlawful.

All the companies listed offer a telephone betting system with a toll-free 800 number, live operators to speak to, and a touch tone system to input your own wagers using the keypad on your telephone. Some even have voice activated systems that respond to your commands.

Signing up for an account is easy. Each service provides a simple how-to section for establishing a bet account. First, you must reside in a state that allows phone account wagering (a list of states is provided on each Web site). You need to be at least 18 years old to establish an account, and you must provide your name, address, phone number, and a secret PIN number.

After you've provided this information, you make a deposit to fund your betting account by sending a check or money order, or by using an Internet pay service like Comdata, Global Cash, Access, or PayPal. You want to check with customer service for the ways you're allowed to withdraw money. Each bet service has a toll-free number to place your bets with a clerk.

Autotote on the Wire

Autotote on the Wire is owned by Autotote and is based out of Connecticut. The company operates telephone betting in the state, off-track wagering parlors, and two teletheaters called Sports Haven in New Haven and Bradley Teletheater at Bradley Airport in Hartford. Autotote is a totalisator company that provides parimutuel services to racetracks all over the world. In other words, Autotote provides the computer systems required to handle parimutuel wagering (see Chapter 3 on parimutuel wagering). Autotote on the Wire also has a very good voice activation system. Its toll free phone number is 800-468-2260, and its Web address is www.ctotb.com.

Capital OTB

One of the regional off-track betting companies in the state of New York, Capital OTB covers the Albany area with the Albany Teletheater and numerous branches. Its toll free phone number is 800-292-BETS, and its Web address is www.capitalotb.com.

eBetUSA

Penn National Gaming owns and operates eBetUSA. Penn National is known for the racetrack of the same name in Grantville, Pennsylvania. It also owns Pocono Downs harness in Wilkes-Barre, Pennsylvania, and Charles Town Racetrack in Charles Town, West Virginia. The company owns and operates eight casinos throughout the U.S.

Penn National bypassed American technology in contracting with eBet Gaming Systems in Australia. An added feature of eBetUSA is that you can wager over your computer and watch live streaming of up to eight different simulcast signals. eBetUSA's toll free phone number is 800-946-9772. Check it out on the Web at www.ebetusa.com.

Interbets Catskill OTB

The Catskill Off-Track Betting Corporation (in upstate New York) owns and operates Interbets Catskill OTB. Catskill OTB is famous, but for unfortunate reasons (see the sidebar, "Catskill OTB's dubious claim to fame"). Its toll free phone number is 888-FUN-2BET. Check out Catskill OTB on www.interbets.com.

New York City OTB

The first of the off-track wagering divisions in New York state, New York City OTB covers Manhattan with three attractive teletheaters — The Inside Track, The Winner's Circle, and The Yankee Clipper. New York City OTB also operates 65 OTB shops and 10 restaurants throughout New York City (which includes the boroughs of the Bronx, Brooklyn, Manhattan, Queens, and Staten Island). NYC OTB's toll free phone number is 800-OTB-8118. Check it out on the Web at www.nycotb.com.

NYRA One

Owned and operated by the New York Racing Association, NYRA One racetracks include Aqueduct, Belmont Park, and Saratoga. I recommend this account provider in New York state because more money is returned to the horseman in purse money, and it supports live racing. NYRA One's toll free phone number 800-THE-NYRA, and its Web site is www.nyra.com.

Philadelphia Park Phonebet

Phonebet is recognized as the first phone betting system in the U.S. It has been in the forefront of technology — first offering bet operators, then a touch tone system, and finally an Internet system coupled with live streaming of the horse races. Because Phonebet was first and is very reliable, it's the largest account wagering service in the U.S. Phonebet's toll free phone number is 888-346-7737, and its Web site is www.phonebet.com.

Catskill OTB's dubious claim to fame

Catskill OTB, a company that offers horse racing account wagering, may never live down its role, or its reputation, in the biggest scam in the history of U.S. horse racing. When Volponi, a 43/1 long shot, won the 2002 Breeders' Cup Classic at Arlington Park in Arlington Heights, Illinois, a chain of events in the Breeders' Cup Ultra Pick 6 started and led directly to the offices of Catskill OTB.

Originally, there were six winners in the 2002 Breeders' Cup Ultra Pick 6 paying out $3.1 million. But what's incredulous is that all six tickets came from Catskill OTB and were purchased by the same account holder — Derrick Davis, who lived in Baltimore, Maryland. Just as unusual was the betting pattern of the winning ticket. Davis used a single horse in the first four races and then all-all, meaning the entire field, in the final two legs. The ticket was a $12 denomination. No one plays pick 6 tickets in that manner, meaning that Davis singled two long shots — Mile winner, Domedriver, at $54.00 to win and Filly and Mare Turf winner, Starine, at $28.40 to win. Red flags indicating fraud went up everywhere, and within 48 hours, the Breeders' Cup froze the $3.1 million Ultra Pick 6 money and began an investigation.

The investigation uncovered that three former Drexel University fraternity pals — Chris Harn, Derrick Davis, and Glen DaSilva — had schemed to take advantage of weaknesses in horse racing's parimutuel system. Harn was the ringleader who worked as a programmer at Autotote, which gave him full access to the parimutuel computer system. But the most important factor was that he knew that Catskill

OTB's phone betting system was about the only betting service that didn't record phone-in bets. (Betting services have a recording device to protect themselves in case of a dispute with an account holder over a transaction.)

Because Catskill OTB had no recording device, Harn knew that after a bet was placed on the Breeders' Cup Ultra Pick 6, the wager was untraceable. Davis set up a Catskill OTB account, and Harn then placed the now infamous "single-single-single-single-all-all" Breeders' Cup Ultra Pick 6 ticket. After the fourth race in the Breeders' Cup Ultra Pick 6, Harn went into the Autotote computer system and changed the four singles on the Breeders' Cup Ultra Pick 6 ticket to the four winning horses. In other words, the ticket was now a sure winner.

But then the unthinkable happened. At 43/1 odds, Volponi (the longest odds horse in the Classic), won the race. When Harn discovered that they had the only winning Breeders' Cup Ultra Pick 6 tickets, he knew they were dead meat. If not for Volponi, the perpetrators probably wouldn't have been caught, because many winners would have emerged in the Ultra Pick 6, and the spotlight wouldn't have shone on Derrick Davis and eventually Harn and DaSilva.

Harn, Davis, and DaSilva pleaded guilty and served jail sentences. Autotote and the horse racing industry spent millions of dollars fixing flaws in the betting system and establishing more security safeguards. Then almost two years after the scam, Catskill OTB finally installed a recording device to monitor phone bets.

Suffolk OTB

Another one of the New York state account wagering systems, Suffolk OTB is located in Suffolk County on Long Island. Its toll free phone number is 800-TEL-BETS. You can visit Suffolk OTB's Web site at www.suffolkotb.com.

Television Games Network

Television Games Network, better known as TVG, is an off-shoot of the television network that's on a growing number of cable systems. The master plan was for TVG to attract a high level of accounting wagering to finance the television network. The National Thoroughbred Racing Association (NTRA) was aligned with it from the start.

Other accounting wagering services that were members of the NTRA protested that TVG was cannibalizing into their own business. Everything has been resolved, and TVG is focusing on getting its network into more homes. I recommend TVG because it returns money back to racetracks through a Source Market Fee program and supports live racing. TVG's toll free phone number is 888-PLAY-TVG. TVG is located in Los Angeles, and its Web site is www.tvgnetwork.com.

Winticket.com

Winticket.com began as Ohio TAB in 1994, and Ohio racetracks Beulah Park, River Downs, Scioto Downs, and Thistledowns were the original owners. Now only Beulah Park and River Downs remain as owners. Beulah Park is located near Columbus, and River Downs is in Cincinnati. Its corporate name is America TAB. The company has a working relationship with AmTote and Bloodstock Research Information Services. One advance in dealing with Winticket.com is free information and past performances from BRISNET, which is part of Bloodstock Research. Winticket.com's toll free phone number is 866-891-5100, and you can check out its Web site at www.winticket.com.

XpressBet

XpressBet is owned by Magna Entertainment Corporation based out of Ontario, Canada. Magna owns a fleet of U.S. racetracks including Bay Meadows in San Mateo, California; Golden Gate Fields in Albany, California; Great Lakes Downs in Muskegon, Michigan; Gulfstream Park in Hallandale, Florida; Laurel Park in Laurel, Maryland; Lone Star Park in Grand Prairie, Texas; Pimlico in Baltimore, Maryland; Remington Park in Oklahoma City, Oklahoma; Santa Anita Park in Arcadia, California; and Thistledowns in North Randall, Ohio. Magna also owns and operates Horse Racing Television, better known as HRTV. It televises exclusively its own branded racetracks. XpressBet's toll free phone number is 866-889-7737. You can visit XpressBet's Web site at www.xpressbet.com.

Youbet.com

Youbet.com was founded in 1987 and went public in 1995. Its stock is sold on NASDAQ under the symbol UBET. The company is slowly gaining a foothold in the marketplace and has done some good things with its technology. It shows a live streaming of the races with its strategic partners. Its toll free phone number is 888-968-2388. Visit Youbet.com at `www.youbet.com`.

Getting the best deal

Competition for wagering customers is fierce, and in a competitive marketplace, service companies need to offer things to you, the customer, to make them stand out. That's what's happening in the telephone account wagering category. You're in the driver's seat, so you can shop and compare services, see who's offering the best promotion, and sign up accordingly. You can probably even do an Internet search and find out from other horseplayers which betting services grade out higher than others in customer satisfaction.

Every company I list in this chapter has promotions running of some kind. Here's a useful checklist of items to ask for and consider before choosing your future telephone account provider:

- ✔ Cash back for referring a new customer
- ✔ Cash rebate to you or into your opening account just for signing up
- ✔ Player rewards program and perks, such as free points for signing up or referring a new customer
- ✔ Free gifts of any kind
- ✔ Free additional services of any kind
- ✔ Free video to watch the races on your computer over the Internet
- ✔ Free race replay service
- ✔ Toll-free calling numbers and tape recorded phone calls
- ✔ No surcharge on placing bets
- ✔ No minimum balance
- ✔ Ease in depositing money into your account
- ✔ Ease in withdrawing money from your account
- ✔ A complementary Internet site that's useful and easy to use
- ✔ All racetracks available for you to wager on so you don't have to open more than one account
- ✔ Hours of service from first race to last if you want to bet that many horses

Watching the Race in Your PJs

Since the inception of the National Thoroughbred Racing Association (NTRA), broadcast hours for horse racing have skyrocketed. The NTRA was sharp enough to see opportunities with the major networks to add more horse racing to their programming hours. In addition, two networks that broadcast nothing but horseracing have emerged.

Of course, the main benefactors in the increased broadcasting are you and the horse racing industry. Horse racing is making a resurgence in popularity, and there are many newcomers to the sport. Being on television remains one of the best ways to promote a product, and horse racing is finally getting with it. For horseplayers, life is made simpler when they can bet in their pajamas and watch the races live on their TV sets.

Studies have shown that when a horse race is on television, the handle for the race goes up, meaning horseplayers bet on races when they can watch them. Lots of horse bets are placed on races that the bettor doesn't see. But it's human nature that if you place a bet, you want to see the outcome.

I count four basic sources of watching horse racing on TV: network television, cable, TVG, and HRTV. In this section, I describe each source in more detail.

Network television

Horse racing appears on all the networks at some point of the year. NBC airs the first two legs of the Triple Crown — the Kentucky Derby and Preakness — and the Breeders' Cup World Thoroughbred Championship. ABC has picked up the Belmont Stakes (the third leg of the Triple Crown) and some ESPN horse racing hours. And CBS has a summer series of top handicap races that the NTRA sells to horseplayers as a national pick 4 — one pick 4 wager using all four TV races — on special Saturdays. From time to time, FOX shows horse racing.

Cable

Horse racing was one of the first sports to jump onto the ESPN bandwagon when the all-sports network began in late 1979. A little more than a year later, Jim Wilburn and Chris Lincoln formed Winner Communications in Tulsa, Oklahoma. Their first broadcast for ESPN was championship Quarter Horse racing.

The two men saw the light and quickly expanded into the Thoroughbred industry, providing a valuable conduit for the sport onto ESPN. That was the start of horse racing on cable television, and it has grown unabated ever since.

In 1999, the NTRA acquired the racing assets of Winner Communications and has run with the ball even further. The number of programming hours horse racing produces for ESPN and ESPN2 goes a long way towards increasing the popularity of the sport.

FOX Sports Network is also now a major player in the horse racing's cable realm. FOX airs a one to two hour block of time in the afternoon during these California meetings: Fairplex in Pomona, Hollywood Park in Inglewood, Del Mar in Del Mar, and Oak Tree at Santa Anita in Arcadia. At night, FOX airs Quarter Horse racing from Los Alamitos in Los Alamitos, California.

Television Games Network

Television Games Network (TVG) bills itself as the interactive horse racing network. It's available on many cable systems throughout the U.S. and on satellite via the DISH Network and Direct TV.

When TVG first broadcast during the summer of 1999, it was niche programming for horse racing that followed on the heels of The Golf Channel, The Food Network, The Travel Channel, and so on. Cable opened the doors for new channels created to focus upon these narrowly defined market segments.

Horse racing was long overdue for such programming because of its sizable built-in audience (millions of established horse racing fans) and large amount of product (horse races) available for next to nothing because the cost of satellite transmission of the races is already being paid for as a simulcast product. Each racetrack has a television production unit in place and satellite capabilities to beam the broadcast signal out.

The winners of this launch are you and I. I get TVG and HRTV (see following section) through the Dish Network, and I can watch the horse races at home all day long. It's a proven fact that horseplayers bet more money on horse races they can see. So combining TVG and HRTV with a telephone betting account (see "Wagering by Telephone," earlier in the chapter) is a perfect marriage for you the horseplayer.

TVG averages between six and eight live horse races per hour and a few more on tape delay. It provides expert commentary from a host and one or two handicappers, plus on the scene reports from reporters at the racetracks.

One of the best programs aired on TVG is called "The Works," which airs for two weeks prior to the Kentucky Derby (see Chapter 18 on picking a Derby winner) and the Breeders' Cup World Thoroughbred Championships. "The Works" shows the training and workouts of contenders leading up to the events with expert commentary to analyze what the horses have just done.

HorseRacing TV

Magna Corporation started HorseRacing TV (HRTV) to showcase its own stable of racetracks. None of those racetracks are available to be shown on TVG (see preceding section), and a preponderance of the racetracks on TVG can't be shown on HRTV. So what gives?

If you, the horseplayer, want to watch all the racetracks, you need to subscribe to both TVG and HRTV. The same goes for telephone account wagering. You need to open separate accounts at XpressBet (see "Considering your options," earlier in the chapter) to bet the Magna racetracks and TVG to bet all the others.

The most popular simulcast signals that HRTV shows are from Santa Anita Park in Arcadia, California, and Gulfstream Park in Hallandale, Florida. Ironically, both operate at roughly the same time of the year — January through April. The rest of the year, you get a steady diet of Maryland racing, Northern California racing, and outposts like Remington Park in Oklahoma City, Oklahoma, and Thistledowns in North Randall, Ohio.

HRTV and TVG show international racing from Hong Kong, England, Australia, and Dubai to name a few examples. Expect more foreign horse racing to be imported into your home in the coming years.

Chapter 23

Viva Las Vegas

For a town that doesn't have a racetrack, Las Vegas is an incredibly popular place for betting on horse racing. It makes sense that out of 35 million annual visitors to Las Vegas, a lot of the tourists are horse-racing fans.

In addition, thousands of locals who live in town frequent the Vegas race books on a daily basis. Here, you can watch the races live on television monitors, have plenty of free seating to spread out your *Daily Racing Forms,* and drink, eat, and relax for practically nothing.

Las Vegas race books save seats for their regular horseplayers and offer big bettors free comps for food and amenities. If you play your cards right, Las Vegas is the best place in the world for playing the horses, and in this chapter, I tell you why.

Finding the Race Books That Suit Your Needs

Nearly every casino in Las Vegas has a *race book* — a place where you can watch horse races from around the country on live TV. I like to judge the attitude of a casino by how much it cares about its horseplayers. Some of my measures include the size of its race book, its comfort level, the customer service, and how much it caters to the horseplayers.

So, when you check out a race book for the first time, eyeball some of these amenities:

- **Tables and chairs:** Counter tops should be available to spread out your *Daily Racing Forms,* overnights, and other handicapping materials. The chairs should be comfortable and easy to move in and out of, because you get up and down constantly to make wagers.

- **Daily Racing Forms:** Race book management should provide the *Daily Racing Form* (see Chapter 11 on the *DRF*) for free. At worst, you have to provide a $1 deposit per *Daily Racing Form,* and you get your money back when you turn in your used copy. If the race book tries to charge you full price for the *Daily Racing Form,* I'd go gamble somewhere else.

- **Overnights:** The race book should have printed overnights for each racetrack open that day and a set of overnights for the next day's racing. An *overnight* is a sheet listing the next day's races and includes information about the horses entered for the day, the jockeys, the weights, and the track morning line odds.

- **Televisions:** If you don't have an individual monitor at your seat, then a bank of TVs should show all the races available to be wagered upon. The preference is to have your own monitor.

- **Lighting:** Don't laugh. Some race books are so dark you can't read your *Daily Racing Forms.* And if you drop a $20 bill on the carpet, you may not see it again.

- **Ticket writers:** At the racetrack, they're called *mutuel clerks;* in a race book, they're called *ticket writers* (see the sidebar, "An old-fashioned book bet," later in the chapter). Enough ticket writers should be available so that they're not the cause of you getting shut out of a wager. They should be alert, courteous, and conscientious about their job. Leave a tip for them once in a while to say thank you.

- **Drinks:** In Las Vegas casinos, you can drink for free, but always tip your server!

- **House bets:** It's a big plus for you if the race book offers *house bets* (betting against the casino) in horse racing. House bets come in the form of house quinellas and parlays, which I cover later in "Betting Against the Casino."

- **Comps:** If you're new to the race book, introduce yourself to the supervisor. Let her know you want your wagering tracked so you can become eligible for comps. She'll let you know how your wagering translates into *comp dollars* (points), which are traded in for meals, rooms, and so on (see the following section for more on comps).

An old-fashioned book bet

Before *parimutuel wagering* (betting against one another) became legal in Nevada in 1990, all horse racing bets were *book bets* (betting against the casino or house).

Taking horse bets was a laborious process for the race book operators. The bet sheets or tickets were on three-ply paper. One copy went to the horseplayer as his receipt of the wager. A second sheet went into a secure box that went to the Nevada Gaming Control Board at the end of the day. No one else was supposed to have access to it. A third sheet was for the casino to grade the wager.

A race book needed three types of workers to handle bets. The people at the counter were called *ticket writers,* because they hand wrote the tickets as people called out their bets. The wagers had limits because the casinos didn't want to take unlimited liability. Supervisors had to make an educated guess on the spot whether to accept or reject large wagers.

The second type of worker was the grader. He received copies of the bets and graded them for winners when the race results came in from a disseminator company. The Nevada Gaming Control Board ruled that a disseminator company was required to filter the racing information. This system, in theory, would guarantee that correct information was being sent to the race books and, in particular, would eliminate any past posting of results (meaning that posting of results are delayed on purpose).

The third worker was the cashier who paid off on winning horse bets. He'd make sure the horseplayer's ticket and the graded ticket matched. Lots of horseplayers tried to beat the system, and a few did. But that's for another story.

On rare occasions, race books must revert to this old fashion system of handling horse bets, so this information is good for you to know.

Almost everything at the race books is available for free. The legend of Las Vegas was built upon value and getting more than your money's worth. If you've done your Las Vegas homework right, you'll be sitting in a brightly lit, spacious race book, reading your free *Daily Racing Forms,* sipping a free drink, and watching the races on your own TV monitor — and you won't have spent a dime. At a racetrack, you'd be out $20 to $30 already.

Earning Comps: Using What's Rightfully Yours

Comps — which are freebies and perks a casino gives to its better gamblers — and Las Vegas have been synonymous for a long time. But the entrepreneur who shaped the tradition was Benny Binion, who opened Binion's Horseshoe

---

When free drinks cost you

Casinos have a reason for offering their guests free alcoholic beverages, and they're not just trying to be nice. Mixing alcohol and gambling isn't a good idea. You need all your mental faculties to win at betting on horse racing, and alcohol impairs your judgment. If you're playing the horses and having an excellent day, what better way to celebrate than by having some drinks with friends *afterwards* to relax.

---

casino in downtown Las Vegas in 1951. Binion was renowned for his generosity, offering big and small gamblers alike comps for food and drinks. If a visitor gambled away too much money, he'd buy him a meal and a bus ticket home. Binion's good nature and good business acumen combined to make him generous with comps. He knew every comp offered to a stranger would build brand loyalty and spread the gospel of Binion's Horseshoe casino when that person returned home.

When comps first became popular, there were no computers or player tracking systems. Casino operators had to know their players and how much they bet. Now, however, everything is computerized, and if you're not entered into the casino's computer, you aren't earning any *comp dollars* (points) based on how much money you bet. Unfortunately, you don't have any way around it. To get comped in a Las Vegas casino, you must apply for a *player tracking card* and use it whenever you're gambling. Even if you consider yourself a $2 bettor, earning points doesn't hurt.

After you're entered into a player tracker system, your address is added to a mailing list. The casino marketing department sends you promotional mailers, offers for free gifts, room discounts, and so on. If you're going to gamble on horses or anything else at a casino, play it the right way, and earn everything you have coming to you.

Playing in Contests and Twin Quinellas

The competition among the casino race books for horseplayers is fierce, and you come out the winner. Many casino companies offer free contests, contests with nominal entry fees, and twin quinellas for horseplayers to make a score without trying very hard.

A *twin quinella* is exactly as it sounds — winning two quinellas (see Chapter 15 on exotic wagers) in races designated by the casino. When racetracks have offered the twin quinella as a parimutuel bet, it usually flops because they don't put any seed money or guaranteed money to start the pot. In Las Vegas, the race books put up prize money and create a positive expectancy for the bettor right from the start.

Two twin quinella offerings have been around a long time in Las Vegas — at the Plaza in downtown Las Vegas and at Station Casinos. If the twin quinella isn't won on the first day, then a carryover pool grows from a percentage of the money bet plus the guaranteed money put up by the casino. If the twin quinella has more than one winner, the entire pool is divided equally among the winners.

When you come to Las Vegas, check out the *Daily Racing Form* for a schedule of weekly horse handicapping contests and twin quinellas. Also, two local radio shows — Race Day Las Vegas and Race Day Las Vegas Wrap Up — cover the contest scene. Someone has to win the contests, so you may as well come out on top.

Contest formats change, and because this book has a permanent shelf life in your own library, I won't dwell on specific contest rules. However, in January 2004, the Nevada Gaming Control Board implemented a contest rules amendment that made a lot of local horseplayers grumble. Any contest that charges a fee to enter must have a computerized grading system of the entries. Before the new rule, casino employees hand graded the contest entries. The rule temporarily ended some fee-based contests until the computer software needed to grade the contest entries is in place. Many casinos, for the time being, are offering free contests to legally circumvent the rule.

The leading Las Vegas companies in horse handicapping contests are the Coast Casinos and Station Casinos chains, which each have a number of large casino hotels dotted around Las Vegas. In general, both Coast and Station put a lot of time and money into catering to local horseplayers.

Some Strip hotels that frequently offer horse contests include Bally's Las Vegas, the Excalibur, the Imperial Palace, and the New Frontier. Off the Strip, the Las Vegas Hilton, the Hard Rock, Terrible's, and Sam's Town have contests from time to time.

Wagering the Kentucky Derby and Breeders' Cup in Las Vegas

The two most special days in horse racing are the first Saturday in May when the Kentucky Derby is run and the day in late October or early November when the Breeders' Cup World Thoroughbred Championship takes place. As you can imagine, the folks in Las Vegas like to get in on the action.

Placing future book bets

Many Las Vegas casinos offer a future book bet on the Kentucky Derby, Kentucky Oaks, and Breeders' Cup races. When you place a *future book bet*, you bet on a horse well in advance of the special race and get *fixed odds* (meaning when you place the bet, you get the current odds at that time) on that horse. Fixed odds are usually higher because your bet is final regardless of whether the horse even makes it to the starting gate for the special race.

Some big scores have been made on future book horses. In 1988, some California horseplayers reportedly went to Tijuana, Mexico and made large future wagers on a filly named Winning Colors to win the Kentucky Derby. They bet her at 100/1 odds. The filly went on to win the Kentucky Derby and paid only $8.80 to win, or 3/1 odds, at Churchill Downs. In 1990, an unnamed Las Vegas horseplayer bet Unbridled after the colt had a horrendous trip in the Fountain of Youth. When Unbridled won the Kentucky Derby, the bettor collected nearly $50,000 in future book winnings.

The earliest Kentucky Derby and Breeders' Cup future books are at Bally's Las Vegas, Coast Resorts, and the Plaza. By earliest, I mean they open their future books far in advance of the race or races.

Dipping into the parimutuel pool: Kentucky Derby and Oaks Future Wagers

Churchill Downs racetrack in Louisville, Kentucky hosts its own Kentucky Derby Future Wager and Kentucky Oaks Future Wager. While the Las Vegas future book odds are fixed, the Kentucky Derby and Oaks Future Wagers are *parimutuel pools*, meaning the odds are final after the pools close.

The Derby and Oaks Future Wagers are offered three weekends each spring. You can bet them in nearly all racetracks and off-track betting parlors around the country and, of course, in Las Vegas.

Las Vegas horseplayers have a unique advantage because the Derby and Oaks Future Wagers and future book pools are open simultaneously, creating a shopping frenzy for the best odds on Derby and Oaks horses.

Catching the race in the next best place: Kentucky Derby and Breeders' Cup parties

The race books advertise that if you can't attend the Kentucky Derby or the Breeders' Cup in person, then the next best place to watch the races is in

Las Vegas. Many major race books host big parties for the two events. If they charge admission, the cost isn't very much. But if you're a regular horseplayer in the race book or are included on its marketing mailing list, you'll probably receive an invitation. One aspect that makes attending these parties more enjoyable than being at the actual races is that you don't have to wait in long lines to bet, get your food and beverage, or use the rest room. And the casino service is second to none.

Why the casinos root for horseplayers to win

When you're on the casino floor playing black-jack, roulette, craps, the slot and video poker machines, and so on, you're betting against the casino, also called the *house*. Regardless of how friendly the dealers are to you at the card table, he represents your mortal enemy.

Casino megaresorts weren't built on the sweat equity of their shareholders and investors. They were built on the spending habits of you, me, and millions of people who lose money gambling. Resorts want you to spend money on rooms, restaurants, shows, and so on (which is why you should cash in your comps and never feel guilty about it).

The philosophy changes 180 degrees in the casino race book. The house really wants you to win, and here's why: In *parimutuel wagering*, you bet against the other horseplayers. The racetrack, or in this case the casino race book, holds the takeout (see Chapter 3) percentage and pays out the rest of the wagering pool to winning horseplayers.

The *blended takeout rate,* meaning the average takeout rate combining all the parimutuel wagering pools, is around 20 percent. For example, at Saratoga, the takeout is 14 percent for straight bets; 17.5 percent for daily doubles,

exactas, and quinellas; and 25 percent for the trifecta, superfecta, pick 3, pick 4, and pick 6. If all the money bet at Saratoga were added up and the takeouts deducted, the blended takeout for the overall wagering pool would average to be about 20 percent.

The race book pays the host racetrack 3 percent as a rights fee for allowing betting on its simulcast signal. So the race book theoretically keeps 17 percent. But hold everything. What if the horseplayers in the race book do really well, and what if they do really poorly?

That's the kicker for the casino race book. If horseplayers do really badly, then the race book has to wire the profit or extra money back to the racetrack. If horseplayers do really well, then the racetrack has to wire money to the race book to balance its accounting. Believe me — the race books prefer money to come in than to go out.

Successful horseplayers don't sit on their winnings; they bet back race after race — known in the industry as *churning*. When horseplayers churn back the same money over and over again with a blended takeout rate of 20 percent, you're talking about large profits for the race book.

Betting Against the Casino

Most horse racing bets in Las Vegas are made into the parimutuel wagering pools. However, horse bets are made against the casino or house when no parimutuel wagering is offered. The two examples I cover here are house quinellas and parlay wagering. Not all Las Vegas race books offer these two house bets, so check with the race book supervisor ahead of time.

House quinellas

House quinellas (see Chapter 15 on exotic wagers) and *parlays* (see Chapter 4 on placing a bet) are among the best horse racing bets you can make in Las Vegas. Both wagers are *book bets,* meaning you're betting against the house.

The two bets aren't offered in every race book in Las Vegas. For example, most Strip hotel race books don't offer them. The thought is that most of their horseplayers are tourists. Where tourists come from, the racetracks don't offer similar wagers. Race books that cater to local horseplayers do offer house quinellas and parlays. (The locals think that the tourists are squares because they don't know about this kind of betting action, but now readers of this book know!)

You probably wonder how house quinellas are any different from racetrack quinellas. Racetrack quinellas are their own separate *parimutuel pool,* meaning the odds become final after the pool closes. For example, if you bet a racetrack quinella using a 2/1 favorite with a 14/1 long shot, your winning quinella pays the same regardless of which horse finishes first or second.

Not so with a Las Vegas house quinella. You can see a typical example of a house quinella payoff in Table 23-1.

Table 23-1	The Payoff for a House Quinella		
	Win Payoff	*Place Payoff*	*House Quinella Payoff*
Favorite horse (2/1 odds)	$6	$3	--
Long shot horse (14/ 1 odds)	--	$10	$30

Here's the formula for figuring a house quinella payoff:

1. **Multiply the win price of the first horse times the place price of the second horse.**
2. **Divide the total by two.**

Using the information in Table 23-1, I multiply $6, the win price of the first horse, by $10, the place price of the second horse, and get $60, which I divide by two to get $30.

A house quinella is a tremendous advantage over a racetrack quinella when the long shot horse wins the race. See the difference in the house quinella payout in Table 23-2.

Table 23-2	A House Quinella Payoff Changes When the Long Shot Wins		
	Win Payoff	*Place Payoff*	*House Quinella Payoff*
Long shot horse (14/ 1 odds)	$30	$10	--
Favorite horse (2/1 odds)	--	$3	$45

In Table 23-2, if the long shot wins, I multiply $30, the win price of the long shot, by $3, the place price of the favorite, and get $90, which I divide by two to get $45.

In the preceding two examples, the house quinella payoff increased from $30 to $45 when the long shot won. The racetrack quinella would've paid the same amount either way.

One play that Las Vegas horseplayers love, and the race books hate, is called a *lock 'em up Q.* In this play, you take two heavy favorites and bet a big house quinella. A lock 'em up Q invariably pays more than a racetrack exacta box (see Chapter 15 on exotic wagers) or a racetrack quinella.

Parlays

The parlay wager can be a useful weapon in your betting arsenal. A two-horse win parlay, in essence, is making your own daily double wager (see Chapter 15 on exotic wagers).

Something that I like to do is make place and show parlays (see Chapter 4 on placing a bet). The parlay isn't my main bet, but it's a complementary wager that rewards me if I'm almost right with the horses I like.

For example, if I part-wheel some horses in a pick 3 (see Chapter 15 on exotic wagers), I may choose the longer price horses — one from each race — and make a three-horse place or show parlay. My main strategy is to win the pick 3. But, if my price horses run well but don't win, I can be rewarded if they finish second or third depending on my parlay wager.

Sometimes I win the pick 3 but lose the parlay. Other times the parlay wins, but the pick 3 loses. The best result is to win both wagers. I've found that allowing yourself to almost be right and cash tickets is a fun and profitable way to play.

Comparing Las Vegas with Other Locales

In 1977, when casino gambling expanded into Atlantic City, New Jersey, Wall Street analysts predicted doom and gloom for Las Vegas. They predicted that tourists on the east coast would flock to the Jersey Shore to gamble and forsake Las Vegas entirely.

If you've been to Las Vegas recently, you know the analysts were 100 percent wrong. Instead of stealing tourists away from Las Vegas, Atlantic City and eventually other locales that introduced casino and riverboat gambling to newcomers are creating new customers for Las Vegas.

Las Vegas remains the mecca of gambling in America. All the outposts are nice to visit from time to time, but Americans know that if you're going to shoot dice, play the ponies, see a few shows, and really let your hair down, there's only one Las Vegas.

One edge that Las Vegas has is sports gambling. Sports gambling is illegal in every state but Nevada. Race books here are placed next to the sports books, creating an excitement that can't be duplicated. Where else but Las Vegas can you win the daily double at Aqueduct and then take your winnings and parlay them, legally, on the New York Giants minus three points over the Washington Redskins. If you like to gamble, it doesn't get any better.

Part VI
The Part of Tens

The 5th Wave   By Rich Tennant

"He prefers it to trotting."

In this part . . .

For Dummies books are renowned for their lists of tens, and because many readers review the lists first, I've highlighted three areas that may really interest newcomers. The first list is the ten best bets to make, and it entails some common handicapping situations that can be very profitable. The second list is made up of the ten best racetracks to visit — all of which I've been to. So when you're traveling around the country for business or for pleasure, make sure you stop by these racetracks. The third list is the ten most common betting mistakes — some that are obvious and some that can slip under the mental radar.

Chapter 24

Ten Best Bets and Betting Angles

. . . .

In This Chapter

▶ Discovering the best betting angle in horse racing

▶ Betting to win

▶ Placing the right kind of wagers

▶ Recognizing scenarios that can win you money

. . . .

When I do public handicapping for the *Las Vegas Review-Journal,* I select a best bet every day on the Southern California card. To me, that best bet is a horse that's a surest winner. I seldom factor the horse's morning line odds into the play.

In this chapter, I identify what I consider to be the ten best bets as far as winning money and cashing a lot of tickets too. Throughout this book, I write under the premise that you have $100 to gamble with for a single day of horse racing action. To a hardcore gambler, that's not much money to work with. But for a newcomer to horse racing, $100 is enough to win some money and have fun.

My idea for this chapter isn't just to list the wagers themselves but to present the handicapping scenarios too. In reality, you have barely more than ten types of parimutuel bets to choose from. But some scenarios exist that maximize the winning probability of certain wagers. The odds of the horses you use can also increase the profitability potential. In previous chapters, I cover the race shape and the good betting scenarios that you can identify with basic handicapping. I've listed some of the best situations here.

Lone Speed

When I open up the *Daily Racing Form* and start handicapping the races, the first thing I do is break down the running styles of the horses into three classifications: speed horses, pace horses, and dead late closers (see Chapter 12). After I do that, the race shape forms when I contrast the horses' different running styles.

The best betting angle in horse racing is a *lone speed horse*. Lone speed means he's the only speed horse in the race. Lone speed can show up in any size field and at a race of any distance. When a speed horse gets out in front and faces no early opposition, he dictates the pace and is very difficult to beat.

The most obvious example of a lone speed horse is when a horse has all ones in its *Daily Racing Form* past performance lines, and all the other horses in the race do not. Unless one of the other jockeys sacrifices his chances by going after the lone speedball early, the leader has a free shot at an easy advantage.

Unfortunately, if the lone speed horse is too obvious, it can be a low-odds favorite. Yet if certain factors appear — like the lone speed horse is moving up in class, trying a new distance, or has a new jockey or trainer — they may buffer the odds.

An example where a lone speed horse may not be so obvious is in a two-turn distance race. At first glance, the field may not appear to have a lot of early speed. The kind of horse that slips beneath the handicapper's radar screen is a sprinter stretching out in a two-turn distance race for the first time.

Until this race, the sprinter may have been running in races with very fast fractions, like a half-mile in 45 seconds. The routers in today's distance race may be used to a more leisurely half-mile of 47 seconds. The sprinter stretching out may find itself galloping along in front at a slow pace for him, but a fast pace for the other horses.

At the top of the stretch, the come-from-behind horses will commence their rally. But the stretch out horse has something in reserve because it hasn't been pressured hard like it has been in faster sprint races. Often times, the lone speed horse keeps going, winning at attractive odds.

Win Bets

Professional horseplayers have learned that to beat the takeout (see Chapter 3) in horse race betting over the long run, going for big scores in the exotic pools — such as pick 6, pick 4, and superfecta wagers — is necessary (see Chapter 15). You need a lot of know-how and a lot of bankroll to successfully go for big scores. That translates into you needing a lot of staying power to ride out the inevitable long losing streaks that accompany the kind of feast or famine wagering in exotic pools.

You may not be ready for that kind of commitment just yet. In the beginning, you're better off finding winners and betting on winners — simple as that.

For bettors with less experience and finite bankrolls, win bets on fast horses at fair odds is a good formula. Cashing win bets stretches your bankroll and gives you lots of action during the racing card. And if you want to take that shot at a score, hopefully you have the finances to do so.

Daily Double

The *daily double* (see Chapter 15) was the first exotic wager in American racing. It began as a link between the first two races on the card as a marketing tool to ensure that horseplayers came to the racetrack early. If bettors didn't get to the racetrack in time for the first race, they'd miss their daily double opportunity.

The beauty of the daily double is that it hasn't lost its value despite the large number of exotic wagers now available. If you can beat a favorite in one of the two daily double races, you're paid more than a parlay (see Chapter 4) of the two win prices. If you can beat both favorites, the daily double payoff zooms upward.

If you bet on Southern California races, you have access to a daily double bet rolling through the entire card that begins in race one. It's not unusual to have two 3/1 odds horses win and see the daily double pay $40 or more, especially if neither horse was the favorite. A natural parlay between two $8 win prices is $32.

A big advantage of the daily double is that the racetrack shows the probable payoffs on the television monitors. You can see the potential payoff before you place your wager.

I know some horseplayers who chart the daily double pool and can tell you which are the hot horses. They create a big edge by knowing which horses are getting bet in an exotic pool.

Pick 3

The *pick 3* is basically a daily double with one more race added onto it (see Chapter 15 for more on this type of bet). Betting on three winners in a row on a single ticket isn't easy, but the rewards can be great.

One big difference between a daily double and a pick 3 is that you can bet a pick 3 for a $1 base unit, but the daily double is $2 in nearly all jurisdictions.

The pick 3's cheaper price allows you to place more horses on the mutuel ticket and keep the cost affordable. For example, you can play two horses in each race of a pick 3, and the ticket costs only $8.

You can bet the pick 3 lots of ways to gain maximum value. You may love a horse in the sequence and single that race. Then if you go three horses deep in the other two legs, the ticket costs just $9. Even if you go four horses deep in the other two races, the ticket costs only $16, and you have a chance to catch one or two long shots with the horse you favor.

On a limited bankroll, the pick 3 is one way to make a small score on short money. Your probability of winning is pretty good, and you're stretching your resources to maximum usage.

Pick 4

Much of the same philosophy of the pick 3 extends to the *pick 4* (see Chapter 15). The bet takes you out one more leg into a fourth race winner. Like the old saying goes — no guts, no glory.

The pick 4 can be bet in a $1 unit. So, playing two horses in each of the four races costs you $16. The pick 4 has become enormously popular among horseplayers, because the payoffs can reach five figures without a huge outlay of capital.

In keeping with the premise of a $100 betting bankroll for the day, $16 out of $100 is a high percentage. But if you want to try for a score, the pick 4 is an excellent vehicle. Just know the risk is higher, but the rewards are a lot greater.

House Quinella

A *quinella* is betting on the first two finishers in a race, in either order. So, for example, if you bet a 1-2 quinella, you win if the race finishes 1-2 or 2-1. Quinella betting is offered at many racetracks, but except for in California, it isn't available on all the races.

You can only make a house quinella bet in a Las Vegas race book (see Chapter 23 to find out all about betting in Vegas). The bet is so popular there, its nickname is the "House Q."

The big advantage of a house quinella comes when one of the top two finishers is a long shot horse, and the horse wins the race at high odds. At the racetrack or OTB, you can bet an exacta box (see Chapter 15), but in Las Vegas, the house quinella gives you a tremendous advantage in value.

For example, consider the 2004 Breeders' Cup Juvenile race won by long shot Wilko at 28/1 odds with the logical Afleet Alex coming in second. Wilko paid $58.60 to win, and Afleet Alex paid $5 to place at Lone Star Park. A $1 exacta box returned $127. In computing a $2 house quinella payoff, you multiply $58.60 by $5 to get $293 and divide by 2 to get $146.50.

So, a $2 house quinella payoff of $146.50 outperformed a $1 exacta box payoff of $127 at Lone Star Park. That kind of advantage to the horseplayer holds up around 75 percent of the time with the House Q.

Third Start off a Layoff

One of my handicapping mentors, Brad Thomas, taught me the simple *third start off a layoff* angle, which to my chagrin, has actually been around for a while. It just goes to show you that your education in the "University of Horse Handicapping" never ceases.

When horses are laid off for a long period (meaning they don't run for many months or more), they usually need racing action to regain peak conditioning. This situation is comparable to professional athletes using pre-season football or exhibition baseball games for conditioning.

Some trainers use fast morning workouts to prepare a horse to win the first time off a layoff. Winning the first time off isn't easy to do, and some trainers are better at preparing their horses than others. The *Daily Racing Form* provides statistical trends in the past performances that show this winning percentage.

The third start off a layoff angle works well with horses that ran well, but hard, in their return. Invariably, the horse will regress next time out in the second start, because it worked its muscles hard in the returning race and wasn't back to peak condition just yet. The time between races may not be sufficient to shake off the soreness and rest in time for the second start off the layoff.

The best time to step in and bet is in the third start off the layoff. The horse's muscles should be finely tuned by now, and even if the trainer didn't prepare enough for the first start comeback, the animal has literally raced itself into good condition.

I don't bet a horse blindly on the third start off a layoff. You still must apply basic handicapping skills to ensure the horse is ready to win (see Chapter 12 for the basics on handicapping). The trainer has to run the horse in a race it can win, and the horse must have shown some spark in the two prior races to hint that it's improving. Also, the odds must merit a win bet. An old racetrack axiom says, "There's not a man alive that can pay the rent at 4/5."

Running First Time for a Claiming Price

Dropping into a *claiming race,* a race where the horses are for sale for a claiming price, for the first time is the biggest class drop in horse racing but is often times overlooked by the betting public (see Chapter 2 for more on the classifications of horse races). Horsemen don't want to give their horses away, so they run them instead in nonselling races like maiden special weight races, if they're *maidens* (have never won a race before), and allowance and optional claiming races, if they're winners.

If a racehorse isn't running to its potential, at some point the owner and trainer must decide if dropping the horse in class is necessary. The trainer may want to win a race to boost the horse's confidence, and the owner wants to win a race to get some purse money back for his monetary investment.

Regardless, when a horse runs in a claiming race for the first time, it's a good time to step in and see if the horse is a worthwhile bet. You still need to apply basic handicapping to the race, but in this case, you may need to be a forgiving handicapper.

The horse is being dropped into a claiming race for the first time because it isn't winning. Also, for the first time, the owner and trainer are risking giving the horse away. You may be faced with the past performances of a horse that's been badly beaten in its prior starts.

I like to make a judgment not only on the horse, but on the jockey and trainer too. A *live horse,* meaning a horse with a chance to win, usually has a *live rider,* meaning a jockey who wins races. If I'm going to take a leap of faith, I still want basic handicapping angles going in my favor along with a generous mutuel price.

Speed Horse Turning Back in Distance

My handicapping tournament partner, Lou Filoso, got me interested in betting on speed horses that have *turned back in distance* (run a shorter-length race). This betting angle comes up with some nice-priced horses that many handicappers summarily dismiss as quitting sprinters.

The theory is to look for speed horses that fight for the early lead and then tire late in the race. When their trainers turns them back in distance, the horses often have some new-found stamina left for the finish. Some horses even change their running style. They stalk the pace and then finish with energy.

I apply this angle to one-turn races only and to the shortening up in distance of at least one furlong.

In some cases, you need to be a forgiving handicapper, but the higher odds of the winners more than make up for the horses that run poorly and don't win.

First-Time Gelding

When horses are *gelded*, meaning they're castrated, horseplayers call it "the ultimate equipment change" (see Chapter 10). Horses that have blue-collar pedigrees are quite often gelded because their future is on the racetrack and not in the breeding shed.

The first-time gelding angle is a key handicapping tool when horses have above average pedigree (the horse's sire and dam). The horse's owner tries to win at all costs without gelding the animal with the dream of developing a stakes horse and future stallion prospect. But things don't always work out.

Horses are gelded if they're mean and cantankerous, refuse to train, and aren't focused on racing. Sometimes a horse is gelded if it has a problem with his testicles.

Risk versus reward

There's a big difference between winning a bet and winning money. Often times, the opportunity to cash a bigger winner supercedes the lower probability of cashing a ticket. I call this betting decision one of risk versus reward. A decision like this is similar to the ones stock market investors make. Some investors prefer riskier stocks with a chance of higher yields, while others buy mutual funds or bonds and try for a safer return.

In horse racing wagering, you're not necessarily betting more money to make more money. Having a bigger bankroll helps. You can buy more combinations and use more horses in exotic wagers. What the size of your bankroll can do is raise or lower your own expectations.

For example, if you play the state lottery hoping to turn $1 into $1 million, you better have low expectations. Your actual odds of winning the jackpot are lousy.

In horse racing, you don't have many chances to win a million dollars. But making five-figure or six-figure payoffs is conceivable, and your chances of winning are much more realistic than playing the lottery. But you have to take risks like including many long shot horses and trying to beat the favorites.

Horse racing can be played on so many levels, and that fact contributes to its tremendous mass appeal. To increase the reward, you know ahead of time you need to increase the risk.

Gelding is a last resort, but doing so sometimes unlocks a horse's talent and creates a great betting opportunity for handicappers. The trainer may finally be able to train the animal now that it has been gelded. The gelding is more focused on racing, and if its testicles were bothering him — well — they aren't anymore. A first-time gelding can sometimes explode with ability that hasn't been seen in any of its prior races.

Gelding information isn't always timely or available. The folks at the *Daily Racing Form* do their best to have current information. If an unpublished first-time gelding is in the race you're betting on, the information appears on the information crawl on the racetrack's television sets when late changes are given.

Chapter 25

Ten Best Racetracks to Visit

In This Chapter

▶ Making sure you get the complete experience

▶ Previewing the ten best racetracks you should visit

During my horse racing career, I've had the chance to work at and visit some of the finest racetracks in the country. So everything you read in this chapter is from first-hand experience. I hope *Betting on Horse Racing For Dummies* has nurtured your interest in the sport and made you want to personally visit every one of these racetracks and any others that didn't make this list due to space reasons. (By the way, politically, it's bad enough for me to only list ten racetracks, so I'm certainly not going to try and rate them one through ten. The way they appear is in alphabetical order.)

Remember that horse racing and betting on horse racing are played best outdoors. So when you go, in addition to taking a couple nice pens and highlighters to handicap with, throw in some sun screen, and wear comfortable clothing, because you're going to be moving around a lot as you take in all the sights and sounds. And if you feel a bit intimidated going to the track for the first time, bookmark some of the key sections in this book and take it along with you. I'm happy to be your guide.

Arlington Park

The original Arlington Park (www.arlingtonpark.com) opened on October 13, 1927. It burned to the ground on July 31, 1985. The new Arlington Park reopened on June 28, 1989, under the leadership of former chairman Richard L. Duchossois, who merged the racetrack in 2000 with Churchill Downs, Inc.

Located in Arlington Heights in the western suburbs of Chicago, Illinois, Arlington markets to families and a younger demographic as well or better than any racetrack in America. Mr. Duchossois demands a high level of customer service from his employees, and they deliver. Arlington is the cleanest racetrack you'll ever visit, and its food service may be the best in the country. No matter what you eat at this racetrack, the food is tasty, fresh, and reasonably priced.

The complete experience

With some sporting events, the television coverage is so good that you feel like you're at the game. Well, that won't happen with horse racing, and that's not a knock against the fine TV coverage. Horse racing is such a visual and sensory experience that watching it from home or at an OTB (off-track betting) parlor can't match the electricity of being at the racetrack. When you go to the racetrack, I hope you get out of your chair and enjoy the complete experience.

Here I've provided you a brief check list. When you go to the racetrack, I want you to see the sights, hear the sounds, and even get a slight whiff of the horse manure if you have to. After you return home, you'll be glad you did.

❑ If the racetrack offers a free morning tour of the backstretch, please take it. You'll love seeing the horses and the people working during the morning hours.

❑ During one of the early races, make sure you get close to the action from the start to the finish.

❑ Go down to ground level and watch the horses being led into the paddock to be saddled. You'll be close enough to say hi to the grooms as they walk their horses by you.

❑ Go to the rail and watch the post parade close up. Listen to the chatter among the riders and the pony people. Watch the racehorses closely.

❑ Go downstairs during a route race that's starting right in front of the stands. You can situate yourself a few yards from all the action.

❑ Watch the loading of the horses into the starting gate. Hear the noise and feel the excitement when the starter springs open the gates and the horses come flying out of their stalls.

❑ Stay in position to see the stretch run as the horses whiz by you. Watch the jockeys riding their horses; hear the snap of the whip and the chirping of the jockeys as they urge their horses to run faster.

❑ Move down the rail to where the horses are being brought back after the race to be unsaddled. You'll hear the by-play between the jockeys and trainers, including some of their excuses for losing the race.

❑ Get a look at the winner's circle as the winning team celebrates victory. The feeling is unbeatable.

In 1981, Arlington hosted the world's first seven-figure purse, the Arlington Million. Another highlight came when it hosted the 2002 Breeders' Cup World Thoroughbred Championships. Races are held at Arlington from early May through September.

Contact information: Arlington Park, Euclid Avenue & Wilke Rd, Arlington Heights, IL 60006; phone 1-847-255-4300; e-mail track@arlingtonpark.com.

Belmont Park

The first thing you notice about Belmont Park (www.nyra.com) is how big it is. The original track opened in 1905 and was rebuilt in 1968 on 430 acres in Elmont, New York. The grandstand and clubhouse are so huge that the track can easily handle the 100,000 fans that attend the Belmont Stakes — the third jewel in racing's Triple Crown — each June.

The Belmont main track is a 1½-mile oval — the biggest in North America. If you don't have a pair of binoculars, the horses running down the backside will look like ants. For the handicapper, Belmont races tend not to have a track bias because of the size of the main track. Horses racing wide at Belmont isn't a negative like at many other tracks.

Belmont will host the Breeders' Cup again on October 29, 2005. The European horses love racing here because of two wide sweeping turf courses. Each fall, Belmont schedules Breeders' Cup prep races like the Beldame, Champagne, Flower Bowl, Frizette, Jockey Club Gold Cup, and Turf Classic on the same weekend.

In a way, Belmont is a dinosaur among racetracks, because no one would attempt to build a place this big again. Belmont is one of my favorite racetracks. If you're visiting New York City in the summer, I recommend you reserve at least one day for an outing to Belmont.

Contact information: Belmont Park, 2150 Hempstead Turnpike, Elmont, NY 11003; phone 1-516-488-6000; ; fax 1-516-352-0919 ; e-mail cserv@nyrainc.com.

Churchill Downs

Churchill Downs (www.kentuckyderby.com) calls itself "The World's Most Legendary Racetrack" and understandably so. It was first built in Louisville, Kentucky, in 1874 and has raced every year since then. It's the home of the Kentucky Derby — America's greatest horse race — and it's the first jewel of the Triple Crown. The feeling you get from historic Churchill Downs will deliver a chill up your spine.

Racing at Churchill Downs is from late April to early July and late October to late November. The Kentucky Derby is always run on the first Saturday in May, and the Kentucky Oaks is held the Friday before that. Churchill Downs will host the Breeder's Cup in 2006. Seating for these races is as hard to get as

Super Bowl tickets. To accommodate the huge crowds, the track is completing a massive renovation in time for the 2005 Kentucky Derby that will fully modernize the facility with luxury boxes, improved seating, and top of the line amenities. The infield can hold another 50,000 fans on these special occasions.

If you really want to see history, go to the Kentucky Derby Museum, which is on the grounds and is open year round.

Contact information: Churchill Downs, 700 Central Avenue, Louisville, KY 40208; phone 1-502-636-4000; fax 1-502-636-4430; for e-mail, go to www. churchilldowns.com.

Del Mar

Built by singer Bing Crosby and some of his Hollywood cronies, Del Mar (www.delmarracing.com) opened on July 3, 1937. Del Mar is about as laid-back as racetracks come. The track is known as "where the turf meets the surf" because it's located right next to the Pacific Ocean, just 20 miles north of San Diego in Del Mar, California. It draws people from Los Angeles and Las Vegas, and I know lots of people who plan summer vacations based upon the Del Mar meeting.

The nightlife around Del Mar is about as famous as the daytime horse racing. The restaurants, bars, and taverns are full of racing fans and a bunch of well-known jockeys, trainers, and owners enjoying themselves.

Del Mar's racing season lasts from late July to early September. The biggest race of the meet is the $1 million Pacific Classic for 3-year-olds and older. Del Mar is also famous for 2-year-old racing. The early West Coast hopefuls for the Kentucky Derby usually make their debuts here.

Contact information: Del Mar, Via De La Valle & Jimmy Durante Blvd., Del Mar, CA 92014; phone 1-858-755-1141; fax 1-858-792-1477; e-mail marys@ dmtc.com.

Gulfstream Park

When bettors think winter horse racing, they think south Florida and Gulfstream Park (www.gulfstreampark.com). Here, snowbirds can leave the frigid climates and enjoy handicapping in the warm Florida sunshine. The racing season runs from early January to late April.

Gulfstream opened on February 1, 1939, but shut down after four days. It reopened four years later and hasn't missed a beat since. Owner Frank Stronach is orchestrating an extensive modernization — literally tearing down the grandstand and starting all over again. I've seen the old Gulfstream plenty of times, but now I have a good reason to visit the new one.

Gulfstream is a key player on the road to the Triple Crown. Races like the Florida Derby, Fountain of Youth, and Holy Bull attract top 3-year-olds that are getting ready for the Kentucky Derby.

You also see top riders from the east coast and Midwest at Gulfstream. The quality of racing is superb, and the jockey colony is the best you see all season long.

Contact information: Gulfstream Park, 901 South Federal Highway, Hallandale Beach, FL 33009; phone 1-800-771-8873; fax 1-954-454-7827; e-mail dlang@ gulfstreampark.com.

Keeneland

Just to give you a sense of how traditional Keeneland (www.keeneland.com) is, it went 61 years without a track announcer until the April 1997 meeting. That's like watching a football game on TV without any commentators. Visiting Keeneland in Lexington, Kentucky, is like going to Wrigley Field. It's a shrine to the sport of horse racing.

I've always enjoyed the food at Keeneland, especially the steaming burgoo on a cool afternoon of racing. And the crowd is surprisingly young here. The University of Kentucky is in session during the racing season (April and October), and seemingly half the students from the university are at the races.

The horse races are terrific to bet on because the purse money paid to horsemen is the highest in the country due to profits from the Keeneland Sales horse auctions. Bigger purses attract more horses and bigger fields, which make for good handicapping and betting. The biggest stakes all year is the Blue Grass in April, an important Kentucky Derby prep race.

Keeneland has two treasures that are free for you to enjoy, so take advantage. The Keeneland Library houses the finest collection of research materials about horse racing, and Keeneland has the only stable area that's open for the public to walk through.

Contact information: Keeneland, 4201 Versailles Road, Lexington, KY 40588; phone 1-800-456-3412; fax 1-859-255-2484; e-mail marketing@keeneland.com.

Lone Star Park

Lone Star Park (www.lonestarpark.com) is the only new racetrack to make this top ten list. Opened in 1997, it took only seven years to earn the industry's trust of hosting the 2004 Breeders' Cup. That, in itself, is a remarkable achievement.

I've been to Lone Star several times to work network telecasts. The number of Texans in cowboy hats and boots at the racetrack never ceases to amaze me. The crowd is friendly and has a deep respect for the horses.

At Lone Star, the Thoroughbred racing season is from early April through July. Lone Star is also the only track on this list that works extensively with another horse breed, Quarter Horses. The Quarter Horse races are run in October and November.

Lone Star is located very close to Arlington, Texas, where the Texas Rangers play baseball. I can visualize a day-night doubleheader of horse racing and baseball. You can't beat that.

Contact information: Lone Star Park, 1000 Lone Star Parkway, Grand Prairie, TX 75050; phone 1-972-263-7223; fax 1-972-262-5622; for e-mail, go to www.lone starpark.com.

Monmouth Park

Monmouth Park (www.monmouthpark.com) is a track that races under the radar screen of many horseplayers. Because Monmouth runs in the summer from late May to late September, it can get overshadowed by New York's Belmont Park and Saratoga. A coming out party will be held in 2007 when Monmouth hosts the Breeders' Cup.

Monmouth is at the north end of the Jersey Shore, only a mile or two from the Atlantic Ocean. The area is a great place to vacation and a better place to live.

The track architecture is definitely old school in a scenic sense. Monmouth has parterre boxes in the clubhouse, which are the forerunners to the luxury boxes that are currently the rage in sports arenas and stadiums. The parterre boxes at Monmouth are among the best places to watch live racing of any track in the United States.

The biggest race of the season at Monmouth is the $1 million Haskell Invitational, which typically showcases many of the top Triple Crown runners.

Contact information: Monmouth Park, 175 Oceanport Avenue, Oceanport, NJ 07757; phone 1-732-222-5100; fax 1-732-870-2814; e-mail mpinfo@njsea.com.

Santa Anita Park

The first thing you notice as you look out over Santa Anita Park (www.santa anita.com) are the majestic San Gabriel Mountains in the backdrop of Arcadia, California. There's no more breathtaking view in American horse racing.

The track opened in 1934 — a year after the legalization of parimutuel wagering in California. You can't say Santa Anita without thinking of the Strub family. Dr. Charles H. Strub founded the track, and his son, Robert Strub, continued the family legacy of class and integrity by offering the finest in horse racing until his death in 1993.

Santa Anita is now owned and operated by Frank Stronach and his racing conglomerate, Magna Entertainment. Santa Anita remains part of the rotation for hosting the Breeders' Cup. It's a stately and magnificent venue, and like Belmont Park in New York, you likely won't see anyone attempt to build a racetrack like this one again.

Santa Anita holds races from December 26 through April and from late September to early November. Santa Anita is a key stop on the road to the Kentucky Derby. The San Rafael, the San Felipe, and the Santa Anita Derby for 3-year-olds often times produce the Derby favorite. The Santa Anita Handicap, also called the "Big Cap," is one of the most prestigious races for older horses.

Contact information: Santa Anita Park, 285 W. Huntington Drive, Arcadia, CA 91066; phone 1-626-574-7223; fax 1-626-821-1514; e-mail info@santaanita.com.

Saratoga

You know a place is special when Hollywood movie makers wax poetic about it. Movies that feature Saratoga (www.nyra.com) include *Saratoga, Saratoga Trunk,* and *Billy Bathgate.*

The tradition and history run very deep at Saratoga, where the first meet was held back in 1863. Saratoga was an easy choice for home of the National Museum of Racing. Hall of Fame ceremonies are held there each August to induct new members.

Saratoga Springs is located in upstate New York, about an hour north of Albany. About 30,000 people live in Saratoga Springs year-round, which is also the home of Skidmore College. During the racing season, the population nearly triples. Saratoga Springs is one city where you don't have to apologize for being a horse racing fan. And no one in town is going to ask you "What's a *Daily Racing Form?*" The people know racing, enjoy racing, and most of all respect the sport of racing.

Going to Saratoga Springs, New York, is almost like stepping back in time. The architecture of the buildings and homes reflects a bygone era. More than 1,000 buildings in the area are on the National Register.

The quality of racing is second to none at Saratoga. Saratoga runs from late July to early September. After the Churchill meet ends, many Kentucky horsemen and jockeys join the New York horsemen and jockeys to present the best racing product you'll see all year. The $1 million Travers Stakes for 3-year-olds, called the Mid-Summer Derby, is the highpoint of the racing season. And like Del Mar in California, trainers start their most promising 2-year-olds during this meet.

You can tell I have a deep appreciation for Saratoga and what it represents in horse racing. If I had to rate the ten racetracks in this chapter by personal preference, I admit I'd rank Saratoga as the number one best racetrack to visit.

Contact information: Saratoga Race Course, 267 Union Avenue, Saratoga Springs, NY 12866; phone 1-518-584-6200; fax 1-718-322-3814; e-mail cserv@nyrainc.com.

Chapter 26

Ten Common Betting Mistakes

- -

In This Chapter

▶ Placing the wrong bets at the wrong times

▶ Making poor decisions that affect your betting

- -

Although luck plays a big part in betting the races, winning requires a sequence of doing the right things at the right times. Handicapping and betting are highly skilled activities that when done correctly lead to a lot of wins and profits.

However, in your betting journey, a lot of factors can trip you up, causing you to lose money and ask yourself, "What did I do wrong?" One mistake can ruin a perfect plan. In this chapter, I list ten of the most common betting mistakes people make that can leave them shaking their heads.

Not Betting a Horse to Win

Picture this: You're handicapping a race and like a nice 9/1 long shot. You make all the right decisions. You hook the horse up in daily doubles, a pick 3, and trifectas (see Chapter 15 for more on exotic wagers). You watch the race and see that your horse is going to win, so you start looking for the second and third place horses to fill out your trifecta. You have the second horse, but wait — some improbable long shot runs third, and you don't have it on your ticket. You lose all your trifecta bets.

Not to worry. You're live with daily doubles and the pick 3. In the next race, you have four horses — a couple logical horses and a couple pricey runners — in an eight-horse field. One of the horses you left off the ticket wins, and your daily doubles and pick 3 go down in flames. You've turned a $20 winner into a total loss.

It's okay for any horseplayer to go for a score in trying to win a lot of money. A $20 horse to start a pick 3 promises a nice payout even if the favorite wins one of the next two races or even wins both of the races.

The mistake lies in not making a win bet on the horse you like. The story would be different if the horse you like has 5/2 odds. But when the horse is good odds, you should start with a win bet. Then you can make additional exotic bets to try to really make some money.

Some horseplayers I know bet half of the amount of money they intend to invest in a particular race to win. I know others who bet one-third. For example, if you're going to invest $50 in a race or races on a horse, your win bet should be between $16 and $25. You then put the rest on exotic wagers.

A $15, $20, or $25 winner is nothing to sneeze at. Too many horseplayers overlook win betting and put all their eggs in the exotic wager basket.

Betting Too Many Racetracks

In a simpler era not long ago, the only races you could bet on were at the local racetrack. You had a menu of nine or ten races with about 30 minutes between each race. You had plenty of time to handicap and reflect on your decisions.

Now in the age of simulcasting, where tracks transmit their races via satellite for wagering, scores of races fill your horse-racing day. I consider today's racing a parimutuel buffet with lots and lots of choices. You have too many races to choose from and not enough time to give them all what I consider "handicapping justice."

In big money handicapping tournaments (see Chapter 17), you're offered seven or eight racetracks to handicap and make your tournament plays from. That large number comes with the territory of playing for a six-figure first prize. After three days and nights at these tournaments, even the best professional handicappers are mentally and physically drained. So in my opinion, for you to handicap a large number of races and racetracks during a simulcast day and expect to make money is nearly impossible. I recommend you focus on a few racetracks you know well and feel confident about.

Don't spread yourself out so thin that you do a poor job of handicapping and betting all the racetracks. Focus on your strengths. Remember the object is to make money, not make a whole bunch of bets just to have action on them. You have to be able to show discipline and patience.

Betting On Bad Favorites

To make money betting on horse racing, you need to beat favorites much more often than you bet on them. When you bet on favorites, you're in with the majority, which depresses your odds and your value. So the favorites you bet on better win.

Known by veteran handicappers as "sucker" horses, here are two of the worst kinds of favorites to play:

✔ The first is the professional maiden, a horse that has never won a race, that shows a steady diet of second and third place finishes but never wins. The thought that he'll win the next time may be appealing, but it seldom ever occurs. And when he does win, his odds are no value at all.

The only time you should even consider betting on a professional maiden that never wins is when it's running in maiden special weight races (see Chapter 2) and drops in for a claiming price (see Chapter 2) for the first time. That class drop is so big that even the herd mentality, the natural instinct where horses prefer to run with the pack, may not be enough to prevent this horse from winning.

✔ The second example is a horse stuck in a non-winners of two races lifetime condition. The whole field in this type of race is usually ugly, because all the starters have only one lifetime win.

In this situation, the betting public gravitates to the most consistent horse, meaning the one with a lot of second and third place finishes on its resume. That angle isn't strong enough for me to play the favorite at short odds, though. I suggest trying to beat the favorite instead by betting on other horses in the race that are juicy overlays.

Figure 26-1 features the *Daily Racing Form* past performances for the types of horses that keep getting bet to favoritism.

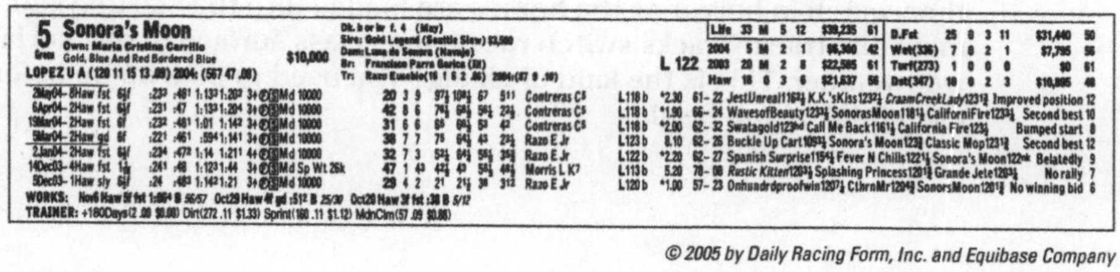

Figure 26-1:
Daily Racing Form past performances for Sonora's Moon.

© 2005 by Daily Racing Form, Inc. and Equibase Company

Sonora's Moon is a good example of a bad favorite that you try to beat. Five times she was heavily favored (denoted by asterisk) while running in an Illinois-bred maiden claiming $10,000 class level. Horseplayers call bad favorites like this one *money burners,* because the money you bet on them to win goes up in smoke.

Getting Shut Out

When you wager on horse racing long enough, you get *shut out* at the betting window (the race goes off before you could bet on it). In fact, you probably get shut out a lot.

When you do get shut out, often your first inclination is to blame the mutuel clerk, the bettor in front of you, or the racetrack or race book for not having enough windows open. You shouldn't blame other people, however, because getting shut out is something you can control by standing in the betting line early enough and adjusting if the betting lines are long. If you intend to make a serious wager, don't wait until one or two minutes to post and take the high risk of not getting your bet in.

Not Looking at the Race Changes

One of the first things you should do as a horseplayer is check the late changes for the racetracks you want to bet. In Las Vegas race books, you can get these changes off the boards. But if you're at a racetrack or OTB (off-track betting parlor), you probably need to monitor the television simulcast signals. You get up-to-the-minute information about scratches, rider changes, overweights, equipment changes, and other factors that may heavily influence your handicapping.

Not following through on checking the race changes can be an expensive lesson. For example, imagine if you handicap a turf race, make your bets, and then watch in horror as the horses are loaded into the starting gate on the main dirt track. Tracks switch races from grass surface to dirt surface during wet weather. This is the kind of change you need to pick up on before you even think about betting.

Practicing Bad Money Management

Everyone stumbles in the money management department at some point. When you go to the racetrack or OTB, the key is to have a finite amount of money in your pocket to gamble with. It doesn't matter if the amount is $100, $500, or more as long as you don't spend more money than what you've allotted yourself.

If you do some preparatory handicapping, you know which horses and races look best to you. Good money management dictates that you reserve enough money to make your strongest bets. You can make some action bets — small plays just to have something to root for — but you must get your primary bets in on the horses and races you like the most to maximize your chances of winning.

Bad money management is going through your bankroll before your strongest plays come up. Not saving your money for your best bets shows a total lack of discipline, which prevents you from becoming a winning horseplayer. And using your bank ATM card as a crutch to get more cash is bad money management too.

Chasing Your Losses by Betting More Money

Anyone who gambles will inevitably enjoy winning streaks and suffer from losing streaks. The nature of gambling is to have peaks and valleys. When you do run into a losing streak, I advise you to cut back on the size of your wagers. Not only does your bankroll shrink when you're losing, but you also often have bad karma going on.

Bad karma can come in many forms. Perhaps the horse you like wins but gets disqualified. Or the horse you like gets a terrible ride and just misses. Or maybe you handicap and bet a race correctly, but some impossible 50/1 long shot beats you out. Betting lower amounts will at least slow down the spiral until the situation improves, and the situation will improve.

The only time you should increase your wagers is when you're winning. If you're playing within a measured percentage of your bankroll, your bets are getting bigger because your bankroll is growing.

A point may come when the size of your bets reaches the top of your comfort level. A veteran horseplayer once told me early in my gambling career that if you're a $2 bettor, just because you hit a hot winning streak, you don't automatically become a $10 or $20 bettor overnight. He said you are what you are, and you'll know when the stakes get too high.

A common betting mistake is to increase the size of wagers when you're losing. The idea is to win back your losses as quickly as possible. This seldom works because you're betting under pressure and your decision making may get clouded.

Overlooking a Winning Horse

Bettors often overlook a horse that just won its last race. Why's that, you ask? Invariably a horse that just won is moving up in class in its next start. The belief is the horse can't run back and win again. Another reason bettors may overlook a horse that just won is because a win may earn a horse a top Beyer Speed Figure (see Chapter 11) and maybe even a career best. Some people call this kind of horse a bounce (see Chapter 11) candidate and therefore don't want to bet on it.

Although many reasons exist to knock a horse that just won, the fact is that any horse that won its last start should be in good condition. An animal moving up in class should help, not hinder, the parimutuel value. And you should like the fact that the horse wanted to pass or run away from other horses in his last race.

Betting a horse that just won is a simple and solid betting angle. This type of no-brainer bet can snap you out of a losing streak, because this type of horse often wins at fair odds.

Forgetting to Check Your Tickets

You see signs at the betting windows reminding you to check your tickets, and even the mutuel clerk or ticket writer says, "Check your tickets please" before you leave the window. But how many times do you actually look over your tickets? Not too often I bet.

Everyone has been burned at some point — even myself. Last summer I made a $20 quinella bet on a Del Mar race. The horses came in like clockwork, so I went up to cash my ticket, thinking I was going to collect $110. The ticket writer told me the ticket was a loser. I looked at it and saw that it was a $20 quinella on a race at Delaware.

To my disappointment, the ticket writer who sold me the ticket thought I said Delaware instead of Del Mar. Ultimately, though, the mistake was mine, because I didn't check my ticket.

Betting lines are set up next to one another. The mutuel bay is extremely noisy, so it's hard to hear. Mistakes can and do happen. Also, most horseplayers wait to bet until a couple minutes to post, so everyone is in a hurry to get his or her bet down — only multiplying the chances of errors occurring.

Getting Touted Off a Horse

Picture this: You do all the handicapping work. You know which horse or horses you like. You design some nice plays to maximize profit potential, including making a win bet. You go up to the betting window, and then someone you know gives you a tip on another horse in the race. What do you do?

Unfortunately, some people take the tip to heart and change their bets. The information may be well intended, but it goes against what you just handicapped. My advice: Trust yourself. Why go through all the work if you allow yourself to get touted off, meaning talked off, the horse you like. Changing your decisions is a recipe for disaster.

John Kelly, a respected sports handicapper in Las Vegas, has a saying that goes, "Listen to everyone; follow no one." And he's right. You can listen to what all the other people are saying. But when the time comes to bet, make your own decisions based upon the facts as you know them.

If you don't want the tip horse to beat you, include him in your wagers if you can afford it.

Appendix

A Glossary of Horse Racing Lingo

• •

Horse racing lingo has worked its way into everyday usage and you likely didn't even know it. Political elections are commonly called a *horse race* and if its a close election the vote could come *down to the wire* in a *photo finish*. Sports teams are said to *spit the bit* when they quit trying on the field. The person who didn't get promoted is an *also ran*. The terms used here are all common to horse racing. You can read their definitions, and more, in this handy glossary.

Across the board: Consisting of three straight bets — to win, place, and show — all on a single horse.

All button: Betting all of the horses in a race in a multiple race wager. Also, to use all of the horses in the field in the win, place, or show spot in a multiple horse wager.

Allowance race: A non-claiming race where the racing secretary writes, in a condition book, the race's weights, conditions, and eligibility.

Also eligible: A horse drawn outside of the body of the race that can't start unless a horse within the body of the race scratches out and doesn't run.

Also ran: A horse that finishes out of the money in fourth place or higher.

At the post: When the racehorses reach the starting gate.

Backside: The barn or stable area where the horses are housed.

Backstretch: The straight part of the racetrack opposite from where the finish line is; also means the stable area where the racehorses are kept.

Bearing in: Failure of a horse to run a straight path by veering toward the inside rail.

Bearing out: Failure of a horse to run a straight path by veering toward the outside rail.

Beyer Speed Figures: Speed figure ratings that measure the quality of a horse's race. They appear in the *Daily Racing Form* past performances.

Bit: A metal bar, from which the reins are attached, that fits into a horse's mouth. Used to help the rider control the horse.

Bleeder: A horse that suffers pulmonary bleeding during a race or workout due to ruptured blood vessels.

Blinkers: A piece of equipment consisting of two cups attached to the bridle or around a horse's head to restrict the horse's acute peripheral vision.

Bloodline: A horse's pedigree that starts with its sire and dam and includes their extended family.

Blowout: A short and fast morning workout done a day or two before a race.

Bounce: When a horse follows a very good race with a poor one.

Box: To use designated horses in all positions (first, second, third, fourth), depending if the bet is an exacta, quinella, trifecta, or superfecta, of a multiple horse wager.

Breeze: A light morning workout when a horse runs without the rider's encouragement.

Broodmare: A filly or mare used for breeding.

Bugboy: An apprentice rider.

Bute: Short for phenylbutazone, a commonly used anti-inflammatory drug for horses.

Calk: A cleat on the bottom of a horseshoe allowing the horse to gain more traction. Mud calks, also called stickers, are worn on a wet track.

Chalk: The betting favorite.

Checked: A horse pulled back by its jockey after getting interfered with or running in tight quarters; also called steadied.

Chute: An extension of the course — both on the main track and turf course — that allows for a longer straight run from the starting gate.

Claim: To buy a horse out of a claiming race.

Claiming race: A race where every starting horse is eligible to be purchased — or claimed — for a specified price.

Clockers: Persons who time the morning workouts.

Closer: A horse that likes to run from behind the field and find its best stride during the latter part of the race.

Clubhouse turn: The first turn to the right of the finish line where the clubhouse is normally located.

Colors: A hat and shirt worn by the jockey during the race to represent the horse owner; also called silks.

Colt: A male horse, four years old and younger, that hasn't been castrated.

Condition book: A book put out by the racing secretary that details the races the racetrack is offering over the next three or four weeks.

Conditioner: A horse's trainer.

Connections: The owner, trainer, and other people associated with a racehorse.

Coupled: An entry of two or more horses because of common ownership.

Cuppy: A main track condition where the dirt breaks away in clods from under a horse's hoofs.

Cushion: The surface of the racetrack above the base.

Daily double: A single bet where you're trying to pick the winners of two consecutive races.

Dam: The mother of a horse.

Dead-heat: When two or more horses finish on exact, even terms. A photo finish camera substantiates the tie.

Derby: A stakes race for 3-year-old horses.

Distanced: A defeated horse losing by so many lengths that the jockey stops riding before the wire.

Distaff: Refers to a female horse or to the female side of a horse's family.

Dogs: Orange traffic cones used during morning workouts on the dirt track and turf course to protect the inner-part of the surface. Dogs are usually placed 15 to 20 feet off the inner rail during wet weather.

Driving: A finish where the jockey vigorously uses his hands and whip to urge the horse to the finish line.

Dwelt: When a horse breaks very slowly from the starting gate.

Eighth pole: A large pole located one furlong from the finish line.

Entry: A horse entered to race by its trainer; also, when an owner has two or more horses in the same race, they run as a single betting unit.

Exacta: A single bet in which you trying to pick the first two finishers of a race in exact order.

Far turn: The final turn in a race right before the horses enter the home stretch.

Farrier: A blacksmith or horseshoer.

Fast: Term describing a dry, main dirt track in optimum condition.

Field: All of the horses in a single race.

Filly: A female horse, four years old and younger.

Firm: Term describing a turf course in optimum condition.

First turn: Refers to the first turn in a route race that starts in front of the grandstand/clubhouse; also called the clubhouse turn.

Foal: A newborn horse.

Fractions: The clocking at various intervals during a horse race.

Front runner: A horse that prefers to race on the lead.

Furlong: One-eighth of a mile; also called a panel.

Gallop: A horse's easy gait while not being timed.

Gelding: A castrated male horse.

Good: Term describing a dirt track or turf course that's too wet from the rain to be called fast or firm.

Graded race: The most prestigious stakes races in North America. Stakes earn a grading of I, II, or III based on the quality of fields from prior years.

Grass course: A turf course. Grass is considered the natural surface for horses to run over.

Groom: A stable employee who tends to the daily needs of a racehorse; also describes the daily cleaning and hygiene a horse needs to keep healthy.

Half-mile pole: A large pole located four furlongs — a half-mile — from the finish line.

Halter: A strap or rope by which horses are led. Also the action of claiming a horse by another trainer.

Handicap: A race where the racing secretary assigns weights to all the horses with the theoretical goal of creating a dead heat at the finish.

Handicapping: Studying all the different factors involved in trying to decipher the winner of a horse race.

Handily: Term describing a workout that shows more effort than breezing; also describes when a horse wins a race as the rider pleased.

Hanger: A horse in the stretch that refuses to pass other horses.

Hat trick: Also called an equador, a jockey, trainer, or owner who wins three races or more on a single race card.

Head of the stretch: The top of the stretch where horses turn for home, meaning the finish line.

Homebred: A racehorse that's owned and bred by its owner.

Home stretch: The final straightaway in a race located right in front of the stands.

Horse: A male horse five years old and older.

Horse identifier: Person who checks each horse's lip tattoo in the paddock to confirm its identity.

Horseman: An owner, trainer, or breeder.

Horseplayer: A person who handicaps and bets on the horse races.

Hung: The action of a horse that wouldn't extend itself in the stretch.

In foal: A pregnant mare.

In the money: When a horse finishes in first, second, or third.

Inquiry: When the stewards investigate whether an infraction occurred during the running of a race.

Irons: The stirrups.

Jockey agent: The person who books the mounts for a jockey and normally gets paid 25 percent of the jockey's earnings.

Juvenile: A two-year-old racehorse.

Key: To use a horse in one spot (first, second, third) in a vertical, multiple horse wager.

Lasix: The common name for Furosemide, a diuretic used to prevent pulmonary bleeding in a racehorse.

Length: A measure describing the span of a horse from end to end — nose to tail — that's around eight or nine feet long.

Lone speed: A horse who looks like the only early speed in the race.

Long shot: A horse going off at high odds, whether it's in the racetrack morning line or in the actual betting.

Maiden: A horse that has never won a sanctioned race.

Mare: A female horse five years old or older.

Minus pool: A mutuel pool, typically for show, where people bet so much money on one horse that after the takeout is deducted, there's isn't enough left to make a minimum payoff. The racetrack is required to make up the difference out of its own funds creating the minus pool.

Morning line: The odds given to horses in a race prior to the start of betting. It's a prediction how the linemaker thinks the public will bet.

Mudder: A horse that runs well in the mud.

Muddy: Describes a mushy, drying out main track that doesn't show surface water like a sloppy track.

Mutuel clerk: Also called a mutuel teller, a person who punches out your bets from a parimutuel machine. In a Las Vegas race book, this person is called a ticket writer.

Mutuel field: Extra horses that are bundled together in a single interest for betting purposes only. It's created when a racetrack can accommodate up to 12 or 14 betting interests, but the field has more starters than that.

Name: To enter a horse in a race or to select a jockey to ride.

Neck: A margin used in a result chart and past performance for a horse that's considered a quarter of a length.

Nose: The smallest margin between two horses without being a dead-heat, typically a fraction of an inch up to six inches.

OTB: An acronym for "off-track betting," where horseplayers can bet on horse races away from the racetrack.

Oaks: A stakes race for 3-year-old fillies.

Objection: A claim of foul lodged typically by a jockey — and once in a while by a trainer — in a race against another jockey.

Odds-on: A horse going off at less than even money. On the tote board, the odds will show 4-to-5 or lower.

Off time: The starting time of the race.

Off track: A very wet racing surface, comparable to muddy or sloppy; also refers to betting away from the racetrack.

Official: What a race is declared when the stewards have given their final approval and horseplayers can start cashing their winning tickets.

Open company: A race with no restrictions regarding which state a horse was bred in.

Overlay: A horse going off at higher odds than its perceived chances of winning.

Overnight: A sheet listing the next day's races that's available out of the racing secretary's office and in Las Vegas race books.

Overweight: The extra weight carried by a horse above its assigned weight typically caused by the weight of the jockey.

Pace: How fast the lead horses are running at each stage of the race — quarter-mile, half-mile, and so on.

Pace horse: A horse that likes to race a couple lengths off the leaders.

Paddock: The saddling enclosure, which is in full view of the public.

Parimutuel wagering: A wagering system invented in France where all bets are pooled together, and after a deduction by the house called the takeout, the rest of the pool is paid out to the winning bettors. Betting on horse racing in the United States is based upon parimutuel wagering.

Parlay: To take your winnings from one horse or race and bet it all back on another horse or race.

Part-wheel: Using a few horses in one spot of a multiple race or multiple horse wager.

Path: A running lane on the racetrack equal to the width of a horse's body. Thus, a horse racing in the four-path, also called four-wide, should have room to fit three more racehorses inside him.

Pick 3: A wager where you must select the winners of three straight races.

Pick 4: A wager where you must select the winners of four straight races.

Pick 5: A wager where you must select the winners of five straight races.

Pick 6: A wager where you must select the winners of all six designated races.

Place: Finishing second in a race.

Place pick 8 (or all): A wager where you must select a horse to finish either first or second in all eight races on the program. If there are more than eight races, you must do the same for all races on the card.

Pole: Markers at specific distances around the racetrack, usually every sixteenth of a mile, that aid the jockeys and racing fans in knowing how much distance remains in the running of a race.

Pony: To assist a jockey on a racehorse with a lead pony and pony rider.

Positive expectancy: Betting into a parimutuel pool when there's a carryover. If you win, you receive a higher payout because of the carryover amount.

Post parade: When the horses leave the paddock and walk in front of the stands single file in post position order.

Post position: A horse's assigned stall in the starting gate.

Post time: The time when a race is supposed to start.

Purse money: Money put up for the racetrack in each race that the horses' owners, trainers, and jockeys try to win.

Quarter crack: A crack in the wall of the hoof.

Quarter-pole: A large pole at the top of the stretch to signify a quarter-mile remaining to the finish line.

Quinella: A single bet where you're trying to select the first two race finishers in either order.

Race book: Betting parlors in Las Vegas specifically designed for use by horseplayers.

Rank: A fractious horse that fights the control of the jockey.

Rate: To restrain a horse slightly to conserve energy for later in the race.

Rider: The jockey on a horse.

Ridden out: Winning a race with slight urging from the jockey.

Rogue: A horse that constantly misbehaves.

Route: A race run around two turns.

Saddle cloth: A cloth used underneath the saddle on which a number designating the post position is visible to the public.

Save ground: When a jockey rides close to the rail, which is the shortest way around the racetrack.

School: To teach a horse to behave calmly in the starting gate or in the paddock.

Score: Winning a lot of money, as in making a score or trying for a score.

Scratch: When a horse is taken out of a race due to illness, injury, or a trainer's decision and approved by the stewards.

Send: When a jockey rides hard for the early lead at the start of a race.

Set down: When a jockey asks for his horse's best in the stretch run.

Sex allowance: A weight concession granted to a female horse running against males.

Shadow roll: A wool roll attached above a horse's nostrils to prevent the horse from looking down and seeing shadows on the racetrack.

Shed row: The part of the barn area where the horses reside in individual stalls.

Ship: To send a horse to another track for a race.

Shipper: A horse that comes in for a race from another racetrack.

Short: A horse that tires in a race due to a possible lack of fitness.

Show: Finishing third in a race.

Shuffled back: A horse that's forced to drop back and lose ground because of being stuck behind slower running horses.

Shut off: When one horse cuts in front of another horse during a race forcing the other horse and rider to take up sharply.

Shut out: When a horseplayer failed to wager because the race began before he or she was able to get to the betting window.

Silks: A hat and shirt worn by the jockey in a race to represent the horse owner; also called colors.

Single: To use only one horse in a race as part of a horizontal, multiple race wager.

Sire: A horse's daddy.

Sixteenth pole: A pole indicating to the jockeys and fans ⅟₁₆ mile to the finish line.

Sloppy: A very wet racetrack with standing water visible to the naked eye.

Sophomore: A 3-year-old horse.

Spit out the bit: A tired horse who stops pressing against the bit. The jockey then knows the horse is no longer giving its best effort.

Sprint: A one-turn race that's less than one mile.

Stakes: A race where the purse consists of nomination fees and entry fees paid by the owner of each starter, plus money put up by the racetrack.

Stallion: A male horse that hasn't been castrated and is used for breeding after his racing career.

Starting gate: A mechanical device with up to 14 padded stalls for horses to stand in located where the races are started from.

Steadied: When a horse is taken up by its jockey due to traffic problems during a race.

Stewards: Racing officials who adjudicate each horse race and enforce the rules of racing during the meet.

Straight bets: Betting to win, place, or show.

Stretch: Also known as the home stretch, it's the final straightaway in a race that's located right in front of the stands.

Stretch runner: A come from behind horse that finishes fast in the stretch.

Stud: A stallion.

Superfecta: Correctly betting the top four finishers, in exact order, of a race.

Suspension: A penalty handed out by the stewards to jockeys, trainers, and backstretch employees for a racing infraction or rules violation.

Syndicate: When horseplayers pool money together to wager on multiple horse and/or multiple race bets.

Take back: A jockey maneuver to place his horse off the early pace or further back, as in the back of the field.

Take down: To disqualify a horse for an infraction in a race after a ruling by the stewards.

Taken up: When a jockey pulls its horse up sharply because of traffic problems.

Takeout: A commission deducted by the racetrack that's divided among the racetrack for operations, local and state agencies, horsemen's purses, and so on.

Teletimer: An electronic timer that times the races and flashes on the infield tote board.

Ticket writer: What a mutuel clerk is called in a Las Vegas race book.

Tightener: A prep race that helps a horse get ready for a bigger engagement.

Tongue tie: A cloth strip used to literally tie a horse's tongue down so he can't swallow it during a race.

Totalizator: A linked system of parimutuel machines that accepts wagering from the public and prints a ticket or voucher as a receipt for the horse-player; also spelled totalisator.

Tote board: The board in the infield that shows the odds, betting pools, prob-able payoffs, and other information; also known as an odds board.

Trainer: A person who trains the horse on behalf of the horse's owner.

Trifecta: A single bet where you must select the first three finishers in exact order.

Triple: Has two connotations — can either mean the same as a trifecta or a pick three.

Triple Crown: The Kentucky Derby, Preakness, and Belmont Stakes for 3-year-olds. Eleven Triple Crown horses have won all three races.

Turf course: A grass course.

Underlay: A horse going off at lower odds than its perceived chances of winning.

Under wraps: A horse running under restraint by its rider, which is extremely impressive.

Walking ring: A circular walk path for horses located next to the paddock.

Washed out: When a horse breaks out in a nervous sweat before the race, sometimes to the point of dripping water from its belly.

Weight: The assigned load a horse carries in a race, including the jockey, saddle, and equipment.

Wheel: A style of betting where a horse is used with all other horses in a two-horse or two-race exotic wager.; also, a horse that pivots sharply and unexpectedly with a rider aboard.

Whip: A stick a jockey uses to hit the horse and encourage it to run faster.

Workout: A horse's morning exercise that's a predetermined distance.

Yearling: A one-year-old horse.

Index

BUSINESS, CAREERS & PERSONAL FINANCE

0-7645-5307-0

0-7645-5331-3 *†

Also available:
- Accounting For Dummies †
  0-7645-5314-3
- Business Plans Kit For Dummies †
  0-7645-5365-8
- Cover Letters For Dummies
  0-7645-5224-4
- Frugal Living For Dummies
  0-7645-5403-4
- Leadership For Dummies
  0-7645-5176-0
- Managing For Dummies
  0-7645-1771-6

- Marketing For Dummies
  0-7645-5600-2
- Personal Finance For Dummies *
  0-7645-2590-5
- Project Management For Dummies
  0-7645-5283-X
- Resumes For Dummies †
  0-7645-5471-9
- Selling For Dummies
  0-7645-5363-1
- Small Business Kit For Dummies *†
  0-7645-5093-4

HOME & BUSINESS COMPUTER BASICS

0-7645-4074-2

0-7645-3758-X

Also available:
- ACT! 6 For Dummies
  0-7645-2645-6
- iLife '04 All-in-One Desk Reference
  For Dummies
  0-7645-7347-0
- iPAQ For Dummies
  0-7645-6769-1
- Mac OS X Panther Timesaving
  Techniques For Dummies
  0-7645-5812-9
- Macs For Dummies
  0-7645-5656-8

- Microsoft Money 2004 For Dummies
  0-7645-4195-1
- Office 2003 All-in-One Desk Reference
  For Dummies
  0-7645-3883-7
- Outlook 2003 For Dummies
  0-7645-3759-8
- PCs For Dummies
  0-7645-4074-2
- TiVo For Dummies
  0-7645-6923-6
- Upgrading and Fixing PCs For Dummies
  0-7645-1665-5
- Windows XP Timesaving Techniques
  For Dummies
  0-7645-3748-2

FOOD, HOME, GARDEN, HOBBIES, MUSIC & PETS

0-7645-5295-3

0-7645-5232-5

Also available:
- Bass Guitar For Dummies
  0-7645-2487-9
- Diabetes Cookbook For Dummies
  0-7645-5230-9
- Gardening For Dummies *
  0-7645-5130-2
- Guitar For Dummies
  0-7645-5106-X
- Holiday Decorating For Dummies
  0-7645-2570-0
- Home Improvement All-in-One
  For Dummies
  0-7645-5680-0

- Knitting For Dummies
  0-7645-5395-X
- Piano For Dummies
  0-7645-5105-1
- Puppies For Dummies
  0-7645-5255-4
- Scrapbooking For Dummies
  0-7645-7208-3
- Senior Dogs For Dummies
  0-7645-5818-8
- Singing For Dummies
  0-7645-2475-5
- 30-Minute Meals For Dummies
  0-7645-2589-1

INTERNET & DIGITAL MEDIA

0-7645-1664-7

0-7645-6924-4

Also available:
- 2005 Online Shopping Directory
  For Dummies
  0-7645-7495-7
- CD & DVD Recording For Dummies
  0-7645-5956-7
- eBay For Dummies
  0-7645-5654-1
- Fighting Spam For Dummies
  0-7645-5965-6
- Genealogy Online For Dummies
  0-7645-5964-8
- Google For Dummies
  0-7645-4420-9

- Home Recording For Musicians
  For Dummies
  0-7645-1634-5
- The Internet For Dummies
  0-7645-4173-0
- iPod & iTunes For Dummies
  0-7645-7772-7
- Preventing Identity Theft For Dummies
  0-7645-7336-5
- Pro Tools All-in-One Desk Reference
  For Dummies
  0-7645-5714-9
- Roxio Easy Media Creator For Dummies
  0-7645-7131-1

* Separate Canadian edition also available
† Separate U.K. edition also available

Available wherever books are sold. For more information or to order direct: U.S. customers visit www.dummies.com or call 1-877-762-2974.
U.K. customers visit www.wileyeurope.com or call 0800 243407. Canadian customers visit www.wiley.ca or call 1-800-567-4797.

SPORTS, FITNESS, PARENTING, RELIGION & SPIRITUALITY

0-7645-5146-9

0-7645-5418-2

Also available:
- Adoption For Dummies
  0-7645-5488-3
- Basketball For Dummies
  0-7645-5248-1
- The Bible For Dummies
  0-7645-5296-1
- Buddhism For Dummies
  0-7645-5359-3
- Catholicism For Dummies
  0-7645-5391-7
- Hockey For Dummies
  0-7645-5228-7

- Judaism For Dummies
  0-7645-5299-6
- Martial Arts For Dummies
  0-7645-5358-5
- Pilates For Dummies
  0-7645-5397-6
- Religion For Dummies
  0-7645-5264-3
- Teaching Kids to Read For Dummies
  0-7645-4043-2
- Weight Training For Dummies
  0-7645-5168-X
- Yoga For Dummies
  0-7645-5117-5

TRAVEL

0-7645-5438-7   0-7645-5453-0

Also available:
- Alaska For Dummies
  0-7645-1761-9
- Arizona For Dummies
  0-7645-6938-4
- Cancún and the Yucatán For Dummies
  0-7645-2437-2
- Cruise Vacations For Dummies
  0-7645-6941-4
- Europe For Dummies
  0-7645-5456-5
- Ireland For Dummies
  0-7645-5455-7

- Las Vegas For Dummies
  0-7645-5448-4
- London For Dummies
  0-7645-4277-X
- New York City For Dummies
  0-7645-6945-7
- Paris For Dummies
  0-7645-5494-8
- RV Vacations For Dummies
  0-7645-5443-3
- Walt Disney World & Orlando For Dummies
  0-7645-6943-0

GRAPHICS, DESIGN & WEB DEVELOPMENT

0-7645-4345-8   0-7645-5589-8

Also available:
- Adobe Acrobat 6 PDF For Dummies
  0-7645-3760-1
- Building a Web Site For Dummies
  0-7645-7144-3
- Dreamweaver MX 2004 For Dummies
  0-7645-4342-3
- FrontPage 2003 For Dummies
  0-7645-3882-9
- HTML 4 For Dummies
  0-7645-1995-6
- Illustrator cs For Dummies
  0-7645-4084-X

- Macromedia Flash MX 2004 For Dummies
  0-7645-4358-X
- Photoshop 7 All-in-One Desk
  Reference For Dummies
  0-7645-1667-1
- Photoshop cs Timesaving Techniques
  For Dummies
  0-7645-6782-9
- PHP 5 For Dummies
  0-7645-4166-8
- PowerPoint 2003 For Dummies
  0-7645-3908-6
- QuarkXPress 6 For Dummies
  0-7645-2593-X

NETWORKING, SECURITY, PROGRAMMING & DATABASES

0-7645-6852-3

0-7645-5784-X

Also available:
- A+ Certification For Dummies
  0-7645-4187-0
- Access 2003 All-in-One Desk
  Reference For Dummies
  0-7645-3988-4
- Beginning Programming For Dummies
  0-7645-4997-9
- C For Dummies
  0-7645-7068-4
- Firewalls For Dummies
  0-7645-4048-3
- Home Networking For Dummies
  0-7645-42796

- Network Security For Dummies
  0-7645-1679-5
- Networking For Dummies
  0-7645-1677-9
- TCP/IP For Dummies
  0-7645-1760-0
- VBA For Dummies
  0-7645-3989-2
- Wireless All In-One Desk Reference
  For Dummies
  0-7645-7496-5
- Wireless Home Networking For Dummies
  0-7645-3910-8

HEALTH & SELF-HELP

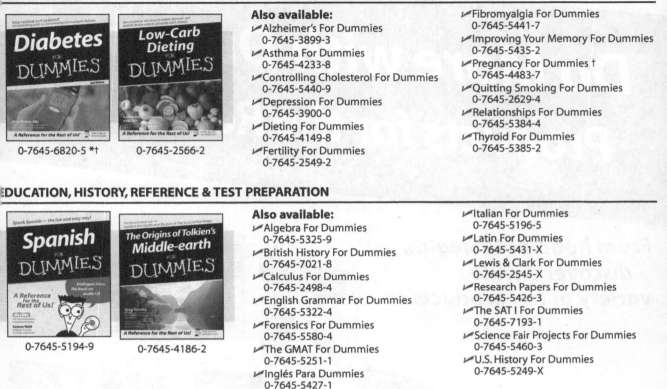

0-7645-6820-5 *†

0-7645-2566-2

Also available:
- Alzheimer's For Dummies
  0-7645-3899-3
- Asthma For Dummies
  0-7645-4233-8
- Controlling Cholesterol For Dummies
  0-7645-5440-9
- Depression For Dummies
  0-7645-3900-0
- Dieting For Dummies
  0-7645-4149-8
- Fertility For Dummies
  0-7645-2549-2

- Fibromyalgia For Dummies
  0-7645-5441-7
- Improving Your Memory For Dummies
  0-7645-5435-2
- Pregnancy For Dummies †
  0-7645-4483-7
- Quitting Smoking For Dummies
  0-7645-2629-4
- Relationships For Dummies
  0-7645-5384-4
- Thyroid For Dummies
  0-7645-5385-2

EDUCATION, HISTORY, REFERENCE & TEST PREPARATION

0-7645-5194-9

0-7645-4186-2

Also available:
- Algebra For Dummies
  0-7645-5325-9
- British History For Dummies
  0-7645-7021-8
- Calculus For Dummies
  0-7645-2498-4
- English Grammar For Dummies
  0-7645-5322-4
- Forensics For Dummies
  0-7645-5580-4
- The GMAT For Dummies
  0-7645-5251-1
- Inglés Para Dummies
  0-7645-5427-1

- Italian For Dummies
  0-7645-5196-5
- Latin For Dummies
  0-7645-5431-X
- Lewis & Clark For Dummies
  0-7645-2545-X
- Research Papers For Dummies
  0-7645-5426-3
- The SAT I For Dummies
  0-7645-7193-1
- Science Fair Projects For Dummies
  0-7645-5460-3
- U.S. History For Dummies
  0-7645-5249-X

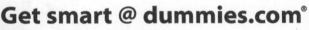

Get smart @ dummies.com®

- **Find a full list of Dummies titles**
- **Look into loads of FREE on-site articles**
- **Sign up for FREE eTips e-mailed to you weekly**
- **See what other products carry the Dummies name**
- **Shop directly from the Dummies bookstore**
- **Enter to win new prizes every month!**

* **Separate Canadian edition also available**
† **Separate U.K. edition also available**

Available wherever books are sold. For more information or to order direct: U.S. customers visit www.dummies.com or call 1-877-762-2974.
U.K. customers visit www.wileyeurope.com or call 0800 243407. Canadian customers visit www.wiley.ca or call 1-800-567-4797.